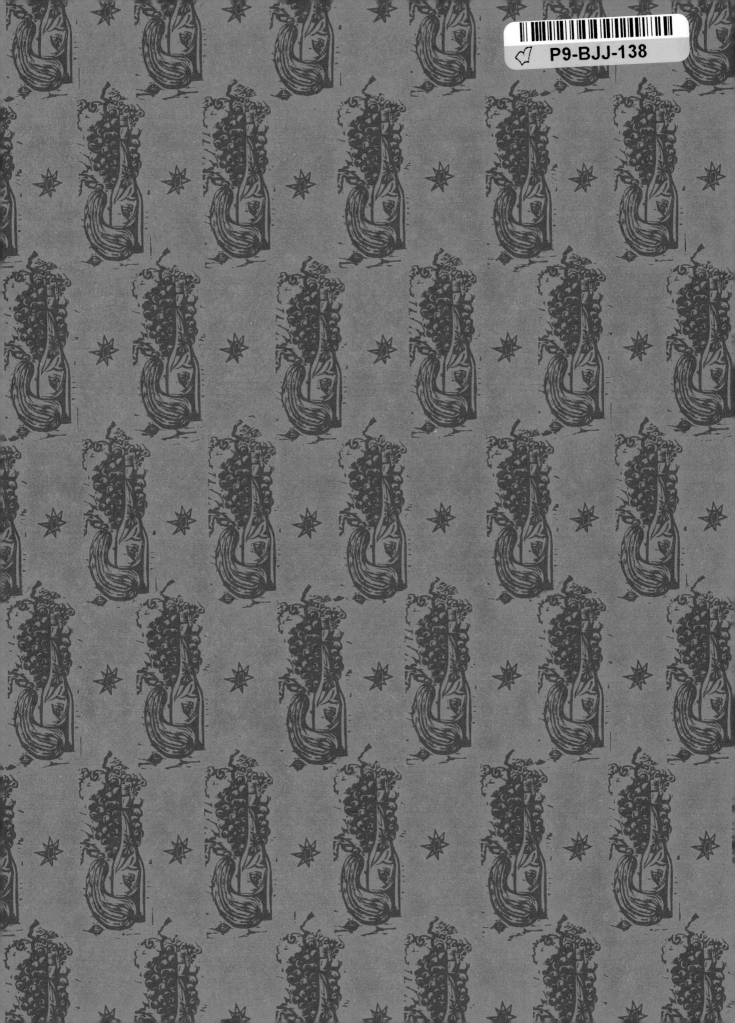

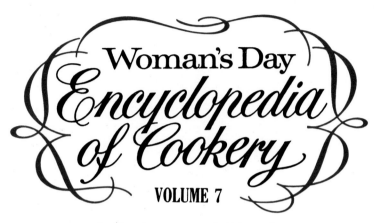

Woman's Day
Encyclopedia of Cookery
VOLUME 7

in 12 volumes—over 2,000 pages—
with more than 1,500 illustrations in color,
1,000 entries and 8,500 recipes
1,200 menus, 50 specialty cook books
and a host of delightful features by distinguished food writers.

Prepared and edited by the Editors of Woman's Day
Editor: EILEEN TIGHE
Managing Editor: EVELYN GRANT   *Food Editor:* GLENNA MCGINNIS
Art Consultant: HAROLD SITTERLE   *Photographic Editor:* BEN CALVO
Associates: OLIVIA RISBERG, CHARLOTTE SCRIPTURE,
CAROLYN STORM, JOHANNA BAFARO

SPECIAL PROJECT STAFF
Editor: NIKA STANDEN HAZELTON   *Art Director:* LEONARD A. ROMAGNA
Associates: L. GERALDINE MARSTELLER, HELEN FEINGOLD,
SUSAN J. KNOX, INEZ M. KRECH

FAWCETT PUBLICATIONS, INC.   NEW YORK

*Direct all correspondence regarding
recipes, sale of replacement volumes
or complete gift sets to:*

Woman's Day Encyclopedia of Cookery
Fawcett Publications, Inc.
One Astor Plaza
New York, New York 10036
(212) 869-3000

Printed in U.S.A. by
FAWCETT PRINTING CORPORATION
Rockville, Maryland

Table of Contents

VOLUME 7

KIDNEY TO MOCHA

Definitions and 740 Recipes
How to buy, store, prepare, cook, and serve •
Nutritive Food Values • Caloric Values

To help you plan more varied meals
with the recipes in this volume

Foreword

To the best of our knowledge, no work of this magnitude ever has been undertaken by any author, editor, or publisher in America. The editors of Woman's Day, with a special staff of experts, present to you this Encyclopedia of Cookery, a comprehensive and colorful library on all culinary matters. The twelve-volume encyclopedia contains in its 2,000 pages over 8,500 recipes from all over the world, 1,500 food illustrations in color, 1,200 menus, 50 special cook books and over 1,000 food definitions. In addition, there are full details about all foods, their nutritive and caloric values, how to buy, serve, prepare, and cook them. There is a history of food and cooking, articles on nutrition, diet, entertaining, menu planning, herbs and spices. Every topic of culinary interest is covered. Five years of intensive work have gone into its preparation, backed by twenty-five years of food and cookery experience in the publication of Woman's Day.

We think you will find this Encyclopedia of Cookery the most complete and authoritative work ever published on the subject. It is a library for everyone who cares about good food and the fine art of preparing it.

The Editors

VOLUME 7

KIDNEY—Known as a variety meat, this is one of the glandular organs of animals. The kidneys of beef, lamb, veal, and, less frequently, pork are used in cookery. Kidneys may be served alone or combined with other meats or in omelets. In addition to being very nutritious, they are inexpensive and when well prepared, very flavorful.

Availability and Purchasing Guide—Kidneys are widely available and should be fresh when purchased. They should be light in color and firm; avoid dark red or soft kidneys.

☐ Beef kidneys average 1 to 1¼ pounds and make 3 or 4 servings.
☐ Lamb kidneys weigh about 2 ounces; allow 2 or 3 per serving.
☐ Pork kidneys weigh about 4 ounces and make 1 serving.
☐ Veal kidneys weigh 8 to 12 ounces and make 1 or 2 servings.

Storage—Kidneys should be loosely wrapped and kept in the refrigerator. Plan to cook the day of purchase.

☐ Refrigerator shelf, raw: 1 day
☐ Refrigerator shelf, cooked: 2 to 3 days
☐ Refrigerator frozen-food compartment, raw, prepared for freezing: 2 to 3 weeks
☐ Freezer, raw, prepared for freezing: 6 months

Nutritive Food Values—Good source of protein, phosphorus, iron, vitamin A, thiamine, and riboflavin.

☐ Beef, 3½ ounces, raw = 130 calories
☐ Lamb, 3½ ounces, raw = 105 calories
☐ Pork, 3½ ounces, raw = 106 calories
☐ Veal, 3½ ounces, raw = 113 calories

Basic Preparation—Remove skin and excess fat with knife or small scissors. Beef kidneys should be soaked for at least 15 minutes in cold water before cooking; change water several times. Drain, and dry before using.

☐ **To Cook**—Braise or simmer beef kidney for 1 to 1½ hours.

Lamb and veal kidneys are very tender; braise or broil for 10 to 12 minutes; or cook in liquid for 45 minutes to 1 hour.

Pork kidneys should be sliced and cooked for 1½ hours. When combined with other ingredients they should only be used in dishes which are thoroughly cooked.

Avoid overcooking beef, lamb, and veal kidneys as this causes toughening.

Kidney Tour of Europe

by Helen Evans Brown

Our trip had been planned as a gastronomic tour, and so it was for me. For my husband Philip, it was a kidney tour. He ordered them at every stop in Denmark, England, Spain, France, and Italy. He didn't have them at every meal, but there were few days when he missed an order of them. Always a kidney *aficionado,* he became a kidney expert. Philip has a theory about kidneys, one he has tested many times at home. He judges restaurants by their kidneys. He is convinced that if a chef prepares them to perfection, everything he cooks will be flawless. But if Philip is served tough overcooked kidneys, he will never darken that restaurant door again. On this particular trip he proved his theory backward. Starting with Q.E.D., he ordered kidneys at some of the world's great restaurants. Always they were sublime. Only once in all the countries we visited did he have a poorly prepared kidney; that was at a hotel in Aix-en-Provence, one with a good reputation, too. And much to Philip's glee, the rest of the meal was also poor.

I was invited to taste each order, so that I could duplicate the dish for him in my own kitchen. Sometimes a gracious chef gave me his recipe, sometimes I had to rely on my palate, and sometimes I found a similar recipe in one of the books on classic cuisine.

One thing that did not surprise us was that all the famous French chefs serve kidneys juicily pink within, and that the famous recipes for kidneys invariably admonish, "Do not overcook," or "Kidneys should be served underdone." There's a good reason for this: kidneys toughen if they are cooked too long. True, they can reach a second stage of tenderness by continued long cooking, but the flavor suffers in the stewing, and the tenderness is more nearly mushiness. French chefs cook kidneys quickly, over a high heat,

until they are "seized" (*saisir,* the French call it). This means until the cut surfaces are seared and the actual blood stops running; then, pink and juicy, they are kept hot while the sauce is finished.

Although veal and lamb kidneys are considered the choicest, beef kidneys are also delicious when properly prepared. Because they have a stronger flavor than those of veal or lamb, many cooks soak them in salted or acidulated water, or in wine, before cooking them. As for pork kidneys, they are flavorsome, but there is the danger of trichinosis, so it is not very smart to use them unless you want them for soup or stew. In this case, cook them to that tender-again stage.

All kidneys spoil easily, so be sure they are very fresh. As for cleaning kidneys, don't try to remove every bit of the white core; if you do, you'll end up with *hachis de rognons.* In fact, many cooks do not remove the core at all. One favorite way of cooking veal kidneys is in the fat which envelopes them, leaving the core intact. If, however, you want every bit of white removed, try using a pair of small pointed scissors. Lamb kidneys are easily prepared by making a slit in the skin on the rounded side opposite the core. Peel the skin back to the core and, leaving it attached to the core, pull out as much as possible and snip off all the core that can be reached with the point of a knife or scissors. Pork kidneys can be cleaned in the same way, but veal or beef kidneys don't need skinning. The tough part of the core may be cut out with a sharp knife or, again, with scissors. Some cooks think manicure scissors the perfect tool for this task.

MUSHROOM AND KIDNEY PIE

Philip had this pie at Simpson's, in London.

2 veal kidneys or 1 beef kidney
⅓ cup chopped onion
1 cup sliced mushrooms
2 tablespoons butter
1 tablespoon minced parsley
Beef gravy
2 tablespoons port
Pastry

Cut kidneys into small pieces. (If beef kidney is used, it may be soaked in salted water for 30 minutes.) Sauté the onion and mushrooms in the butter, combine with kidneys and parsley, and to the juices in the pan add enough beef gravy (canned may be used) to make 1 cup. Add port, put in a 1½-pint or 1-quart casserole, cover with pastry rolled about ¼ inch thick, and bake in preheated moderate oven (350°F.) for 35 minutes for rare kidneys, or 45 minutes for well done. Makes 4 servings.

ROGNONS FLAMBÉS AU RUBAN BLEU
A famous Parisian kidney dish.

Blanch ¾ pound sliced mushrooms in water and a little lemon juice for about 2 minutes. In another pan melt ⅓ cup butter, and add 1 pound veal kidneys. Cook over high heat for 2 minutes; remove kidneys to a cutting board and, with a very sharp knife, cut into pieces, discarding core. Return to pan along with the mushrooms, drained. Remove fat and cook for 4 or 5 minutes over low heat. Season with a little salt and freshly ground white pepper. Add 3 soupspoons of brandy, and flame, shaking the pan all the time. Now add 3 soupspoons of the coldest, heaviest cream you can find. Add 1 teaspoon strong prepared mustard and ½ teaspoon Worcestershire. Simmer gently until the kidneys are done to your liking, shaking the pan. Makes 4 servings.

KIDNEY TURBIGO
This Italian way with kidneys has also become popular in France and England.

    2 veal kidneys
      Melted butter
    1 cup brown sauce or beef gravy
    ¼ cup tomato purée
    2 tablespoons Madeira or sherry
    1 tablespoon butter
      Dash of cayenne
    ½ pound chipolata (Italian sausage),
      cooked
    8 mushroom caps, sautéed
    8 artichoke hearts, cooked tender
    4 small tomatoes, baked

Split kidneys and remove the unsightly part of the core. Then dip them into melted butter and broil, cut side first, for 3 to 4 minutes on each side, or until done to your liking. Remove them to a platter and keep warm. Combine brown sauce, tomato purée, wine, 1 tablespoon butter, and dash of cayenne. Heat, and pour over kidneys. Surround with sausage and vegetables. Makes 4 servings.

NYRE SAUTÉ, GAMMELTOFT
In the home of a charming Danish friend in Copenhagen, we had this lovely kidney sauté.

Slice 1 pound mushrooms and 2 veal kidneys. Cook them together in ¼ cup butter for about 5 minutes. Add 1 tablespoon flour, stir, and pour in ¼ cup Madeira and 1 cup heavy cream. Season with salt and pepper, heat gently, and serve at once. Makes 4 servings.

KIDNEY AND HAM RAGOUT
This is another Danish recipe.

Dice 1 pound ham and brown it lightly in 2 tablespoons butter or ham fat, along with 1 small chopped onion. Add 1 tablespoon flour, 2 cups consommé, and ½ cup sherry; simmer for 30 minutes. In the meantime, slice 2 veal kidneys and sauté quickly in 3 tablespoons butter. Add to the ham mixture, season with salt and pepper and a little hot pepper sauce or cayenne, and serve with rice or noodles. Makes 6 servings.

KIDNEY STEW
This old-fashioned dish is still a favorite in England.

Cut 1 pound kidneys, any kind, into pieces about the size of walnuts, and sauté in 3 tablespoons butter with 1 chopped onion. When the kidneys are done, remove and keep warm. To the onion, add 2 tablespoons flour and 1 can (10½ ounces) consommé. Also add ½ cup white wine or tomato juice. Simmer for 10 minutes, add kidneys, and heat but do not boil. Serve in a ring of rice, sprinkled with minced parsley. Makes 4 servings.

KIDNEY CASSEROLE JEREZ
We had this at a restaurant in Leicester, England.

    2 veal kidneys
    ½ pound mushrooms
    1 carrot
    1 celery stalk
    1 small onion
    1 tablespoon butter
    4 thin slices of lemon
    ¼ cup sherry
    ½ cup beef bouillon

Leave kidneys whole, and trim so that a layer of fat about ¼ inch thick remains. Clean and chop mushrooms, carrot, celery, and onion and spread on the bottom of a well-buttered casserole. Dot with butter and top with kidneys. If the kidneys do not have their fat, spread thickly with cold butter. Bake in preheated moderate oven (350°F.) for 30 minutes. Add the remaining ingredients to the juices in the pan. If you wish, you may also bind the sauce with 1 tablespoon flour that has been kneaded with 2 teaspoons butter. Serve in the casserole, slicing the kidneys as you would a pot roast. Crusty bread should be provided so that not a drop of the precious juices will be lost. Makes 4 servings.

VEAL KIDNEY BONNE FEMME
This French country recipe makes a delicious luncheon dish.

Slice 1 veal kidney and sauté in 2 tablespoons butter. In butter or margarine in another pan, brown 1 cup diced potatoes, 4 slices of bacon cut into pieces, and 1 cup small mushroom caps. Combine with the kidneys, season with salt and pepper, and sprinkle with 1 tablespoon minced parsley. Makes 2 generous servings.

BROCHETTES DE ROGNONS PANÉS ET GRILLÉS
This interesting way of doing kidneys is very popular in the seaport of Marseilles.

Allow 1 veal kidney for each 2 servings. Slice each kidney into 5 or 6 lengthwise slices. Top each slice with a slice of Canadian bacon and thread 2 or 3 of these on a skewer. Brush thoroughly with olive oil and roll in fine bread crumbs. Broil slowly for about 15 minutes, taking care that the crumbs don't burn. Serve with Maître d'Hôtel Butter. To make ¼ cup Maître d'Hôtel Butter cream ¼ cup butter and beat into it ¼ teaspoon salt, 1 tablespoon minced parsley, and a dash of white pepper; add 1½ teaspoons fresh lemon juice drop by drop.

VEAL KIDNEYS WITH ANCHOVIES
This recipe comes from Nice.

Slice 2 veal kidneys about ⅓ inch thick and cook in 2 tablespoons olive oil to which a crushed garlic clove has been added. When desired degree of doneness has been reached, season with salt and pepper and add 1 tablespoon each of fresh lemon juice, minced parsley, butter, and minced anchovies. Stir and cook for another few seconds, just long enough to heat. Makes 4 servings.

ROGNONS D'AGNEAU À LA LULLY
This is a recipe from the Champagne region of France.

Split 8 lamb kidneys and cook them for 3 minutes in ¼ cup butter. Remove and keep warm. To the pan add 1 tablespoon minced parsley, ½ cup thinly sliced mushrooms, and 2 chopped shallots or 2 tablespoons minced onion. Cook for 5 minutes, add the juice of 1 lemon and the kidneys, and season with salt and pepper. Add 1 more tablespoon butter and cook just long enough for the kidneys to become pink. Serve with tiny potato croquettes, or with frozen French-fried potato puffs. This makes 4 servings.

KIDNEYS WITH EGGS, GUETARIA
In a tiny town on the Bay of Biscay we had this dish for lunch.

Sliced lamb kidneys were sautéed quickly in a mixture of butter and olive oil, leaving them less done than usual. They were put in buttered cocottes, allowing 1 kidney for each, 1 egg was broken over each, 1 tablespoon heavy cream poured on, and they were baked in a moderate oven (350°F.) until the eggs were set. Try this for a breakfast dish.

RIÑONES À LA PAMPLONA
This dish is named after the famous Spanish bullfighting town, where we had it.

    8 lamb kidneys
    2 cups cooked peas
    1 cup sliced mushrooms
    ½ cup tomato sauce
    ¼ cup chopped cooked ham

Riñones á la Pamplona

¼ cup minced onion
1 teaspoon minced parsley
1 tablespoon butter
1 tablespoon olive oil
¼ cup sherry
Cooked rice

Slice kidneys. Heat peas, mushrooms, and tomato sauce. Sauté the kidneys with the ham, onion, and parsley in the butter and olive oil. When pink, add wine and combine with vegetables. Serve with rice. Makes 4 servings.

BRAISED PORK KIDNEYS

This is an Italian dish in which the kidneys are cooked for a long time, which is as it should be with pork.

4 pork kidneys
3 tablespoons olive oil
½ cup chopped onion
1 garlic clove, minced
1 tablespoon tomato purée
1 cup red wine
¼ teaspoon dried rosemary
Salt and pepper to taste
2 tablespoons minced parsley

Cut kidneys into quarters and sauté in the oil along with the onion and garlic. Add liquids and rosemary. Cover and simmer slowly for about 30 minutes, or until tender. Season with salt and pepper and sprinkle with minced parsley. Serve with rice. Makes 4 servings.

FRITTI ROGNONI

1 cup all-purpose flour
1 egg
⅔ cup milk
2 teaspoons cooking oil
½ teaspoon salt
2 veal or 8 lamb kidneys, sliced
¼ inch thick
Shortening for deep frying

Combine first 5 ingredients. Dip slices of kidney into batter and fry in deep hot fat (370° F. on a frying thermometer) until nicely browned. Drain on paper towels and serve at once. Makes 4 servings.

ROGNONCINI DI VITELLO TRIFOLATO

3 veal kidneys
2 tablespoons olive oil
1 garlic clove, crushed
3 anchovy fillets
Salt and pepper to taste
1 tablespoon chopped parsley
2 teaspoons red-wine vinegar

Slice the kidneys thin and sauté them in the olive oil with the crushed garlic. When the blood stops running, add the remaining ingredients. Mix well, and serve. Makes 6 servings.

KIELBASA, KOLBASI, or KOLBASSY—

A highly seasoned sausage of Polish origin, made of coarsely ground lean pork and beef, flavored with garlic and other spices. It comes fresh or smoked, uncooked or cooked.

Kielbasa is sold in straight links four to five inches long, and about one and a half inches in diameter. It should be stored in the refrigerator and eaten as soon as possible.

To prepare kielbasa cover with water and bring to a boil. Lower heat and simmer for 30 minutes, or until thoroughly cooked. Drain, and cut into slices. Use hot or cold.

Caloric Value

☐ 3½ ounces = 304 calories

POLISH BIGOS

2 pounds fresh or about 3½ cups (one 1-pound, 13-ounce can) sauerkraut
2 cups meat stock
2 cups (one 1-pound can) tomatoes
1 large onion, chopped
1 large apple, peeled and chopped
1 tablespoon bacon fat
1 pound kielbasa
2 cups diced leftover cooked meat
Salt to taste
Dash each of black pepper and cayenne
1 tablespoon sugar
1 tablespoon flour
2 cans (4 ounces each) sliced mushrooms, drained
Boiled potatoes

Drain and rinse sauerkraut. Put in heavy pot with stock and liquid from tomatoes; simmer. Sauté tomatoes and onion with apple in fat for a few minutes. Cut kielbasa into 1-inch chunks and add with meat to vegetables; simmer for 10 minutes. Add seasonings, sugar, and flour to vegetable-meat mixture; stir. Add mushrooms and stir; cook until slightly thickened. Add to sauerkraut. Simmer mixture for 1½ to 2 hours, adding more stock if dry. Let stand in cool place overnight. When ready to use, reheat slowly and serve with hot boiled potatoes. Makes 6 to 8 servings.

Note: This dish can be frozen, if desired. When ready to use, let stand for several hours at room temperature before reheating over low heat.

KINGFISH—

The name of a number of salt-water food fishes of the Atlantic and Pacific coasts. They are related to the Spanish mackerel and may weigh up to seventy-five pounds or more. The Florida kingfish is a notable game fish. Kingfish has a distinctive flavor with a small amount of bones. It can be broiled, sautéed, baked, stewed, or poached.

Availability and Purchasing Guide—

Available November to March. Can be purchased whole, in fillets, and in steaks.

Select fresh-smelling firm fish, elastic to the touch.

Storage—

Should be wrapped tightly and refrigerated.

☐ Refrigerator shelf, raw: 1 to 2 days
☐ Refrigerator frozen-food compartment, raw, prepared for freezing: 2 to 3 weeks
☐ Freezer, raw, prepared for freezing: 1 year
☐ Refrigerator shelf, cooked: 3 to 4 days

Nutritive Food Values—

Good source of protein.

☐ 3½ ounces, raw = 105 calories

Freezing—

Clean and wash fish. Eviscerate. Dip fish into a solution of 4 cups cold water to 1½ teaspoons ascorbic acid for 20 seconds. Wrap in moisture-vapor-proof wrapping, excluding as much air as possible. Seal.

BAKED KINGFISH STEAKS AU GRATIN

4 kingfish steaks
All-purpose flour
Butter or margarine
Salt and pepper
1½ cups milk
½ cup buttered soft bread crumbs
2 tablespoons grated Parmesan cheese

Dip steaks in flour, and arrange in shallow broilerproof baking pan. Dot with butter and sprinkle with salt and pepper. Bake in preheated moderate oven (375° F.) for 25 minutes, or until fish flakes easily with a fork. Meanwhile, melt 3 tablespoons butter, and blend in 3 tablespoons flour. Gradually add milk, and cook, stirring, until thickened. Season to taste with salt and pepper. Pour over fish steaks. Sprinkle with crumbs and cheese. Put under broiler until crumbs are lightly browned. Makes 4 servings.

KIPPER—

As a verb the word means to cure fish by cleaning, salting, spicing, and then drying or smoking. The best-known kippered fish is herring, and when the word kipper is used alone, it refers to kippered herring.

The cured kipper is golden-brown and the taste is delicate and smoky. Kippers are eaten grilled, fried, baked, or poached, either plain or with a sauce. Kippers are one of the great English breakfast foods and the British dote on them at home and pine for them in countries where they are not available. Apart from this national emotion, kippers make a tasty dish for breakfast, lunch, or supper.

Since proper smoking is what gives kippers their exclusive taste, the processing of kippers is regulated by law so that they are completely colored by wood smoke and not artificially colored with dyestuffs.

Availability—

Kippered alewife, anchovy, bloater, bowfin, butterfish, carp, cod, eel, garfish, haddock, hake, halibut, mullet, pollock, roe, salmon, sardines, shad, sturgeon, trout, and whitefish are all available kippered, most as fillets. Some, however, such as halibut are sold in chunks.

Kippered herring is also available canned.

Purchasing Guide—Fillets or chunks should not be dry-looking. The skin should be fairly smooth, and fish should have an appetizing smoky aroma.

Storage

☐ Canned, kitchen shelf: 6 months
☐ Mildly smoked fillets and canned, opened and covered, refrigerator shelf: 2 to 3 days
☐ Heavily smoked fillets, refrigerator shelf: 4 to 5 days

Caloric Value

☐ Kippered haddock, 3½ ounces = 103 calories
☐ Kippered halibut, 3½ ounces = 224 calories
☐ Kippered herring, 3½ ounces = 211 calories
☐ Kippered mackerel, 3½ ounces = 219 calories
☐ Kippered salmon, 3½ ounces = 176 calories
☐ Kippered sturgeon, 3½ ounces = 149 calories
☐ Kippered whitefish, 3½ ounces = 155 calories

Basic Preparation—Kippered fish that are heavily smoked should be soaked in boiling water for a few minutes before cooking.

☐ **To Grill**—Wash fish and remove heads. Brush fish on both sides with melted butter. Put fish on a rack, 6 inches below the source of heat. Grill for 3 minutes on one side, turn, and grill for the same length of time on the other side. Brush fish occasionally during cooking. Season with pepper and serve with lemon wedges and toast.

☐ **To Fry**—Melt enough butter in a large frying pan just to cover the bottom. Place fish side by side, skin side down, in the hot butter. Fry for 3 to 4 minutes on one side, turn, and fry for the same length of time on the other side. Add more butter to the pan if necessary. Serve fish with pan juice poured over them.

KIPPER SOUFFLÉ

3 kippers
6 tablespoons all-purpose flour
2 cups milk
2 egg yolks, beaten
2 egg whites, beaten until stiff
Pepper

Cover kippers with boiling water for 2 to 3 minutes. Drain. Cover with fresh water and cook until kippers are soft enough to remove skin and bones. Put flour in a saucepan and gradually stir in milk. Cook over low heat, stirring constantly, until smooth and thick. Beat some of the hot sauce into egg yolks. Pour into the remaining sauce and cook over low heat until smooth and thick. Mash boned kippers until smooth and

fold into sauce. Beat egg whites until stiff but not dry. Add pepper to taste. Fold into fish mixture. Pour mixture into buttered 1-quart soufflé dish. Bake in preheated moderate oven (375°F.) for 30 to 35 minutes, or until lightly browned. Makes 4 servings.

KIPPERED SALMON WITH RICE

¼ pound kippered salmon
2 hard-cooked egg whites
2 cups hot cooked rice
¼ cup butter
⅛ teaspoon paprika
⅛ teaspoon powdered thyme
Tomato wedges
1 sour pickle, sliced lengthwise

Have salmon cut very thin. Dice half with a sharp knife and cut remainder into ¼-inch strips. Chop egg whites and press yolks through coarse sieve. Put rice in mixing bowl and add diced salmon and chopped egg whites. Melt butter and add paprika and thyme. Add rice mixture and cook, stirring, until lightly browned. Pile in serving dish and garnish with salmon strips, tomato wedges, and pickle. Makes 4 servings.

Note: Kippered trout, bowfin, or whitefish may be flaked and prepared as above.

KIPPERED HADDOCK WITH BACON

1 kippered haddock (1½ pounds), not too heavily smoked
2 slices bacon, diced
8 ripe olives, diced
1 tablespoon chopped parsley

Put fillet in shallow baking dish. Sprinkle with bacon. Bake in preheated hot oven (400°F.) for 15 minutes, or until fillet is thoroughly heated and bacon is browned. Arrange on hot platter and sprinkle with olives and parsley. Makes 4 servings.

Note: Kippered hake may also be prepared as above.

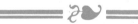

KISS—A small chewy mound-shape confection prepared with egg white and sugar. To these basic ingredients coconut, chopped nut meats, chopped dates, and chocolate or chopped nut candy are added. Since the name is derived from the shape, other small mound-shape confections may be referred to as kisses.

Kiss also refers to a bite-size piece of candy, including commercially produced chocolate, fondant, or peanut-butter candy, usually wrapped in paper or foil.

COCONUT KISSES

½ teaspoon salt
4 egg whites
1¼ cups very fine granulated sugar
1 teaspoon vanilla extract
2 cups shredded coconut
24 candied cherries, halved

Add salt to egg whites, and beat until stiff but not dry. Add sugar, 1 tablespoon at a time, beating until granules are dis-

solved. Add vanilla and coconut, mixing lightly. Drop by teaspoonfuls onto ungreased brown paper on cookie sheets. Bake in preheated moderate oven (350°F.) for about 20 minutes. Slip paper onto wet table or board. Let stand for 1 minute. Loosen kisses with spatula; remove to wire racks. Top each with cherry half. Makes about 4 dozen.

DATE-NUT KISSES

4 egg whites
Dash salt
1½ cups sugar
1 teaspoon vanilla extract
½ pound dates, cut in pieces
1 cup coarsely chopped walnuts

Beat egg whites until foamy. Add salt. Gradually add sugar, beating until very stiff and glossy. Fold in vanilla, dates, and nuts. Drop by teaspoonfuls onto buttered cookie sheets and bake in preheated slow oven (300°F.) for about 25 to 30 minutes. Makes about 4 dozen.

COCOA KISSES

3 egg whites
1 cup sugar
⅛ teaspoon salt
1 teaspoon vanilla extract
3 tablespoons cocoa
¾ cup chopped pecans

Beat egg whites to soft moist peaks; gradually beat in sugar and salt. Continue beating until mixture is thick and glossy and egg whites will stand in peaks. Fold in vanilla, cocoa, and pecans. Drop from teaspoon onto buttered cookie sheets. Bake in preheated very slow oven (250°F.) for about 30 minutes, or until kisses are partly dry and retain their shape. Remove from the pan while hot. Makes about 40.

KIWI BERRY or CHINESE GOOSEBERRY—The kiwi berry was discovered in China in 1847 by an English botanist. It grows on trees and is the same shape and size as a lime. The berry has a thin brown skin covered with coarse fuzz. It can be peeled or spooned out of the skin. The flesh is soft, brilliant green in color, and is filled with tiny edible black seeds. It has a refreshing tart-sweet subtle taste.

In New Zealand where kiwi berries are very popular, the favorite way of serving them is in a Pavlova cake; a meringue baked until crisp, filled with sweetened whipped cream, and topped with peeled and thinly sliced kiwi berries.

Kiwi berries are available at gourmet fruit stores. They can be kept for several days in the refrigerator.

KNACKWURST—A smoked and cooked sausage also called knockwurst, or knoblauch, made from a formula similar to that used for the frankfurter. The chief differences between a frankfurter and knackwurst are in the size and the seasoning: knackwurst is larger around and shorter, and it contains more garlic. The name is of German origin, *knack* meaning to "crackle" or to "make a noise when breaking," or, in this case, when bitten into. *Wurst* means "sausage."

Availability and Purchasing Guide— Knackwurst is available in food stores throughout the country all year round. May be sold in pairs by the pound, or packaged. May be skinless or stuffed into natural casing. May be all meat, all beef, or contain fillers and meat.

Storage—Should be used as quickly as possible to prevent fat from becoming rancid and to prevent molding.

☐ Refrigerator shelf, well wrapped in foil or in original wrapper: 1 week
Freezing is not recommended.

Caloric Value

☐ 3½ ounces = 278 calories

Basic Preparation—Knackwurst is fully cooked and may be eaten as purchased, but it is usually served heated.

☐ **To Cook**—Simmer in water to cover for about 7 minutes, or until heated through.

☐ **To Broil**—Split knackwurst and place on rack 3 to 4 inches below heat. Broil each side for about 3 minutes. Turn only once.

☐ **To Panbroil**—Split knackwurst and place in preheated skillet. Cook over moderate heat for about 4 minutes per side, or until heated through. Turn only once.

☐ **To Bake**—Bake as part of a casserole. Baking time and temperature vary according to the other ingredients in the casserole.

Serve with potato salad, sauerkraut, or in any way you would serve frankfurters.

KNEAD—A method of mixing with the palms and heels of the hands to make dough or fudge smooth. In culinary language, the word is most often applied to the working of a yeast dough with the hands in order to develop the gluten of the flour and give better grain and texture to the final product.

To knead yeast dough, shape it first into a ball. Press out the dough so it is flat. Pick up the edge farthest from you and fold over top of the edge nearest you. Then using both hands, press down with heels of palms, pushing the dough away from you. Press lightly as you push. With both hands, give the dough a quarter turn. Now repeat folding, pushing, turning, until the dough is smooth and elastic. Kneading is finished when the dough is smooth, springy, and elastic, and like satin to the touch. It should not stick to your hands or to the board. Generally kneading will take five to ten minutes depending on the type of flour used: whole grains such as whole-wheat or rye take longer to develop the gluten.

To knead fudge, work in the same manner. Form candy into a ball, then fold, press, and turn as for yeast. Candy should be well mixed and smooth at the end of kneading.

KNIFE—A knife is a cutting instrument with a blade and a handle. Some knives, such as pocketknives, have the handle attached with a hinge. The functioning part of a knife is the blade, which is usually of steel, often stainless steel. In other days, knife blades were made of iron, bone, silverplate, or gold plate. Prehistoric man has left behind knives made of chipped stone and flint, and sailors on long voyages have carved knives of ivory. Knife handles can be as elaborate as taste and pocketbook permit. The Babylonians used richly ornamented hilts, some carved out of bone and garnished with golden pins and studs.

Knives have existed almost as long as man. Their first use was for hunting and self-defense rather than for cooking and eating. The knife as we know and use it today is a development of this early tool.

As applied to food, the knife is a cutting or spreading tool. For table service it may be a dinner knife, a luncheon, a steak, a butter, or a fruit knife. For serving there are carving knives, slicers, cheese knives, cake knives. And in the kitchen the variety of knives is almost endless, including paring knives, bread, utility, boning, chef's knives, peelers, corers, scoops, and cleavers. They come in different sizes, shapes, weights, and materials to fit special uses. Blades are most often of steel but handles and sometimes blades may be of silver, wood, bone, ivory, horn, other metals, mother-of-pearl, plastic, or plastic-impregnated wood.

KOHLRABI—This member of the cabbage family is a native of northern Europe. The name comes from the German and means "cabbage turnip." Kohlrabi has an unusual appearance which distinguishes it from other members of the cabbage family. Instead of a head of closely packed leaves, there is a globular swelling of the stem, about three to four inches in diameter, just above the ground, and the leaves sprout from this. The leaves are similar to turnip leaves.

Kohlrabi is a popular vegetable in Europe. It makes an excellent accompaniment to roast or broiled meats when cut into julienne strips or thin slices and steamed and buttered. It may also be served with a sauce, or made into a salad.

Availability—May through November. Peak months are June and July.

Purchasing Guide—Look for small kohlrabi with fresh tops and rind that can easily be pierced with a fingernail. Large heads tend to be tough and woody. Avoid kohlrabi with blemishes or growth cracks.

Storage—Store in cool dry area with enough space for good air circulation.

☐ Cool dry area: 2 weeks

☐ Refrigerator frozen-food compartment, prepared for freezing: 2 to 3 months

☐ Freezer, prepared for freezing: 1 year

Nutritive Food Values—Kohlrabi is a good source of vitamin C. The greens are a good source of iron.

☐ 3½ ounces, raw = 29 calories

Basic Preparation—Remove leaves; save young tender ones to cook separately. Pare thickened stem and cut into slices or julienne strips. May be boiled, baked, steamed, or fried, dressed with butter or a sauce. Young kohlrabi may be eaten raw as a salad, cut into julienne strips and marinated in a French dressing.

☐ **To Freeze**—Select young, tender vegetables. Remove leaves, pare, and cut into ½-inch cubes. Drop into boiling water for 1 minute. Chill in cold water for 5 minutes. Drain. Pack in containers, leaving ½-inch headspace.

SPICED KOHLRABI WITH CHEESE

4 kohlrabi
Salt
Water
2 tablespoons butter
2 tablespoons all-purpose flour
1 cup milk
¼ cup grated American cheese
1 tablespoon chopped parsley
⅛ teaspoon ground nutmeg

Cut off tops and pare the thickened stems of kohlrabi. Slice stems and drop into boiling salted water to cover. Cook for about 20 minutes, or until barely tender. Drain well. Boil tender leaves separately in the same manner; drain well. Chop leaves very fine and combine with cooked stems. Melt butter in small saucepan over low heat. Add flour and stir well. Gradually add milk and cheese and cook, stirring constantly, until cheese is melted. Add cooked kohlrabi and cook until heated through. Garnish with parsley and ground nutmeg. Makes 4 servings.

KOREAN COOKERY

by Peter Hyun

The lovely peninsula of Korea is a land of rugged mountains and sparkling waters, bounded by Manchuria and Siberia on the North, China across the Yellow Sea, and Japan across Korea Straits. It is the size of all New England plus New Jersey and Delaware and the climate has the same variety, although it is a little colder than the climate between Portsmouth, New Hampshire, and Charleston, South Carolina. People who have lived there say it is one of the healthiest climates in the world. In other words, Korea is not a tropical country, but it is a lovely one, filled with the beautiful monuments of its ancient civilization, which is quite different from that of other countries of the Far East.

One of the reasons for this is that the Koreans are an ancient and homogeneous race, distinct from both the Chinese and Japanese. They are thought to be the descendants of two strains, the nomadic tribes of Mongolia and the Caucasian people of western Asia, and they have both occidental and oriental characteristics. The Korean national dress reflects this; the short, close-fitting bolero jackets and the colorful, flowing skirts of the women make for one of the most beautiful female costumes to be found anywhere.

The loveliness of the Korean landscape is such that the islands off its shores are said to be the home of the immortals. It is matched by Korean art, from the Buddhist temples with their perfect symmetry and serene classical lines, to the famous Korean lacquer ware, which is delicately inlaid with mother-of-pearl and said to be the world's most exquisite. Korean ceramics are found in all major museums, and the rich heritage of ancient music survives; the Yi Palace orchestra, founded 500 years ago, still performs today. And one of the oldest existing astronomical observatories, dating from the 7th century, still stands at Kyongju.

The idyllic character of much of Korea is reflected in the luxurious flower gardens and in the houses, which are often decorated with ink paintings and calligraphy. The furniture is sparse; since there are no beds or chairs, people sit on mats on the floor and mattresses are brought out at night. Clothes are kept in very ornately decorated chests, there

are low reading desks, and the brass and porcelain ware in the kitchen is of fine and artistic quality and considerable diversity. Interestingly, Korean houses have been heated for 1,500 years with a kind of central heating. The floor is paved with bricks, and under the top layer of bricks are flues which connect with a tunnel under the floor level. This tunnel carries heat from the kitchen to the main chimney.

Today the traditional way of life as a whole is on the wane. The impact of Western culture and civilization is felt, particularly in large cities. The Western influx began in the latter part of the 19th century when Korea—long known as the "Hermit Kingdom"—opened its door to the West.

In 1910, however, this modernization of Korea was interrupted when the Japanese occupied the country and converted it into a military governorship, which tried unsuccessfully to control the thoughts and feelings of every Korean.

Korea today is a divided country; the allied victory in 1945 resulted in the tragic division of the small peninsula into North and South Korea.

In North Korea the communist system has replaced nearly all traditional customs with new values and practices, while in the South, where in most cases any change of traditions is left to individual choice, the process of modernization has been steady but relatively slow.

Traditional Korean home life is ruled by the "Five Codes of Confucius." There ought to be, according to the codes, "justice between ruler and subject, affection between father and son, prudence between husband and wife, order between old and young, and trust between friends."

Good manners are strictly observed by everyone—so much so that at one time Korea had a ministry of etiquette in the government.

At home, older members of the family —usually grandparents or parents—are considered "superiors," and as such absolute obedience is accorded to them by the rest of the family. In the presence of the "superiors" no drinking, smoking, singing, or loud talking is allowed. The "superiors," on their part, treat the younger members of the family with discretion and affection. They may be strict but they are not cruel.

The Korean mother is always tolerant with her children, while the father is, at least outwardly, an uncompromising disciplinarian. In the event that the mother becomes a widow, she automatically inherits the father's role.

The eldest son, as the heir to the family name, is treated with respect even

in his childhood. Since he is expected to support his aged parents eventually, he inherits most of the family property. If a family has no son, the parents adopt one—often their daughter's husband—in order to preserve the family name.

The birth of a son is greeted with more rejoicing than that of a daughter. In fact, the Korean woman suffers from the status of inferiority imposed on her by social convention.

The primary function of Korean women is to serve their men. They do so by bringing up their children properly and by preparing excellent meals for their families—especially their husbands. It is often said that the happiness of a family depends on the quality of food served in the household. Like the French, the Koreans take food very seriously. Well-fed Korean husbands are known to be more considerate and affectionate towards their wives than ill-fed ones.

Despite the impact of the West upon Korea, the traditional Korean cuisine has not changed at all. True, some sophisticated people living in the cities take coffee and toast for breakfast, but they constitute a small minority. Most Koreans eat three hearty meals—breakfast, lunch, and dinner—each day.

The Korean equivalent of Western bread is rice. Steamed rice is served with a variety of vegetable and meat dishes. The most famous vegetable dish is *kimchi,* a highly seasoned and fermented pickle of cabbage, turnip, and cucumber, which provides a large amount of the vitamins in the Korean diet. Soups, containing seaweed, meat, or fish, are always served. Vegetables are never overcooked. Vegetable dishes are seasoned with red and black pepper, garlic, sesame-seed oil, and soy sauce. Beef, pork, and fish courses are generally grilled over burning charcoal.

Steamed rice is served in an individual china or brass bowl and is placed in front of each diner. The other dishes are placed in the center of the table. A spoon with a long handle and chopsticks made of silver or brass are the usual eating utensils. A knife is not needed since all meats and vegetables are served thinly sliced.

The differences between Chinese, Japanese, and other Far Eastern and Korean food are interesting. The Chinese are great pork eaters and the Japanese fish consumers, but Koreans prefer vegetables, both wild and cultivated. While the Chinese use rich sauces in cooking and the Japanese eat many things raw or deep fried, most Korean dishes are grilled. Unlike the flamboyant and spicy foods of Siam, Korean cooking is spicy in a discreet way. Spices are used solely to enhance the taste of the meat.

Korea has never been a tea-drinking nation. In the old days, in China and Japan, the water had to be boiled in order to make it fit to drink. Blessed with pure mineral waters, however, Korea had no use for tea.

One of the most widely known native drinks is ginseng, made from a perennial herb of the same name. Festive drinks are sikhe (sweet wine), a sweetened and fermented rice water, and haangchae (flower drink), a molasses-sweetened, magnolia-flavor beverage.

The native alcoholic beverages are the rather weak yakju (medicinal wine) brewed from rice and the strong soju (distilled wine) made from grain. Often fruits and flowers are added to the soju to brew such flowery wines as igangju (plum-ginger wine), omiju (magnolia wine), paekhwaju (hundred-flower wine) and kukhwaju (chrysanthemum wine).

Generally, a meal is prepared in the kitchen and brought to the room on a small table. The typical Korean house has no dining room as such and a central room or a living room is used for the purpose. The most common dining table is square and, regardless of its size, is usually ten inches high. It is finished in black lacquer. Another and more elaborate type is hexagonal, finished in vermilion with mother-of-pearl inlays of flowers, birds, or landscape.

"A majestic view has no charm when the table is bare," warns a Korean proverb. Korean cuisine takes heed of that warning and offers a superb wealth of excellent food.

GROUND TOASTED SESAME SEED
1 cup white sesame seeds
1 tablespoon salt

Remove any sand found among the seeds. Wash, if necessary. Put in heavy skillet and brown slowly, stirring constantly. When seeds are brown and rounded, remove at once from the heat. Add salt. Mash seeds until pulverized. Sesame seed is used in this form in most recipes.

SOUP

KORI KUK
(Oxtail Soup)
1 oxtail (about 2 pounds)
10 cups water
¼ cup soy sauce
1 tablespoon sesame-seed oil
1 tablespoon ground toasted sesame seed
½ teaspoon pepper
2 tablespoons minced onion
1 tablespoon minced garlic

Have butcher cut oxtail into 8 pieces. Wash and add water. Bring to a boil,

lower heat, and simmer for 2 hours, removing scum. Do not add extra water while oxtail is cooking. When the pieces can be pierced easily by a fork or a chopstick, take them out and roll in a mixture of 1 tablespoon soy sauce, the sesame oil, ground sesame seed, pepper, onion, and garlic until well coated. Add 3 tablespoons soy sauce to the broth. Put oxtail back into the pan and bring to boil before serving. Makes 6 to 8 servings.

FISH AND SHELL FISH

DOMI JUN
(Sea Bream Fried in Egg Batter)
1 sea bream, 7 to 8 pounds
Salt and pepper
2 eggs
½ cup all-purpose flour
Sesame-seed oil
Parsley
1 cup soy sauce
¼ cup vinegar

Skin fish, wash, and pat dry. Bone with a thin sharp knife. Cut into thin pieces diagonally and sprinkle with salt and pepper. Whip eggs lightly with 1 teaspoon salt. Flour the fish slices on both sides and dip into the beaten egg. Fry in shallow (about ¼ inch deep) sesame-seed oil. Garnish with parsley and serve with soy sauce mixed with vinegar. Makes 6 to 8 servings.

KUL JUN
(Oysters Fried in Egg Batter)
1 pint shelled oysters, drained
Salt and pepper
¼ cup all-purpose flour
2 eggs, well beaten
3 tablespoons sesame-seed oil
½ cup soy sauce
2 tablespoons vinegar

Wash oysters and drain well. Sprinkle them with salt and pepper and roll in flour. Dip oysters into eggs mixed with ½ teaspoon salt, then fry on both sides in sesame-seed oil. Serve with soy sauce mixed with vinegar. Makes 6 servings.

SAEWU JUN
(Shrimps Fried in Egg Batter)
1 pound large shrimps, in shell
Salt and pepper
⅓ cup all-purpose flour
2 teaspoons ground toasted sesame seed
1 egg, well beaten
3 tablespoons sesame-seed oil
1 cup soy sauce
¼ cup vinegar

Remove head, shell, and black line from each shrimp, but leave the tail. Cut each open on the underside and flatten out. Sprinkle with salt and pepper. Holding shrimp by its tail, dip into flour mixed with sesame seed and then into beaten egg. Sauté on both sides in sesame-seed oil. Serve with soy sauce mixed with vinegar. Makes 4 servings.

MEAT AND POULTRY

TON JUN
(Beef with Soy-Bean Cake)
2 soy-bean cakes* (¼ cup canned bean cake or 2 bean-curd cakes)
½ pound ground beef round
2 tablespoons minced onion
1 teaspoon minced garlic
½ teaspoon minced gingerroot
2 tablespoons ground toasted sesame seed
1 tablespoon soy sauce
¼ to 1 teaspoon pepper (depending on taste)
2 tablespoons sesame-seed oil

Wrap soy-bean cakes in several thicknesses of cheesecloth and weight them for 30 minutes to drain. Add ground beef to soy-bean cakes. Add onion, garlic, gingerroot, sesame seed, soy sauce, pepper, and 1 tablespoon sesame-seed oil. Mix thoroughly and shape into small cakes. Fry on both sides in remainder of sesame-seed oil. Makes 3 to 4 servings.

* Korean foods can be bought in oriental food stores.

PUL KOKI
(Fire Beef)
1 pound beef sirloin (boneless steak)
¼ cup minced onion
2 teaspoons minced garlic
¼ cup soy sauce
2 tablespoons sugar
1 teaspoon black pepper
Dash of red pepper
2 tablespoons ground toasted sesame seed
2 tablespoons sesame-seed oil

Cut sirloin into paper-thin slices. This is easier to do if meat is first frozen until hard. Combine onion, garlic, soy sauce, sugar, black and red pepper, sesame seed, and oil; mix well. Pour over beef slices, coating each slice with the sauce. Grill on skewers over charcoal. Or broil in a broiler 6 inches from source of heat, turning occasionally to brown on all sides. Makes 4 servings.

JANG PO
(Beef Broiled in Sauce)
1 pound beef rump
2 tablespoons sugar
¼ cup soy sauce
2 tablespoons minced onion
1½ teaspoons minced garlic
1 teaspoon minced gingerroot
2 teaspoons ground toasted sesame seed
½ teaspoon pepper
1 tablespoon sesame-seed oil
Minced pine nuts

Cut meat into ⅛-inch slices. This is easier to do if meat is first frozen until hard. Mix with sugar. Let stand for a minute or two. Grill lightly until surface of meat is just seared and then pound. Dip meat into sauce made of soy sauce, onion, garlic, gingerroot, sesame seed, pepper, and sesame-seed oil. Grill

Sam Saek Namul

San Juk

Boiled rice

Kori Kuk

lightly once more, turning meat to brown on both sides. Pound and dip again into the same sauce and grill once more. Cut into 1-inch squares and sprinkle lightly with minced pine nuts. Makes 4 to 6 servings.

KALBI KUI
(Broiled Short Ribs)

    3 pounds beef short ribs
    ¼ cup sugar
    ½ cup soy sauce
    ½ tablespoon minced garlic
    6 tablespoons minced onion
    2 tablespoons ground toasted sesame seed
    2 teaspoons minced gingerroot
    ¼ teaspoon pepper
    2 tablespoons sesame-seed oil

Have butcher cut short ribs into about 3-inch squares. Make deep cuts into the meat without cutting through to the bone. Mix sugar, soy sauce, garlic, onion, sesame seed, gingerroot, pepper, and sesame-seed oil, in that order. Brush mixture over and into cuts in meat. Let stand for 1 hour. Grill over charcoal, turning occasionally to brown on all sides. Meat should be medium-rare to be tender and should be broiled at least 8 inches above coals to prevent scorching. Or place on rack in roasting pan and roast in preheated slow oven (325°F.) for about 2 hours. Makes 6 servings.

SAN JUK
(Meat on Skewers)

    1 pound tender beef steak, in one piece
    8 scallions
    4 large carrots
    6 mushrooms
    ¼ cup soy sauce
    2 tablespoons sugar
    1½ tablespoons sesame-seed oil
    3 tablespoons minced onion
    1 tablespoon ground toasted sesame seed
    2 teaspoons minced garlic

Cut beef into 1½-inch cubes. Cut scallions and carrots into 2-inch lengths. Cut mushrooms into halves. Parboil carrots until tender but firm. Arrange scallions, meat, carrots, and mushrooms alternately on skewers. Prepare a skewer or two per person. Dip into sauce made of soy sauce, sugar, sesame-seed oil, onion, sesame seed, and garlic, and grill over an open fire 6 to 8 inches above the coals, turning skewers occasionally to brown on all sides. Or broil meat 6 inches away from source of heat, turning skewers occasionally. Makes 4 servings.

TONGDAK JUK
(Roasted Chicken)

    1 large roasting chicken (about 6 pounds)
    2 tablespoons sesame-seed oil
    3 tablespoons sugar
    ¼ cup soy sauce
    3 tablespoons minced onion
    2 teaspoons minced garlic
    1 teaspoon minced gingerroot
    1 to 2 teaspoons pepper (depending on taste)
    1 tablespoon ground toasted sesame seed

Steam chicken for 1 hour. Combine all other ingredients to make basting sauce. Pour some sauce over the chicken. Skewer chicken and grill over charcoal, turning and basting often, for 1 hour. A rotisserie can also be used, or roast on rack in preheated slow oven (325°F.) for 3½ to 4 hours, turning and basting frequently. Before serving, brush with sesame-seed oil to give chicken a good color and a special flavor. Makes 4 to 6 servings.

DAK CHIM
(Steamed Chicken)

    1 large roasting chicken (about 6 pounds)
    3 tablespoons sugar
    ¼ cup soy sauce
    3 tablespoons minced onion
    2 teaspoons minced garlic
    ½ teaspoon minced gingerroot
    2 tablespoons ground toasted sesame seed
    ¼ teaspoon pepper
    1 tablespoon sesame-seed oil
    8 mushrooms
    3 ounces cooked canned bamboo shoots
    2 carrots
    ¾ cup water
    1 egg, beaten with 2 tablespoons water

Disjoint chicken into 13 pieces and mix with sauce made of sugar, soy sauce, onion, garlic, gingerroot, sesame seed, pepper, and sesame-seed oil. Cut mushrooms into 3 or 4 pieces each. Chop bamboo shoots and carrots into 1-inch pieces. Carrots should be cut into shapes of flowers or plants. Pour water into a large pan. Bring water to boil. Add the chicken and cook over high heat for 4 to 5 minutes. Cover and simmer for 15 minutes. Add vegetables and cook, covered, for 30 to 40 minutes. Remove lid and continue cooking until chicken is tender and water is almost evaporated. While chicken is cooking, pour egg into a lightly buttered 6-inch skillet and prepare a thin omelet. Turn out omelet and cut it into diamond shapes about 1 inch long. When serving, decorate the dish with "egg diamonds." Makes 4 to 6 servings.

VEGETABLES, SALAD, AND SAUCE

OI BOKUM NAMUL
(Cooked Cucumbers)

    3 cucumbers
    2 teaspoons salt
    1 tablespoon sesame-seed oil
    3 tablespoons soy sauce
    1½ teaspoons sugar
    ½ tablespoon minced onion
    ¼ teaspoon red pepper
    1 tablespoon ground toasted sesame seed

Peel cucumbers and cut into thin round slices; sprinkle with salt. Set aside for 1 or 2 hours until cucumbers become soft. Press out liquid. Heat sesame-seed oil in frying pan and cook cucumbers while adding sauce made by combining soy sauce, sugar, onion, and red pepper. When cucumbers are tender, sprinkle with ground sesame seed and serve. Makes 4 to 6 servings.

KIM KUI
(Toasted Seaweed)

    10 sheets seaweed (1 package)
    3 tablespoons sesame-seed oil
    1 teaspoon salt

Brush seaweed with sesame-seed oil, sprinkle with salt, and toast over open flame, in hot frying pan, or in a broiler, until the seaweed turns green. Cut into quarters. Makes 6 to 8 servings.

SAM SAEK NAMUL
(Tricolored Vegetables)

    2 carrots
    2½ tablespoons sesame-seed oil
    ¼ cup soy sauce
    1 tablespoon sugar
    2 tablespoons minced green onion
    1 teaspoon minced garlic
    1½ teaspoons red pepper
    2½ tablespoons ground toasted sesame seed
    ½ pound fresh spinach, washed and drained
    1 tablespoon vinegar
    1½ cups drained bean sprouts*

Cut carrots into very thin slices and cook in 1 tablespoon sesame-seed oil until tender crisp. Add 2 tablespoons soy sauce, 2 teaspoons sugar, 1 tablespoon green onion, the garlic, and ½ teaspoon red pepper. Cook until liquid is absorbed. Stir in 1 tablespoon ground sesame seed. Cook spinach slightly in salted boiling water for 2 minutes. Drain well and cut into strips. Add ½ teaspoon sesame-seed oil, 1 tablespoon soy sauce, remaining sugar, and the vinegar, ½ tablespoon green onion, 1 tablespoon sesame seed, and ½ teaspoon red pepper. Cook bean sprouts in ½ cup water for 10 minutes. Drain. Combine remaining sesame-seed oil, soy sauce, minced green onion, ground sesame seed, and red pepper. To serve, arrange vegetables in 3 different color sections on a platter. Makes 6 servings.

*BEAN SPROUTS

Bean sprouts may be grown from 2 kinds of beans, the small green Chinese mung bean, or the larger yellow soy bean. One cup of dry beans will yield 2 to 3 cups of sprouts. Beans that are old will not sprout well. Examine beans and discard any that are cracked or broken. Wash beans thoroughly, put into 2-quart large-mouthed jar, and soak for 12 hours. Pour off water. Place jar on its side and raise bottom several inches to permit all water to drain off. Keep in this position until beans are sprouted. Three times a day pour lukewarm water over beans and drain. Beans should be kept damp, not wet. At night, add a pinch of chlorinated lime to water used to rinse beans. Keep jar in a dark place where air circulates freely. Sprouting time depends upon the temperature. In cool weather 3 to 5 days are sufficient. When sprouts have formed, wash thoroughly and remove skin from beans and also the hairlike end from each sprout.

KEJA CHAE
(Salad with Mustard)

Carrots, cucumbers, cabbage or
  lettuce, and celery
Pear
Cooked meat
Cooked shrimps
Egg, made into thin pancake and
  cut into thin strips
Powdered mustard
Salad oil
Vinegar
Sugar
Salt

Cut carrots, cucumbers, cabbage, celery, pear, and meat into very fine strips 1½ inches long. Shred shrimps. Arrange all artistically on a serving plate. Garnish with egg strips. For dressing, mix mustard with a little salad oil, vinegar, sugar, and salt to taste. Pour dressing over ingredients in serving plate. Toss at the table.

VINEGAR-SOY SAUCE

6 tablespoons soy sauce
6 tablespoons vinegar
2 tablespoons sugar
1 tablespoon chopped pine nuts

Combine soy sauce, vinegar, and sugar. Mix well and put 2 tablespoons of sauce into individual dishes. Chop pine nuts into fine pieces. Sprinkle over the top of each dish of soy sauce. The vinegar-soy sauce is served in individual dishes so that the individual diner may dip fried foods into the sauce just before eating.

KIMCHI
(Korean Pickle)

2 pounds vegetables: cabbage, yellow
  turnip, and cucumber
2 tablespoons salt
1½ tablespoons minced onion
1 teaspoon minced garlic
⅔ teaspoon minced gingerroot
½ to 1 tablespoon ground red pepper

Wash and drain vegetables. Peel turnip and cucumber. Slice vegetables into small pieces. Sprinkle with 2 tablespoons salt and let stand for 3 to 4 hours. Press out liquid. Mix vegetables well with onion, garlic, gingerroot, and red pepper. Put vegetables in a large glass jar with a tight lid. Leave jar in the refrigerator for 3 to 4 days. Serve with meals. Makes about 2 pints.

KOSHER—From the Hebrew word *kasher* meaning "fitting," "lawful," or "pure." The word is applied most often to food and utensils which have undergone the operations and rituals laid down for orthodox Jews in conformity with the laws of the Talmud. The regulations as to the types of food which may or may not be eaten and to those foods which may or may not be eaten together derive from interpretations of Biblical injunctions.

Kosher foods of all kinds are available in Jewish and many non-Jewish stores. They are often marked by a *U* in a circle, by a *K* in a circle, or simply by a K.

KUMQUAT—The smallest of the citrus fruits, the kumquat grows on small evergreen shrubs which have aromatic white flowers. The kumquats themselves are oblong and the size of a small plum. They have a thick golden-orange spicy rind, acid, rather dry flesh, and small seeds. Kumquats are grown for the ornamental qualities of the shrub and for the fruit, which usually is eaten cooked whole in a sugar syrup, candied, or in marmalade.

Kumquats, like sweet and mandarin oranges, were eaten in China thousands of years ago. The word itself comes from the Chinese and it incorporates the meaning of "gold." Preserved kumquats are a staple dessert of Chinese restaurants.

Generally speaking, kumquats are better eaten cooked than raw. If used raw, they should be very ripe or else they will be unpalatable. They can be cut up or sliced and used for salads and fruit cups. Cooked kumquats are delicious either as a compote, or as a relish with meats and game. They make an excellent dessert when served with cream cheese and are used to make jellies, marmalades, conserves, and crystallized fruit.

Availability and Purchasing Guide—Fresh kumquats are available November through February. Choose firm fruit, heavy for its size.

Kumquats are also available preserved.

Storage—Refrigerate fresh kumquats to avoid drying and wrinkling.

☐ Fresh, refrigerator shelf, uncut: 1
  month

☐ Preserved, kitchen shelf, unopened: 3
  years

Nutritive Food Values—Contains potassium and vitamins A and C.

☐ Fresh, 3½ ounces, raw = 65 calories

Basic Preparation—Wash and dry.

☐ **To Stew**—Put 1 quart kumquats in saucepan and add water. Bring to boil and drain. Repeat this process two more times. In last amount of water, cook kumquats for 5 minutes, or until tender. Drain. Mix ¾ cup water and 2 cups sugar. Cook for 5 minutes, or until a syrup is formed. Add kumquats and simmer for 5 minutes. Chill. Serve whole, or cut in half and remove seeds. Makes 8 servings.

KUMQUAT, ORANGE, AND APPLE COMPOTE

3 preserved kumquats, sliced
1 cup orange sections
2 large tart apples, cut in thin slices
  Toasted slivered almonds

Mix fruits and chill. Just before serving, sprinkle with nuts. Makes 4 servings.

KUMQUAT-GINGER RELISH

4 cups kumquats (about 1 pound)
2 cups sugar
1 cup water
½ to 1 teaspoon ground ginger,
  depending on taste

Remove all stems and leaves from kumquats. Wash fruit thoroughly. Combine sugar, water, and ginger and boil for 5 minutes. Add kumquats. Simmer, covered, over low heat for 45 minutes, or until tender. Serve as a relish with roast chicken, duck, or pork, or as a sauce for ice cream. Makes about 1 quart preserves.

ALMOND-STUFFED KUMQUAT PRESERVE

2 quarts whole kumquats
2 pounds sugar
4 cups water
  Blanched almonds

Wash kumquats; rinse well; drain. Prick each kumquat with a sharp fork to prevent bursting. Drop into enough boiling water to cover and simmer until tender. Drain. Boil sugar and water together for 10 minutes. Add drained kumquats. Cook, partially covered, until fruit is transparent. Remove from heat, cover tightly, and let plump for 24 hours. Remove kumquats from syrup, slit lengthwise, and remove seeds. Fill each fruit with a blanched almond. Replace fruit in syrup, reheat, then pack in hot sterilized jars. Fill jars with strained hot syrup. Seal tightly immediately. Process jars for 10 minutes at a simmering temperature (180°F.). Makes about six ½-pint jars.

CANDIED KUMQUATS

4 cups whole kumquats (about 1
  pound)
  Sugar
1 cup water
  Pecan halves (optional)

Stem and wash kumquats. Cover with water and bring to a boil. Boil for 5 minutes. Drain and cut into halves lengthwise. Combine 2 cups sugar and the water and boil until sugar is dissolved. Drop kumquats into boiling syrup. Cook over low heat for 10 minutes. Cover and let stand overnight. Cook for 20 more minutes and lift from syrup. Place on wax paper to cool. If desired, place half a pecan in each piece of kumquat. Roll in sugar. Store in container. Makes about 2 pounds.

LAMB—A lamb is a young sheep of either sex that has not reached maturity. Generally the flesh from sheep under one year of age is considered to be lamb, while flesh from sheep of greater maturity is referred to as mutton. Spring lamb is the meat of young animals slaughtered between March and September.

Sheep are among the earliest of man's animal foods. There are remains that indicate that primitive man in prehistoric times ate the now extinct "bighorn" sheep. Throughout Asia bands of wild sheep were followed by nomadic tribes, who later domesticated the woolly animals. Sheep spread from Asia Minor to the Mediterranean countries and throughout Europe. In America the Spanish, famous for their sheep, introduced them into the Southwest. And in Colonial days, the smuggling of sheep into the eastern seaports by adventurous sea captains (the English had put strict restrictions on the importation of the profitable animals) was a brisk business.

Lambs are surrounded by many customs and traditions. In the Christian religion they have long been a symbol of Christ, who is known as the Lamb of God. They also symbolize innocence. But the pagans included lambs among the animals who were sacred to Juno, scarcely an innocent goddess. Her other favorite, in fact, was the lordly peacock.

Since sheep were among the animals that flourished in the arid lands of the Middle East, it is not surprising that they figure largely in the folklore and religions of all of these countries. As we know from the Bible, the ancient Israelites were for a large part shepherds, and lamb played a great role as a ceremonial meat. One of the earliest recorded directions for eating lamb is found in the Old Testament. Before the flight of the Jews from Egypt the Lord instructed them "In the tenth day of this month they shall take to them every man a lamb, according to the house of their fathers, a lamb for an house" (Exodus 12:3). He further ordered them to kill the lambs and mark their doors with the blood. Then, said the Lord: "And they shall eat the flesh in that night, roast with fire, and unleavened bread; and with bitter herbs they shall eat it" (Exodus 12:8).

One of the first cook-book writers, the 1st-century A.D. Roman, Apicus, records recipes for lamb stew basted with pepper, hazelwort, ginger, parsley, asafoetida, oil, and a sort of fishy brine called liquamen; boned whole lamb; and lamb braised in milk, honey, pepper, salt, and asafoetida.

The 13th-century author of the Baghdad cookery book published in 1226, Muhammad ibn al-Hasan ibn Muhammed ibn al-Karim al-Katib al-Babhadi to quote his full name, includes a recipe for lamb fattened with pistachio nuts, which is thin cubes of lamb wrapped around the nuts. This was a popular dish among the Persians and Arabs, for it is mentioned at that time in *The Arabian Nights.*

Lamb seems to have an affinity for stuffings and sauces. One of the three musketeers, Porthos, in Dumas' mid-19th-century novel of 17th-century France, *The Vicomte de Bragelonne,* tells of a cook who "first stuffs the lamb in question with small sausages which he procures from Strasburg, forcemeat-balls which he procure from Troyes, and larks which he procures from Pithiviers, by some means or other . . . he bones the lamb as he would bone a fowl, leaving the skin on." This is merely an elaboration of the 1st-century classic Roman preparation. The stuffing of a whole lamb was popular in England as well, for in 1609 Sir Hugh Platt describes how "to boyle a legge of Mutton after the French fashion." It is stuffed with ox suet, bread, cream, egg yolks, "a few sweete hearbes," currants, raisins, nutmeg, mace, pepper, and sugar. Directions are to serve "dry with caret rootes sliced, and cast grosse pepper upon the rootes." Another 17th-century English recipe, that of John Murrel in 1631, calls for a roast lamb seared, and then stewed with "halfe a pinte of white wine, Vinegar, a handfull of French Capers, a dozen Raisins of the Sun, the stones being pickt out, five or six Dates broken in quarters, five or sixe Olives sliced, five or sixe blades of Mace, an handfull of powder Sugar." He directs: "Stew all these untill they be halfe stewed away; then dish your Shoulder, and poure this sauce on the toppe of the meate, throw on Salt, and serve it hot to the Table."

One of the characters in *Pendennis,* Thackeray's novel of 1850, is a French chef, Alcide Mirobolant, formerly Chef to His Highness the Duc de Borodino and to His Eminence Cardinal Beccafico. He describes a lamb dish, "the only brown thing" in a white dinner prepared for his love Blanche, "a little roast of lamb, which I laid in a meadow of spinaches, surrounded with croustillons, representing sheep, and ornamented with daisies and other savage flowers."

English lamb, served with the traditional mint sauce, is one of the favorite dishes of the British Isles. Norwegian lamb too, is excellent, and it seems a fact that the farther north you go in Europe, the more delicate the lamb. The *présalé* lamb of northern France, very young spring lamb raised on salt-marsh farms, is unparalleled for flavor and it lends itself to the French way of cooking it: rare and pink.

Lamb is the chief meat of the Middle East, whose meat cookery is based upon it. From roast skewered lamb to lamb roasted with fragrant herbs, lamb stews, ground lamb cooked alone or with vegetables, Middle Eastern cookery offers a bewildering number of lamb dishes.

Availability—All year round. Most plentiful between January and March. For information on the cuts of lamb available, see chart on Retail Cuts of Lamb, page 1026.

The lamb variety meats available are brains, heart, kidneys, liver, tongue, and sweetbreads. Lamb tongues are available pickled.

Canned lamb products available include stew, Scotch broth, and baby and junior foods.

Purchasing Guide—The color of lean lamb meat varies with the age of the animal, becoming darker with increasing age. Young, milk-fed lamb will have light pink lean. Spring lamb will have deeper pink lean and the average market lamb will have pinkish-red lean. The texture should always be fine and velvety. The fat should be smooth, firm, white, rather brittle but of a waxy consistency. The outer fat is covered with a parchment-like tissue called the fell, which helps keep the wholesale cut fresh and protected if the lamb is aged. This is sometimes removed from retail cuts before they are offered for sale.

Storage—Remove from market paper or loosen wrapper; store unwrapped or loosely wrapped in coldest part of refrigerator.

☐ Raw, ground lamb, stew meat, and variety meats, refrigerator shelf: 2 days

☐ Raw, chops and steaks, refrigerator shelf: 2 to 4 days

☐ Raw, roasts, refrigerator shelf: 5 to 6 days

☐ Cooked, lamb and gravy; and canned, opened and covered, refrigerator shelf: 4 to 5 days

☐ Raw, refrigerator frozen-food compartment, prepared for freezing: 2 to 3 weeks

☐ Raw, all types except ground, freezer, prepared for freezing: 6 to 7 months

☐ Raw, ground, freezer, prepared for freezing: 3 to 4 months

☐ Cooked, lamb and gravy, freezer, prepared for freezing: 2 to 3 months

☐ Canned, kitchen shelf: 1 year

Lamb, once thawed, should not be refrozen.

Nutritive Food Values—Lamb is an excellent source of protein, iron, and niacin, a fair source of riboflavin.

☐ Breast of lamb, 3½ ounces, stewed = 285 calories

☐ Leg of lamb, 3½ ounces, roasted = 319 calories

☐ Loin lamb chops, bone in, 3½ ounces, broiled = 302 calories

☐ Rib lamb chops, bone in, 3½ ounces, broiled = 423 calories

☐ Shoulder, lean and fat, 3½ ounces, roasted = 374 calories

☐ Brains, 3½ ounces, raw = 125 calories

☐ Heart, 3½ ounces, raw = 162 calories

☐ Kidneys, 3½ ounces, raw = 105 calories

☐ Liver, 3½ ounces, raw = 136 calories

☐ Sweetbreads, 3½ ounces, raw = 94 calories

☐ Tongue, 3½ ounces, raw = 199 calories

☐ Tongue, 3½ ounces, braised = 254 calories

Basic Preparation—The cuts of lamb generally used for roasting and broiling come from shoulder, rib, loin, or leg sections. The cuts used for stuffing, braising, cooking in liquid, and grinding generally come from the heart, neck, flank, and shanks. See chart of Retail Cuts of Lamb, page 1026.

☐ **To Roast Lamb**—Remove any fell from cut selected for roasting and wipe meat with a damp cloth. Put on a rack in shallow roasting pan and sprinkle with salt and pepper. If desired, rub meat with a cut garlic clove or sprinkle with herbs such as rosemary, thyme, or marjoram. Do not cover or add water. Insert a meat thermometer into center of thickest part of meat. Roast in preheated slow oven (300° to 325°F.) until thermometer registers degree of doneness desired. See Timetable for Roasting for interior temperature and time. Plan to have roast done 15 to 20 minutes before serving time to allow for making gravy.

☐ **To Make Gravy**—For each cup of gravy desired, use 2 tablespoons drippings, 2 tablespoons all-purpose flour, and 1 cup liquid. Lift roast from pan and pour off all fat except the amount needed. Leave any brown bits in the pan. Blend in flour completely. Put pan over moderately low heat and cook and stir until mixture bubbles and begins to brown. Remove from heat and gradually stir in

TIMETABLE FOR ROASTING LAMB

CUT	APPROXIMATE WEIGHT (POUNDS)	OVEN TEMPERATURE	INTERNAL TEMPERATURE	APPROXIMATE COOKING TIME (MINUTES PER POUND)
Leg	5 to 8	300°F. to 325°F.	175°F. to 180°F.	30 to 35
Shoulder	4 to 6	300°F. to 325°F.	175°F. to 180°F.	30 to 35
Rolled Shoulder	3 to 5	300°F. to 325°F.	175°F. to 180°F.	40 to 45
Cushion	3 to 5	300°F. to 325°F.	175°F. to 180°F.	30 to 35

water or other liquid; combine thoroughly. Return pan to heat. Continue cooking and stirring over low heat until gravy thickens and is cooked, 3 to 5 minutes. Season and strain, if desired.

Note: If pan drippings are not brown, a liquid gravy coloring may be added to attain desired color.

☐ **To Roast Lamb in an Electric Rotisserie**—Any of the cuts that can be roasted in an oven lend themselves to rotisserie roasting. Since rotisseries vary greatly from each other in size, strength of heating unit, etc., all of which affect the cooking times of the meat, consult manufacturer's directions to obtain accurate cooking times.

☐ **To Broil Lamb Chops and Patties**—Remove any fell covering on chops and slash fat edge at 1-inch intervals to keep chops from curling. If desired, rub meat with cut garlic clove. Rub preheated broiler rack with small amount of fat cut from chops. Arrange chops or patties on rack and put in preheated broiler about 3 inches from unit. Broil, using Timetable for Broiling. Turn meat when browned and a little more than half the broiling time is up. Sprinkle with salt and pepper and complete broiling.

☐ **To Panbroil Lamb Chops and Patties**—Put meat in a heavy skillet. (Skillet need not be preheated.) Cook meat slowly, turning occasionally, until well browned on both sides and done. Pour off any fat as it accumulates. When done, season with salt and pepper. (Panbroiling will take about half the time required for oven-broiling.)

☐ **To Braise Lamb**—Meat is browned slowly, seasoned and a little liquid such as water, broth, or vegetable juice is added; the heat is lowered to the point where the meat barely simmers, the pan is covered tightly and cooking continues until meat is completely tender. The meat cooks by steam. For cooking time see Timetable for Cooking Lamb.

☐ **To Cook in Liquid**—The procedure is almost exactly as above, but a larger quantity of liquid is added, usually enough to cover the meat. Recipes, however, are usually required because of the differences in flavors, other foods to be added, the size, shape, and thickness of the meat, and a few changes in procedure, such as flouring the meat. The cut of meat is also usually specified, although this may be interchangeable within a group and according to size and taste.

☐ **To Prepare Brains**—Soak in cold salted water for 15 minutes. Wash in cold running water. Drain, cool, and remove outer membrane. Simmer for 10 minutes in boiling salted water. Drain, cut into slices, and dredge with seasoned flour. Or dip in fine dry bread crumbs seasoned with salt and pepper. Sauté in butter or margarine until lightly browned, sprinkle with parsley, and serve with lemon wedges.

☐ **To Prepare Hearts**—Slice hearts and dredge with seasoned flour. Sauté in butter until browned and done. Add a little Madeira and steak sauce to the drippings and pour over hearts. Or braise hearts in small amount of water for 1½ to 2 hours, or until done.

☐ **To Prepare Kidneys**—Cut kidneys almost in half lengthwise, remove the white core with scissors, then wash kidneys. Keep halves open by threading them side by side on a small skewer. Dip each kidney into butter and sprinkle with salt. Broil under high heat for about 3 minutes on each side. Serve with herb butter or with lemon wedges.

☐ **To Prepare Liver**—Sold sliced, this can be prepared the same way as any other liver. It is tender and has a delicate flavor.

☐ **To Prepare Tongue**—This is generally braised in salted water for 1¼ hours, or until tender. Seasonings such as a few peppercorns, an onion stuck with cloves, a bay leaf, a sliced carrot, and a celery stalk can be added to the water.

☐ **To Prepare Sweetbreads**—These should first be soaked in cold salted water for 15 minutes. Then bring to boil in salted water to cover and boil for 10 minutes. Drain, cool, and remove outer membrane. Slice, brush well with butter, and broil for 3 to 5 minutes on each side.

RETAIL CUTS OF LAMB—WHERE THEY COME FROM

TENDER
1. Shoulder Section
Square-cut shoulder roast
Rolled shoulder roast
Cushion shoulder roast
Saratoga chops
Blade chops
Arm chops
Mock duck
2. Rib Section
Rib roast
Crown roast
Rib chops
3. Loin Section
Loin (saddle) roast
Rolled double loin roast
English chops
Loin chops
Sirloin chops
Sirloin roast
Rolled double sirloin roast
4. Leg Section
Sirloin half of leg roast
Leg roast, sirloin on
Leg roast, sirloin off
American leg roast
Center leg roast

Combination leg
Rolled leg roast
French leg roast
Leg chop (steak)
Shank half of leg
Hind shank
5. Breast Section
Breast
Rolled breast
Breast with pocket
Stuffed breast
Stuffed chops
LESS TENDER
Neck slices
Ribs (for barbecue)
Riblets (single ribs)
Brisket pieces (front of breast section)
Fore shank
GROUND LAMB (generally from neck, breast, shanks, and flank)
Ground lamb
Lamburgers
CUBE STEAKS (generally from brisket)
LAMB FOR STEW (generally from forequarter cuts)

TIMETABLE FOR BROILING LAMB

Set oven regulator for broiling. Adjust broiler pan and rack so that top of meat is approximately 2 inches below heat for 1- to 1½-inch cuts, 3 inches for thicker cuts.

CUT	WEIGHT (OUNCES)	APPROX. COOKING TIME Minutes—Medium done
Shoulder chops		
1 inch	5 to 8	12
1½ inches	8 to 10	18
2 inches	10 to 1 pound	22
Rib chops		
1 inch	3 to 5	12
1½ inches	4 to 7	18
2 inches	6 to 10	22
Loin chops		
1 inch	4 to 7	12
1½ inches	6 to 10	18
2 inches	8 to 14	22
Ground lamb, patties		
1 by 3 inches	4	18

Lamb chops are not usually served rare.

TIMETABLE FOR BRAISING LAMB

CUT	AVERAGE WEIGHT OR THICKNESS	APPROX. TOTAL COOKING TIME
Breast—stuffed	2 to 3 pounds	1½ to 2 hours
Breast—rolled	1½ to 2 pounds	1½ to 2 hours
Neck slices	¾ inch	1 hour
Shanks	¾ to 1 pound each	1 to 1½ hours
Shoulder chops	¾ to 1 inch	45 to 60 minutes
COOKING IN LIQUID		
for stew	1 to 2 inch pieces	1½ to 2 hours

Roast Leg of Lamb

LAMB
COOK BOOK

Mouthwatering recipes for tempting chops, succulent steaks, tender juicy roasts, and those wonderful money-saving cuts: neck, breast, riblets, and shanks

LEG, LOIN (SADDLE), RIB, AND CROWN ROAST OF LAMB

RARE ROAST LEG OF LAMB

5- pound leg of lamb
4 garlic cloves
  Salt and pepper
  Flour
½ cup dry red wine
1 tablespoon butter

Cut slits in lamb and insert garlic cloves. Put on rack in roasting pan and sprinkle with salt, pepper, and flour. Roast in preheated moderate oven (350°F.) for 20 minutes. Add wine and roast for 40 minutes longer, basting occasionally with drippings in pan. Remove to a hot platter and top with butter. Slice very thin and serve with the drippings. Makes 6 to 8 servings.

ROAST LAMB WITH HERB MUSTARD GLAZE

1 leg of lamb (about 6 pounds)
⅓ cup prepared mustard
2 tablespoons soy sauce
1 garlic clove, crushed
1 teaspoon crushed rosemary or thyme
¼ teaspoon ground ginger

Put lamb on rack in shallow baking pan. Roast in preheated slow oven (325°F.) for 1 hour. Combine remaining ingredients and spread over lamb. Roast 1½ hours longer, or until done. Baste with its own drippings once or twice during roasting time. Makes 6 to 8 servings.

BOILED LEG OF LAMB WITH CAPER SAUCE

Trim all skin and fat from a leg of lamb. Cover with boiling salted water. Add 1 each for each pound of meat: medium carrots, onions, small turnips, 2-inch pieces of celery and leeks (optional). Simmer, covered, for 15 to 20 minutes for each pound of meat. Skim frequently to preserve color of meat. Drain, reserving the broth. Serve with mashed or boiled potatoes and Caper Sauce made with the lamb broth.

Caper Sauce

Make medium white sauce, using half milk, half lamb broth. To each cup, add 2 tablespoons capers, 1 teaspoon caper liquid.

POLISH ROAST LEG OF LAMB

5- pound leg of lamb, trimmed of all fat
  Salt and pepper
3 garlic cloves, cut into slivers

20 juniper berries, crushed
2 cups cider or white wine vinegar
2 large onions, sliced
½ pound salt pork, cut into thin slices

With a sharp knife cut pockets in lamb. Rub with salt and pepper. Insert garlic slivers and crushed juniper berries. Heat vinegar to boiling point and pour over lamb. Arrange onion slices on lamb. Marinate for 1 or 2 days, turning occasionally. Discard onion and reserve marinade. Dry lamb. Wrap in salt-pork slices and tie with kitchen string. Roast in preheated hot oven (400°F.) for 2 to 2½ hours, basting very frequently with marinade. Makes 6 to 8 servings.

LEG OF LAMB, CREOLE

½ cup chili sauce
2 tablespoons cider vinegar
½ cup dry red wine
2 tablespoons olive oil
1 cup beef bouillon
1 tablespoon sugar
1 teaspoon salt
½ teaspoon pepper
1 bay leaf
2 onions, minced
2 garlic cloves, minced
8- pound leg of lamb

Mix all ingredients except lamb. Pour over meat. Let stand in refrigerator for at least 6 hours, basting meat occasionally with the sauce. Put lamb on rack in roasting pan. Add sauce and roast, uncovered, in preheated slow oven (325°F.) for about 4 hours, basting occasionally with the sauce. Add boiling water if liquid evaporates. Remove lamb to a hot platter. Thicken gravy. Makes 8 to 10 servings. Can be frozen.

LOIN OF LAMB, BÉARNAISE

6- pound loin of lamb
1 garlic clove
¼ cup dry white wine
¼ cup melted butter
  Sauce Béarnaise

Have lamb cut and tied by butcher. Rub with garlic and put on rack in roasting pan. Roast in preheated slow oven (325°F.) for about 2½ hours, basting occasionally with wine and butter mixed. Serve with Sauce Béarnaise. Makes 8 servings.

Sauce Béarnaise

3 tablespoons each of water and tarragon vinegar
4 egg yolks, slightly beaten
½ teaspoon salt
⅛ teaspoon each of paprika and onion salt
¼ cup butter, creamed

Heat water and vinegar to boiling. Pour over egg yolks, stirring. Add seasonings and cook over hot water until thickened,

stirring constantly. Stir in butter, about 1 tablespoon at a time. Serve at once.

GARNISHED COLD ROAST LOIN OF LAMB

Arrange thin slices of lamb on platter. Place 1 tablespoon chopped jellied consommé or madrilene on each slice. On platter border, arrange alternating mounds of jellied consommé or madrilene and minted cucumbers. Serve with cold green beans with French dressing made with lemon juice to which prepared mustard has been added.

RIB ROAST (RACK) OF LAMB WITH CHUTNEY GLAZE

About 2 cups (one 1-pound can), sliced cling peaches
⅔ cup chutney
3- pound rib roast of lamb, trimmed of excess fat

Drain peaches; reserve syrup. Combine peach syrup and chutney. Place lamb on rack in shallow roasting pan. Baste with some chutney mixture. Bake in preheated slow oven (325°F.) for 1½ to 2 hours, depending on degree of doneness desired, basting frequently with chutney mixture. During last 10 minutes of cooking time, arrange peaches around lamb. Continue basting peaches and lamb. Makes 4 servings.

CROWN ROAST OF LAMB

¼ cup cooking oil
½ cup chopped green pepper or pimiento
1 cup chopped mushrooms
1 cup small white onions, cooked
2 cups cooked wild or brown rice
  Salt and pepper
½ teaspon dried marjoram
5- to 6-pound crown roast of lamb

Heat oil. Cook green pepper and mushrooms in it until barely tender. Add onions, rice, salt, pepper, and marjoram. Fill lamb with this mixture. Place on rack in roasting pan. Bake in preheated slow oven (325°F.) for 2½ to 3 hours, depending on degree of doneness desired. Makes 6 servings.

SHOULDER OF LAMB, IN LARGE PIECES

LAMB HARICOT

1½ cups dried white beans or baby Limas
¼ pound salt pork, diced
2 pounds lamb shoulder, cut into pieces
1½ teaspoons salt
  Pepper to taste
1 cup chopped onions

1 Scotch Broth
2 Savory Turkish Lamb Pilaf
3 Brunch Lamb Kidney Stew
4 Baked Orange Lamb Steaks
5 Stuffed Lamb Chops
6 Mexican Lamb Stew

3

4

5

1 tablespoon flour
4 cups water
   Herb bouquet (parsley, bay leaf, and
   thyme or marjoram)
3 tablespoons minced parsley

Cook beans in salted water for 30 minutes; drain. Brown diced pork in a flame-proof casserole; remove and reserve. In the pork fat brown the lamb; season with salt and pepper and add onions. Cook for 10 minutes and drain off surplus fat. Stir in flour; add water, herb bouquet, and beans. Cover and bake in preheated moderate oven (350°F.) for 1½ to 2 hours, or until the meat is tender. Discard herbs; correct seasoning; add pork. Sprinkle with minced parsley and serve from the same dish. Makes 6 servings.

SPICY ROAST LAMB SHOULDER
   Boned and rolled shoulder of lamb
   (about 3¼ pounds)
2 teaspoons salt
½ teaspoon ground ginger
1 teaspoon each of paprika, pepper,
   and celery salt
2 teaspoons dried marjoram
2 garlic cloves, minced
2 tablespoons water

Put meat, fat side up, on rack in roasting pan. Mix seasonings and water and spread on meat. Roast in preheated slow oven (325°F.) for 2½ to 3 hours. Remove meat to a warm platter. Drain off all except 2 tablespoons of the brownest drippings, add 2 tablespoons flour, and brown lightly. Add 2 cups hot water and cook until thickened. Season. Serve gravy with meat. Makes 8 servings.
Note: Seasonings can be omitted, if desired. Roast meat as directed above.

BARBECUED LAMB IN FOIL
4 pounds lamb shoulder, cut into 6
   serving pieces and trimmed of excess
   fat
⅓ cup flour
1 tablespoon cooking oil
6 small onions, peeled
6 small potatoes, peeled
6 small tomatoes
1 large eggplant, peeled and cut into
   large serving pieces
¼ cup chopped green pepper
1 teaspoon each of salt and seasoned
   salt
½ teaspoon pepper
2 bay leaves, crushed
½ to 1 teaspoon dried thyme or
   marjoram

Cut aluminum foil into 6 pieces 15 inches square. Dredge lamb with flour and brown on all sides in oil. Place each piece on a sheet of foil. To each add 1 onion, 1 potato, 1 tomato, and 1/6 of eggplant pieces. Sprinkle with chopped green pepper. Combine seasonings and

sprinkle over each portion. Wrap each portion and fold over foil to fasten securely. Place in foil-lined baking pan and cover with more foil. Cook on top of barbecue coals for 2½ to 2¾ hours. Or bake in preheated moderate oven (350° F.). Makes 6 servings.

HERBED LAMB SHOULDER
4 pounds boned and rolled lamb
   shoulder
1 garlic clove
2 tablespoons fat
½ teaspoon ground sage
1 teaspoon each of ground rosemary,
   thyme, and marjoram
1 bay leaf
   Salt and pepper
½ cup water

Rub lamb with cut garlic clove; brown on all sides in hot fat in heavy kettle; remove meat and pour off fat. Put rack under meat in kettle. Add herbs and sprinkle meat with salt and pepper. Add water; cover and simmer for 3 hours, or until meat is tender. Remove meat and thicken liquid with a flour-and-water paste. Season with salt and pepper to taste. Makes 6 servings.

CANTONESE BROILED LAMB
2 pounds shoulder of lamb
2 garlic cloves, crushed
6 tablespoons soy sauce
1 tablespoon sugar
1 teaspoon salt

Cut the lamb into 1-inch cubes, and then into slices ¼ inch thick. Add garlic to soy sauce, sugar, and salt. Marinate meat in this mixture for 30 minutes, turning frequently. Remove meat from marinade and place under a very hot broiler for about 5 minutes, turning once or twice. Serve in a shallow dish immediately. Makes 4 servings.

LAMB NAVARIN
2½ pounds boneless lamb shoulder
3 tablespoons clarified butter or
   cooking oil
3 tablespoons chopped shallots or
   onion
2 tablespoons all-purpose flour
2 cups water
1 cup peeled seeded chopped tomatoes
   or 1 cup tomato puree
½ cup dry white wine
1 garlic clove
   Herb bouquet (1 bay leaf, 2 parsley
   sprigs, 1 thyme sprig)
   Salt and pepper
6 carrots
4 white turnips
12 small onions
3 tablespoons butter

Cut the lamb into 1½- to 2-inch cubes and brown in the clarified butter. Add shallots and brown; then add flour, water,

tomatoes, wine, garlic, and herb bouquet. Simmer for 45 minutes, remove meat, and strain liquid back over it. Season to taste. Scrape carrots and cut into 1-inch slices; peel turnips and quarter; peel onions. Brown vegetables in the butter, then add to meat and liquid. Cover and simmer until tender, 30 to 45 minutes, adding water or bouillon if necessary. Skim off fat and serve with crusty bread. Makes 4 to 6 servings.

LAMB STEAKS

GARLIC LAMB STEAKS
Lamb loves garlic and steaks are no exception. Crush 1 garlic clove and let it rest in ½ cup olive oil. Tie some celery leaves, a bunch of parsley, and a good sprig of rosemary or marjoram together in a fagot, and use this to brush the garlic oil on steaks while they are cooking. Cook steaks over a brisk fire from 3 to 6 minutes on a side, basting them with garlic oil. Season.

BAKED ORANGE LAMB STEAKS
2 lamb steaks, trimmed of excess fat
   and cut into halves
1 teaspoon salt
2 medium oranges, sliced
2 tablespoons brown sugar
1 tablespoon grated orange rind
½ teaspoon ground ginger
¼ teaspoon ground cloves
1 teaspoon dried mint flakes
¼ cup melted butter or margarine

Arrange lamb in shallow baking dish. Sprinkle with salt. Top with orange slices. Combine all other ingredients and pour over lamb and orange slices. Bake in preheated slow oven (325°F.) for about 40 minutes, basting often. Makes 4 servings.

LAMB STEAKS IN MARINADE
2 pounds lamb sliced from leg, 1 inch
   thick
3 tablespoons each of olive oil and
   vinegar
½ teaspoon salt
1 onion, minced
   Few parsley sprigs, chopped
   Few rosemary leaves, chopped
   Butter or margarine

Pound meat to about ¾-inch thickness. Put in bowl. Mix remaining ingredients except butter and pour over meat. Refrigerate for several hours or overnight. Sauté meat quickly on both sides in small amount of hot butter in skillet. Put on hot platter. Heat marinade in skillet and pour over meat before serving. Makes 4 servings.

LAMB CHOPS

LANCASHIRE HOT POT

2 pounds lamb shoulder chops
3 lamb kidneys
6 medium potatoes
3 medium onions
½ pound mushrooms, sliced
½ cup minced ham
Salt and pepper
1 cup undiluted canned consommé
¼ cup butter or margarine

Put a layer of chops in the bottom of a casserole. Peel and slice the kidneys, potatoes, and onions and arrange half in the casserole with half of the mushrooms and ham, with salt and pepper sprinkled over. Add another layer of chops. Top with remaining vegetable, kidney, and ham mixture. Pour the consommé over all and dot with butter. Cover and bake in preheated slow oven (300°F.) for 1½ hours. Remove cover, increase heat to hot (400°F.), and bake for 15 minutes. Thicken gravy if desired. Makes 6 servings.

STUFFED LAMB CHOPS

6 thick loin lamp chops
1 tablespoon butter
2 tablespoons each of minced onion and celery
2 tablespoons fresh white bread crumbs
1 teaspoon grated lemon rind
1 tablespoon chopped parsley or chives
Salt and pepper
1 egg yolk or enough light cream to moisten stuffing
Tomato wedges

Cut a pocket in each chop. Heat butter and cook onion in it until soft and golden. Combine with all other ingredients except last 2. Bind with egg yolk. Stuff chops and broil as usual. Serve with tomato wedges. Makes 6 servings.

BARBECUED LAMB CHOPS

1 can (8 ounces) tomato sauce
½ cup minced green onions
1 garlic clove, chopped
½ cup chopped fresh mushrooms or
¼ cup canned mushrooms
2 tablespoons cooking oil
1 tablespoon molasses
2 tablespoons vinegar (preferably tarragon vinegar)
1 teaspoon steak sauce
1 teaspoon salt
½ teaspoon powdered mustard
Dash of hot pepper sauce
4 Saratoga or shoulder lamb chops, at least ¾ inch thick

Combine all ingredients except chops. Cook over low heat, stirring occasionally, for about 15 minutes. Brush lamb with sauce. Broil 3 to 4 inches from heat for 5 to 7 minutes on each side. Brush frequently with barbecue sauce. Makes 4 servings.

Broiled Lamb Chops with broiled tomatoes and stuffed baked potatoes

LAMB CHOPS WITH APPLES AND POTATOES

4 shoulder, blade, or arm lamb chops trimmed of excess fat
2 tablespoons butter or margarine
8 medium potatoes, thinly sliced
4 medium onions, thinly sliced
Salt and pepper
4 apples, peeled, cored, and quartered
1 tablespoon all-purpose flour
1¼ to 1½ cups bouillon
½ cup apple juice or cider
¼ cup grated American cheese

Brown chops quickly in hot butter. Keep hot on separate dish. Cook potatoes and onions in the same butter until golden. Place a layer of vegetables in buttered baking dish. Top with chops and cover with remaining vegetables. Season with salt and pepper. Arrange apples around top of dish. Sprinkle flour into frying pan in which chops were browned and cook until medium brown. Pour in bouillon and boil up once, stirring constantly. Add apple juice and strain liquid into baking dish. Sprinkle with cheese. Bake in preheated moderate oven (375°F.) for about 1 hour, or until tender to the touch of a skewer. Serve from dish. Makes 4 servings.

EAST INDIAN MARINATED LAMB CHOPS

½ cup olive oil
3 tablespoons vinegar
½ teaspoon dried marjoram
4 thick loin or shoulder lamb chops, trimmed of excess fat
1 cup soft stale bread crumbs
½ teaspoon ground mace
2 teaspoons minced parsley
1 teaspoon instant onion
1 tablespoon grated lemon rind
½ teaspoon salt
⅛ teaspoon cayenne
3 tablespoons butter or margarine

Combine olive oil, vinegar, and marjoram. Marinate lamb chops in liquid for at least 4 hours. Combine all other ingredients except butter. Dip marinated chops into mixture and shake free of excess crumbs. Brown chops in melted butter over high heat for 2 minutes; lower heat and cook for 5 to 8 minutes on each side. Makes 4 servings.

BREAST OF LAMB

BAKED STUFFED BREAST OF LAMB

2 cups soft bread crumbs
1 tablespoon grated lemon rind
1 can (2 ounces) flat anchovies, drained and chopped
½ cup chopped parsley
1 egg, beaten
Pepper to taste

2 pounds breast of lamb, cut for stuffing

Combine all ingredients except lamb. Mix well. Stuff lamb with mixture. Fasten with skewers. Place on rack in shallow roasting pan. Bake in preheated moderate oven (350°F.) for about 2 hours. Makes 4 servings.

BAKED SWEET-SOUR BREAST OF LAMB

3 pounds breast of lamb
1 can (8 ounces) tomato sauce
½ pound mushrooms, sliced
½ cup honey
½ cup dry sherry or ½ cup hot bouillon
1 garlic clove, finely chopped
2 tablespoons soy sauce

Trim lamb of excess fat. Place on rack in shallow pan. Bake in preheated moderate oven (350°F.) for 1½ hours. Drain off drippings. Combine all other ingredients and pour over lamb. Bake for about 45 minutes longer, basting frequently. Makes 4 servings.

BRAISED BREAST OF LAMB WITH VEGETABLES

2 pounds breast of lamb, cut into serving pieces
Salt, pepper, and dried rosemary to taste
1 onion, sliced
1 package (10 ounces) frozen whole green snap beans
1 package (10 ounces) frozen cut wax snap beans
1 package (10 ounces) frozen baby Lima beans
16 whole cherry tomatoes

Brown lamb slowly in skillet. Pour off all fat and sprinkle meat with salt, pepper, and rosemary; add onion. Cover and simmer for 1½ hours, or until tender. Remove more fat if necessary. Add a little water to pan drippings. Add beans and sprinkle with salt. Cover and simmer for about 20 minutes, or until meat and vegetables are tender. During last few minutes of cooking, add cherry tomatoes and heat gently. Makes 4 servings.

BREAST OF LAMB ROSÉ

3 pounds breast of lamb
Salt and pepper
1 cup chicken or other bouillon
¼ cup currant jelly
¼ cup boiling water
½ cup rosé wine
Few parsley sprigs, chopped

Brown meat on all sides in heavy kettle. Pour off fat and sprinkle meat with salt and pepper. Add bouillon, cover, and simmer for 2 hours, or until meat is tender. Dissolve jelly in boiling water; add wine and parsley; pour over meat. Simmer for about 15 minutes longer, basting

several times with the liquid in kettle. Serve meat with the liquid; thicken, if desired, with a small amount of flour blended with cold water. Makes 4 servings.

LAMB SHANKS

LAMB SHANKS MILANAISE

2 tablespoons butter or margarine
4 lamb shanks, trimmed of all excess fat
Salt and pepper
2 tablespoons flour
1 cup dry white wine
¼ cup hot bouillon
1 tablespoon minced parsley
1 garlic clove, minced
Rind of 1 medium lemon, minced

Heat butter in heavy casserole or Dutch oven. Season shanks with salt and pepper and roll in flour. Brown on all sides. Pour off excess butter. Cover shanks with wine and cook, uncovered, over medium heat for 5 minutes. Add bouillon, cover, and cook for about 2 hours, or until tender. Ten minutes before serving time, combine parsley, garlic, and lemon rind and place on shanks. Cook for 5 minutes longer. Check sauce and add a little more hot bouillon if too thick. If too thin, stir in mixture of 1 tablespoon butter and ½ tablespoon flour, blended together into a smooth paste, and cook for 5 minutes longer. Makes 4 servings.

BRAISED LAMB SHANKS

12 lamb shanks
½ cup all-purpose flour
1 teaspoon salt
Pepper
1 teaspoon crumbled dried oregano or basil
1 garlic clove
½ cup shortening
2 large onions, chopped
2 cups red wine or bouillon
1 cup water
Herb bouquet of parsley, thyme, bay, and celery leaves

Wash shanks and pat dry. Mix flour, salt, pepper, and oregano. Dredge shanks with mixture. Mince garlic and add to shortening. Heat shortening and brown shanks on all sides. Remove shanks to a roasting pan; add remaining ingredients. Cover and roast in preheated moderate oven (350°F.) until meat is tender, 1½ to 2 hours, basting 2 or 3 times during the cooking with the liquid in the pan. Makes 12 servings.

BARBECUED LAMB SHANKS

4 lamb shanks
2 tablespoons fat
2 onions, sliced
¾ cup ketchup
1½ cups water
2 teaspoons salt
1 tablespoon Worcestershire
½ cup cider vinegar
¼ cup firmly packed dark brown sugar
1 teaspoon powdered mustard
Dash of cayenne

Brown the shanks in the hot fat in heavy kettle. Pour off fat. Add remaining ingredients. Cover and simmer for about 2 hours, spooning some of the sauce over the meat several times during the cooking. If desired, shanks can be baked, covered, in preheated moderate oven (350°F.) for about 2 hours. Makes 4 servings.

RICE-STUFFED LAMB SHANKS

4 short-cut lamb shanks
   (about 2½ pounds)
1 tablespoon olive oil
   Boiling water
2 lemon slices
3 whole cloves
1 teaspoon salt
¼ teaspoon pepper
1 cup uncooked rice
   Celery leaves

Brown meat on all sides in hot oil in heavy kettle. Cover with boiling water; add lemon, cloves, salt, and pepper. Cover and simmer for 1½ hours. Lift out shanks; cool slightly and remove bones. Skim fat from broth; bring broth to boil, add rice, and cook until tender, about 20 minutes, adding more water if necessary. Drain rice, reserving broth. Mix rice with a few chopped celery leaves; season. Stuff boned shanks with the mixture; put in shallow baking dish and add 1 cup of reserved broth. Bake in preheated moderate oven (350°F.) for 15 minutes. Makes 4 servings.

INDIAN STEAMED RICE AND LAMB

2 pounds lamb shanks
½ cup yogurt
4 cups cold water
2½ teaspoons salt
2 cups uncooked long-grained rice
2 tablespoons butter or margarine
4 whole cardamoms, cracked
6 whole cloves
1 cinnamon stick
¼ teaspoon caraway seeds
1 bay leaf
4 cups lamb broth and water
4-ounce can white mushrooms

Purchase lean lamb shanks and trim off all excess fat. Mix with yogurt and marinate for 30 minutes. Add 2 cups cold water and 1 teaspoon salt. Cover and simmer for 3 hours. Cool; trim all lean meat from bones. Discard bones. Save

meat to use later. Chill broth. Lift off all the hardened fat and discard it. Set broth aside. Soak rice for 30 minutes in remaining cold water. Drain well. Melt butter or margarine in 4-quart saucepan. Tie cardamoms and cloves in cheesecloth bag and add to butter along with cinnamon, caraway seeds, and bay leaf. Sauté for 2 minutes. Add well-drained rice. Stir and cook for 3 to 4 minutes. Add lamb broth and water, remaining salt, meat trimmed from bones, and mushrooms. Cover, bring to boiling point, and boil for 15 minutes, or until rice is tender and grains stand apart. Do not stir. Lift out spice bag and loose spices. Serve hot. Makes 8 to 10 servings.

SMALL CHUNKS OR CUTS OF LAMB: NECK SHOULDER RIBLET

LAMB-NECK SLICES WITH VEGETABLES

3 pounds of lamb-neck slices, trimmed of excess fat
1 teaspoon salt
½ teaspoon pepper
3 tablespoons butter or margarine
2 cups (one 1-pound can) Lima beans or peas, drained
4 medium carrots, cooked
1 teaspoon dried basil
1 tablespoon dried parsley flakes
1 teaspoon grated lemon rind
2 tablespoons fresh lemon juice

Sprinkle lamb with salt and pepper. Melt butter and cook lamb in it over medium heat until browned on all sides. Cover and cook over low heat for 20 minutes. Add all other ingredients and simmer, covered, for about 30 minutes. Makes 4 servings.

BRAISED LAMB IN SOUR CREAM

2 pounds lamb neck
¼ cup all-purpose flour
2 teaspoons salt
¼ teaspoon pepper
   Pinch each of ground thyme and tarragon
2 tablespoons butter
¼ teaspoon caraway seeds
2 bouillon cubes dissolved in 1 cup boiling water
1 onion, minced
   Juice of ½ lemon
1 cup dairy sour cream
2 tablespoons dry white wine

Trim some of fat from lamb and cut meat into 1-inch pieces. Dredge with flour seasoned with salt, pepper, and herbs. Brown in hot butter in heavy

skillet. Add remaining ingredients, cover, and cook over very low heat for 1½ hours. Makes 4 servings.

ARMENIAN LAMB STEW

2 pounds lamb shoulder, cut up and trimmed of excess fat
2 tablespoons cooking oil
1 cup sliced onions
2 pounds spinach, cut into large pieces
1 cup tomato juice or sauce
   Salt and pepper
1 cup water

Cook meat in oil until brown on all sides. Add onions; cover and cook over medium heat for about 10 minutes. Onions should be tender but not brown. Add spinach, tomato juice, salt, pepper, and water. Cover and simmer until tender. Depending on the lamb, this may take from 40 minutes to 1 hour. Makes 4 servings.

IRISH LAMB STEW

1 pound lean lamb shoulder
1 pound beef chuck
2 teaspoons salt
¼ teaspoon pepper
½ cup all-purpose flour
2 tablespoons cooking oil
2 yellow onions, sliced
2 teaspoons paprika
½ garlic clove, minced
4 cups water
12 white onions
½ cup diced celery
1 white turnip, peeled and diced
2 carrots, peeled and diced
¼ head cabbage, cut into small pieces
2 leeks, sliced
½ cup canned tomatoes
4 medium potatoes, peeled and diced

Cut meat into 2-inch cubes. Dredge with salt, pepper, and flour. Brown in hot oil. Add sliced onions, paprika, garlic, and water. Bring to boil, cover, and simmer for 1½ hours. Add white onions and cook for 30 minutes. Add remaining ingredients and simmer for about 30 minutes longer. Makes 6 servings.

LAMB IN WHITE WINE

3 pounds boneless lamb shoulder, cut into pieces and trimmed of excess fat
   Salt and pepper
1 garlic clove, chopped
3 tablespoons olive oil
1 cup dry white wine
1½ teaspoons dried rosemary
   Dash of hot pepper sauce
3 eggs
1 tablespoon grated lemon rind

Season lamb with salt and pepper. Sauté garlic in hot oil until golden. Add lamb pieces and brown over medium heat. Add wine, rosemary, and hot pepper sauce. Cover and simmer over low heat until lamb is tender, stirring occasionally. If meat is drying out, add a little more wine. There should be 2 tablespoons of

broth left when the lamb is cooked. Beat eggs in a bowl. Add lamb broth and lemon rind. Pour sauce over lamb and heat to thicken, but do not boil. Makes 4 to 6 servings.

LAMB PIE WITH HERB CRUST

- 2 pounds boneless lamb shoulder or neck
- 3 tablespoons all-purpose flour
  Salt and pepper
- 1 garlic clove, puréed
- 3 tablespoons shortening
- 2 cups bouillon or water (½ may be red or white wine)
  Herb bouquet (bay leaf, thyme, parsley)
- 18 small white onions, parboiled
- 18 very small new potatoes, scraped or 3 large potatoes, cut into good-size cubes
- 2 cups peas
- 1 cup pitted ripe olives
  Herb Crust
- 1 egg yolk
- 2 tablespoons milk or water

Roll meat in flour seasoned with salt and pepper. Sauté along with garlic in the shortening, using a deep flameproof baking dish. When brown, add remaining ingredients except last 3, and simmer until thickened, adding a little more bouillon if necessary to make enough gravy. Remove herb bouquet and correct seasoning. Cool. Roll Herb Crust rather thick and cut into 1-inch strips. Arrange lattice-fashion on pie, trimming ends. Glaze top with egg yolk beaten slightly with milk. Bake in preheated hot oven (400°F.) until browned. Makes 6 servings.

Herb Crust

Mix 1 package (3 ounces) cream cheese, ½ cup butter, 1¼ cups all-purpose flour, ½ teaspoon salt, and 1 teaspoon each of chopped chives and dill. Chill before rolling.

LAMB AND BEAN RAGOUT

- 1 cup dried white beans
  Water
- 2 pounds boneless lamb shoulder, cut into cubes
- ¼ cup bacon fat or butter
- 2 onions, sliced
- 1 garlic clove, minced
- 2¼ cups (one 1-pound, 4-ounce can) tomatoes
- 1 bay leaf
- 1½ teaspoons salt
- ½ teaspoon each of pepper and paprika
- ½ teaspoon herb seasoning
- 1½ cups lamb or chicken broth
- 3 tablespoons flour

Wash beans; cover with water. Bring to boil and boil for 2 minutes. Let stand for 1 hour; cook until tender. Brown lamb in hot fat. Add onions and garlic; cook for a few minutes. Add drained beans and all ingredients except flour.

Lamb Pie with Herb Crust

Cover and bake in preheated moderate oven (350°F.) for 2 hours. Thicken broth with flour blended with ¼ cup cold water. Stir into lamb mixture; bake for 15 minutes. Makes 6 servings.

SCOTCH BROTH

2 pounds breast of lamb, cut up
1 lamb shank
2 quarts water
  Salt
  Peppercorns
½ cup pearl barley
1 package soup greens
1½ cups diced carrots
½ cup diced rutabaga
3 onions, chopped
1½ cups sliced celery

Brown breast of lamb in heavy kettle, stirring frequently. Pour off fat. Add shank, water, 1 tablespoon salt, peppercorns, barley, and soup greens. Bring to boil; cover and simmer for about 2 hours. Remove meat; cool. Trim off any excess fat, remove bones, and put meat back in kettle. Add vegetables, bring to boil and simmer for 30 minutes. Season to taste. Makes about 2½ quarts.

DEVILED LAMB RIBLETS

3 pounds lamb riblets, cut into serving pieces
2 tablespoons prepared mustard
1 cup all-purpose flour
2 teaspoons salt
½ teaspoon pepper
⅓ cup cooking oil
½ cup chili sauce
½ cup fresh lemon juice
2 tablespoons Worcestershire
1 teaspoon paprika
⅓ cup chopped onion
2 cups water

Trim lamb of excess fat. Brush with mustard. Sprinkle with flour, salt, and pepper. Heat oil. Cook lamb in it until browned on all sides. Combine all other ingredients and pour over lamb. Cover and simmer over low heat for about 1½ hours. Makes 4 to 6 servings.

MEXICAN LAMB STEW

4 cups milk
1 onion, chopped
2 bay leaves
½ teaspoon dried thyme
  Salt and pepper
¼ cup butter or margarine
2 pounds lamb, cut into pieces and trimmed of excess fat
½ cup chopped canned or fresh peaches
2 tablespoons raisins, plumped in water
½ cup chopped toasted walnut meats
2 tablespoons capers
  Hot cooked rice

Combine milk, onion, bay leaves, thyme, salt, and pepper. Heat but do not boil. Heat butter and sauté lamb until golden. Add lamb to hot milk and simmer, uncovered, over low heat until lamb is

tender and milk has cooked away, about 1 hour or more. Place lamb on hot serving dish and sprinkle with peaches, raisins, walnuts, and capers. Serve over rice. Makes 4 to 6 servings.

SAVORY TURKISH LAMB PILAF

¼ cup butter or margarine
½ pound boneless lamb, cut into julienne strips
3 medium onions, chopped fine
¼ cup pine nuts or walnut pieces
2 cups uncooked rice
1 large fresh tomato, peeled, seeded, and chopped, or 1 large canned tomato, chopped
¼ cup dried currants or chopped seedless raisins
2 teaspoons salt
1 teaspoon pepper
½ teaspoon ground sage
¼ teaspoon ground allspice
4 cups boiling bouillon or water
  Chopped parsley or mint (optional)

Heat butter and sauté lamb strips in it until golden brown. Remove and keep hot. In the same butter cook onion until soft but not brown. Add nuts and rice and cook over medium heat for 5 minutes, stirring constantly. Add tomato, currants, salt, pepper, sage, allspice, and bouillon. The dish will sizzle. Stir thoroughly and cover tightly. Cook over lowest possible heat until rice is tender and liquid absorbed. Depending on the rice used, this takes 20 to 30 minutes. Return lamb strips to rice and heat thoroughly. Re-cover and let stand in warm place without cooking for about 15 minutes. Before serving, sprinkle with 1 to 2 tablespoons parsley or mint. Makes 6 to 8 servings.

LAMB AND EGGPLANT STEW

1 tablespoon olive oil
2 pounds lamb stew meat, cubed
1 eggplant, unpeeled and cut into cubes
1 garlic clove, minced
1 large onion, chopped
1½ teaspoons salt
1 can (6 ounces) tomato paste
1½ cups hot water
¼ teaspoon each of pepper and crumbled dried thyme

Heat oil and brown meat cubes on all sides. Add remaining ingredients. Bring to a boil, cover, and simmer for 1½ hours, stirring often. Serve on hot rice cooked with a few raisins and pine nuts. Makes 6 servings.

LEFTOVER LAMB

LAMB AND VEGETABLE SOUP

  Bone from roast lamb
2 quarts water

1 cup dried split peas
2 celery stalks with leaves, chopped
2 large carrots, diced
2 medium onions, chopped
2 cups cubed potatoes (3 medium)
3 teaspoons salt
¼ teaspoon pepper
  Lamb scraps

Crack bone in several places. Put in kettle with water and peas. Bring to boil, cover, and simmer for 2 hours. Add remaining ingredients and simmer for 30 minutes longer, or until vegetables are tender. Remove bone.

■ **To Make Soup in Pressure Cooker—** Put bone, 1½ quarts water, and celery in pressure cooker. Cook at 15-pound pressure for 15 minutes. Reduce pressure and remove bone. Trim off any scraps of meat that cling to bone and put meat back in cooker. Add remaining ingredients. Cook at 15-pound pressure for 5 minutes. Makes 2 quarts.

LAMB AND RED-BEAN STEW

2 cups cubed roast lamb
2 tablespoons lamb fat
1½ teaspoons salt
  Dash of cayenne
2¼ cups (one 1-pound, 3-ounce can) tomatoes
1 green pepper, chopped
2½ cups (one 1-pound, 5-ounce can) red kidney beans

Brown lamb in fat in large saucepan. Add remaining ingredients except beans. Bring to boil, cover, and simmer for 1 hour. Add beans and simmer for about 35 minutes, or until liquid is nearly absorbed. Makes 4 servings.

LAMB ROLL WITH BROWN SAUCE

2 cups ground roast lamb
¾ teaspoon salt
¼ teaspoon pepper
1 tablespoon lamb fat
⅓ cup (one 2-ounce can) chopped mushrooms, drained
1 small onion, minced
1 parsley sprig, chopped
2 tablespoons chopped stuffed olives
2 tablespoons chopped sweet pickles
¼ teaspoon powdered mustard
  Biscuit Dough
1 tablespoon milk
  Brown sauce

Put all ingredients except dough, milk, and sauce in heavy skillet. Cook over low heat for 10 minutes. Cool. Turn Biscuit Dough out on lightly floured board and roll into rectangle ¼ inch thick. Spread meat mixture over dough to within ½ inch of edge. Roll up like jelly roll; moisten edges with water and seal. Put roll in greased shallow pan and brush with 1 tablespoon milk. Bake in preheated hot oven (425°F.) for about 30 minutes, or until crust is nicely browned.

Slice while hot and serve on heated platter with Brown Sauce poured over slices; or serve sauce in separate dish if desired. Makes 4 to 6 servings.

Biscuit Dough
1½ cups all-purpose flour
1½ teaspoons baking powder
¼ teaspoon poultry seasoning
¾ teaspoon salt
3 tablespoons lamb fat
½ cup milk (about)

Sift dry ingredients together. Cut in fat until mixture is in coarse crumbs. Add milk and mix to soft dough.

Brown Sauce
2 tablespoons lamb fat
1 small onion, minced
1 parsley sprig, minced
½ carrot, grated
Pinch of dried thyme
1 bay leaf
1½ tablespoons flour
1 bouillon cube, dissolved in 1½ cups boiling water
Salt and pepper

Put all ingredients except liquid, salt, and pepper in skillet. Cook slowly for 10 minutes, or until browned. Add liquid and bring to boil. Season to taste and simmer for 2 minutes. Strain.

CREAMED LAMB IN PUFF SHELLS
2 tablespoons lamb fat
¼ cup all-purpose flour
2 cups milk
½ teaspoon salt
Dash of pepper
1 teaspoon Worcestershire
½ green pepper, chopped
1 pimiento, chopped
2 cups cubed roast lamb
Puff Shells
Parsley

Melt fat in top part of double boiler. Blend in flour. Add milk gradually; cook over boiling water, stirring constantly, until thickened. Add remaining ingredients except shells and parsley. Continue cooking over boiling water until thoroughly heated. Cut a small piece from top of each shell and fill with creamed lamb. Garnish with parsley. Makes 4 to 6 servings.

Puff Shells
½ cup water
¼ cup butter
¼ teaspoon salt
½ cup sifted all-purpose flour
2 eggs

Combine water, butter, and salt in saucepan and bring to boil. Add flour all at once and cook, stirring constantly, until mixture leaves sides of pan. Remove from heat. Add eggs, one at a time, beating thoroughly after each addition. Heap in 6 mounds on greased cookie sheet.

Bake in preheated very hot oven (450° F.) for 15 minutes, then at moderate (375°F.) for 20 minutes.

BARBECUED LAMB ON RICED POTATO
1 large onion, chopped
½ cup tomato sauce
¾ cup water
1 tablespoon sugar
1 tablespoon vinegar
½ teaspoon salt
⅛ teaspoon red pepper
2 cups cubed roast lamb
Hot riced potatoes

Combine first 7 ingredients in skillet and cook over moderate heat for 5 minutes. Add meat; cover and simmer for 15 minutes. Serve over potatoes. Makes 4 servings.

CURRIED LAMB AND LIMAS
2 tablespoons butter or margarine
1 cup cooked Lima beans
2 cups leftover lamb gravy
1 teaspoon instant minced onion
¼ teaspoon ground mace
1 teaspoon salt
¼ teaspoon pepper
2 cups diced cooked lamb
1 small head lettuce, shredded
½ teaspoon curry powder softened in 1 tablespoon water
Hot cooked rice

Simmer first 7 ingredients together for 10 minutes. Add remaining ingredients except rice, cover, and simmer for 10 minutes. Serve with rice. Makes 4 to 6 servings.

RED NOODLES AND LAMB
2 cups diced roast lamb
2 tablespoons lamb fat
2 garlic cloves, minced
1 can (6 ounces) tomato paste
3½ cups water
1½ teaspoons salt
⅛ teaspoon pepper
2 teaspoons paprika
8 ounces broad noodles
Grated Parmesan cheese

Brown lamb lightly in fat. Add garlic, tomato paste, water, and seasonings. Bring to boil; cover and simmer for 1 hour. Add noodles and continue cooking until noodles are tender, stirring occasionally to prevent sticking. Add more water if necessary. Sprinkle with cheese just before serving. Makes 4 servings.

LAMB HASH DE LUXE
1 onion, minced
3 tablespoons butter or margarine
3 cups diced cooked lamb
1 cup diced cooked potato
1 pimiento, chopped
1 cup lamb broth
1 cup undiluted evaporated milk
2 egg yolks, slightly beaten
Salt and pepper
Hot toast

Cook onion in butter for 2 or 3 minutes. Add lamb, potato, pimiento, and broth. Bring to boil. Mix milk and egg yolks; season with salt and pepper. Stir into hash mixture and simmer for a few minutes. Serve on hot toast. Makes 4 to 6 servings.

LAMB HASH LYONNAISE
1 large onion, minced
2 tablespoons butter or margarine
1 tablespoon chopped parsley
1 can (8 ounces) tomato sauce
1 cup leftover lamb gravy
½ teaspoon salt
⅛ teaspoon pepper
⅛ teaspoon ground marjoram
3 cups ground cooked lamb

Sauté onion in butter until golden. Add parsley, tomato sauce, gravy, salt, pepper, and marjoram. Simmer, covered, over low heat for 5 minutes. Add lamb. Cook, covered, in preheated moderate oven (350° F.) for 45 minutes. Makes 4 servings.

Note: Serve plain or dot with mashed potatoes, top with Parmesan cheese, and brown in broiler.

LAMB-STUFFED GREEN PEPPERS
4 large green peppers
1½ cups ground cooked lamb
¼ cup uncooked rice
1 small onion, minced
1½ teaspoons salt
¼ teaspoon pepper
1 can (8 ounces) tomato sauce
1 cup water
Dash of cayenne
2 basil leaves or pinch of dried basil

Cut off tops and remove seeds from peppers. Mix lamb, rice, onion, salt and pepper. Stuff peppers about three-fourths full. Stand upright in a small heavy saucepan with tight-fitting lid. Pour combined sauce and water and remaining seasonings over peppers. Cover and cook very slowly for 40 minutes, or until rice is tender. Add more water if necessary. Makes 4 servings.

SALMAGUNDI SALAD
1½ cups diced cooked lamb
½ cup each of diced cooked potato, carrots, and peas or green beans
¼ cup French dressing
2 sweet pickles, chopped
1 hard-cooked egg, chopped
½ cup mayonnaise
Salad greens

Marinate meat and vegetables in French dressing for 30 minutes. Add remaining ingredients except greens and mix lightly. Serve on cold crisp greens. Makes 4 servings.

LAMB CHUTNEY
¼ cup chopped chutney
1½ cups leftover lamb gravy
8 slices of leftover roast lamb

Mix chutney and gravy; heat to boiling. Add lamb; heat gently. Makes 4 servings.

CANADIAN LAMB SOUFFLÉ
    Butter or margarine
 2 tablespoons all-purpose flour
 1 cup milk
 2 eggs, separated
 1½ cups chopped leftover lamb
    Salt and pepper
 2 tablespoons dry bread crumbs

Melt 1½ tablespoons butter in saucepan. Stir in flour. Gradually stir in milk. Cook over low heat, stirring constantly, until thickened. Remove from heat and stir in egg yolks and chopped lamb. Season to taste with salt and pepper. Beat egg whites until stiff and fold into first mixture. Pour mixture into a well-buttered 1-quart baking dish. Sprinkle top with bread crumbs and dot with 1½ tablespoons butter. Bake in preheated slow oven (325°F.) for 20 to 25 minutes. Serve immediately. Makes 3 to 4 servings.

LAMB VARIETY CUTS

BRUNCH LAMB KIDNEY STEW
 8 lamb kidneys
    Milk
 ½ pound mushrooms, sliced
 6 tablespoons butter or margarine
 2 tablespoons chopped parsley
 1 tablespoon grated onion
    or 1 teaspoon instant onion
 ¼ to ⅓ cup sherry
 ½ cup heavy cream
    Salt and pepper
    Buttered toast or hot cooked rice

Split kidneys and remove white membrane and cord. Soak in milk to cover for 10 minutes, drain, and dry. Cut into thin slices and sauté with mushrooms in butter. Add parsley and onion and simmer over low heat for 5 minutes. Add sherry and cream and simmer for 2 minutes longer. Season to taste and serve immediately on toast. Makes 3 to 4 servings.

LAMB LIVER WITH RICE
 2 lamb livers (about 2 pounds)
 1½ cups boiling water
    All-purpose flour (about ¼ cup)
 ¼ cup bacon fat or other shortening
 3 parsley sprigs
 1 bay leaf
 ⅛ teaspoon ground thyme
 ¼ teaspoon pepper
 2 teaspoons salt
 1 onion, sliced
    Hot cooked rice

Cover livers with the water. Let stand for 5 minutes. Drain, reserving water. Dry livers and dredge with 2 tablespoons flour. Brown in hot fat in heavy kettle. Add herbs, seasonings, onion, and reserved water. Cover and simmer for 1½ hours, or until done. Remove livers and slice. Thicken liquid with a flour-and-water paste. Season to taste and serve with the liver on hot rice. Makes 6 servings.

FRITTO MISTO
(Mixed Fry)
 1 pound lamb or veal brains
 2 sweetbreads
    Salt
 8 artichoke hearts, canned or frozen, halved
    Pepper
 8 cooked cauliflowerets
 16 slices of zucchini
 8 chicken livers
 2 eggs, beaten
 2 cups dry bread crumbs

Soak brains and sweetbreads in cold salted water for 15 minutes; wash in cold running water. Place in kettle with water to cover and boil for 10 minutes. Drain, cool, remove membrane, and cut into 2-inch pieces. Set aside.

Cook artichokes according to directions on can or package. Drain and season.

Dip brains, sweetbreads, artichoke hearts, cauliflower, zucchini, and chicken livers into egg; roll in bread crumbs and set aside.

Fry all coated foods in deep fat or oil heated to 365°F. on a frying thermometer for 4 to 6 minutes for the meats and 2 to 3 minutes for the vegetables. Drain on absorbent paper; keep fried foods warm in preheated very slow oven (200°F.) until ready to serve. Makes 4 servings.

POTTED LAMB TONGUES
 ¼ cup butter or margarine
 2 cups chopped onions
 2 garlic cloves, minced
    Water
 2 teaspoons salt
 1 teaspoon paprika
 ½ teaspoon pepper
 12 whole fresh lamb tongues

Heat butter in a Dutch oven. Sauté onions and garlic until dark brown. Add 1 cup water, salt, paprika, and pepper. Cook over high heat until water evaporates. Add tongues and enough water to cover. Bring to a boil, cover, and simmer for about 1¼ hours. Serve unsliced, garnished with parsley and with pan juice spooned over tongue. Makes 4 to 6 servings.

LARD—Pork fat from fat backs, clear plates, and leaf kidney fat which has been rendered and clarified is called lard. The quality of lard depends on the location of the fatty tissue in the animal and on the method of heating.

For centuries lard was the main fat used in cooking, either made at home at pig-butchering time or bought from the lard barrel. During Colonial days and into this century, all cooking and baking was done with lard, because it produces tender, flavorful pastry. Many homemakers feel to this day that no other fat can beat lard for pastry making. For cooking too, lard gives a superior flavor to dishes that require preliminary browning, such as pot roasts.

Lard is widely used as a cooking fat in South America and in such European countries as France, Germany, Czechoslovakia, and Hungary. The old bugaboo of lard spoiling easily is no longer true today, thanks to superior production methods and to the high quality of home refrigeration.

Availability and Purchasing Guide—Available year round. After lard has been rendered, it may be alkali-refined, bleached, filtered, hydrogenated, deodorized, plasticized and treated with antioxidants and/or emulsifiers, depending on the end product desired. Lard processed to this extent compares favorably with vegetable shortenings in blandness, stability, and consistency. Variation exists among brands of lard, probably more so than with other types of shortening, and labels should be read.

Storage—Should be wrapped tightly to reduce the possibility of off-odors being absorbed from other foods. Treated lards can be kept at room temperature in a cool dry place. Some lards must be refrigerated, and the label so states.

☐ Refrigerator shelf, well wrapped in tightly covered container or original container: 15 days to 2 months

☐ Refrigerator frozen-food compartment, wrapped for freezing: 4 to 5 months

☐ Freezer, wrapped for freezing: 10 to 12 months

Caloric Value

☐ 3½ ounces = 902 calories

Basic Preparation—Due to its structure, lard is particularly desirable in making flaky textures in biscuits and pastry. For cake baking, it is best to use lards which have been hydrogenated, refined, and emulsified. Other lards do not incorporate air, resulting in a flat cake with a sticky crust.

To substitute lard for butter in cooking, use 20 to 25 per cent less lard than butter.

LARD PASTRY

2 cups all-purpose flour
¾ teaspoon salt
⅔ cup lard
Cold water

Mix first 2 ingredients in bowl. Cut in lard with pastry blender or 2 knives. Mixing with fork, add cold water, a few drops at a time, until just enough is added to hold particles together. Shape into a ball and use as needed. Makes enough pastry for a double-crust 9-inch pie, or for two 9-inch pie shells.

CRISP OATMEAL COOKIES

1½ cups firmly packed brown sugar
¾ cup melted lard
6 tablespoons sour milk
½ teaspoon salt
¾ teaspoon vanilla extract
1½ cups sifted all-purpose flour
¾ teaspoon baking soda
3 cups quick-cooking rolled oats

Combine ingredients in order given and mix thoroughly. Shape into balls about 1 inch in diameter and put on greased cookie sheets. Flatten each cookie to ⅛-inch thickness by pressing with wet spatula or the bottom of a glass dipped into water. Bake in preheated moderate oven (375°F.) for 10 to 12 minutes. Cool. Store in tightly covered container. These keep well. Makes 5 to 6 dozen.

LARDING, TO LARD—This is a process which makes dry meat more succulent by the insertion of lardoons—long strips of pork or ham about one-half inch wide. This is done with a larding needle (which can be bought in hardware or household-goods stores) on which the lardoons are threaded and then inserted across the grain of the meat. It immensely improves the flavor if, before use, the lardoons are rolled in salt and pepper, chopped parsley, and a pinch of ground spice such as cloves or nutmeg, or even soaked in brandy. However, few home cooks like to lard. They prefer to ask the butcher to lard their pot roasts. The French, masters of pot roasts, are great ones for larding, and home cooks in France do it as a matter of course. Larding is one of the reasons why pot roast is so good there.

Since larding really makes a world of difference in the succulence and tenderness of the meat, it is worthwhile to acquire a needle and the technique. In a pinch, meat can be larded with an ice pick or a thick knitting needle. You insert the needle into the meat and poke a hole for the lardoons. Then you push them in with the ice pick or needle. Keep lardoons in a cold place until needed.

LARDED HERB POT ROAST

4 pounds beef for pot roast
¼ pound salt pork

1 teaspoon each of crumbled basil, thyme, and marjoram
½ teaspoon ground sage
2 tablespoons all-purpose flour
1 tablespoon fat
Salt and pepper
3 tablespoons water

With a sharp knife cut gashes in beef about 3 inches long and 1 inch deep. Cut salt pork into 5 or 6 strips. Combine herbs and coat both sides of salt-pork strips with the mixture. Insert strips into gashes in beef and secure with toothpicks. Dredge meat with flour and brown on all sides in fat in heavy kettle. Sprinkle with salt and pepper. Place a trivet in bottom of kettle under meat; add water. Cover and simmer for 4 to 4½ hours, adding water if necessary. Remove meat; thicken liquid with flour-and-water paste if desired. Season to taste. Makes 6 servings.

LASAGNA—A broad noodle, about two inches wide, with a ruffled or a plain edge. The plural of the Italian word is *lasagne;* the name probably stems from the Latin word *lasanum,* "cooking pot."

Lasagna is also used to denote a dish of cooked and drained lasagna noodles, baked with several kinds of cheese and in a tomato sauce. The dish may contain meat.

Lasagna is a substantial dish which can be prepared in advance for a party. A tossed green salad and a simple fruit dessert are sufficient to make the meal complete.

Caloric Values

☐ Lasagna noodles, 3½ ounces, cooked = 67 calories

HEARTY LASAGNA WITH MARINARA SAUCE

8 ounces lasagna noodles
1 pound ricotta cheese
8 ounces Mozzarella cheese, sliced
Marinara Sauce
½ cup grated Parmesan cheese

Cook noodles in boiling salted water for 25 minutes, or until tender, stirring frequently. Drain. Arrange in shallow 2½-quart baking dish, making 3 layers each of cooked noodles, ricotta, Mozzarella, Marinara Sauce, and grated cheese. Bake in preheated slow oven (325°F.) for about 45 minutes. Makes 6 servings.

Marinara Sauce

1 medium onion, minced
2 garlic cloves, minced
2 tablespoons olive oil
1 pound ground beef
3½ cups (one 1-pound, 12-ounce can) Italian-style tomatoes
1 can (6 ounces) tomato paste
2 cups water
1 tablespoon salt
⅛ teaspoon cayenne
1 teaspoon sugar
Pinch of ground basil
1 bay leaf

Brown onion and garlic lightly in oil in saucepan. Add meat and cook until browned, stirring with fork. Add remaining ingredients and simmer, uncovered, for 1½ hours. Remove bay leaf.

MAKE-AHEAD CHICKEN LASAGNA

1 canned whole chicken (about 2¼ pounds)
4 cups (one 32-ounce can) Italian tomatoes
2 garlic cloves, minced
1 bay leaf
Pinch of ground thyme
Pinch of ground rosemary
Dash of cayenne or 1 tiny hot red pepper
3 tablespoons olive oil
½ teaspoon sugar
Salt
½ pound lasagna noodles
All-purpose flour
Pepper
¼ cup chopped parsley
¼ teaspoon monosodium glutamate (optional)
¼ teaspoon soy sauce
½ pound Mozzarella cheese, sliced
½ cup grated Parmesan or Swiss cheese

Open chicken, skim fat from broth, and set aside. Pour off broth and set it aside, too. Remove skin and bones from chicken, leaving meat in as large pieces as possible. Put tomatoes, garlic, bay leaf, thyme, rosemary, cayenne, olive oil, sugar, and ½ teaspoon salt in saucepan. Bring to boil, cover, and simmer for 25 to 30 minutes. Cook lasagna noodles in boiling salted water for 10 minutes, or until done but still chewy. Drain in colander, run cold water over them and put on kitchen towel to dry. Measure chicken broth. There should be 1 to 1½ cups. Thicken with flour blended with a little cold water, using 2 tablespoons flour to each cup of broth. Add salt and pepper to taste, the parsley, monosodium glutamate (if used), and the soy sauce. Into a large shallow baking dish (13 x 9 inches), pour a thin layer of tomato mixture. Cover with lasagna, placed side by side. Then add a layer of chicken. Cover with thin slices of Mozzarella. Top with a layer of chicken gravy. Add another layer of lasagna, more tomato sauce, another layer of chicken, gravy, and so on, until baking dish is full and all ingredients except grated cheese are used. Finish with a layer of lasagna. Sprinkle with cheese. Put in refrigerator until ready to bake. Then bake in preheated moderate oven (375°F.) for 30 minutes, or until lightly browned and bubbly. Makes 8 servings.

LAYER CAKE—A cake baked in layers, held together by filling, and covered with thick luscious frosting is typically American and a favorite dessert in all American homes.

Layer cakes are prepared from shortening, sugar, flour, and a chemical leavening agent. The usual American layer cake consists of two layers, but mutilayered cakes may be made by baking the batter in six, seven, or eight layers, or by splitting a standard-size layer cake into halves or thirds.

Layer cakes may be white, yellow, golden, chocolate, spice cakes, or tortes. A torte is generally a richer batter baked in several thin layers and frosted in the same manner as the standard layer cake.

For a velvety texture, the cake should be baked in a pan appropriate for the amount of dough, and the dough should be at least one inch deep in the pan. If the pan is too big, the cake will not rise properly and may brown unevenly. If the pan is too small, the texture will be coarse and the batter may overflow in the oven.

Cake pans should be at least half full but not more than two-thirds full for best results. The standard layer-cake pans are 8 x 1¼ inches, 9 x 1¼ inches, and 10 x 1¼ or 1½ inches. Layer-cake pans come with stationary or loose bottoms. The loose-bottom pans make cake removing easier.

There are many packaged layer-cake mixes on the market. They come in regular 2-layer size and 1-layer small-family or loaf-pan size which can be baked in a single layer.

Hints for Baking Layer Cakes

■ Equipment—Measuring ingredients accurately is easy when you use standard measuring spoons and cups: a nest of measuring cups for dry ingredients and a liquid measuring cup with the rim above the 1-cup marker. A rubber spatula and a sifter are necessary for preparing batter. Use aluminum pans about 1¼ to 1½ inches deep.

■ Procedure—For best results use only ingredients specified and follow directions exactly. Ingredients such as shortening, milk, and eggs should be at room temperature (72°F. to 80°F.). Measure level. Doubling recipes is not advisable.

■ Preparing Pans—Ready-cut pan liners, special pan-lining paper, wax paper, plain white or brown paper can be used to line pan bottoms. Cut paper slightly smaller than pan so that it will not touch edge but will completely cover bottom. No greasing of pan or paper is necessary.

■ Oven Temperature—Correct oven temperature is of great importance when baking cakes. If your oven has no thermostatic control, try using an oven thermometer and adjusting the heat accordingly. You may want to use a thermometer in any case to check the accuracy of your control.

■ Storing Baked Cakes—For short-term storage frosted cakes keep best. It's helpful to store cakes in a cake saver or deep bowl. Cover the cut surface of cake with *wax paper or transparent plastic wrap;* hold wrapping in place with toothpicks inserted at an angle into cake. Cakes with perishable fillings or frostings should be stored, covered, in the refrigerator.

If you wish to freeze a cake, it is best to freeze it unfrosted.

FRUIT-PRESERVE LAYER CAKE

½ cup soft butter or margarine
1 cup granulated sugar
2 eggs
¼ teaspoon grated orange rind
1 tablespoon orange juice
1½ cups sifted cake flour
1½ teaspoons baking powder
¼ teaspoon salt
½ cup water
  Apricot or other preserves
  Confectioners' sugar

Cream butter and granulated sugar until light. Add eggs, one at a time, beating well after each addition. Beat in orange rind and juice. Add sifted flour, baking powder, and salt alternately with water, beating until smooth. Pour into two 9-inch layer pans lined on bottom with paper. Bake in preheated moderate oven (350°F.) for about 25 minutes. Cool. Spread preserves on one layer. Top with second layer. Sprinkle with confectioners' sugar.

ORANGE GOLD LAYER CAKE

¾ cup soft butter
1¼ cups sugar
8 egg yolks
  Grated rind of 1 orange
⅓ cup orange juice
2¾ cups sifted cake flour
2¾ teaspoons baking powder
½ teaspoon salt
⅔ cup milk
  Orange Butter Frosting

Cream butter and sugar until light. Add egg yolks, one at a time, beating well after each addition. Add orange rind and juice. Add sifted flour, baking powder, and salt alternately with milk, beating until smooth. Pour into two 9-inch layer pans lined on bottom with paper. Bake in preheated moderate oven (375°F.) for about 20 minutes. Cool and spread Orange Butter Frosting.

Orange Butter Frosting

Combine grated rinds of 1 orange and 1 lemon and ¼ cup orange juice. Let stand for 10 minutes; strain if desired. Cream ¼ cup butter until light. Add 1 egg yolk, dash of salt, and 2 teaspoons lemon juice. Gradually beat in 3½ cups (1 pound) confectioners' sugar.

SILVER CAKE

⅔ cup soft butter
1½ cups sugar
1 teaspoon vanilla extract
½ teaspoon almond extract
2½ cups sifted cake flour
2½ teaspoons baking powder
⅔ cup milk
½ teaspoon salt
½ teaspoon cream of tartar
4 egg whites

Cream butter and sugar until light. Add flavorings. Add sifted flour and baking powder alternately with milk, beating until smooth. Add salt and cream of tartar to egg whites. Beat until stiff but not dry. Fold into first mixture. Pour into two 9-inch layer pans lined on bottom with paper. Bake in preheated moderate oven (375°F.) for 20 to 25 minutes. Cool and frost as desired.

Strawberry Cream Cake

Make Silver Cake, substituting ½ cup quick strawberry-flavor mix for ½ cup of the sugar. Spread sweetened whipped cream on one layer and top with sliced fresh strawberries; add more cream. Cover with other cake layer and top with cream and strawberries.

Rainbow Cake

Make Silver Cake, dividing batter into 3 parts. Leave 1 part plain. Color 1 part pink and 1 green. Alternate 3 parts in layer pans and bake as directed. Make Fluffy White Frosting, below. Divide into 3 parts. Color half pink, 1 quarter yellow, and remaining quarter green. Reserve half of pink for sides of cake. Alternate colors on bottom layer of cake and run a knife through colors to get a rainbow effect. Add top layer and repeat frostings. Spread pink frosting on sides and decorate top with crushed peppermint candy.

Fluffy White Frosting

In top part of small double boiler combine 2 egg whites, 1½ cups sugar, ⅛ teaspoon salt, ⅓ cup water, and 2 teaspoons light corn syrup. Put over boiling water and beat with rotary beater or electric mixer for 7 minutes, or until mixture will stand in stiff peaks. Add 1 teaspoon vanilla extract.

BURNT-SUGAR CAKE

1¾ cups sugar
¾ cup boiling water
⅔ cup soft butter or margarine
1 teaspoon vanilla extract
2 eggs, separated
3 cups sifted cake flour
3 teaspoons baking powder
½ teaspoon salt
¾ cup milk
  Burnt-Sugar Frosting
  Pecan halves

In small heavy skillet or saucepan heat ¾ cup sugar, stirring, until a brown syrup forms and mixture begins to smoke.

Layer Cakes. 1. Chocolate Shadow; 2. Burnt Sugar;
3. Rainbow; 4. Ambrosia; 5. Lord Baltimore;
6. Chocolate-Walnut Cake;
7. Chocolate-Filled Eight Layer;
8. Strawberry Cream

Very gradually stir in boiling water and remove from heat. Stir and blend well. Cool thoroughly. Cream butter and 1 cup sugar until light. Gradually beat in ½ cup burnt-sugar syrup. (Reserve remainder for Burnt-Sugar Frosting.) Add vanilla, then egg yolks, one at a time, beating well after each addition. Add sifted flour, baking powder, and salt alternately with milk, beating until smooth, beginning and ending with dry ingredients. Fold in stiffly beaten egg whites. Pour into two 8-inch layer pans lined on the bottom with greased wax paper. Bake in preheated moderate oven (375°F.) for about 25 minutes. Cool and frost. Top with nut halves.

Burnt-Sugar Frosting

Cream ⅓ cup butter or margarine. Beat in 1 pound confectioners' sugar, ½ teaspoon salt, 1 teaspoon vanilla, the reserved burnt-sugar syrup, and enough cream or undiluted evaporated milk (about 2 tablespoons) to give spreading consistency.

AMBROSIA CAKE

¼ cup cooking oil
2 egg yolks
6 tablespoons water
1 tablespoon grated orange rind
½ teaspoon vanilla extract
Flaked coconut
1 cup plus 2 tablespoons sifted cake flour
¾ cup sugar
1½ teaspoons baking powder
4 egg whites
½ teaspoon salt
¼ teaspoon cream of tartar
Sweetened whipped cream or whipped topping
Mandarin oranges
Grated coconut

Put oil, egg yolks, water, grated rind, vanilla, and ½ cup coconut in mixing bowl. Add sifted flour, sugar, and baking powder Beat for ½ minute at low speed of mixer or 75 strokes by hand. Beat egg whites with salt and cream of tartar until very stiff. Fold in first mixture lightly but thoroughly. Pour into ungreased pan (8 x 8 x 2 inches). Bake in preheated moderate oven (350°F.) for about 30 minutes. Cool upside down for 1 hour. Loosen carefully from pan and split into 2 layers. Spread whipped cream between layers and on top. Decorate with oranges and sprinkle with coconut.

CHOCOLATE-FILLED EIGHT-LAYER CAKE

6 eggs, separated
1¼ cups sugar
2 tablespoons fresh lemon juice
¾ cup sifted all-purpose flour
¼ cup cornstarch
½ teaspoon salt
Chocolate Frosting

Beat egg whites until stiff. Beat yolks until thick. Gradually beat in sugar and 1 tablespoon lemon juice. Sift in flour, cornstarch, and salt; add remaining lemon juice and beat until smooth. Fold in egg whites. Spread evenly in 2 pans (1 x 10 x 15 inches lined on bottom with wax paper. (If only 1 pan is available, other half of batter can wait.) Bake in preheated moderate oven (375°F.) for 10 to 15 minutes. Turn out on rack and peel off paper at once. Cool cakes and cut each into 4 even pieces. Spread Chocolate Frosting between layers and on top and sides of cake.

Chocolate Frosting

In top part of double boiler over boiling water melt 4 ounces (4 squares) unsweetened chocolate. Beat 4 egg yolks with ⅔ cup sugar. Stir in ½ cup heavy cream and add to chocolate. Cook, stirring, until thickened. Cream 1¼ cups butter or margarine. Beat in chocolate mixture, 1 tablespoon at a time. Chill until of spreading consistency.

CHOCOLATE SHADOW CAKE

¾ cup soft butter or margarine
2 cups sifted cake flour
1¾ cups sugar
⅔ cup unsweetened cocoa
1 teaspoon baking soda
½ teaspoon baking powder
¾ teaspoon salt
1 cup plus 2 tablespoons buttermilk
3 eggs
1 teaspoon vanilla extract
Fluffy White Frosting (page 1042)

Cream butter. Sift flour, sugar, cocoa, baking soda, baking powder, and salt into butter. Add 1 cup buttermilk and mix until all flour is dampened. Beat 2½ minutes at low speed of electric mixer. Add remaining 2 tablespoons buttermilk, eggs, and vanilla. Beat for 2½ minutes. Pour into two 9-inch layer pans, lined on the bottom with paper. Bake in preheated moderate oven (350°F.) for 35 to 40 minutes. Cool, frost with Fluffy White Frosting. Melt 2 ounces (2 squares) unsweetened chocolate with 2 teaspoons shortening. Cool slightly and drizzle over cake, allowing mixture to run down sides.

BROWN-SUGAR FUDGE CAKE

½ cup soft butter or margarine
2¼ cups sifted cake flour
1 teaspoon baking soda
¾ teaspoon salt
2 cups firmly packed light brown sugar
1 cup buttermilk
1 teaspoon vanilla extract
3 eggs
3 ounces (3 squares) unsweetened chocolate, melted
Caramel Frosting
Walnut or pecan halves

Cream butter. Sift flour, soda, and salt onto butter. Add sugar, ⅔ cup buttermilk, and vanilla. Beat for 2 minutes. Add remaining ⅓ cup buttermilk, eggs, and cooled chocolate. Beat for 2 minutes. Pour into two 9-inch layer pans lined on bottom with paper. Bake in preheated

moderate oven (350°F.) for about 30 minutes. Cool, spread Caramel Frosting, and decorate with nuts.

Caramel Frosting

In large saucepan mix 2 cups firmly packed light brown sugar, 1 cup granulated sugar, 2 tablespoons light corn syrup, 3 tablespoons butter, dash of salt, ⅔ cup light cream, and 1 teaspoon vanilla extract. Bring to boil, cover, and cook for 3 minutes. Uncover and cook to 236°F. on a candy thermometer, or until a small amount of mixture forms a soft ball when dropped into cold water. Cool for 5 minutes; then beat until thick. If too stiff, add a little hot water.

CHOCOLATE PEPPERMINT CAKE

½ cup soft butter or margarine
2¼ cups firmly packed light brown sugar (about 1 pound)
3 eggs
3 ounces (3 squares) unsweetened chocolate, melted
2¼ cups sifted cake flour
1½ teaspoons baking soda
½ teaspoon salt
½ cup buttermilk
1 teaspoon vanilla extract
1 cup boiling water
6 ounces of thin chocolate mint wafers
Peppermint Frosting

Cream butter and sugar; add eggs, one at a time, beating well after each addition. Add cooled chocolate and blend. Add sifted flour, soda, and salt alternately with buttermilk; beat until smooth. Stir in vanilla and water. Pour into three 8- or 9-inch layer pans lined on bottom with paper. Bake in preheated moderate oven (350°F.) for about 30 minutes. Remove to racks and press mints on 2 bottom layers. Cool and spread Peppermint Frosting between layers and on top and sides of cake.

Peppermint Frosting

Make Fluffy White Frosting (page 1042), omitting vanilla. Flavor with ½ teaspoon peppermint extract.

CHOCOLATE-WALNUT CAKE

2¼ cups sugar
3 tablespoons water
2 ounces (2 squares) unsweetened chocolate, melted
¾ cup soft butter
1 teaspoon vanilla extract
4 eggs, separated
2¼ cups sifted cake flour
1 teaspoon cream of tartar
½ teaspoon each of baking soda and salt
3 cups milk
1 box vanilla-pudding and pie-filling mix
Chocolate Cream-Cheese Frosting
Colored Walnuts

Stir ¼ cup sugar and the water into chocolate. Cream butter and remaining 2 cups sugar. Add vanilla, then egg yolks, one at a time, beating well after each addition. Add chocolate mixture and blend. Add sifted flour, cream of tartar, soda, and salt alternately with 1 cup milk; beat until smooth. Fold in stiffly beaten egg whites. Pour into three 9-inch layer pans lined on bottom with paper. Bake in preheated moderate oven (350° F.) for about 35 minutes. Prepare pudding with 2 cups milk; cool. Put cooled layers together with pudding; spread Chocolate Cream-Cheese Frosting. Sprinkle with Colored Walnuts.

Chocolate Cream-Cheese Frosting

Cream ¼ cup soft butter and 8 ounces cream cheese. Add 3 ounces (3 squares) unsweetened chocolate, melted, dash of salt, 3 cups sifted confectioners' sugar, ⅓ cup light cream, and 1 teaspoon vanilla extract. Beat until smooth.

Colored Walnuts

Add green food coloring to 2 teaspoons warm water; add ¾ cup chopped walnuts and blend well. Dry in moderate oven (350°F.) for 8 minutes.

SOUTHERN CHOCOLATE CAKE

    6 ounces (1 small package) semi-sweet
        chocolate pieces
    ½ cup butter or margarine
    4 egg yolks
    ⅔ cup sugar
    1 cup sifted cake flour
    1¼ teaspoons baking powder
    ½ teaspoon baking soda
    ¼ teaspoon salt
    ½ cup milk
    1 teaspoon vanilla extract
    2 egg whites
        Fluffy White Frosting (page 1042)

Melt chocolate and butter; cool. Beat egg yolks until thick. Gradually beat in ⅓ cup sugar and beat until very thick. Add sifted flour, baking powder, soda, and salt alternately with milk and beat until smooth. Add chocolate mixture and vanilla. Beat egg whites until stiff. Gradually beat in remaining ⅓ cup sugar. Fold into batter. Pour into two 8-inch layer pans lined on bottom with paper. Bake in preheated moderate oven (375° F.) for about 25 minutes. Cool and spread Fluffy White Frosting.

COMPANY GOLD CAKE

    11 egg yolks
    2 cups sugar
    ½ cup butter or margarine
    1 cup milk, scalded
    2⅓ cups sifted cake flour
    3 teaspoons baking powder
    ½ teaspoon salt
    1 teaspoon vanilla extract
        Caramel Frosting (page 1044)

Beat egg yolks until thick and lemon-colored. Gradually beat in sugar. Add butter to hot milk and let stand until butter melts. Add sifted flour, baking powder, and salt to first mixture alternately with milk and butter. Add vanilla. Pour into 3 ungreased pans 8 x 8 x 2 inches. Bake in preheated slow oven (325°F.) for 30 minutes. Cool and spread Caramel Frosting.

COFFEE SPICE CAKE

    ½ cup soft butter
    1 cup firmly packed light brown sugar
    2 eggs
    ½ teaspoon each of vanilla and lemon
        extracts
    1½ cups sifted all-purpose flour
    1½ teaspoons baking powder
    ½ teaspoon salt
    1 teaspoon ground cinnamon
    ¼ teaspoon each of ground ginger,
        cloves, and nutmeg
    ⅓ cup undiluted evaporated milk
    ¼ cup strong coffee
        Coffee Frosting

Cream butter and sugar until light. Add eggs, one at a time, beating well after each addition. Add flavorings. Add sifted flour, baking powder, salt, and spices alternately with milk and coffee, beating until smooth. Pour into two 8-inch layer pans lined on bottom with paper. Bake in preheated moderate oven (350°F.) for 25 minutes. Cool and spread Coffee Frosting.

Coffee Frosting

Cream ⅓ cup butter. Add dash of salt and ½ teaspoon vanilla extract. Gradually beat in 2½ cups confectioners' sugar and enough strong coffee to moisten (about 2 tablespoons).

GOLDEN LORD BALTIMORE CAKE

    ½ cup butter or margarine (at room
        temperature)
    2¼ cups sifted cake flour
    2 teaspoons baking powder
    ¾ teaspoon salt
    1 cup sugar
    1 teaspoon grated orange rind
    5 egg yolks, unbeaten
    ⅔ cup milk
        Fluffy White Frosting (page 1042)
    ½ cup almond-macaroon crumbs
    ¼ cup chopped walnuts
    ¼ cup chopped blanched almonds
    12 candied cherries, quartered
    ¼ teaspoon orange extract
    1 tablespoon sherry
        Whole candied cherries
        Strips of angelica

Stir butter just to soften. Sift in dry ingredients, including sugar. Add orange rind, egg yolks, and half of the milk; mix until all flour is dampened. Then beat for 2 minutes in electric mixer set at low speed, or with 300 vigorous strokes by hand. Add remaining milk and beat for 1 minute longer in the mixer or 150 strokes by hand. Bake in two greased and floured 9-inch layer pans in preheated moderate oven (375°F.) for about 25 minutes. Make Fluffy White Frosting. Add macaroon crumbs, nuts, cherries, orange extract, and sherry to one third of the Frosting and stir. Spread between cooled cake layers. Use remaining Frosting for top and sides of cake. Decorate top with whole cherries and angelica.

HIMMEL TORTE

    2 cups butter or margarine
    2 cups granulated sugar
    8 eggs

    2 cups sifted cake flour
    1 teaspoon cream of tartar
    ½ teaspoon baking soda
        About 5 jars (8 ounces each) currant
        jelly
        Confectioners' sugar

Using an electric mixer, cream the butter and gradually beat in the sugar. Add the eggs one at a time, beating well after each addition. Sift the flour with the cream of tartar and baking soda; add to the butter mixture. Beat for 10 minutes. Bake only 2 layers at a time. With batter, cover just the bottoms of two inverted ungreased 9-inch layer-cake pans. Bake in preheated moderate oven (375° F.) for 10 to 12 minutes, or until lightly browned. Remove from pans at once and spread each layer with currant jelly while warm. Put layers together. There is enough batter for 14 to 16 layers. Sprinkle with confectioners' sugar. Cut into small slices to serve as torte is very rich.

LEAVEN, LEAVENING AGENTS—

These are various substances which lighten dough or batter while it is baking and make it more palatable. The word comes from the Latin *levare* which means "to raise."

Though air and steam act as leavening agents to a certain extent, the oldest and best-known ingredient used for leavening is yeast, as essential to the baking of bread now as it was in the remote days when first discovered, probably by accident, in a batter that had fermented.

Leaven and leavening agents are part of the history of civilization due to their effects on the making of bread, mankind's basic food. Their importance is best seen in the many ways in which the word leaven has been used figuratively and symbolically in much of the world's mythology and literature. Perhaps the most touching one is found in the Bible (Matthew 13:33): "The kingdom of heaven is like unto leaven, which a woman took, and hid in three measures of meal, till the whole was leavened."

Leavening agents increase the surface area of dough through the release of gases within the dough. The expansion of these gases during baking increases the size of the finished food, and gives a desirable porous structure. Of the gases created the principal one is carbon dioxide; the others are air and water vapor or steam.

Air is a physical means of leavening. It may be incorporated into the batter by means of an egg-white foam or to a lesser degree by creaming fat and sugar. Chiffon, angel food, spongecakes, and soufflés are examples of air used as leavening.

Steam, another physical leavening, occurs when water is exposed to high temperatures. Popovers and cream puffs are leavened by steam.

Baking soda, also known as sodium bicarbonate or bicarbonate of soda, is a chemical leavening agent. When the soda is heated in the presence of moisture, carbon dioxide gas is produced. When used by itself, soda leaves a disagreeable taste and produces a yellow color. To prevent this, an acid substance, such as cream of tartar, sour milk, or molasses, is usually used in combination with the soda.

Baking powder, another chemical leavening agent, is sold in three forms. The tartrate powders, containing cream of tartar and tartaric acid, react quickly in batter or dough at room temperature. The phosphate powder, containing calcium acid phosphate, releases two thirds of its gas at room temperature and the remainder when heat is applied. The double-acting powder contains sodium aluminum sulfate and calcium acid phosphate; it releases a small portion of gas when ingredients are combined, but the greater amount is released in the oven.

Yeast is a living plant which can produce carbon dioxide under suitable environmental conditions. It is available in two forms, active dry and compressed. Active dry yeast may be substituted for compressed yeast, using one ¼-ounce package for each cake of compressed yeast.

Yeast should be reactivated in warm water (temperatures that are too high will destroy it), 105° to 115°F. if dry and 80° to 90°F. if compressed.

Sourdough is a fermented dough which produces carbon dioxide under suitable environmental conditions.

***Availability and Purchasing Guide*—** Baking powder is available canned; baking soda is sold in packages; active dry yeast is available in foil envelope packages, and compressed yeast is available in cakes.

***Storage*—**Baking powder and baking soda should be tightly wrapped or covered to prevent moisture absorption which causes loss of quality of leavening power.

- ☐ Baking powder, kitchen shelf, tightly covered: 8 to 12 months
- ☐ Baking soda, kitchen shelf, tightly covered: indefinitely
- ☐ Active dry yeast, kitchen shelf, in original package: until expiration date on package
- ☐ Compressed yeast, refrigerator shelf, in original container: until expiration date on package
- ☐ Compressed yeast, freezer, in original container: indefinitely

Caloric Values

- ☐ Baking powder, 1 ounce = 11 to 25 calories, depending on type
- ☐ Dry yeast, 1 ounce = 80 calories
- ☐ Compressed yeast, 1 ounce = 25 calories

LEBKUCHEN—A spicecake of German origin and one of the oldest of cakes. Originally it was always made with honey. The word comes from Middle High German, an obsolete language, predecessor of modern German, and it is a contraction of two words, *lebe* meaning "loaf" and *kuoche* meaning "cake."

Lebkuchen belongs to the category of medieval honey cakes which were the pride of the Bakers' Guilds in many European cities. They were baked in different shapes and molds, some of which were beautifully carved. The shape of the lebkuchen depended on the occasion for which it was baked; for St. Nicholas Day and Christmas, the shape was a Santa Claus. Lebkuchens were luxury cakes, since their ingredients included spices, citron, and almonds, all of which were too expensive for nonfestive occasions.

Lebkuchen, like their cousin the gingerbread, ornamented the fairs of the past, the red-letter events of those earlier days when communications and travel were possible only at rare intervals. All European countries have their own version of lebkuchen, as a loaf cake, a flat cake, or a cookie.

HONEY LEBKUCHEN

3⅓ cups sifted cake flour
¼ teaspoon baking soda
1 teaspoon ground cinnamon
¼ teaspoon ground nutmeg
⅛ teaspoon ground cloves
½ teaspoon salt
⅔ cup honey
½ cup firmly packed brown sugar
2 tablespoons water
1 egg, slightly beaten
¾ cup shredded candied orange peel
¾ cup shredded candied citron
½ cup almonds, blanched and shredded
Glaze

Sift flour with soda, spices, and salt. Mix honey, sugar, and water; bring to boil and boil for 5 minutes. Cool. Add dry ingredients, egg, fruits, and nuts. Press dough together and wrap in wax paper. Store in refrigerator for 2 to 3 days to ripen. Roll ¼ inch thick on lightly floured board, and cut into 3- x 1-inch strips. Bake on greased cookie sheet in preheated moderate oven (350°F.) for about 15 minutes. Cool and spread with Glaze. Makes about 4 dozen.

Glaze

Mix 2 cups sifted confectioners' sugar and 3 tablespoons boiling water until smooth. Add 1 teaspoon vanilla extract and spread on cookies while warm.

DROPPED ALMOND LEBKUCHEN

1 cup white sugar
2 eggs
Grated rind of ½ lemon
1½ cups blanched almonds, finely ground
¼ cup candied lemon peel, finely ground
1 teaspoon ground cinnamon
½ teaspoon ground nutmeg
¼ teaspoon ground cloves
⅛ teaspoon salt
Lemon Frosting
Colored sugar

Beat white sugar, eggs, and lemon rind with electric mixer for 15 minutes. Stir in remaining ingredients except Lemon Frosting and colored sugar. Drop by teaspoonfuls onto greased cookie sheets. Bake in preheated moderate oven (350° F.) for 10 minutes, or until very lightly browned. Remove at once from cookie sheet and spread with a little Lemon Frosting. Sprinkle with colored sugar. Makes about 3 dozen.

Lemon Frosting

Mix 1 cup confectioners' sugar and 3 tablespoons fresh lemon juice until smooth and blended.

CHOCOLATE LEBKUCHEN

1¼ cups white sugar
¾ cup honey
2 tablespoons water
2 cups semisweet chocolate pieces
1 cup chopped unblanched almonds
½ cup finely chopped mixed candied fruit
2 eggs, well beaten
¼ cup fresh orange juice
2¾ cups sifted all-purpose flour
2 teaspoons each of ground cinnamon and cardamom
1 teaspoon ground cloves
1 teaspoon each of baking soda and baking powder
Thin Orange Frosting
Red candy shot
Green sugar

Combine sugar, honey, and water in large saucepan. Bring to a boil. Remove from heat; cool. Stir in chocolate, almonds, candied fruit, eggs, and orange juice. Sift in flour, spices, soda, and baking powder and blend thoroughly. Store dough in tightly closed container at room temperature for 3 days to ripen. Spread in greased and floured pan (15 x 10 x 1 inch). Bake in preheated slow oven (325°F.) for 35 to 40 minutes. Cool. Spread Thin Orange Frosting, cut into diamonds, and decorate with red shot and green sugar. Makes about 4 dozen.

Thin Orange Frosting

To each 1 cup sifted confectioners' sugar, add 1 to 2 tablespoons fresh orange juice, stirring until of the right consistency. Tint as desired.

LEEK—This first cousin of the onion and garlic has a cylindrical stalk with a small simple bulb, and flat, juicy, compactly rolled-up leaves which are dark green at the top and white towards the bulb. Leeks have a mild onion flavor and are used as a seasoning or a vegetable. The whole leek is used in cooking, with the exception of the tough part of the leaves and the roots.

Leeks are native to the Mediterranean regions, and they have been enjoyed by Egyptian, Greek, and Roman gourmets for thousands of years. The Emperor Nero consumed them in great quantities, believing they would improve his singing voice. The use of leeks continued through the centuries, and became one of the favorite Italian, English, and French vegetables; the French call leeks "the asparagus of the poor."

Leeks are also the emblem of Wales. The Welshmen, who in the 6th century A.D. won a victory over the Saxons, attributed their strength to the leeks they wore to distinguish them in battle. They were probably brought to Wales by Phoenicians trading in tin along the Welsh coast.

Availability—Leeks are sold in bunches and are available all during the year. The peak season is winter and early spring.

Purchasing Guide—Select crisp, young leeks with fresh green tops. Avoid those with wilted or discolored tops.

Storage—Cut off rootlets and the unusable part of the tops, leaving about 2 inches of green leaves. Do not wash until ready to use. Put in moisture-proof wrapping and keep in the vegetable compartment of the refrigerator.

☐ Refrigerator shelf or vegetable compartment, raw: 3 to 8 days

☐ Refrigerator shelf, cooked: 1 to 2 days

☐ Refrigerator frozen-food compartment, prepared for freezing: 2 to 3 months

☐ Freezer, prepared for freezing: 1 year

Nutritive Food Values—The green part has some vitamin A.

☐ 3½ ounces, raw = 52 calories

Basic Preparation—Wash leeks thoroughly in several changes of water to remove sand from leaves. Leeks may be cut into halves lengthwise, cut into 1-inch pieces, or left whole. Leeks can be served in any way asparagus is served.

☐ **To Cook**—Place washed and trimmed leeks in 1 inch of boiling salted water. Cover and cook until tender, about 15 minutes. Drain well and season to taste. Serve with butter or margarine, or cover with any white or cheese sauce, and brown in oven or under broiler. Or chill and serve with French dressing as an appetizer or salad.

☐ **To Braise**—Place washed and trimmed leeks in butter in a heavy skillet, with

water that clings to the leaves. Cover and simmer for 10 to 15 minutes, until leeks are tender. Season to taste.

☐ **To Freeze**—Slice white part of leeks in ⅛-inch pieces. Cover with boiling water and drain; or steam over boiling water for 2 minutes, or until leeks are limp. Chill thoroughly in ice water, drain, and wrap securely. Pack in polyethylene bags inserted in boxes and then wrapped in freezer paper so that the odor will not penetrate other foods.

LEEK SOUP

      6 leeks, white part only, cut into thin rounds
      1 white onion, sliced
    ¼ cup butter or margarine
      6 potatoes, peeled and sliced
      6 cups chicken bouillon
    ½ cup chopped parsley
      1 egg yolk, beaten
        Salt and pepper
        Dash of ground nutmeg
      2 cups light cream
        Crumbled crisp bacon

Sauté leeks and onion in butter until soft but not brown. Add potatoes, bouillon, and parsley, and simmer until vegetables are soft. Strain and sieve vegetables and return purée to broth. Add some broth to egg, stirring, then add egg to broth with seasonings. Add cream and reheat but do not boil. Garnish in tureen with bacon. With salad and rolls, this is a hearty meal. Makes 2 quarts.

SCOTCH COCK-A-LEEKIE

      1 stewing chicken (about 5 pounds), cut up
      3 onions, quartered
    ¼ cup chopped parsley
      2 celery stalks, slivered
    ¼ cup chopped celery leaves
    ½ teaspoon poultry seasoning
        Salt and pepper
      1 bay leaf
    2½ quarts cold water
      2 tablespoons barley
    12 leeks with tops, cleaned and sliced
      3 potatoes, peeled and diced
        Chopped parsley

Place all ingredients except barley, leeks, potatoes, and parsley in kettle; bring to boil, then simmer for 2 hours, or until chicken is tender. Remove chicken and slice thin; put aside. Strain broth; add barley, leeks, and potatoes, and continue to simmer for 30 minutes. Place sliced chicken in tureen, pour over soup, and garnish with chopped parsley. With crusty bread and a salad this is a one-dish meal. Makes about 3 quarts.

LAMB AND LEEK SKILLET

      1 pound lean lamb, cubed
      2 tablespoons butter
      2 bunches of leeks, white part only, cut into pieces
        Salt and pepper
      2 ripe tomatoes, peeled and quartered
      2 cups bouillon
        Juice of ½ lemon
      2 eggs, beaten
        Hot cooked rice

Brown lamb in butter; add leeks, season, and stir. Add tomatoes and cook for a few minutes, stirring. Add bouillon, cover, and simmer for 1 hour. Just before serving add lemon juice to eggs; add a little broth, then add eggs to liquid in pan. Cook until just thick. Serve over rice. Makes 4 servings.

LEEK AND GREEN-PEA PURÉE

      6 leeks, white part only, thinly sliced
    ¼ cup butter or margarine
      4 cans (10½ ounces each) condensed green-pea soup
      4 cups rich milk
        Salt and pepper
        Dash of curry powder
        Dairy sour cream
        Poppy seeds

Sauté leeks gently in butter until soft but not brown. Combine soup, milk, and seasonings in top part of double boiler. Add leeks and heat. Serve with garnish of sour cream and poppy seeds. Makes about 2 quarts.

LEEK AND CHICKEN CASSEROLE

      1 lemon
      1 roasting chicken (4 to 5 pounds)
      2 cups water
      4 leeks, white part only, cut into 1-inch pieces
      2 onions, sliced
      4 carrots, peeled and sliced
      4 celery stalks
    ¼ cup butter or margarine
        Salt and pepper
      1 bay leaf
        Pinch of crumbled dried thyme
      4 whole cloves
      3 cups dry white wine
        Chives
        Thin lemon slices

Rub half of lemon over whole chicken and put with water in covered casserole or Dutch oven (cover must be tight). Put over low heat and, while coming to boil, sauté leeks, onions, carrots, and celery in butter, just until leeks begin to yellow. Add with seasonings and half of wine to casserole. Bake, covered, in preheated moderate oven (350°F.) for 2 hours. Remove chicken and carve. Add rest of wine to broth and reheat. Season to taste. Pour over chicken in a tureen and serve with garnish of chives and thin lemon slices. Makes 4 to 6 servings.

FORDHOOK LIMAS AND LEEKS

      2 packages (10 ounces each) frozen Fordhook Lima beans
      2 leeks, cleaned and sliced thin
      2 table spoons butter or margarine
      1 tablespoon all-purpose flour
    ¼ teaspoon paprika
        Salt and pepper

Cook Fordhook Limas as directed on the label. Drain, reserving ½ cup liquid. Sauté leeks in butter or margarine for 5 minutes. Blend in flour. Gradually stir in bean liquid and cook over low heat, stirring constantly, until thickened. Add paprika, beans, and salt and pepper to taste; heat. Makes 6 servings.

What Every Woman Should Know About LEFTOVERS: A Matter of Simple Arithmetic

12 basic recipes that can be made with any leftover cooked meat or poultry

Multiplication gives you variety. Because the twelve recipes given here are completely flexible, you can produce more than 100 different main dishes. If you multiply twelve by turkey, chicken, duck, beef, veal, ham, pork, lamb, tongue, and sausage, you'll see that you have 120 possibilities. And with a freezer, you can have a whole assortment at once from which to choose.

Division saves you money. A roast is a luxury if it goes for only one dinner. But use the leftovers for a second main dish, and you divide the cost per meal in half. Some of these recipes take as

little as two cups of meat, yet they serve from four to six people.

Addition lets you be creative in the kitchen. Besides cooked meat and poultry, you can add other leftovers: gravy, broth, rice, macaroni, vegetables, and the constant collection of vegetable cooking water, high in nutrients.

Subtraction cuts down on working and cooking time. When you've studied these recipes, you'll see that most of them call for a short cooking time because the meat is already cooked. So if you're going to have a busy afternoon, you can select one of the twenty-minute dishes,

Pancake Roll Ups

prepare it in the morning, and slip into the kitchen just half an hour before dinnertime. The short cooking time subtracts from your fuel bill, too. These recipes are work savers because the preparation of most takes only about fifteen minutes. And some of them save you both time and work in still another way: they're one-dish meals that need only salad, bread, dessert, and beverage to complete the menu.

RICE CASSEROLES

1 cup uncooked rice
1 can cream of celery or mushroom
  soup
¾ cup milk
1 teaspoon instant minced onion
2 to 3 cups cut up leftover cooked
  meat or poultry
1 box frozen mixed vegetables, cooked
  Dash of hot pepper sauce
1 teaspoon Worcestershire

Cook rice according to your favorite method and put it in a 1½-quart baking dish. Mix soup, milk, onion, meat, vegetables, and seasonings; put on rice. Bake in preheated moderate oven (375°F.) for about 40 minutes, or until hot and bubbly. Makes 4 to 6 servings.

Note: Sprinkle top with buttered bread crumbs, grated cheese, or chopped nuts, if desired. Cream of chicken soup can be substituted for the cream of celery or cream of mushroom.

PINWHEELS

3 cups all-purpose flour
1½ teaspoons salt
4½ teaspoons baking powder
½ cup shortening
  Milk
2 cups ground or minced cooked
  meat or poultry
2 cans cream of mushroom soup
3 green onions, chopped
1 tablespoon prepared mustard

Mix flour, salt, and baking powder. Cut in shortening well. Mix in 1 cup milk to make a stiff dough. Roll out into rectangle 6 x 10 inches. Spread with meat mixed with remaining ingredients, using ¾ cup soup. Roll up lengthwise. Cut in 8 to 10 slices. Bake on cookie sheet in preheated hot oven (425°F.) for about 20 minutes. Thin remaining soup with milk, heat, and serve with pinwheels. Makes 4 servings.

SHEPHERD'S PIES

2 cups cut up leftover cooked meat
  or poultry
2 cups leftover gravy
  or canned soup
1 cup sliced carrots, cooked
½ cup cooked peas
1 can (1 pound) onions, drained
  Salt and pepper
1 egg yolk
2 cups leftover mashed potatoes
  or 1 package instant mashed potato

Combine meat, gravy, carrots, peas, and onions. Heat. Season to taste with salt and pepper. Pour into a 2-quart casserole. Beat egg yolk into potatoes and top casserole with potatoes put through a pastry tube or spooned lightly on top.

Bake in preheated hot oven (425°F.) until potatoes are browned and gravy bubbles, about 25 minutes. Makes 4 servings.

PANCAKE ROLL UPS

1 cup all-purpose flour
½ teaspoon salt
1 cup milk
2 eggs
  Fat for frying
2 cups ground or minced cooked meat
  or poultry
1 cup minced celery
¾ cup cream of mushroom soup
2 tablespoons chopped pimiento
  Salt and pepper
  Cheese Sauce
  Toasted almonds

Mix flour and salt. Add milk, and beat until smooth. Add eggs, and beat thoroughly. Heat about 1 teaspoon fat in a 6-inch frying pan. Pour in just enough batter to cover bottom of pan, tilting so mixture spreads evenly. Turn, and cook other side. Remove, and make remaining pancakes. Mix remaining ingredients except last 2. Put some of mixture in center of each pancake, roll up, and place close together in shallow baking dish. Heat in preheated moderate oven (350°F.) for 20 minutes. Serve with Cheese Sauce and sprinkle with toasted almonds. Makes six to eight 6-inch roll ups.

Cheese Sauce

Melt 2 tablespoons butter or margarine, and blend in 2 tabelspoons all-purpose flour and ½ teaspoon powdered mustard. Gradually add 1 cup milk and cook, stirring, until thickened. Stir in ⅓ cup shredded sharp Cheddar cheese and salt and pepper to taste. Makes 1 cup.

CREOLE-STYLE LEFTOVERS

1 medium onion, chopped
1 garlic clove, minced
1 green pepper, chopped
2 tablespoons cooking oil
1 cup canned tomatoes
½ teaspoon thyme
1 teaspoon salt
¼ teaspoon pepper
  Dash of hot pepper sauce
3 cups water
2 cups cut up cooked meat or poultry
1 cup uncooked rice
1 pound cleaned shelled shrimps

Brown onion, garlic, and green pepper in oil. Add remaining ingredients except rice and shrimps. Bring to boil and stir in rice. Cover and simmer for about 20 minutes. Add shrimps and cook for 10 minutes longer, or until rice is tender and mixture is quite dry. Makes 4 to 6 servings.

CHOW MEINS

1 large onion, sliced
3 tablespoons cooking oil
2 cups sliced celery
2 bouillon cubes
1½ cups water
2 cans (1 pound each) Chinese
  mixed vegetables, drained
2 tablespoons soy sauce
2 cups cut up leftover cooked meat
  or poultry
1 cup small spinach leaves
  Salt, pepper, and soy sauce

Cornstarch
Chow mein noodles

Cook onion in oil until lightly browned. Add celery, bouillon cubes, and water; cover, and cook for 5 minutes. Add remaining ingredients, except last 5. Bring to boil; season with salt, pepper, and soy sauce. Thicken with cornstarch mixed with a little cold water. Serve with chow mein noodles. Makes 4 to 6 servings.

MEXICAN PIES

1 cup yellow cornmeal
1 cup milk
3 cups boiling water
  Salt
3 slices bacon
½ cup diced celery
1 onion, chopped
½ green pepper, chopped
1 cup tomatoes
½ cup corn
1½ teaspoons chili powder
  Pepper to taste
¼ cup sliced ripe or stuffed olives
1½ cups minced leftover cooked meat
  or poultry
1 cup grated process cheese

Mix cornmeal with milk; add to boiling water with 1 teaspoon salt. Cook until thickened, stirring. Cover; simmer for 10 minutes. Use to line baking dish. Dice and fry bacon; add celery, onion, and green pepper; cook for 10 minutes. Simmer for 5 minutes with 1½ teaspoons salt and remaining ingredients except cheese. Put in baking dish. Add cheese. Bake in preheated slow oven (325°F.) for 45 minutes. Makes 4 to 6 servings.

CURRIES

1 small onion, minced
¼ cup butter or margarine
¼ cup all-purpose flour
2 to 3 tablespoons curry powder
½ teaspoon powdered ginger
1 teaspoon salt
2 cups meat stock or 2 bouillon cubes
  and 2 cups water
1 cup light cream
3 to 4 cups cut-up leftover cooked
  meat or poultry
  Juice of ½ lemon
4 cups cooked rice
1 small green pepper, chopped

Cook onion in butter. Stir in flour, curry, ginger, and salt. Add stock and cream; cook until thickened, stirring constantly. Add meat and lemon juice; heat. Push curry mixture to one side of serving skillet or dish. Add rice and garnish with the green pepper. Makes 4 to 6 servings.

NOODLE CASSEROLES

2 to 3 cups cut up leftover cooked
  meat or poultry
1 can (6 ounces) tomato paste
1 garlic clove, minced
3 cups water
½ teaspoon onion salt
1½ teaspoons salt
¼ teaspoon pepper
1 bay leaf
  Dash of cayenne
8 ounces wide noodles
½ cup cooked peas
  Grated Parmesan cheese

Combine all ingredients, except last 3. Bring to boil. Add noodles; be sure sauce covers them; add more water if necessary for noodles to cook thoroughly. Cover, and cook slowly until noodles are tender, about 20 minutes. Add hot peas, and sprinkle with grated cheese. Makes 4 to 6 servings.

BARBECUE-STYLE LEFTOVERS

1 small onion, chopped
2 tablespoons butter or margarine
1 teaspoon salt
1 teaspoon chili powder
½ teaspoon celery salt
1 can (8 ounces) tomato sauce
2 tablespoons brown sugar
3 tablespoons vinegar
2 tablespoons Worcestershire
½ cup ketchup
1 cup water
  Dash of hot pepper sauce
2 cups cut up leftover meat or poultry
1 can (1 pound) whole potatoes, drained

Cook onion in butter. Add remaining ingredients, except meat and potatoes. Simmer for ½ hour, or until quite thick. Add meat and potatoes, simmer about 10 minutes longer, or until meat and potatoes are heated. Makes 4 servings.

À LA KING LEFTOVERS

½ green pepper, cut up
½ cup butter or margarine
⅓ cup all-purpose flour
3½ cups milk
2 to 3 cups cut up leftover meat or poultry
1 can (4 ounces) sliced mushrooms, drained
2 pimientos, cut up
  Salt and pepper
  Worcestershire
  Cooked rice, toast, or waffles

Cook green pepper in butter for 3 minutes; remove pepper. Make a cream sauce by stirring flour into butter; then add milk, and cook until thickened, stirring constantly. Add green pepper, meat, mushrooms, and pimientos; bring to boil. Season to taste with salt, pepper, and Worcestershire. Serve over rice. Makes 4 to 6 servings.

STUFFED VEGETABLES

6 large onions or tomatoes, or 4 green peppers
½ cup diced celery
2 tablespoons fat
2 cups ground leftover cooked meat or poultry
1 can (3 or 4 ounces) chopped mushrooms
  Chopped parsley
1 cup soft stale bread crumbs
1 tablespoon Worcestershire
  Dash of hot pepper sauce
1 teaspoon powdered mustard
1 cup gravy
  Salt and pepper

Peel and cook onions until almost tender; remove centers; or cut slice off tops of tomatoes and scoop out centers; or cut slice off tops of peppers, remove seeds, and boil for 5 minutes. Cook celery in fat; mix with rest of ingredients, using only enough gravy to moisten. Stuff vege-

tables. Put with rest of gravy in casserole. Bake in preheated moderate oven (375°F.) for 25 minutes. Makes 4 to 6 servings.

LEGUME—Food plants which have pods that open along two seams when the seeds are ripe are called legumes. The seeds are usually the edible part of the legume. Peas, chick-peas, beans, Lima beans, soybeans, peanuts, and lentils are the best-known food legumes. There are more than 11,000 species of legumes. Many, such as clover and alfalfa, are used as fodder for animals; others are used for medicinal purposes. Another name for legume is pulse.

Next to cereals, legumes are the most important food plant for humans. They contain proteins, carbohydrates, fats, minerals, and some vitamin B. All in all, they supply a great part of the food essentials man must have to survive.

Legumes are easily grown under varying soil or climatic conditions and when dried, they store easily, thanks to their small size, their low water content, and their hard coating.

Legumes are a food essential in countries where little meat is eaten. They are wholesome, inexpensive and, when properly cooked, delicious food. They can serve as a substitute for potatoes, rice, and pastas; they can be combined with any number of other foods, stretching more costly ones; and they can be cooked in endless ways.

LEMON—The lemon tree, a member of the citrus family, is a small tree which grows ten to twenty feet in height. It has short spines and large, fragrant, white and purple flowers. The light yellow fruit is small, oval, and ends in a blunt point. The pulp of the fruit is juicy and acid, containing half of one per cent sugar and five per cent citric acid. From antiquity, the lemon has been used as a fruit for preserves. Lemon marmalade, a pleasant change from orange marmalade, was known as early as 1609. Lemon juice has been used as a flavoring, medicinal agent, and stain remover.

There are many varieties of lemons. Some have thin skins and others very thick ones. The first are used for their juice, the second for making candied lemon peel which is used in baking and for desserts. Oil for flavoring is extracted from the rind; it takes about 1,000 lemons to make one pound of oil.

The exact birthplace of the lemon is not known although it is probable that the home of this beloved fruit was some-

where near northern Burma. It is said to have been present in China as early as 971 A.D., according to a later court chronicle which reported: "In the fourth year of K'ai Pao two bottles of lemon juice were allowed to be presented to the Emperor."

About 1,000 A.D. Arab writers record the lemon, which flourished in Syria, Egypt, Palestine, and Persia. Between the years 1,000 and 1200 lemons were introduced into the Mediterranean regions of Europe, brought there by the Crusaders.

Columbus, on his second voyage to America to set up a colony, stopped off at the Canary Islands where he gathered up seedlings of lemons as well as oranges. Then he established his colony on the northern coast of Hispaniola, or Santo Domingo, the modern Haiti and Dominican Republic. The plants were spread by the Spanish to Mexico and Central America in the early 16th century. In 1565 when the Spanish established themselves in St. Augustine, Florida, they introduced the lemon to this country. Later the Spanish Franciscans carried fruit seeds with them when they moved north from Mexico in 1769 to establish a mission at San Diego in California. From this small beginning California has grown to be one of the largest suppliers of lemons in the world. It produces over half the world's lemon crop.

The lemon has a long history of medicinal use. In Colonial days, sailors on long voyages, and the colonists themselves, were often overcome by scurvy. It was discovered that an ounce of lemon juice a day was a preventative. In the 15th century lemon peel was often used for toothpaste; English apothecaries found the juice useful in dissolving pearls for an epilepsy remedy. And witches in England, Sicily, and Italy were accustomed to writing the name of their victim on a piece of paper pinned to a lemon. This was reputed to cause misfortune and death.

The unholy practices of witchcraft are more than offset today by the joy a lemon can give to a diet-conscious cook. A trickle of lemon juice over asparagus or broccoli, soups, or salads improves flavor immensely, and is a worthy substitute for other nonslimming seasonings. Lemon juice in a French dressing points up the delicate taste of greens. Grated lemon rind added to cakes and desserts, to stew, meatballs, meat loaves, and spaghetti sauces makes a world of flavor difference. Fruit, whether fresh or canned, sparkles when lemon juice and grated lemon rind are added, and a little lemon rind added to stewed fruit as it cooks makes a subtle change in the taste.

The beauty of the lemon is more than skin deep; few fruits add so much zest to foods and beverages.

Availability—All year round with peak crop in June and July.

Lemon juice is available in canned, bottled, and frozen varieties. Frozen concentrates are available for lemonade, pink lemonade, and punches. Available also is lemon gelatin dessert, lemon pudding and pie filling, and dried grated lemon rind.

Purchasing Guide—Lemons of good quality are firm, heavy for their size, and fine textured. Do not purchase fruit with green tinges since it is not fully ripened.

☐ 12 medium lemons = about 3 pounds = 1 pint juice
☐ 1 medium lemon = 3 tablespoons juice

Storage—Refrigerate to avoid drying and wrinkling.

Canned citrus is best stored in a cool, dry, well-ventilated place. Once juices are squeezed or canned juices are opened, vitamin C combines with air and forms a new compound which has no vitamin value. After 24 hours in refrigerator: 20% vitamin C loss; after 24 hours at room temperature: 60% vitamin C loss. Opened cans retain vitamin content best when tightly covered.

☐ Fresh, room temperature, juice: 1 day
☐ Fresh, refrigerator shelf, juice: 5 to 6 days
☐ Fresh, refrigerator shelf, whole fruit, uncut: 1 month
☐ Canned, kitchen shelf: 1 year
☐ Canned, refrigerator shelf, opened and covered: 1 to 4 days
☐ Frozen juice, refrigerator frozen-food compartment: 3 weeks
☐ Frozen juice, freezer: 1 year

Nutritive Food Values—An excellent source of vitamin C. One lemon provides 40 to 80 per cent of one day's need for vitamin C.

☐ 1 lemon = 20 calories
☐ Lemon juice, 3½ ounces = 25 calories

Basic Preparation—Squeeze lemon just before using to prevent loss of flavor and vitamin C. If juice and rind are to be used in a recipe, grate the rind first and then squeeze the juice from the lemon. Grate only the outermost portion of the rind on the finest part of grater.

Slices or wedges of fresh lemon are fashioned into decorative designs and used as garnishes in meat, poultry, and fish dishes. Lemon juice is used to prevent cut fruits, such as bananas, pears, apples, etc., from darkening. Lemon juice can be used to sour fresh milk for cooking and baking purposes. Use 2 tablespoons juice to 1 cup milk.

LEMON COOK BOOK

GREEK LEMON SOUP

4 cups strained well-flavored chicken
  bouillon
¼ cup uncooked rice
3 eggs
  Juice of 1 medium lemon
  Salt and white pepper

Heat bouillon in saucepan. Add rice, cover, and simmer until rice is tender, about 25 minutes. Beat eggs and lemon juice; add ½ cup hot bouillon, 1 tablespoon at a time, stirring constantly. Then stir this mixture into remaining hot soup. Season to taste. Serve at once. Makes about 1 quart.

LEMON-BROILED SHRIMPS

1 cup soy sauce
¼ cup fresh lemon juice
1 onion, minced
2 pounds fresh or frozen raw shrimps

Mix soy sauce, lemon juice, and onion in glass bowl. Shell and devein shrimps. Marinate in soy mixture for at least 2 hours. String on skewers and broil for 10 minutes, or until shrimps are tender. Makes 6 to 8 servings as an appetizer, or 4 to 6 as a main dish.

FISH STEAKS WITH LEMON BUTTER

¼ cup butter or margarine
3 tablespoons fresh lemon juice
2 teaspoons salt
¼ teaspoon pepper
2 pounds fish steaks
2 tablespoons sesame seeds
6 lemon slices

Combine first 4 ingredients in a small saucepan. Heat until butter melts. Brush both sides of fish with lemon-butter sauce. Arrange fish on a greased broiler rack. Place under broiler 4 inches from source of heat. Broil for 5 minutes. Turn, brushing both sides with sauce. Sprinkle sesame seeds over top. Broil for 5 more minutes, or until seeds have lightly browned and fish is flaky. Garnish each serving with a slice of fresh lemon. Makes 6 servings.

VEAL SCALOPPINE MILANESE

1½ pounds veal for scaloppine, pounded
  flat
  Flour
2 tablespoons olive oil
6 tablespoons butter
1 tablespoon grated lemon rind
6 thin slices of peeled lemon
1 teaspoon dried tarragon
3 tablespoons fresh lemon juice
1 tablespoon white wine or dry
  vermouth
  Salt and pepper
  Lemon slices, unpeeled
  Watercress

Dip the escallops of veal into flour and sauté very quickly on both sides in mixture of olive oil and butter. Add lemon rind and turn the escallops again. Add lemon slices, tarragon, and liquids and turn the escallops several times in the mixture. Season with salt and pepper to taste. Simmer for 3 to 4 minutes and transfer to a hot platter. Pour pan juices over all and garnish with lemon slices and watercress. Serve with crisp Italian bread and chopped spinach seasoned with lemon, garlic, and butter. Makes 4 servings.

INDONESIAN SKEWERED PORK

1 cup salted peanuts
2 tablespoons ground coriander
2 garlic cloves
1 teaspoon crushed red pepper
1 cup sliced onion
¼ cup fresh lemon juice
2 tablespoons brown sugar
¼ cup soy sauce
½ teaspoon pepper
½ cup butter or margarine
½ cup bouillon or water
2 pounds lean pork, cut into 1-inch
  cubes

Combine all ingredients except last 3 in container of electric blender. Whirl to a fine purée. Transfer purée to a saucepan and bring to boil. Stir in butter; add bouillon and remove from heat. Cool and pour over pork. Marinate for at least 3 hours. Thread pork on skewers and broil slowly over charcoal or under broiler for 25 to 30 minutes turning frequently to brown and cook on all sides. If any marinade remains after cooking, heat and pour over meat. Makes 4 to 6 servings.

JELLIED PORTUGUESE LEMON CHICKEN

1 stewing chicken (5 pounds), cut into
  pieces
  Chicken bouillon
2 celery stalks, including tops
1 large carrot, chopped
1 medium onion, chopped
2 teaspoons dried tarragon
1 teaspoon curry powder
1½ tablespoons salt
1½ teaspoons pepper
2 tablespoons grated lemon rind
½ teaspoon ground saffron
  Juice of 1 lemon
½ cup cornstarch
1 cup cooked peas
4 cooked carrots, sliced
12 tiny white onions, cooked
½ cup chopped watercress
2 tablespoons port

Put chicken pieces into deep kettle. Add enough bouillon to cover, as well as celery, carrot, onion, tarragon, curry powder, and salt and pepper. Simmer, covered, for 2½ to 3 hours, or until chicken is tender. Strain broth; chill and remove fat. Discard chicken back, wing tips, and neck. Strip off skin. Cut chicken into bite-size pieces. Add lemon rind, saffron, and lemon juice to strained chicken broth. Simmer, covered, for 10 minutes. Add a little water to the cornstarch and stir into broth. Cook, stirring constantly, until thickened and smooth. Cool. Combine broth with chicken pieces, peas, carrots, onions, and watercress. Work gently so as not to break vegetables. Stir in port. Put in deep serving dish. Chill until set. Makes 8 servings.

CHICKEN IN LEMON-CAPER BUTTER

½ cup butter
2 tablespoons fresh lemon juice
1 teaspoon salt
1 garlic clove
⅛ teaspoon pepper
½ teaspoon paprika
1 can (6 ounces) sliced mushrooms,
  drained
1 tablespoon drained capers
1 frying chicken (about 3 pounds),
  cut up

Put all ingredients except chicken in skillet and bring to boil. Arrange chicken in skillet; bring again to boil; cover. Simmer for 30 minutes, or until chicken is tender, turning several times. Makes 4 servings.

LEMON AND ORANGE SALAD

1 bunch of mint
¼ cup olive oil
3 large lemons, chilled
3 large oranges, chilled
  Sugar, salt, and pepper
  Watercress, chicory, or endive

Set aside several sprigs of mint and place remaining leaves, chopped, in a mortar or similar arrangement. With the pestle or back of a wooden spoon press and rub until most of the juice has been extracted. Add to the olive oil and let stand. With a very sharp knife slice lemons and oranges (their skins must be quite plump and smooth) into thinnest possible rounds. Seed, cut into halves, and place in salad bowl. Sprinkle lightly with sugar (the oil balances the tartness; do not oversweeten), pour over olive oil, and season well with salt and pepper. Toss gently, adding more oil or seasoning if desired. Do not let this salad stand. Serve, topped with reserved sprigs of mint, in a white bowl garnished with watercress. This salad is a savory accompaniment to the sweeter meats—turkey, chicken, pork, and lamb. Makes 6 servings.

LEMON-ORANGE-COTTAGE-CHEESE MOLD

3 envelopes unflavored gelatin
¾ cup fresh orange juice

1½ cups hot water
6 tablespoons sugar
6 tablespoons fresh lemon juice
½ teaspoon salt
1½ cups creamy cottage cheese
1½ cups halved seedless grapes
1 pimiento, seeded
2 cups diced mixed fresh fruit

Soften gelatin in orange juice. Stir in hot water. Mix well to dissolve gelatin. Add sugar, lemon juice, and salt. Put cottage cheese through a sieve and add. Mix well. Chill until the mixture begins to thicken. Beat with a rotary or electric beater. Fold in grapes. Rinse a 1-quart ring mold in cold water. Fill with mixture. Chill until firm and ready to serve. Just before serving turn out onto serving plate. Garnish as desired with designs cut from pimiento. Fill center with diced mixed fresh fruit. Makes 8 servings.

GREEK POTATO SALAD
2 pounds potatoes (4 medium)
¼ cup olive oil
¼ cup fresh lemon juice
¼ cup finely chopped green onion
1 tablespoon minced parsley
½ teaspoon dried oregano
Salt and pepper

Boil potatoes in their skins until tender. Drain, peel, and quarter. Cut into slices. While still warm, pour olive oil, and lemon juice over potatoes. Toss to coat each slice. Add onion, parsley, oregano, and salt and pepper to taste, and toss again. Chill before serving. Makes 4 servings.

LEMON FRENCH DRESSING
½ cup fresh lemon juice
1½ cups salad oil
2 teaspoons salt
¼ teaspoon pepper
1 teaspoon dry mustard
1 teaspoon paprika
Dash of cayenne

Beat all ingredients together thoroughly, or shake in a glass jar. Refrigerate. Makes about 2 cups.

LEMON-HONEY DRESSING
1 egg yolk
¼ cup honey
2 tablespoons fresh lemon juice
1½ tablespoons milk
½ cup cottage cheese
Dash each of salt and ground mace

Beat egg yolk with fork in top part of double boiler. Gradually add honey and lemon juice. Cook over boiling water until thickened, stirring constantly. Cool. Blend milk and cottage cheese. Add to egg-yolk mixture; mix well. Season to taste with salt and mace. Serve with fruit salad. Keep in refrigerator. Makes about 1 cup.

FRESH-LEMON BARBECUE SAUCE
½ cup minced onion
1 garlic clove, minced
2 tablespoons each of butter or margarine and salad oil
2 tablespoons brown sugar
1 teaspoon salt
1 teaspoon celery salt
½ teaspoon cayenne
½ teaspoon powdered mustard
⅓ cup fresh lemon juice
2 tablespoons cider vinegar
1 tablespoon horseradish
1 cup water

Sauté onions and garlic in butter and oil until onions are transparent. Add sugar, salt, and spices. Mix well. Stir in remaining ingredients. Simmer for 10 to 15 minutes. Use to barbecue beef, lamb, pork, or chicken. It may also be used as a marinade for meats. Makes 1½ cups.

BROWNED-BUTTER FRESH-LEMON SAUCE
¼ cup butter or margarine
2 tablespoons fresh lemon juice
Salt and pepper

Brown butter or margarine. Stir in lemon juice and salt and pepper to taste. Serve over vegetables or fish. Makes enough sauce for 4 servings.

SAFFRON BREAD
½ cup boiling water
1 teaspoon saffron shreds
3 cups sifted all-purpose flour
½ teaspoon salt
3 teaspoons baking powder
½ teaspoon baking soda
½ cup shortening
1 cup sugar
2 eggs, beaten
½ cup fresh lemon juice
½ cup shredded fresh lemon peel

Add boiling water to saffron and steep for 30 minutes. Sift dry ingredients together. Cream shortening and sugar until light and fluffy; add eggs, beat well. Combine saffron and water with lemon juice and peel. Add with dry ingredients to creamed mixture, stirring just enough to moisten. Turn into two greased and floured loaf pans (7½ x 3½ x 2¼ inches). Bake in preheated moderate oven (350°F.) for 40 to 45 minutes.

LEMON MERINGUE PIE
1 cup sugar
2 tablespoons cornstarch
¼ teaspoon salt
1½ cups hot water
1½ cups crumbs from soft-type bread (no crusts)
3 eggs, separated
1 tablespoon butter
Grated rind of 1 lemon
Juice of 2 medium lemons
9- inch pie shell, baked
Meringue

In top part of double boiler mix well sugar, cornstarch, and salt. Stir in hot water and beat until smooth. Add bread crumbs. Cook over boiling water, stirring, until smooth and thickened. Stir small amount of mixture into beaten egg yolks. (Reserve whites for Meringue.) Then combine the two mixtures in boiler; cook for 2 or 3 minutes. Add butter, lemon rind, and juice. Cool slightly. Pour into baked shell. Pile Meringue lightly on pie, covering filling completely. Bake in preheated hot oven (400°F.) for 5 minutes, or until lightly browned.

Meringue
Beat 3 egg whites with ¼ teaspoon salt until frothy. Gradually add 6 tablespoons sugar, and beat until stiff but not dry.

SLICED-LEMON PIE
1¾ cups sugar
½ cup all-purpose flour
¼ teaspoon salt
1¼ cups boiling water
3 small lemons
Pastry for 2-crust 9-inch pie, unbaked
2 tablespoons butter

Mix well first 3 ingredients. Add water and beat with rotary beater until smooth. Grate rind of 1 lemon and add to first mixture. Cut peel and white membrane from all 3 lemons and slice lemons paper-thin, discarding seeds. There should be about ⅔ cup lemon slices. Stir into first mixture. Line 9-inch pie pan with half of pastry, pour in filling, dot with butter, and adjust top crust. Bake in preheated very hot oven (450°F.) for 10 minutes. Reduce heat to moderate (350°F.) and bake for about 45 minutes longer. Serve warm. Makes 6 to 8 servings.

LEMON CREAM PIE
⅓ cup all-purpose flour
2 tablespoons cornstarch
¾ cup sugar
¼ teaspoon salt
2½ cups milk, scalded
4 egg yolks, beaten
½ cup fresh lemon juice
2 teaspoons grated lemon rind
3 tablespoons butter or margarine
Yellow food coloring (optional)
9- inch pie shell, baked
Whipped cream

In heavy saucepan mix first 4 ingredients. Gradually stir in milk and cook, stirring, over medium heat until thickened. Stir small amount of mixture into egg yolks; then combine the two mixtures and cook, stirring, for 1 minute. Add lemon juice, rind, and butter. Stir in a few drops of food coloring and pour into baked shell. Top with whipped cream. Makes 6 servings.

LEMON SPONGE PIE
¾ cup sugar
¼ cup melted butter or margarine
¼ cup all-purpose flour
Grated rind of 2 lemons
¼ cup fresh lemon juice
1 cup milk
2 eggs, separated
⅛ teaspoon salt
Pastry for 1-crust 9-inch pie, unbaked

Mix sugar, butter, flour, lemon rind and juice, milk, and egg yolks. Beat egg whites with salt until stiff but not dry. Fold into first mixture; pour into pastry-lined pie pan. Bake in preheated moderate oven (350°F.) for 40 minutes. Cool. Makes 6 servings.

LEMON CHEESE PIE

2 tablespoons soft butter
1½ cups shredded coconut
12 ounces cream cheese
3 eggs
¾ cup sugar
¼ teaspoon salt
Grated rind of 1 lemon
3 tablespoons fresh lemon juice
Sweetened whipped cream

Spread a 9-inch pie pan with the butter. Sprinkle with coconut and press firmly into the butter. Beat cheese until light and fluffy. Add eggs, one at a time, beating thoroughly after each addition. Gradually beat in sugar; blend in salt, lemon rind, and juice. Pour into coconut pie shell. Bake in preheated moderate oven (350°F.) for 30 minutes, or until firm. Cool and spread with cream. Chill. Makes 6 servings.

LEMON CHIFFON PIE

1¾ cups water
1 cup sugar
¼ teaspoon salt
6 eggs, separated
2 boxes (3 ounces each) lemon-flavored gelatin
⅓ cup fresh lemon juice
1 tablespoon grated lemon rind
10-inch Crumb Crust
Whipped cream

In top part of double boiler put water, ½ cup sugar, salt, and egg yolks. Beat slightly to blend. Put over simmering water and cook, stirring constantly, until slightly thickened. Remove from heat and pour over gelatin. Stir until dissolved. Add lemon juice and rind. Chill until thickened but not firm. Beat egg whites until foamy; gradually add remaining sugar, beating until stiff but not dry. Fold this meringue into gelatin mixture. Pile lightly in prepared Crumb Crust and chill until firm. Top pie with whipped cream and sprinkle with crumbs reserved from crust mixture. Makes 8 servings.
Note: For an 11-inch pie use 2½ cups water, 1½ cups sugar, ¼ teaspoon salt, 9 eggs, 3 boxes lemon-flavored gelatin, ½ cup fresh lemon juice, 1 tablespoon grated lemon rind, and an 11-inch Crumb Crust. For ease in handling, divide egg-yolk mixture to chill. Fold half of meringue into each.

Crumb Crust

On wax paper or in a plastic bag, roll enough graham crackers, gingersnaps, vanilla wafers, or zwieback to make 1¾ cups. With spoon or finger tips, thoroughly mix crumbs with ½ cup soft (not melted) butter or margarine. Add ⅓ cup sugar with grahams or 3 tablespoons with zwieback. Reserve ⅓ cup of mixture to use as garnish on top of the pie. Using back of spoon, press mixture firmly and evenly on bottom and sides of buttered deep 10- or 11-inch pie pan. Press edge with finger tips to extend a little above pan. Bake in preheated moderate oven (350°F.) for about 10 minutes; crust should not brown. Chill. Makes one 10- or 11-inch crust.
Note: For a 9-inch pie shell, use 1¼ cups graham-cracker crumbs, ⅓ cup soft butter or margarine, and ¼ cup sugar with grahams or 2 tablespoons with zwieback. Reserve ¼ to ⅓ cup of mixture for top.

LEMON SOUFFLÉ

4 eggs, separated
1 cup granulated sugar
Juice and grated rind of 1 lemon
⅛ teaspoon salt
Confectioners' sugar

Beat egg yolks until thick and lemon-colored; gradually beat in ½ cup granulated sugar; add lemon juice and rind. Beat egg whites with salt until frothy; gradually beat in remaining granulated sugar. Continue beating until mixture will hold a peak when beater is lifted; fold into egg-yolk mixture. Pour into a straight-sided 1½-quart baking dish, preferably pottery, lightly buttered and sprinkled with sugar. Place dish in pan of hot water and bake in preheated slow oven (325°F.) for 40 minutes. Remove from oven; dust with confectioners' sugar and serve at once. Makes 6 servings.
Note: The French enjoy a soufflé that has a crusty top and sides and a center soft enough to serve as a sauce. To obtain this result bake it at 375°F. for only 20 minutes.

STEAMED LEMON PUDDING

¼ cup soft butter
½ cup sugar
2 eggs
Grated rind of 2 lemons
2 figs, chopped
¼ cup currants
¼ cup chopped walnuts
3 tablespoons fresh lemon juice
3 tablespoons milk
½ cup sifted all-purpose flour
½ teaspoon baking soda
Dash of salt
Dash each of ground allspice, cloves, and cinnamon
Clear Lemon Sauce

Cream butter, then add sugar gradually and continue beating until creamy. Add eggs, one at a time. Add grated rind, fruits, and nuts; then gently stir in juice, milk, and sifted dry ingredients, blending until smooth. Steam in a buttered 1-pound coffee can or suitable pudding mold sealed with aluminum foil and lid, on a trivet in boiling water to ⅓ height of can. Steam for 1½ hours. Serve hot with Clear Lemon Sauce. Makes 6 servings.

Clear Lemon Sauce

¾ cup sugar
2 tablespoons cornstarch
2 cups water
¼ cup butter
Grated rinds of 2 lemons
¼ cup fresh lemon juice
Dash of salt

Mix sugar and cornstarch. Add water and stir until blended. Cook until slightly thickened and clear, stirring constantly. Remove from heat and add remaining ingredients. Serve hot.

LOW-CALORIE FROZEN LEMON CUSTARD

8 saccharin tablets (¼ grain each)
3 tablespoons fresh lemon juice
½ cup evaporated milk, undiluted
Dash of salt
1 egg, separated

Turn refrigerator control to coldest setting. Dissolve saccharin in lemon juice. Chill milk in refrigerator tray until ice crystals form around edge. Pour into a chilled bowl and whip until peaks are formed. Add salt and egg white and beat for 1 minute. Beat egg yolk into sweetened lemon juice. Fold in whipped milk. Freeze in refrigerator tray. Makes 4 servings.
Note: Use 2 teaspoons liquid noncaloric sweetener instead of the saccharin, if preferred.

LEMON BUTTERMILK SHERBET

3 cups buttermilk
½ cup lemon juice
Sugar to taste
1 egg white
⅛ teaspoon salt
Yellow food coloring

Mix buttermilk, lemon juice, and sugar. Freeze until almost firm in freezer, or in freezing compartment of refrigerator with temperature control at coldest setting. Add frozen mixture to egg white and salt; beat with rotary beater or electric mixer until light and fluffy. Add a little food coloring. Return to tray and freeze until firm. Makes 4 servings.

FRESH-LEMON SHERBET

1 envelope unflavored gelatin
2¼ cups cold water
1½ cups sugar
½ cup fresh lemon juice
⅛ teaspoon salt
1 teaspoon vanilla extract
1½ teaspoons grated lemon rind
1 egg white

Soften gelatin in ¼ cup of the cold water. Combine sugar with 1 cup of remaining water and bring to boiling point. Boil for 3 minutes. Remove from heat and stir in gelatin. Add remaining cold water, lemon juice, salt, vanilla, and grated lemon rind. Turn into freezing tray and freeze until almost firm. Turn into a bowl, add egg white, and beat until fluffy and smooth. Return to freezing tray and freeze until firm and ready to serve. Makes 1½ quarts.

BAVAROIS AU CITRON

Grated rind of 2 lemons
⅓ cup boiling water
3 egg yolks

Fresh-Lemon Peach Cooler   **Lemon-Orange-Cottage Cheese Mold**
Lemon and Orange Salad   **Lemon Meringue Pie**

½ cup sugar
½ cup fresh lemon juice
2 tablespoons fresh orange juice
  Dash of salt
1 envelope unflavored gelatin
3 tablespoons cold water
1 cup heavy cream, whipped
½ cup sifted confectioners' sugar
  For garnish, whipped cream,
  strawberries, lemon blossoms, or
  chopped candied gingerroot

Steep grated rind in boiling water. Beat egg yolks until thick and lemon-colored. Add sugar slowly and continue beating until creamy. Blend mixture into steeped rind and liquid; add fruit juices and salt. Cook over hot water, stirring, until thickened, about 15 minutes. Add gelatin that has been soaked in cold water for a few minutes. Stir until dissolved. Chill. When mixture begins to set, fold in whipped cream into which confectioners' sugar has been folded. Put in mold and chill for several hours. At serving time unmold and garnish as desired. Makes 6 servings.

LEMON-ORANGE REFRIGERATOR CAKE

1 egg, separated
½ tablespoon fresh lemon juice
½ teaspoon grated lemon rind
6 tablespoons sifted sugar
3 tablespoons hot water
½ cup sifted cake flour
½ teaspoon baking powder
  Few grains of salt
  Lemon-Orange Filling

Beat egg yolk slightly; add lemon juice and beat until thick and light yellow. Add lemon rind. Continuing to use beater, add sugar, 1 spoonful at a time. Add hot water slowly and dry ingredients sifted together twice. Fold in egg white beaten until stiff but not dry. Pour into 8-inch layer-cake pan which has been greased, lined with wax paper, and lightly greased again. Bake in preheated moderate oven (350°F.) for about 20 minutes. Remove from pan; cool on rack. Cut layer into halves and carefully split each piece, making 4 thin layers. Spread Lemon-Orange Filling between layers and on top and sides of cake; cover and chill overnight.

Lemon-Orange Filling

2 tablespoons cornstarch
½ cup fresh orange juice
2 tablespoons fresh lemon juice
2 tablespoons water
¼ cup honey
  Few grains of salt
1 teaspoon grated orange rind
1 egg, separated

Mix cornstarch with juices and water. Add honey, salt, and orange rind. Cook over hot water for 15 minutes, stirring frequently. Pour gradually over slightly beaten egg yolk. Return to double boiler and cook for 2 minutes longer. Cool slightly. Fold in egg white beaten until stiff.

LEMON CURD

½ cup butter or margarine
1½ cups sugar
  Grated rind of 2 lemons
½ cup fresh lemon juice
6 eggs, slightly beaten

Put all ingredients in top part of double boiler over simmering water. Cook, stirring constantly, until fairly thick. Cool and store in the refrigerator. Use as a filling for tiny tarts, or as a spread on ladyfingers or spongecake. Makes about 3 cups.

LEMON-NUT COOKIES

2 cups pecans, ground
2 eggs, beaten
1 teaspoon lemon extract
2 cups sugar
2 cups sifted all-purpose flour
¼ teaspoon salt
  Lemon Frosting

With hands mix all ingredients except frosting, working mixture thoroughly until soft enough to hold together. Mixture will be dry at first. Shape into 2 rolls about 1½ inches in diameter and wrap in wax paper. Chill for several hours. Cut into ⅛-inch slices. Put on greased cookie sheets and bake in preheated slow oven (325°F.) for 10 minutes. While hot, brush with Lemon Frosting. Makes 8 to 10 dozen.

Lemon Frosting

Mix 2 cups confectioners' sugar, 1 teaspoon grated lemon rind, a little yellow coloring, and enough lemon juice to moisten.

FLUFFY LEMON FROSTING

1½ cups sugar
½ teaspoon cream of tartar
⅛ teaspoon salt
6 tablespoons hot water
2 tablespoons fresh lemon juice
½ cup egg whites (about 4)
½ teaspoon vanilla extract
¼ teaspoon grated lemon rind

Combine first 5 ingredients in saucepan. Cook, without stirring, until a little of mixture dropped into cold water will form a soft ball (240°F. on a candy thermometer). Meanwhile, beat egg whites until stiff but not dry. Add syrup very slowly to egg whites, beating constantly with rotary beater or electric mixer at high speed. Add vanilla and grated lemon rind. Makes enough frosting for tops and sides of two 9-inch layers.

LEMON CUSTARD SAUCE

1 cup milk
  Grated rind of ½ lemon
3 egg yolks
⅛ teaspoon salt
¼ cup sugar

Scald milk and rind in top part of double boiler over hot water or in a heavy saucepan. Beat egg yolks slightly, just enough to mix. Stir in salt and sugar, then hot milk slowly. Return immediately to top

of double boiler over hot, not boiling, water, and cook, stirring constantly, until thick enough to coat a metal spoon. Cool. Cover and chill. Serve on puddings or over ice cream. Makes 1 cup.

FRESH-LEMON DESSERT SAUCE

¾ cup sugar
1½ tablespoons cornstarch
1 cup water
¼ teaspoon salt
2 tablespoons fresh lemon juice
2 tablespoons butter or margarine
1 teaspoon grated lemon rind
  Dash of ground mace

Combine first 4 ingredients. Mix well and cook over medium heat until thickened. Remove from heat and stir in remaining ingredients. Serve warm or cold over cake, puddings, or gingerbread. Makes 1½ cups.

FRESH-LEMON PEACH COOLER

1 cup fresh peach purée
½ cup fresh lemon juice
½ cup sugar
2 egg whites
1 cup finely crushed ice
1 cup water
  Fresh lemon slices
  Fresh mint

Combine first 6 ingredients in jar of electric blender. Blend for 30 seconds to 1 minute. (If an electric blender is not available, place in 1½-quart fruit jar. Tightly screw on top and shake vigorously.) Serve in tall glasses, over additional ice if desired. Garnish with fresh lemon slices and fresh mint. Makes 5⅓ cups.

FRESH-LEMON-AND-ORANGE PARTY PUNCH

1 cup sugar
4 cups water
1¼ cups fresh lemon juice
6 cups fresh orange juice
1 cup fresh raspberry or strawberry juice*
  Fresh lemon and orange slices for garnish
  Fresh strawberries or raspberries for garnish
  Fresh mint for ganish

Combine sugar with 2 cups of the water and ¼ cup of the lemon juice. Mix well and bring to boiling point. Boil for 1 minute. Add remaining water and cool. Stir in remaining fruit juices. Pour into a punch bowl over ice. Float lemon and orange slices and fresh strawberries or raspberries over the top. Garnish with fresh mint. Makes about 3 quarts.
*To make raspberry or strawberry juice, crush berries and push through a fine sieve.

GINGER LEMON JELLY

½ cup fresh lemon juice
2 cups water
6 cups sugar
1 tablespoon ground ginger
1 bottle liquid pectin

Mix lemon juice, water, sugar, and ginger and bring to a boil in a large kettle. Add liquid pectin, bring to a full rolling boil, and boil for ½ minute. Remove from fire, skim, and pour into hot sterilized jars. Cool slightly and seal. Makes six ½-pint jars.

LEMON MARMALADE

1½ cups thinly sliced lemons
    (tightly packed)
  ½ cup thinly sliced lemon peel
  6 cups water
4¼ cups sugar
  4 candied or maraschino cherries,
    sliced (optional)

Remove any seeds from lemon slices. Put sliced lemon, peel, and water in saucepan, bring to boil and boil rapidly, uncovered, for 20 minutes. Measure; there should be 5½ cups of liquid and fruit. Boil for 5 minutes longer. Then add sugar and cook rapidly for 30 minutes, or until mixture sheets from side of spoon. Add cherries, if desired. Cool for 5 minutes. Then pour into hot sterilized jars and seal. Makes 4 half-pint jars.

PICKLED LEMON WEDGES

  6 lemons
  2 tablespoons salt
  2 garlic cloves, minced
  1 teaspoon paprika
  ¼ cup crushed dried hot red pepper
    About 1 cup salad oil, heated

Wash lemons, cut in quarters and remove obvious seeds. Roll in salt and pack in quart jar. Cover and let stand at room temperature for 4 days. Then add remaining ingredients and let stand for 4 or 5 days longer. Store in refrigerator. Makes 1 quart.

LEMONADE—Lemon juice, sugar, and water are the ingredients of one of the most popular and refreshing beverages invented by man. Lemonade is usually served icy cold and often garnished with fruit or mint, but it may also be served hot, as a soothing drink for colds or the simple pleasure of a hot drink.

A glass of frosty lemonade on a day when the air is thick with heat is one of the most exquisite pleasures in the world, and one that is appreciated at any age. To many of us, lemonade also brings back childhood memories of visits to the circus topped by the treat of pink lemonade, or of youthful enterprise expressed in roadside lemonade stands, where homemade lemonade is sold for pennies to provide pocket money.

Despite the excellence and convenience of commercially frozen lemonade, the homemade product still has great charm. The simplest and quickest way to make lemonade is by squeezing lemon juice and adding water and sugar to taste. But lemonade made with a sugar syrup, kept in the refrigerator for ready use, is excellent and eminently worth making.

Availability—Frozen concentrated lemonade, white or pink, is available all year round.

Storage

☐ Refrigerator shelf, covered: 7 days
☐ Refrigerator frozen-food compartment: 3 weeks
☐ Freezer: 1 year

Caloric Value

☐ 3½ ounces, diluted = about 44 calories

LEMONADE SYRUP

2 cups sugar
1 cup water
1 cup fresh lemon juice

Combine sugar and water in saucepan. Bring to boil; boil for 5 minutes. Cool; add lemon juice. Strain the syrup. Store in covered container in refrigerator. When ready to serve, add 2 tablespoons syrup to 1 glass of ice water. Makes 2½ cups syrup.

CLARET LEMONADE

½ cup lemonade
½ cup claret
  Sugar

Moisten rim of glass with lemon juice or water, then dip rim into granulated sugar. Pour lemonade and claret over ice in glass. Makes 1 drink.

LEMON-APPLE PUNCH

Mix 2 cans (6-ounces each) frozen lemonade concentrate and 2 cups canned apple juice. Add ice cubes and 1 bottle (29 ounces) chilled carbonated water. Stir well and serve at once. Makes 6 tall glasses.

PICNIC FRUIT PUNCH

In a large vacuum jug combine 1 can each of frozen pineapple-juice concentrate, orangeade mix, and lemonade mix with 1½ quarts water. Add a 29-ounce bottle of chilled carbonated water and fill with ice. Makes 12 large glasses.

ICED LEMONADE-TEA

Dilute one 6-ounce can frozen lemonade mix according to directions on can. Add to 1 quart iced tea. Pour over ice cubes.

LENTEN COOKERY—In the Christian church, the period of fasting, penitence, and prayer that precedes Easter is called Lent. The word comes from the Old English *lencten,* "the spring season," and since Easter falls in the spring, spring and pre-Easter fasting have become identified. Lent is observed in varying degrees by the Roman Catholic, Greek Orthodox, and Anglican churches and by some of the Protestant denominations.

Lent is a period of forty days beginning on Ash Wednesday and lasting until Holy Saturday. It was observed as a period of spiritual and physical penitence in preparation for Christ's Passion and Resurrection. The number forty is a ritualistic one, for forty were the days of the Flood, the years of the Jews' wandering, the fasts of Elias and Moses and of our Lord in the desert. This period of purification has its analogies in the passing of winter and the coming of spring, when nature has rid herself of the dregs of winter and burst into newness and freshness.

The strictness of keeping the Lenten fast has varied greatly during the centuries. In the Roman Catholic church, the religious observances for the various days of Lent are part of the church ritual, but the amount of fasting has changed considerably. At the time of Irenaeus, an important bishop of the end of the 2nd century, the fast before Easter was as short as it was intense; some people ate nothing at all for the forty hours before Easter morning. Good Friday was always kept as a fast day, and it still is by the great majority of Catholics.

According to the current regulations of the Roman Catholic Church, people should eat to maintain their health. Every Lenten weekday, including Saturday, they may have one main meal with meat except on Fridays, and two smaller meatless meals, which together will not equal the main meal. People should not eat between meals, though liquids do not count as breaking fast.

The standard food for Lent has always been fish. The monasteries of medieval Europe were renowned for their fish ponds, and the excellence of fish cookery in Catholic countries can be traced to the importance of fish during Lent. In those days too, many Lenten fasters subsisted on water, salt, and nourishing whole-grain, dark-brown bread which is almost a meal itself.

In this world in which we live with so much wonderful food, there is very little hardship attached to eating meatless meals. Neither nutrition nor flavor suffer in well-prepared Lenten dishes.

Lentil Salad

LENTIL—This legume is one of the first plants whose seeds were used for food. The plant itself is a slender annual with tendrils, and often serves for animal fodder.

The lentil seed is small and lens-shape. It is never used green, but is dried when it is fully ripe. The lentil is extremely nutritious and is one of the staple foods of the Near East, where a dish called "Esau's Dish of Lentils" is still a favorite.

The lentil is a native of southwestern Asia. The Bible often mentions lentils; the most famous reference is that of Esau who sold his birthright for bread and a "pottage of lentiles" (Genesis 25: 29 to 34). The lentils mentioned in the Bible are of the red variety, widely used in Egypt and the Near East.

In America, lentils are most generally eaten in soup. In Europe and the Near East they appear in stews, as salads, and with other foods. Lentil salad is a standard dish of the French hors-d'oeuvre table, and puréed lentils are served instead of potatoes with pork and other meats in Germany.

Availability—Lentils are available in food stores all year round. There are two varieties: the *French,* gray outside, yellowish inside, and sold with the seed coat on; the *Egyptian,* reddish yellow, smaller and rounder, without a seed coat.

Purchasing Guide—Lentils are available packaged and are also available in bulk. Lentil soup is available in cans. Some minestrone or bean-soup dry mixes include lentils.

Storage—Lentils should be stored in their original container or in a tightly covered container.

☐ Kitchen shelf: 6 to 8 months

Nutritive Food Values—Lentils are a good

source of carbohydrates and incomplete protein, and are a good meat, milk, cheese, and egg supplement. Lentils also contain some B vitamins and are a good source of iron, with fair amounts of calcium and vitamin A.

☐ 3½ ounces, raw = 340 calories

Basic Preparation—Loose lentils should be carefully picked over; discard foreign material and imperfect seeds. Wash thoroughly. Packaged lentils need only be washed. They may or may not need soaking. Follow directions on the package.

☐ **To Cook**—Cook lentils in the water in which they were soaked; if soaking was not necessary, add the water called for in the recipe to the pot of measured lentils. Add salt (allowing 1 teaspoon for each 1 cup dried lentils). Cover, bring to a boil, reduce heat, and cook gently until tender. Lentils used in soup should be cooked until they mash easily. Lentil dishes should be well seasoned.

THICK LENTIL SOUP

½ pound sliced salami or
  frankfurters
1 tablespoon shortening
2 onions, chopped
1 garlic clove, if desired
5 cups water
¾ cup dried lentils
⅓ cup chopped celery and leaves
½ green pepper, chopped
¾ teaspoon mixed pickling spice
1 small hot red pepper, if desired
  Salt and pepper

Cut salami into ¼-inch strips and brown slowly in fat in heavy kettle. Add onions and minced garlic; cook for 5 minutes. Add water, washed lentils, celery, green pepper, and spices. Cover, bring to boil, reduce heat, and simmer for 1½ hours, or until lentils are very well done. Add salt and pepper to taste during last 30 minutes. Makes 4 servings.

CREAM-OF-LENTIL SOUP

1 pound dried lentils
3 quarts water
2 tablespoons beef bouillon
1 onion, chopped
1 garlic clove, minced
1 carrot, chopped
1 celery stalk, chopped
¼ teaspoon powdered mustard
¼ pound bologna, hard salami, or
  boiled ham, cut into thin strips
  Salt and pepper
1 cup light cream

Wash lentils and soak overnight in the water; do not drain. Add bouillon, vegetables, and mustard. Bring to boil and simmer, covered, for 2 hours, or until lentils are very tender. If desired, force through sieve. Add meat; season to taste; simmer for 10 minutes. Add cream just before serving. Makes 2 quarts.

THICK LENTIL AND SPINACH SOUP

1 pound dried lentils, washed
3 quarts water

⅓ cup cooking oil
2 medium-size onions, minced
5 ounces broad egg noodles
1 pound raw spinach, chopped
  Salt and pepper

Put lentils and water in large covered kettle. Simmer for 1½ to 2 hours, or until tender but not mushy. Add more water if necessary to keep a soupy consistency. Heat oil in small skillet; add onions and fry until yellow. Pour into lentil mixture. Add noodles, cover, and cook for 20 minutes. Add spinach and cook for 5 minutes longer. Season to taste. Makes 4 to 6 servings.

LENTIL PURÉE WITH POACHED EGGS

1¾ cups dried lentils
5½ cups water
2 tablespoons shortening
1 onion, chopped
1 garlic clove, minced
1 bay leaf
  Pinch of dried thyme
  Salt and pepper
4 eggs, poached

Wash lentils; soak overnight in the water; do not drain. Cook until lentils are tender and liquid is partly evaporated; do not drain. Melt shortening; add onion, garlic, bay leaf, and thyme, cook for a few minutes; add to lentils. Season to taste with salt and pepper. Press lentil mixture through a sieve or ricer. Top each serving with a poached egg. Makes 4 servings.

LENTILS WITH SAUSAGE

1 cup dried lentils
3 cups water
1 garlic clove, minced
½ pound sausage meat
½ cup bread crumbs
1 medium onion, minced
  Salt and pepper

Wash lentils; add water and garlic. Bring to boil; boil for 2 minutes. Turn off heat; let stand for 1 hour. Combine sausage meat and bread crumbs; shape into 1-inch balls. In skillet brown sausage and onion. Add to undrained lentils; cook for 35 minutes, or until lentils are tender. Season with salt and pepper to taste. Makes 4 servings.

SPICY LENTILS WITH TOMATO SAUCE

1 cup dried lentils
3 cups water
1 bay leaf
3 parsley sprigs
1 onion, chopped
3 tablespoons shortening
1 cup cooked rice
¼ teaspoon ground mace
  Salt and pepper
1½ cups well-seasoned tomato sauce

Wash lentils and soak in water overnight; do not drain. Add bay leaf and parsley, cook until tender, about 1 hour. Brown onion in fat; add lentils, rice, mace, and salt and pepper to taste. Heat thoroughly. Serve with sauce. Makes 4 servings.

LENTIL AND POTATO CASSEROLE

¾ cup dried lentils, washed

3 cups cold water
3 cups diced boiled potatoes
2 tablespoons shortening
2 tablespoons flour
1 medium-size onion, minced
2 cups milk
1 tablespoon salt
¼ teaspoon ground sage
⅛ teaspoon pepper

Simmer lentils in water for about 1 hour, or until tender; add a little more water if necessary. Drain lentils and mix with potatoes. Place in oiled 2-quart baking dish. Heat shortening in heavy skillet; add flour and onion and cook for 1 minute; add remaining ingredients and cook until sauce thickens slightly. Pour over lentils. Bake for 30 minutes in preheated moderate oven (375°F.). Makes 4 servings.

LENTIL CURRY WITH RICE

½ cup dried lentils
½ cup milk
1 onion, chopped
3 tablespoons shortening
1½ cups water
1 teaspoon curry powder
  Salt and pepper
1 tablespoon fresh lemon juice
1½ cups cooked rice

Wash lentils; soak overnight in milk in refrigerator; do not drain. Brown onion in shortening; add water, curry powder, lentils, and milk. Simmer for 1 hour, or until lentils are tender; add more water if necessary; season to taste with salt and pepper. Add lemon juice before serving. Serve on rice. Makes 3 or 4 servings.

LENTIL SALAD

2 cups dried lentils
⅛ teaspoon salt
1 onion stuck with 2 cloves
1 bay leaf
6 scallions, chopped
1 cup chopped parsley
½ cup French dressing
  Salt and pepper
  Salad greens
  Red-pepper strips

Wash lentils and boil for 2 minutes in water to cover. Remove from heat, cover, and let stand for 1 hour. Add the salt, onion, and bay leaf. Bring again to a boil. Lower heat and simmer, covered, until lentils are tender. Do not overcook. Drain and cool. Combine lentils with scallions, parsley, and French dressing. Season with salt and pepper to taste. Toss thoroughly. Chill before serving. Serve on salad greens and garnish with strips of red pepper. Makes 4 to 6 servings.

LENTIL SAUCE

1 onion, chopped
1 garlic clove, minced
¼ cup olive oil
1½ cups dried lentils, washed
1 crumbled dried hot red pepper
2½ teaspoons salt
½ teaspoon pepper
4 cups water
2 beef bouillon cubes
1 teaspoon monosodium glutamate
¼ teaspoon each of crumbled dried

basil and oregano
About 2¼ cups (one 1-pound, 3-ounce
can) tomatoes
1 can (6 ounces) tomato paste
2 tablespoons vinegar
12 ounces spaghetti, cooked
Grated cheese

Cook onion and garlic in olive oil for 5 minutes. Add next 5 ingredients. Cover and simmer for 30 minutes. Add remaining ingredients except spaghetti and cheese and simmer, uncovered, for about 1 hour, stirring occasionally. Serve on spaghetti; sprinkle with cheese. Makes 8 servings.

A POT OF JACOB'S GUILE

by Vance Bourjaily

With a dollar's worth of vegetables and a set of instructions I inherited from my grandmother, you can prove to yourself that the man on the short end of the world's most celebrated bad bargain was a wiser fellow than he sounds. The bargain is the one described in Genesis 25:29-34—the exchange in which Esau swapped his birthright for what has since been villainously described as a mess of pottage.

One can hardly be blamed if, coming across that horrid phrase "mess of pottage," he concludes that Esau was an undiscriminating oaf. For "mess" has one current meaning and only one—outside, perhaps, Army, Navy, and trout-fishing circles, where it may still mean "a quantity of food" as well as "a group of persons who regularly eat together" (Webster's dictionary). As for "pottage," the word has no current culinary meaning at all; but it sounds alarmingly like "porridge," and not a bit like "a dish of vegetables, or vegetables and meat" (again the quote is from Webster).

Ever since boyhood, I have been fully aware that the shifty English language had done Esau wrong. Casual though he may have been about his inheritance, Esau was no lout in his attitude toward food. In fact, with my grandmother's expressive saucepan to back him, the Biblical bargainer becomes a candidate for veneration by food and wine societies; a man who, though he gave up everything, gave it up for a fine meal.

My grandmother was a Lebanese lady, whose life, in the bleak periods between generations when there were no young children in her care, found its fullest expression in cooking. She once told me

that, except when she was staying alone, she never got out of bed in the morning until she had decided what to serve for dinner that night. This decision must generally have been taken along about dawn, for she was always the first up, a short, heavy woman with great physical strength, a wide emotional range, and a slow, tireless, fluid energy.

If the meal she had decided on required a large variety of ingredients, she might spend her whole morning terrorizing greengrocers and outwitting butchers to obtain exactly what was needed. Early in the afternoon, the first leisurely creative steps began—washing, peeling, soaking, cutting—during which my grandmother was relaxed and chatty with whoever might be visiting her in the kitchen. As mealtime approached, however, things moved faster and faster; the atmosphere became one of concentration. The lavishness of her personality was absorbed in mixing and tasting, browning, basting, thickening, testing—until finally everything was ready at once to be heaped on platters and carried in triumph to the table. My stomach still grovels at the memory.

Very often one of these dedicated afternoons would be witnessed from beginning to end by a determined daughter- or granddaughter-in-law, bent on recording the steps that went into producing this or that dish. The technique of observation involved a good deal of jotting down of times and quantities. ("4:15— she picked it up and slapped it" was one of my wife's notations from an afternoon of Syrian bread baking). Only a few of the simpler preparations succumbed to this method, however, and of them the most reliable, and perhaps the most useful, is 'mjeddrah, or Esau's pottage.

The word 'mjeddrah is only a second-generation-Arabic approximation of sounds, some of which cannot be represented in the English alphabet. One authority (cited more fully below) in which I found the word transliterated it mujeddrah, but I cannot conscientiously recall the oo sound as being part of the first syllable as spoken in my own mumbling family. The j, like the one in our name, would be represented by zh in dictionary phonetics, and pronounced like the z in azure. If the word seems troublesome, it would by no means be un-Arabic to invent for the dish a name like "Esau's Downfall" or "Jacob's Guile"; there is at least one commemoratively named dish in the Arab cuisine, an eggplant creation called "The Imam Fainted."

The chief ingredient of 'mjeddrah is (as Genesis says) the red lentil, a vegetable which, in the United States, is sold

from the same shelf as split peas, dried Limas, and kidney beans. I am not relying on the Biblical reference, however, in asserting that my grandmother's 'mjeddrah and Esau's Downfall are the same dish. *The International Standard Bible Encyclopedia,* for example, says: "It was of 'red lentils' that Jacob brewed his fateful pottage, a stew, probably, in which the lentils were flavored with onions and other ingredients, as we find it done in Syria today."

Hastings' *Dictionary of the Bible* says: "In Palestine a kind of 'pottage' known as mujedderah, universally popular, is made from [lentils]. It is of a reddish-brown colour, and is certainly the original 'red pottage' of Esau."

"Universally popular" is, if anything, an understatement. 'Mjeddrah is served daily in many peasant households. As it uses ingredients that can be stored or dried, it may be made the year around, and it may be eaten cold as well as hot.

In Lebanon, my grandmother used to tell us, the fruit and vegetable farmers among whom she grew up customarily take cold 'mjeddrah into the fields for lunch. To keep it moist, they wrap the portion in one of their flat, supple loaves of bread, and, at noon, slice whatever salad vegetables happen to be growing at hand into the sandwich.

Because 'mjeddrah is thought of by Arabic-speaking people as a peasant dish, you will not find it on the menus at Middle Eastern restaurants. My grandmother may, in fact, have thought it rather a quirkish taste of ours when we clamored so for her to make it; but the quirk has been communicated to the non-Arabic ladies who have married into our family and, through them, to a long and generally rapturous list of guests.

There isn't anything much you need to know in shopping for the lentils with which to make a pot of Jacob's Guile, except to avoid the French kind, which are gray rather than reddish-brown. Besides lentils, you'll need a good grade of long-grain white rice, onions, olive oil, butter, and things for salad. The following directions are calculated to feed five people:

In the morning, put one and a half cupfuls of lentils to soak in cold water. By evening, most of the moisture will have been absorbed. About an hour before you are going to serve the dish, drain off whatever remains of the water; put the lentils in a pot; add four cupfuls of cold water and a teaspoonful of salt. Cover the pot; set it on the stove over medium heat, and bring it to a boil. As soon as it boils, reduce the heat, and let the lentils simmer, stirring occasionally to prevent sticking.

Next, cut up two cupfuls of onions, not too finely. Heat a quarter of a cupful of olive oil; add the onions, a teaspoonful of salt; cover, and cook very slowly until soft and yellow. (It is my theory that the smell of onions cooking in olive oil reached the field where Esau was working—which would give strong support to a temporary-insanity plea if anyone cares to enter it for him.)

Wash three quarters of a cupful of rice; drain it, and parch it in one and a half tablespoonfuls of butter. I'm not sure that "parching" is a proper cooking term; by it I mean that you are to sauté the rice in butter for a couple of minutes, until it loses the translucence it will acquire when the butter first coats it, and becomes white again.

Now add rice and onions to the lentils, with enough hot water (perhaps two cupfuls) to finish cooking the rice. The exact amount you must judge for yourself, adding a cupful or less at a time, and being careful to put in no more than rice and lentils will absorb by the time they are cooked soft but not mushy.

Some hold that the dish, now complete, is properly served with crisp-fried (almost burned) onions sprinkled over the top, and salad on the side. My family has less restraint; omitting the final onions, we ladle the 'mjeddrah onto our plates and the salad directly onto the 'mjeddrah. The mixture of hot and cold and the texture contrast are wonderful.

The salad should have greens, tomatoes, and raw onions in it; from there you may be as elaborate as you like. Cucumber, radishes, and celery are all successful additions. My grandmother's dressing for the salad involved three parts of olive oil to two of lemon juice, quite a lot of paprika, and pinches of sugar, mustard, and garlic-rubbed salt. Just before adding the dressing, she crumbled a tablespoonful of dried mint leaves over the salad. In lieu of Syrian bread, hard rolls go well with the meal, as do strong black olives, and the white, goat's-milk cheese sometimes called "Greek cheese."

In addition to serving 'mjeddrah to guests, my wife and I depend fairly steadily on it in the lean times other couples fill in with beans or macaroni products. A hunger for it comes up in non-lean times, too. And someday, some discriminating fellow is going to show up at our house while the onions are cooking, with a birthright on him.

LETTUCE—This is a vegetable whose nutrients are found in the part of the plant that grows above the ground. There are several hundred varieties of lettuce, all originating from a common weed of the roadsides and wastelands of southern Europe and western Asia.

Lettuce is of great antiquity; the Greeks ate lettuce and so did Persian kings as long ago as 300 B.C. The Arabs, great lettuce eaters to this day, developed many varieties, including romaine. Lettuce came to America via the West Indies. Reportedly, it was grown in the Bahamas as early as 1494. Until the 20th century, when lettuce became a large commercial crop, it was extensively grown in home gardens.

Lettuce, and quantities of it, is an accepted part of the American diet. But we delude ourselves about its healthful properties if we eat only the bleached lettuces or the white parts, throwing away the green, tougher outer leaves, where the vitamins are.

Availability—Lettuce is available in food stores all year round. Peak months are generally May through August.

Purchasing Guide—The following types of lettuce are marketed:

Butterhead—A small, soft, loose-leafed head of lettuce. Its outer leaves are light green, its inner leaves light yellow, with a buttery feel. It is a sweet succulent lettuce. The most common butterhead varieties are *Bibb* and *Boston*.

Cos or Romaine—A long, cylindrical head with stiff leaves, dark green on the outside, becoming greenish-white near the center.

Crisphead—The most popular type of lettuce. The outer leaves are medium-green in color with flaring, wavy edges. The inner leaves are pale green and folded tightly. *Iceberg* lettuce is a variety of crisphead.

Lamb's Tongue or Field Lettuce—Comes in small clumps of tiny, tongue-shape leaves on delicate stems. It is not commonly available because it does not ship or keep well and is found only near the areas where it is grown. Most often available in the fall months in eastern markets.

Leaf—A hardy type of lettuce with loose leaves branching from a stalk. It may have a curled or a somewhat smooth leaf of light to dark green. It has a crisp texture.

Stem—With an enlarged stem and no head, this lettuce has long, narrow leaves tapering to a point. The flavor is a combination of celery and lettuce. The main variety is *celtuce*.

Look for fresh, unwilted heads with no discoloration. Butterhead and romaine should have fairly compact heads, although these types naturally have less tightly clustered leaves than iceberg. Crisphead lettuce should be firm, free from rust spots, and heavy for its size. The very large head may be overmature and is apt to be bitter.

Storage—Refrigerate lettuce as soon as possible. Wash, drain well, and place in covered container, a film bag, or the vegetable compartment of the refrigerator.

☐ Refrigerator shelf or vegetable compartment: 3 to 8 days

Lettuce should not be frozen.

Nutritive Food Values—Lettuce has small amounts of vitamins A and C and minerals, if the outer leaves are eaten.

☐ 3½ ounces, raw = 13 to 18 calories

Basic Preparation—Wash lettuce and drain well. To remove whole leaves, remove core. Let water run into the hole and gently spread apart the leaves. Place in a colander in the refrigerator to crisp.

Lettuce can be cut into wedges, or shredded with a sharp knife, or torn apart. This latter method prevents the lettuce from darkening at the cut edges. To keep greens crisp toss them with dressing just before serving.

CREAM-OF-LETTUCE SOUP

      3 tablespoons bacon fat
      6 scallions, finely chopped
      1 medium head crisphead lettuce,
         shredded
      1 teaspoon curry powder
    ¼ teaspoon dried mint
      1 cup chicken bouillon
      1 cup light cream
      4 slices of hard-cooked egg
         Chopped chives

Melt fat in large saucepan. Add scallions and sauté until tender. Add lettuce, curry powder, mint, and bouillon. Stir well and simmer, covered, for 4 to 5 minutes, or until lettuce is wilted and tender. Purée the soup and return to saucepan with 1 cup light cream. Adjust seasoning, bring to a boil, and serve garnished with hard-cooked egg slice and chopped chives. Makes 4 servings.

GARDEN LETTUCE WITH BACON DRESSING

      4 slices of bacon, minced
      2 tablespoons cider vinegar
      2 teaspoons sugar
      1 teaspoon salt
    ¼ teaspoon pepper
    1½ quarts butterhead lettuce

Cook bacon in skillet until crisp and brown. Add vinegar, sugar, salt and pepper and bring to boil. Tear lettuce into small pieces; put in large bowl. Add hot dressing; toss and serve. Makes 4 servings.

GREEN ONIONS, PEAS, AND LETTUCE

      1 bunch of green onions
      1 pound green peas, shelled
         Salt
      1 head crisphead lettuce, cut into
         thick wedges
      2 tablespoons butter or margarine
         Pepper

Trim tops from onions; reserve; put

California Chef's Salad

onions in saucepan. Add boiling water to barely cover. Cook, covered, for 5 minutes. Add peas; do not stir; sprinkle with salt; cover and cook for 10 minutes. Put lettuce and sliced onion tops over peas; cover and cook for about 5 minutes, or until vegetables are tender. Add butter; season with salt and pepper to taste. Makes 4 servings.

GREEN PEAS AND LETTUCE

1 small head crisphead lettuce
1 cup peas
  Salt and pepper
  Boiling water
  Heavy cream

Remove heart from lettuce. Fill with peas. Tie up leaves and place head in 1 inch of boiling water. Cover and steam until peas are tender, about 30 minutes. Season to taste with salt and pepper and serve with cream. Makes 2 or 3 servings.

ASPARAGUS WITH LETTUCE SAUCE

Heat 2½ cups (one 1-pound can) cut asparagus; drain. To 1 cup hot medium white sauce (2 tablespoons butter, 2 tablespoons flour, 1 cup milk, salt and pepper), add ½ cup chopped lettuce and 1 small onion, chopped. Serve over asparagus. Makes 4 servings.

WILTED LETTUCE

2 quarts broken Boston or leaf lettuce (2 heads)
2 tablespoons chopped chives or green-onion tops
3 tablespoons bacon fat
¼ cup vinegar
1 teaspoon sugar
  Salt and pepper

Sprinkle lettuce with chives. Heat fat; add vinegar, sugar, and salt and pepper to taste; heat. Pour over lettuce; toss and serve at once. Makes 4 servings.

CHEESE-STUFFED LETTUCE SALAD

1 medium head crisphead lettuce
1 package (1¼ ounces) blue cheese
2 packages (3 ounces each) cream cheese
2 tablespoons mayonnaise
2 tablespoons minced green-onion tops
1 pimiento, minced
¼ teaspoon pepper
½ teaspoon Worcestershire
  Dash of hot pepper sauce

Hollow out heart of lettuce, leaving 1-inch shell. Beat cheese and mayonnaise together until smooth. Add remaining ingredients and mix well. Fill lettuce shell, wrap well, and chill for 1 to 2 hours, or until cheese is firm. Cut into crosswise slices about ¾ inch thick. Makes 4 to 6 servings.

CALIFORNIA CHEF'S SALAD

2 cups mixed salad greens (butterhead and romaine lettuce and chicory)
1 cup small raw spinach leaves or watercress, stems trimmed
½ cup sliced celery
2 cups orange segments
1 cup cooked ham, slivered

1 cup cooked chicken, slivered
½ cup Swiss cheese, slivered
 Favorite French dressing
 Salt and pepper
2 hard-cooked eggs, sliced

Into large salad bowl tear salad greens with hands into bite-size pieces. Combine with spinach leaves, celery, orange segments, ham, chicken, and Swiss cheese. Toss with French dressing to taste. Season with salt and pepper. Garnish with hard-cooked egg slices. Makes 4 to 6 servings.

GERMAN LETTUCE SALAD

Prepare any lettuce in the usual manner. Dress with a sprinkling of sugar, a little salt and pepper, and either sweet or sour cream. Dairy sour cream, which is thick, may be diluted with lemon juice to the thickness of heavy cream.

LICORICE—The plant, *Glycyrrhiza glabra,* is a perennial herb of the pea family. It grows wild in southern Europe and in western and central Asia. It has long rootstocks, feathery leaves, and flowers of various colors, usually pale violet or blue. Licorice is now cultivated on a large scale, especially in Spain and Italy. Its dried root, or an extract made from it, is used to flavor medicines, tobacco, cigars, cigarettes, soft and alcoholic drinks, candy, and chewing gum.

Licorice has been known as a flavoring since remote times, and its appeal, especially to the young, goes on undimmed through the ages.

LIMA BEAN—This round, full, slightly curved bean is truly an American native, for although a number of beans were known and used in Europe before the voyage of Columbus, Lima beans as well as green beans, kidney, pea, pinto, and others, were unheard of before the New World was discovered.

Lima beans were found in various sections of the Americas as early as 1500. They were named after Lima, Peru, where the European explorers first came across them, but it is now believed that their original home was Guatemala. They spread from there through the Indian trade routes and were adopted by many tribes of American Indians, from the Southwest to the Northeast. Lima beans, both fresh and dry, formed one of the staples of the Indian's diet. Since they are a highly concentrated food and, when dried, easy to store and transport, they made excellent provisions for the ships trading with Europe and the Far East.

Because they require warmer weather and a greater humidity than usually found in Europe, they have never become an important crop there.

Availability and Purchasing Guide
Fresh Lima Beans

Available year round with the peak crop from June to September. They are generally sold in the pod. Pods should be well and evenly filled, firm, crisp, and unspotted, dark green in color. Flabby, yellowed pods are a sign of poor quality.

Frozen fresh Lima beans are available in two varieties: Baby and Fordhook. These are two distinct types (Fordhooks are not grown-up Baby Limas) and both are tender, green fresh beans, the Fordhook being larger and plumper than the Baby. Frozen fresh Limas are also available in various sauces such as cheese or tomato and butter, and in combination with corn, as "succotash," and with other vegetables, as "mixed vegetables."

Small, large (or jumbo) fresh Lima beans are available canned. They are generally labeled "green" Lima beans to distinguish them from dried Limas and the terms "baby," "large," or "jumbo" refer to the size of the bean, not the variety as they do with the frozen beans. Fresh Lima beans combined with corn are also available canned.

☐ 2 pounds in pod = 2 cups shelled

Dried Lima Beans

Available packaged in many size beans: baby, medium, large, etc. Also available canned as jumbo (large) and baby (small). Here again the size, not the variety, of bean is what is being described.

Dried Lima beans are occasionally known as "butter beans," and in the South, large dried Limas mottled with purple are called "calico" or "speckled butter beans."

Dried Lima beans should be clean, uniform in size and quality. Since today they are usually packaged, a reliable brand will guarantee clean, uniformly sized beans.

☐ 1 pound, raw = approximately 2 cups
☐ 1 pound, cooked = approximately 6 cups

Storage—Do not shell fresh Lima beans until ready to use and do not keep too long before cooking. Store in the refrigerator in a moisture-proof container.

☐ Fresh, refrigerator shelf, raw: 3 to 14 days
☐ Fresh or dried, refrigerator shelf, cooked and covered: 4 to 5 days
☐ Fresh, refrigerator frozen-food compartment, prepared for freezing: 1 month
☐ Fresh, freezer, prepared for freezing: 10 months
☐ Canned, fresh, kitchen shelf: 1 year
☐ Frozen, fresh, refrigerator frozen-food compartment: 3 months
☐ Frozen, fresh, freezer: 1 year
☐ Dried, kitchen shelf: 6 to 8 months

Nutritive Food Values—Fresh Lima beans are higher in protein than most vegetables, with fair amounts of vitamins A and C.

☐ Fresh, 3½ ounces, boiled and drained = 111 calories
☐ Fresh (green), canned, 3½ ounces, solids and liquids = 71 calories
☐ Fresh (green), canned, 3½ ounces, solids, drained = 96 calories
☐ Fresh baby Limas, frozen, 3½ ounces, boiled and drained = 118 calories
☐ Fresh Fordhook Limas, frozen, 3½ ounces, boiled and drained = 99 calories

Dried Lima beans are a good source of protein, iron, and thiamine and a good supplement to other protein foods.

☐ Dried, 3½ ounces, cooked = 138 calories

Basic Preparation—Fresh Lima-bean pods are comparatively tough, so the easiest way of removing the beans is to cut a thin strip from the inner side of the pod, give pod a quick twist to open it, then remove the beans.

☐ **To Cook Fresh Limas**—Have about 1 inch of water boiling in a saucepan. Drop beans in; cover pan and cook for 20 to 25 minutes. About ½ teaspoon salt may be added to the cooking water if desired. Drain off liquid, season, add butter and serve.

☐ **To Freeze Fresh Limas**—Open pods and remove beans. Blanch in boiling water:

Small: 1½ minutes
Medium: 2 minutes
Large: 2½ minutes

Chill for 5 minutes in running cold water. Pack in containers, leaving ½-inch headspace. Seal.

☐ **To Cook Dried Limas**—Sort dried beans carefully. Cover beans with water and soak overnight, using the amount of water prescribed on the package. Then cook beans in water in which they were soaked, until tender. For a quick-cook method, add water and bring to a boil. Cover and cook for 2 minutes. Remove from heat and let stand for 1 hour. Reheat and cook until beans are tender.

FRESH LIMA BEANS

CREAMY SUCCOTASH

    2 pounds fresh Lima beans, shelled,
      or 1 box frozen Lima beans
      Salt
    4 or 5 ears of corn
    ½ cup cream
    2 tablespoons butter or margarine
      Salt and pepper

Cook beans (covered) in just enough boiling salted water to prevent sticking for about 20 minutes, or until almost tender. Or cook frozen beans as directed on the label. Cut off corn kernels; scrape liquid from cob with dull edge of knife. Add corn and cream to beans; simmer gently for 5 minutes. Add the butter, and salt and pepper to taste. Heat thoroughly. Makes 4 servings.

PICNIC SUCCOTASH

    ½ pound bacon ends, chopped
      About 1 cup (8-ounce can) small
      onions, drained
    2 cups (1-pound can) green Lima
      beans, drained
    2 cups (one 1-pound can) whole-kernel
      corn, undrained
      Salt and pepper

Cook bacon in large saucepan until crisp. Remove and set aside. Drain off all but ¼ cup fat. Cut onions into halves; add to fat; cook for 5 minutes. Add bacon, beans, and corn; heat thoroughly. Season. Makes 4 servings.

LIMA BEANS WITH EASY WHITE SAUCE

    3 pounds fresh Lima beans, shelled,
      or 2 boxes frozen Lima beans
      Salt
      Water
    1 tablespoon butter
    1 tablespoon all-purpose flour
    1 cup hot milk
      Salt and pepper

Cook beans, covered, for 20 to 30 minutes in 1 inch of boiling salted water. Or, cook frozen beans as directed on the label. Cream butter and flour; add to hot milk in top part of double boiler; do not stir. Cover; cook over boiling water for about 12 minutes. Beat with whisk or rotary beater until well mixed. Drain beans. Add to sauce. Season with salt and pepper. Makes 4 servings.

LIMA BEANS WITH CHEESE

    2 pounds fresh Lima beans, shelled

      or 1 box frozen Lima beans
    ½ teaspoon celery salt
    ¼ cup light cream
    ¼ teaspoon pepper
    ½ cup grated process American cheese
    1 tablespoon melted butter or
      margarine

Cook beans, covered, in 1 inch of boiling salted water for 20 to 30 minutes; drain. Or, cook frozen beans as directed on the label; drain. Mix beans with remaining ingredients. Put in 1-quart casserole and bake in preheated moderate oven (350°F.) for 15 minutes, or until thoroughly heated. Makes 4 servings.

CHILI LIMAS

    2 pounds fresh Lima beans, shelled,
      or 1 box frozen Lima beans
    1 small onion, minced
    3 tablespoons butter or margarine
    ⅓ cup chili sauce
      Dash of cayenne

Cook beans, covered, in 1 inch of boiling salted water for 20 to 30 minutes. Or, cook frozen beans as directed on the label. Cook onion in butter until tender; add chili sauce and cayenne. Drain beans, add sauce, and heat well. Makes 4 servings.

MINTED LIMAS

Not only peas are good when dressed with mint; try frozen baby Lima beans, cooked in a minimum of water with fresh or dried mint, plus sugar, salt, and pepper to taste. Lacking the herb, melt and add a bit of mint jelly. Don't forget that big pat of butter before you send these green morsels to the table.

LIMA BEANS IN LEMON SAUCE

    2 pounds fresh Lima beans, shelled
    ⅓ cup water
    ¼ cup butter or margarine
      Salt and pepper
    ½ teaspoon crumbled dried rosemary
    1 teaspoon cornstarch
    3 tablespoons fresh lemon juice
    3 tablespoons chopped parsley

To Lima beans add water, butter, salt, pepper, and rosemary. Simmer, covered, over low heat for 20 to 30 minutes, or until beans are tender, adding a little more water, if necessary. Mix cornstarch with lemon juice. Gradually stir cornstarch mixture into Lima beans. Cook over low heat, stirring constantly, until mixture thickens. Stir in chopped parsley. Makes 4 servings.

CURRIED LIMA SALAD

    1 box frozen Lima beans, cooked and
      cooled
    2 cups diced celery
    1 pimiento, chopped
    ⅓ cup each of mayonnaise and dairy
      sour cream
    1 teaspoon curry powder
      Salt and pepper to taste
      Watercress

Mix all ingredients except watercress. Serve with cress. Makes 4 servings.

GREEN-LIMA-BEAN SALAD

    ½ peeled cucumber, diced
    ¾ cup sliced celery
    4 radishes, sliced
    ½ medium green pepper, chopped
    2 cups (1-pound can) green Lima beans,
      drained
      Mayonnaise
      Salt and pepper
    2 tomatoes, cut into wedges

Mix first 5 ingredients lightly. Add enough mayonnaise to moisten. Season to taste. Chill. Just before serving, put in bowl and garnish with tomato. Makes 4 servings.

LIMA-BEAN AND EGG SALAD

    2 cups (1-pound can) green Lima
      beans, drained
      French dressing
    ½ cup mayonnaise
      Small amount of minced onion
    4 hard-cooked eggs
    1 cup sliced celery
      Salt and pepper to taste
      Paprika
      Salad greens

Moisten Lima beans with French dressing and let stand for 10 to 15 minutes. Add remaining ingredients except paprika and greens. Chill. Sprinkle with paprika and serve with greens. Makes 4 servings.

DRIED LIMA BEANS

LAMB-BONE AND LIMA-BEAN SOUP

      Bones and trimmings from lamb
      roast
    2 quarts water
    2 cups dried Lima beans
    1 cup chopped onion
    1 cup chopped celery and leaves
    2 cups tomato juice
      Salt and pepper

Put bones and trimmings in soup kettle; add water and beans; let stand for 2 hours. Add onion and celery; bring to boil slowly and skim. Simmer for about 2 hours. Remove trimmings and bone. Mince any bits of meat on the bone and add to soup. If there is fat on soup, cool soup and remove fat. Mash beans slightly with potato masher; do not drain. Add tomato juice. Season to taste with salt and pepper. Heat thoroughly. Makes about 2 quarts.

CODFISH AND LIMA-BEAN CHOWDER

    1 slice of bacon, diced
    1 onion, sliced
    1 garlic clove, minced
    2 potatoes, sliced
    2 cups water
    1 package shredded salted dried
      codfish
    8-ounce can tomato sauce
    2 cups cooked dried Lima beans
      Ground thyme
      Salt and pepper

Cook bacon in heavy saucepan until crisp; add onion and brown lightly. Add garlic, potatoes, and water; bring to boil, cover, and simmer for about 15 minutes until almost tender. Freshen codfish according to package directions and add with tomato sauce and Lima beans; simmer for about 10 minutes. Season with a little thyme and salt and pepper. Makes 4 large servings.

PORK AND LIMA BEANS

1 pound end pork chops (about 3)
1 cup dried baby Lima beans, cooked
¼ teaspoon curry powder
¼ cup ketchup
1 teaspoon salt

Remove pork from bones and cut meat into 1-inch squares. Brown well in skillet without added fat; remove from heat. Add remaining ingredients; mix well. Put in greased casserole. Bake in preheated slow oven (325°F.) for 1 hour. Makes 4 to 6 servings.

SAVORY BEAN AND CHICKEN CASSEROLE

1 pound (2 cups) dried Lima beans
¼ pound diced salt pork
2 medium onions, chopped
1 mashed garlic clove
1 stalk celery, chopped
¼ teaspoon ground thyme
½ pound sausage meat
1 frying chicken (2½ pounds) cut in pieces
¼ cup margarine
½ cup tomato sauce
¼ cup chopped parsley
1 cup dry white wine
½ pound diced ham

Soak beans in deep kettle overnight. The next day, do not drain: Add additional water to cover beans, salt pork, half of the chopped onions, garlic clove, celery, and ground thyme. Simmer, covered, until beans are almost tender. Drain beans; reserve liquid. Fry sausage meat and remaining onions in skillet until sausage meat is browned. Drain off fat. In another skillet, cook chicken in margarine until golden brown on all sides. Add tomato sauce, parsley and white wine. Simmer, covered, stirring frequently, for 15 minutes. Put half of the bean mixture into a 3-quart casserole. Add sausage meat and chicken and tomato sauce. Top with remaining beans. Add enough reserved bean liquid to cover mixture in casserole. Bake covered in a preheated slow oven (325°F.) for 1½ hours. Stir in ham. Bake uncovered for another 30 minutes. Makes 6 servings.

BARBECUED FRANKFURTERS AND LIMA BEANS

1 onion, minced
1 garlic clove, minced
2 tablespoons fat
¼ cup firmly packed brown sugar
2 tablespoons vinegar
½ teaspoon powdered mustard
1 tablespoon Worcestershire
1 can (8 ounces) tomato sauce
2½ cups (one 1-pound, 4-ounce can) dried Lima beans
1 pound frankfurters, cut into 2-inch pieces

Cook onion and garlic in fat in skillet until lightly browned. Add sugar, seasonings, and tomato sauce; bring to boil, and simmer for 5 minutes. Add beans and frankfurters; heat. Makes 4 servings.

INDIVIDUAL HAM AND LIMA-BEAN CASSEROLE

¾ pound ham ends
1 garlic clove, minced
3 tablespoons salad oil
4 cups (two 1-pound cans) large dried Lima beans, drained
¼ cup liquid drained from beans
¼ cup vinegar
1 tablespoon brown sugar
⅛ teaspoon pepper
¼ teaspoon paprika
2 parsley sprigs, chopped
Salt to taste

Trim some of fat from ham, and cut meat into thin strips about 1 inch long. Put ham and garlic in skillet with oil and cook until ham is lightly browned. Add remaining ingredients; mix well and pour into 4 individual baking dishes. Bake in preheated moderate oven (350°F.) for about 30 minutes. Makes 4 servings.

FRENCH BEAN CASSEROLE

1 pound (2 cups) dried Lima beans, washed and drained
6 cups water
½ pound pork-sausage links
1 pound boneless lean lamb, cubed
2 onions, chopped
2 garlic cloves, minced
½ teaspoon crumbled dried rosemary leaves
2 teaspoons salt
Dash of pepper
¾ cup red wine

Cover beans with water, bring to boil, and boil for 2 minutes. Cover pan and let stand for 1 hour. Cook until almost tender, adding more water if necessary. Drain, reserving 1½ cups liquid. Cut sausages into halves and fry until browned. Remove sausage. Brown lamb, onion, and garlic in fat remaining. Put lamb mixture into 3-quart casserole. Add seasonings and wine. Cover and bake in preheated moderate oven (350°F.) for 1 hour. Add beans, sausage, and bean liquid. Cover and bake for 1½ hours more. Makes 6 servings.

BEAN AND BACON CASSEROLE

1 pound (2 cups) dried Lima beans, washed and drained
2 quarts water
1 garlic clove, minced
1 medium onion, sliced
Dash of cayenne
1 bay leaf
¾ pound slab bacon
¼ cup molasses
¼ cup ketchup
2 teaspoons salt
2 teaspoons Worcestershire
⅛ teaspoon pepper
1 teaspoon dry mustard
2 tablespoons brown sugar

Cover beans with water, bring to boil, and boil for 2 minutes. Cover pan and let stand for 1 hour. Add garlic, onion, cayenne, bay leaf, and bacon in one piece. Cook, covered, until beans are tender, stirring occasionally. Remove bacon; drain beans, reserving 1½ cups liquid. To liquid, add remaining ingredients, except brown sugar. Put beans in 2-quart casserole and pour liquid over beans. Remove rind from bacon; cut meat into ¼-inch slices and arrange on beans. Sprinkle with brown sugar. Bake, uncovered, in preheated hot oven (400° F.) for 1¼ hours. Makes 4 to 6 servings.

SUPER LIMA-BEAN CASSEROLE

1 pound (2 cups) dried Lima beans, soaked
3 cups green beans, cut into 1-inch lengths
¼ cup butter or margarine
2 medium onions, chopped
3 tablespoons chopped parsley
3 tablespoons all-purpose flour
Salt and pepper to taste
⅓ cup dry bread crumbs
2 tablespoons grated Parmesan cheese

Cook Lima beans and green beans separately until tender. Drain off cooking liquid, measure, and add enough water to make 3 cups; reserve. Put Lima beans and green beans in layers in 2-quart casserole. Melt butter; sauté onions and chopped parsley until golden brown; stir in flour. Gradually stir in reserved liquid. Cook over low heat, stirring constantly, until smooth and thickened; season with salt and pepper to taste. Pour sauce over beans. Cover. Bake in preheated slow oven (325°F.) for 30 minutes. Uncover and sprinkle with bread crumbs mixed with Parmesan cheese. Bake for 15 minutes longer. Makes 6 servings.

COUNTRY-STYLE BEANS

1 pound (2 cups) dried Lima beans, washed and drained
6 cups water
1 onion, chopped
½ pound salt pork
1 teaspoon salt
¼ teaspoon white pepper
½ teaspoon dry mustard
1 tablespoon brown sugar
½ cup ketchup

Cover beans with water, bring to boil, and boil for 2 minutes. Cover pan and let stand for 1 hour; then cook until tender, adding more liquid when necessary. Drain, reserving liquid. Put half the beans in bean pot or casserole and sprinkle with half the onion. Add salt pork and remaining beans and onion. Mix salt, pepper, mustard, brown sugar, ketchup, and 1½ cups bean liquid. Add to beans. Add more liquid, if necessary, to cover beans. Cover and bake in preheated slow oven (275°F.) for 6 to 8 hours. Remove pork, slice, and broil. Serve with beans. Makes 6 to 8 servings.

LIME—A small bushy and spiny tropical tree which belongs to the citrus family. The tree has small white flowers and its fruit, which measures up to two and a half inches in diameter, is small and compact and resembles the lemon in shape. The rind of the lime is green and thin. The flesh is light green, with a very acid and juicy pulp which yields a pungent juice. Oil is extracted from the rind.

The lime tree originated in eastern and southern Asia where it grew wild. It was brought to the East Indies and domesticated in the 16th century by Portuguese and Spanish explorers. British sailors were called "limeys" because of the limes that were carried on their ships to prevent scurvy.

The tree is very sensitive to cold and can only be grown in tropical and sub-tropical climates. Limes grown in Florida, California, and Mexico supply the United States market. Most of them are a variety called Persian, but there is a smaller, rounder, more acid variety called Key Limes grown on the Florida Keys.

Availability—Fresh limes are generally available in quantity from June to December.

Bottled lime juice, sweetened or unsweetened, is available, as is a frozen lime-juice, limeade, and lemon-and-limeade concentrate, and Daiquiri mix. Lemon-lime carbonated beverages, packaged lime-gelatin dessert, and Key-Lime pie filling are also available.

Purchasing Guide—Look for limes that are green rather than deep yellow because they contain more acid. Brown spots on skin do not affect quality of juice.

Storage—See Lemon, page 1051.

Nutritive Food Values—Excellent source of vitamin C.
☐ Lime juice, fresh or unsweetened, 3½ ounces = 26 calories
☐ Limeade, 3½ ounces, diluted = 41 calories

Basic Preparation—Cut and squeeze limes for fresh juice. Cut lime slices in decorative ways for iced drinks, punches, and sherbets. Grate rind and add with juice for added flavor and sparkle.

FRESH-LIME MELON CUP
2 cups fresh cantaloupe cubes
1 cup fresh pineapple wedges
⅓ cup sugar
¼ cup fresh lime juice
1/16 teaspoon salt
    Fresh mint (optional)

Place cantaloupe and pineapple in a bowl. Combine sugar, lime juice, and salt. Pour over fruit and toss lightly. Chill, and serve in sherbet glasses. Garnish with fresh mint if desired. Makes 4 servings.

CHICKEN STEAMED IN LIME JUICE
½ cup fresh lime juice
½ teaspoon each of salt and paprika
1 teaspoon each of ground coriander and cardamom seed
3 large chicken breasts, halved
    Cooking oil

In mixing bowl combine lime juice, salt, paprika, coriander, and cardamom. Skin chicken breasts and, if desired, bone. Put chicken in bowl and toss to cover with marinade on all sides. Marinate for at least 1 hour. Drain; reserve marinade. Brush each piece of chicken with oil. Place chicken in large skillet. Pour marinade over pieces. Simmer over low heat, tightly covered, for 45 minutes, or until chicken is tender. Makes 3 to 6 servings.

JELLIED LIME AND CHEESE SALAD
1 box (3 ounces) lime-flavored gelatin
    About 2½ cups (one 1-pound, 4½-ounce can) pineapple chunks
12 whole blanched almonds
1 envelope unflavored gelatin
1 pound (2 cups) cream-style cottage cheese
1 tablespoon fresh lemon juice
¾ teaspoon salt
⅓ cup light cream
½ cup chopped blanched almonds

Dissolve lime gelatin in 1 cup hot water. Add ½ cup syrup from pineapple and ½ cup cold water. Chill until slightly thickened. Arrange 12 almonds in bottom of deep 1½-quart mold. Carefully pour in slightly thickened gelatin mixture. Chill overnight, or until very firm. Drain pineapple and dice enough to make 1 cup. Sprinkle unflavored gelatin on ¼ cup cold water; let stand for 5 minutes. Dissolve over hot water. Add to cheese with pineapple and remaining ingredients; mix well. Spoon onto firm gelatin in mold. Chill until firm. Unmold on plate. If desired, garnish with watercress; serve with mayonnaise seasoned with curry powder. Makes 6 to 8 servings.

MINTED FRESH-LIME MOLD WITH WATERMELON BALLS
2 envelopes unflavored gelatin
1 cup cold water
¼ cup chopped fresh mint
2 cups boiling water
1 cup fresh lime juice
1 cup sugar
¼ teaspoon salt
    Few drops of green food coloring
3 cups fresh watermelon balls
    Fresh mint leaves for garnish

Soften gelatin in cold water. Steep mint leaves in boiling water. Strain and pour mint diffusion over softened gelatin. Stir to dissolve gelatin. Blend in lime juice, sugar, salt, and green food coloring. Turn into 1-quart ring mold. Chill until firm and ready to serve. Unmold on serving plate and fill center with watermelon balls. Garnish with fresh mint leaves. Makes 6 to 8 servings.

MOLDED LIME AND BLUEBERRY SALAD
2 boxes (3 ounces each) lime-flavored gelatin
2 cups hot water
1¼ cups cold water
3 tablespoons fresh lime juice
¼ teaspoon salt
3 cups fresh blueberries
    Salad greens
    Mayonnaise or salad dressing

Dissolve gelatin in the hot water. Stir in cold water, lime juice, and salt. Chill until thickened but not firm. Fold in berries and pour into 5-cup mold. Chill until firm. Unmold on greens and serve with mayonnaise. Makes 6 servings.

LIME SALMON-SALAD SPREAD
1 can (1 pound) salmon
1 medium apple, diced
⅓ cup salad dressing
2 tablespoons fresh lime juice
    Salt and pepper to taste

Mix all ingredients. Store in covered jar in refrigerator. Makes about 1½ cups.

FRESH-LIME FRENCH DRESSING
1 cup salad oil
¼ teaspoon salt or salt to taste
½ teaspoon powdered mustard
1/16 teaspoon white pepper
1 garlic clove, peeled
2 teaspoons finely chopped onion
⅓ cup fresh lime juice
1 egg white

Combine first 6 ingredients and let stand for 1 hour. Remove garlic. Add lime juice and egg white and beat with a rotary beater. Chill, serve over vegetable or fruit salad. Makes 1¼ cups.

FRESH-LIME CREAM
1 cup sugar
2 tablespoons cornstarch
⅛ teaspoon salt
1 cup water
¼ cup fresh lime juice
1 egg, lightly beaten
1 teaspoon grated lime rind
1 teaspoon vanilla extract
1 cup heavy cream, whipped
    Whipped cream for garnish
    Grated lime rind for garnish

Combine first 3 ingredients in saucepan or top part of a double boiler. Gradually stir in water. Cook over hot, not boiling, water or medium direct heat until thickened, stirring constantly. Add lime juice and cook until thickened. Add a little of hot mixture to the egg and then stir into remaining hot mixture. Cook for 1 to 2 minutes over low heat, stirring constantly. Remove from heat and add grated lime rind and vanilla. Cool. Fold in whipped cream. Serve in sherbet glasses, garnished with additional whipped cream and a sprinkling of lime rind. Makes 6 servings.

LIME-GINGER FOAM
½ cup fresh lime juice
¼ cup sugar
3 egg whites
1 teaspoon vanilla extract
1 bottle (28 ounces) ginger ale, chilled

Key Lime Pie

Fresh-Lime Froth

Molded Lime and
Blueberry Salad

Fresh-Lime Melon Cup

Combine lime juice, sugar, and egg whites in container of electric blender and whirl until frothy. Add vanilla and divide among 4 tall glasses. Fill glasses with ginger ale. Stir gently to mix ingredients. Makes 4 servings.

Note: If blender is not available, beat egg whites until stiff. Fold in sugar and lime juice.

LIME SHERBET

    3 cups sugar
    4 cups water
    ¾ cup fresh lime juice
      Dash of salt
    2 egg whites

Put sugar and water in saucepan, bring to boil, and boil for 5 minutes. Remove from heat and add lime juice and salt. Pour into freezing trays and freeze until mushy. Put lime mixture in cold bowl, add egg whites, and beat until fluffy. Freeze until firm. Makes about 1¾ quarts.

FRESH-LIME FROTH

    ⅓ cup fresh lime juice
    ½ cup finely crushed ice
    2 tablespoons sugar
    1 unbeaten egg white

Place all ingredients in a shaker or 1-quart fruit jar. Shake well until ingredients are well blended and mixture is frothy. Serve in fruit-juice glasses or in tall stemmed glasses. Garnish with fresh mint if desired. Makes approximately 1 cup.

KEY LIME PIE

    1 cup and 2 tablespoons sugar
    ⅓ cup cornstarch
    ½ teaspoon salt
    ¼ cup cold water
    1½ cups hot water
    6 tablespoons fresh lime juice
    3 eggs, separated
    3 tablespoons butter or margarine
    1 tablespoon grated lime rind
    9- inch pie shell, baked
    6 tablespoons sugar
    ⅛ teaspoon salt
      Fresh lime slices for garnish

Combine first 4 ingredients in a saucepan. Mix well. Add hot water and cook over low heat, stirring constantly, until very thick. Stir in fresh lime juice. Return to heat and cook until thickened. Beat egg yolks lightly. Beat in a small amount of hot mixture. Cook for about 2 minutes, stirring constantly. Add butter and lime rind. Cool. Pour into cold pastry shell. Beat egg whites until stiff but not dry. Beat in remaining sugar and salt gradually, beating until blended. Spread over top of pie. Bake for 20 minutes in preheated slow oven (300°F.). Serve cold, garnished with fresh lime slices.

FLORIDA LIME PIE

    3 egg yolks, beaten
    ⅓ cup sugar
    ¼ cup fresh lime juice

    1½ teaspoons grated lime rind
    1½ cups heavy cream
      Green food coloring
    9- inch Graham Cracker Crust (see Crumb Crust, page 1054)

In top part of double boiler mix egg yolks, sugar, and lime juice. Cook over boiling water, stirring, until thickened but not firm. Stir in lime rind. Whip 1 cup cream and fold in. Add a few drops of green coloring. Pile into shell and chill for about 24 hours. Top with remaining ½ cup cream, whipped, and some more grated lime rind if desired. Makes 6 to 8 servings.

Note: You can make it a day ahead because it tastes even better if it chills for a day.

LIME TARTS

    3 egg yolks
    ¼ cup sugar
    ¼ cup fresh lime juice
    2 teaspoons grated lime rind
    1 cup heavy cream, whipped
      Green food coloring (optional)
    6 tart shells, baked

In top part of double boiler beat egg yolks with sugar until thick. Beat in lime juice. Cook over boiling water until thickened, stirring constantly. Stir in lime rind. Chill. At serving time, fold into whipped cream. Tint green with food coloring, if desired. Spoon into baked tart shells. Makes 6 servings.

LIME JULEP

Thoroughly chill glass or metal tumbler. Fill with finely crushed ice. Squeeze into it juice of 1 lime and add 2 teaspoons or more superfine sugar. Mash in 2 or 3 chopped mint leaves. Cover glass and shake until glass is heavily coated with frost—about 5 minutes. Stick a sprig of fresh mint into ice. Serve at once with a short colored straw.

LIME-ORANGE CONSERVE

    6 oranges
    5 cups water
    6 cups sugar
    ¼ cup fresh lime juice
      One 2-inch piece stick cinnamon
    ½ cup raisins
    ½ cup flaked coconut

Remove orange peel in quarters. Dice pulp, removing center membrane and seeds. Force peel through food chopper, using coarse blade. Cover peel with water and bring to boil. Cook for about 20 minutes, or until peel is tender. Add pulp and juice to undrained rind. Cook for about 20 minutes longer, or until mixture is reduced to about one half its original volume and measures about 6 cups. Add sugar, lime juice, cinnamon, and raisins, stirring until sugar is dissolved, for about 30 minutes, or until mixture sheets from side of spoon. Remove from heat and stir in coconut. Pour into hot sterilized jars and seal. Makes about seven ½-pint jars.

LIQUEUR by *José Wilson*—Liqueurs are spirits that have been sweetened, flavored, and sometimes colored according to formulas which usually remain well-kept secrets. Unlike spirits or wines which are made by straightforward processes of distillation or fermentation, the alchemy of a liqueur lies in the choice and blending of the flavoring ingredients (caraway and orris, aniseed and peppermint, cocoa and coffee beans, to name a few) that give the sweetened spirit a distinctive taste.

The word liqueur comes from the Latin *liquefacere,* "to make liquid, dissolve, or melt," and the flavoring elements of a liqueur are in fact dissolved either by infusion in such spirits as brandy, whisky, or rum, or by infusion followed by distillation. Some flavorings cannot stand up to distillation, since their heavy essential oils become lost in the heat of the process, while others withstand it successfully. When a flavored liquid is distilled, it becomes clear and this has led to confusion between liqueurs and the white brandies or *eaux-de-vie* distilled from cherries, raspberries, strawberries, plums, and pears (Kirsch, Framboise, Fraise, Mirabelle, Quetsch, Slivovitz, and *eau-de-vie de poire),* which are often called liqueurs, but are not. These white alcohols are dry, distilled from a single fruit, unflavored and unsweetened, and potent. True liqueurs, although they can be equally strong, must contain at least two and a half per cent sugar. Like spirits, liqueurs have an alcoholic content of over twenty-four per cent by volume and the proof can vary from forty-nine, for Cherry Heering, to a high of 110, for green Chartreuse.

Within the family of liqueurs, there are varying degrees of sweetness. The *crèmes* (crème de menthe, crème de cacao, crème de cassis, and so on) are distinguished by smooth syrupy sweetness, while the fruit-flavored brandies (made by blending the fruit flavor with the spirit) tend to be lighter and less cloying. *Cordial,* the word purists prefer to use to describe the fruit-flavored liqueurs, has become a favorite synonym today for the whole range, perhaps because its amiable, friendly connotation sounds less esoteric and alcoholic. Cordials call to mind the old-fashioned *liqueurs de ménage* or homemade liqueurs prevalent in those centuries when women put up their own household remedies and drinks and kept in their stillrooms sealed crocks of alcohol in which fruits, flowers, nuts, and herbs lay steeping. These heavy homemade potions, often sipped to seal or ratify a bargain, were known as ratafias. Signatories to Louis XIV's peace treaties quaffed them

in what may have been the first instance of an *entente cordiale.*

In the 17th and 18th centuries, English ladies of fashion started the custom of the after-dinner liqueurs by serving imported French cordials or their own concoctions in little cordial pots, shaped like miniature teapots and matched to their silver tea services. Ratafias, which are not distilled, can be made at home by anyone with a spirituous bent, a garden full of carnations or acacia flowers, green walnuts or quinces, and a spare quart of Cognac.

Although there is no record of the discovery of the first liqueur, credit is usually given to the medieval monks and alchemists, the physicians and medical researchers of their day. According to one account, brandy mixed with the juice of very ripe plums was prescribed as a malaria remedy by Camaldolite monks of the Order of St. Romuald early in the 11th century. Chaucer in the *Canterbury Tales* says "Gold in a physic is a cordial," a highly prophetic remark, for specks of gold, regarded in the Middle Ages as a cure-all, were later to be introduced to a liqueur, Eau de Vie de Danzig, transforming it into Goldwasser or Liqueur d'Or. In the 15th century an ingenious doctor of Padua, beset by a petulant but influential female patient, made up for her a soothing draught of brandy sweetened and flavored with attar of roses and honey, to which he gave the euphonious name *rosolio.* The name became generic in Italy for all flavored sweetened brandies and Catherine de Medeci took along her rosolio experts when she left Florence to marry the Duc d'Orleans, later Henry II of France. An aromatic pink Rosolio liqueur is still a popular tipple in Italy and the Near East.

Two of the world's great classic liqueurs originated with French monks who had learned the curative powers of herbs and discovered the art of distilling their essence. The older, *Benedictine,* took its name from the Benedictine Abbey at Fécamp where it was originally made in 1510 (it is still manufactured there, although on the ruins of the abbey, by a commercial company). The letters D.O.M. *(Deo Optimo Maximo)* on the label are a grateful, graceful dedication "to God, most good, most great."

Equally famous is *Chartreuse,* developed from a family recipe given to the Carthusian monks of the Grande Chartreuse Monastery by the Maréchal d'Estrées in 1605. The jealously guarded formula depends on the herbs (said to number 130) that were gathered by the monks near the monastery in Grenoble. When the monks were expelled by the

French Government in 1903, they tried to make their liqueur in Tarragona, Spain, but with little success. The necessary herbs were lacking. In 1938 they were allowed to return to France and the magic brew regained its old glory. Chartreuse is made in two strengths and colors, the yellow at eighty-six proof and the green at 110.

Other liqueurs, almost equally successful, have a more secular history. One of the most romantically documented is *Drambuie,* a liqueur made from Scotch whisky, honey, and herbs that takes its name from a contraction of *an dram buidheach,* a Gaelic phrase meaning "the drink that satisfies." Tradition has it that Bonnie Prince Charlie, in hiding after the disastrous Forty-Five Rebellion, presented the recipe to a Captain Mackinnon of the Isle of Skye who had generously sheltered him until a rescuing French ship arrived. Treasured for centuries as a festive drink by the Mackinnon Clan, the recipe was finally bottled and marketed in 1906 by the then-current Mackinnon, proprietor of an Edinburgh whisky firm.

Cherry Heering's sweet success began in the more prosaic atmosphere of a 19th-century grocer's shop in Copenhagen. Young apprentice Peter F. Heering was given by the grocer's wife her special recipe for cherry liqueur. When he opened his own store, his customers, mostly seafaring men, found the drink to their taste and carried it in their ships to ports on the seven seas. The demand grew; young Mr. Heering abandoned groceries and went into the large-scale production of Cherry Heering.

The 19th century, due to improved techniques for refining sugar and distilling alcohol, saw a boom in the liqueur business that has continued ever since. There are now so many liqueurs made around the world (new ones are added every year) that it would be impossible to list or classify them all. The following are the best known and they have been roughly grouped in general categories.

The Crèmes—Crème d'ananas (pineapple), crème d'amande (almond), crème de banane (banana), crème de cacao (chocolate), crème de cassis (black currant), crème de cerise (cherry), white, green, and red crème de menthe (peppermint), crème de noyaux (made from fruit kernels, with a nutty bitter-almond flavor), crème de vanille (vanilla), and crème de violette (oil of violets).

The Flavored Brandies—Apricot, blackberry, cherry, ginger, peach.

The Herb-Flavored Liqueurs—Anis, Anisette, Benedictine, B&B (Benedictine and

Brandy), Centherb, green and yellow Chartreuse, Drambuie, Fior d'Alpe, Galliano, Goldwasser, Irish Mist, Izarra, Kümmel, Liqueur d'Or, Trappistine, Vielle Cure.

The Fruit-Flavored Liqueurs—Aurum, Cointreau, Cordial-Médoc, Curaçao, Grand Marnier, Mandarine, Triple Sec, Van der Hum (orange or tangerine flavor); Apry, Abricotine (apricot flavor); Cherry Heering, Maraschino (cherry flavor); Framberry (raspberry flavor); peach liqueur; sloe gin; Parfait Amour and Rock and Rye (citrus flavor, although the latter can also be a mixture of rock candy and rye whiskey).

The Coffee-Flavored Liqueurs—Expresso, Kahlua, Kona Coffee Liqueur, Luana, Tia Maria.

Also listed as a liqueur but a curiosity that defies classification is the Dutch Advocaat, a thick yellow mixture of eggs, sugar, and brandy that is more like an eggnog.

LITCHI or LICHEE NUT—The fruit of a handsome ornamental tropical tree, the litchi, which grows up to forty feet in height and which has a broad round crown and shiny leaves. The litchi is a native of southeastern Asia, and has been an important fruit in China and Asia for over 2,000 years.

The litchi is a very distinctive fruit. It is round and one to two inches in diameter. The rough shell is bright red and leathery. Inside, the shimmery firm white flesh surrounds a single seed. It is juicy and it has a pleasant mildly aromatic and slightly acid flavor.

The fresh litchi is considered a great delicacy in China. The pulp is seeded and canned and it forms a standard dessert in Chinese restaurants, where each nut is usually served speared on a toothpick.

Dried litchi nuts are also very popular in Chinese cookery and reasonably well known in the United States. The white flesh, in drying, becomes brown and leathery, with a raisinlike consistency and flavor. The surrounding shell, when dried, is brown and brittle.

Availability—Occasionally available fresh in Chinese food stores. Fresh pitted litchis canned in heavy syrup and dried litchi nuts are available in specialty food stores.

Caloric Values

☐ Fresh, 3½ ounces = 64 calories
☐ Dried, 3½ ounces = 277 calories

LITCHI SALAD

1 envelope unflavored gelatin
¼ cup sugar
½ teaspoon salt
1¼ cups water
¼ cup vinegar
1 tablespoon fresh lemon juice
½ cup finely shredded cabbage
1 cup chopped celery
2 tablespoons chopped green pepper
12 fresh litchi fruit, peeled and pitted, or canned litchi

Mix gelatin, sugar, and salt thoroughly in saucepan. Add ½ cup of the water. Place over low heat, stirring constantly until gelatin is dissolved. Remove from heat and stir in remaining water, the vinegar, and lemon juice. Chill mixture to consistency of unbeaten egg white. Fold in shredded cabbage, celery, green pepper, and fresh litchi fruit. Turn into 2-cup mold or individual molds and chill until firm. Unmold on serving plate. If desired, garnish with watercress and serve with salad dressing. Makes 4 servings.

LITCHI GELATIN DESSERT

1 envelope unflavored gelatin
⅓ cup sugar
Juice of 1 can litchis; add water to make 1¾ cups
2 tablespoons brandy
12 fresh litchi fruit, peeled and pitted, or canned litchi

Mix gelatin and sugar thoroughly in a small saucepan. Add ½ cup of the litchi juice. Place over low heat, stirring until gelatin is dissolved. Remove from heat and stir in remaining juice. Chill until slightly thicker than unbeaten egg white. Mix in brandy and beat with electric beater until light and fluffy and doubled in volume. Spoon into dessert dishes and chill until firm. Garnish with fresh litchi which have been peeled and pitted, or use canned pitted fruit. Makes 4 servings.

JELLIED LITCHI AND PEACH DESSERT

1 can (11 ounces) litchis in heavy syrup
1 can (1 pound) sliced peaches
1 envelope unflavored gelatin
Water
¼ cup sugar
2 tablespoons fresh lemon juice

Drain fruits, reserving syrups. Chill fruits and add enough water to syrup to make 1¾ cups. Soften gelatin in ¼ cup water. Heat syrup and pour over gelatin. Add

sugar and lemon juice, and stir until gelatin and sugar are dissolved. Chill until slightly thickened. Fold in fruits and chill until firm. Makes 4 to 6 servings.

LIVER—Both in animals and in man, the liver is one of the most important internal organs and essential to the health of the body. Liver has outstanding nutritional properties and, when properly prepared, it is delicious. Beef, calf's, lamb, pork, and poultry livers are used in the cookery of many nations. Goose liver is used in France and Hungary to make the famous *pâtés de foie gras*. In America, beef or calf's liver is often served with bacon or onion.

Availability—Fresh beef, calf's, chicken, lamb, and pork livers are all generally available. Fresh duck livers are occasionally available. Chicken livers may be sold separately or in combination with other giblets.

Frozen beef and chicken livers are available. Sautéed chicken livers; chicken livers with mushrooms; chicken, goose, and turkey liver pâtés; goose livers, whole or puréed, are also available canned.

Purchasing Guide—Beef, lamb, and pork livers are usually marketed in slices. Poultry livers are sold whole. Beef liver is less tender than calf's or lamb livers and has a more pronounced flavor. Beef liver ranges in color from light to dark red, the former usually being more tender. Pork liver has a strong flavor and is less tender than the other kinds.

Poultry livers are tender and mild in flavor.

Storage—Keep liver loosely wrapped in the refrigerator.

☐ Refrigerator shelf, raw: 1 to 2 days
☐ Refrigerator shelf, cooked: 2 to 3 days
☐ Refrigerator frozen-food compartment, prepared for freezing: 2 to 3 weeks
☐ Freezer, prepared for freezing: 6 months

Nutritive Food Values—Nutritionally, liver is one of the most valuable foods. It is an excellent source of protein, iron, vitamin A, riboflavin, and niacin; it contains good vitamin C and fair amounts of thiamine.

☐ Beef liver, 3½ ounces, panfried = 229 calories
☐ Calf's liver, 3½ ounces, panfried = 261 calories
☐ Chicken liver, 3½ ounces, simmered = 165 calories
☐ Goose liver, 3½ ounces, simmered = 215 calories
☐ Lamb liver, 3½ ounces, panfried = 270 calories

☐ Pork liver, 3½ ounces, panfried = 241 calories
☐ Turkey liver, 3½ ounces, simmered = 174 calories

Basic Preparation—Remove membrane from outer edge and cut out veins if present.

☐ **To Panfry or Sauté**—All livers can be panfried. Have beef, calf's, lamb, and pork livers sliced ¼ inch thick. Sprinkle with flour seasoned with salt and pepper. Heat small amount of fat in skillet. Using tongs, put liver in skillet. Cook quickly, turning once, until crisp and brown on both sides, 4 minutes in all. Cook pork liver a little longer.

☐ **To Broil**—Calf's, lamb, and poultry livers can be broiled. Have calf's or lamb livers sliced ½ inch thick. Put on broiler rack and broil with melted butter or margarine. Broil 3 or 4 inches from unit, turning once, until of desired doneness, for 4 to 8 minutes in all.

☐ **To Braise**—All livers can be braised. Have beef, calf's, lamb, or pork livers sliced ½ inch thick. Sprinkle with flour seasoned with salt and pepper. Brown liver quickly on both sides in a little hot fat. Add ⅓ cup water or bouillon; simmer, covered, until tender.

☐ **To Freeze**—Wash well and pat dry. Wrap individual portions in moisture-vapor-proof wrapping, excluding as much air as possible. Seal.

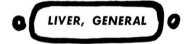

BRAISED LIVER IN CURRY-TOMATO SAUCE

2 onions, sliced
½ green pepper, sliced
3 tablespoons butter or margarine
1 pound beef, pork, or lamb liver, thinly sliced
2 tablespoons all-purpose flour
2 teaspoons salt
¼ teaspoon pepper
½ teaspoon curry powder
1 bay leaf
1 can (19 ounces) tomatoes

Cook onion and pepper in 1 tablespoon butter until lightly browned. Remove onion and pepper. Remove membrane and tendons from liver. Dredge liver with flour, 1 teaspoon salt, and ⅛ teaspoon pepper. Brown on both sides in remaining butter. Add onion mixture, remaining salt and pepper, curry powder, bay leaf, and tomatoes. Bring to boil, cover and simmer for 1 hour, or until liver is tender. If desired, thicken sauce with a flour-and-water paste. Makes 4 servings.

LIVER AND MUSHROOMS

1 pound cooked liver, cut into pieces
1 cup broiled fresh mushrooms
1 cup brown sauce (gravy from cooking the liver is

good, thickened and well seasoned)
2 tablespoons fresh orange juice
1 tablespoon fresh lemon juice

Combine ingredients. Heat thoroughly. Serve with baked potatoes or on toast. Makes 3 or 4 servings.

DEVILED LIVER IN CROUSTADES

2 onions, sliced
2 tablespoons butter
  or margarine
1 pound beef, pork, calf's,
  or lamb liver, diced
2 tablespoons all-purpose flour
2 teaspoons powdered mustard
1 cup hot water
½ teaspoon salt
⅛ teaspoon pepper
⅓ cup dairy sour cream
4 croustades (toast cups)

Lightly brown onion in 1 tablespoon butter. Push to side of skillet. Add remaining butter. Roll liver in the flour, and brown in the butter. Add mustard, water, salt, and pepper. Bring to boil, stirring constantly. Add sour cream and serve in croustades. Makes 4 servings.

LIVER AND BROWN-RICE RING

4 cups cooked brown rice
  Leftover liver (any kind),
  finely diced (about 1½ cups)
1 tablespoon grated onion
¼ cup minced green pepper
½ cup minced celery
2 tablespoons melted butter or
  margarine
  Salt and pepper
1 can (10½ ounces) concentrated
  tomato soup
½ lemon, thinly sliced

Mix rice, liver, onion, green pepper, celery, and butter. Season to taste with salt and pepper. Add a little water if necessary to make mixture of right consistency to hold together. Press into well-greased 1½-quart ring mold or bowl. Heat in preheated hot oven (400°F.) for 10 minutes. Unmold. Serve with sauce made from soup heated with lemon slices. If desired, add a bit of minced onion and a crumbled bay leaf to the sauce; dilute a little with vegetable cooking water if a thinner sauce is desired. Makes 4 servings.

SMOTHERED LIVER AND ONIONS

5 medium onions, sliced
3 tablespoons shortening
1 pound thinly sliced beef liver
2 tablespoons all-purpose flour
1 teaspoon salt
⅛ teaspoon pepper
¾ cup water

Cook onions in 1 tablespoon hot shortening until golden-brown; remove. Cut away membrane and large tubes from liver. Dredge with flour, salt, and pepper, mixed together. Fry in remaining shortening until browned on both sides. Add

onions and water; cover and simmer for 30 minutes, or until liver is tender. Add more water, if necessary, to prevent sticking. Makes 4 servings.

FRENCH-FRIED LIVER

After pulling off outer skin, with scissors cut 1½ pounds beef liver into strips about 3 x 1½ inches. Snip out any tubes. Dip strips into buttermilk seasoned with salt and pepper. Then roll in dry pancake mix. Fry in hot deep fat (375° F. on frying thermometer) for about 2 minutes, or until lightly browned. Serve with succotash and cooked sweet potatoes browned in fat after removing liver. Makes 4 servings.

PIQUANT LIVER AND VEGETABLES

¼ cup (2 ounces) diced
  salt pork
¾ pound beef liver
2 teaspoons salt
¼ teaspoon pepper
2 tablespoons all-purpose flour
  Fat for frying
3 medium potatoes
3 carrots, scraped
1 can (4 ounces) sliced mushrooms
1 cup canned tomatoes
2 celery stalks, diced
4 small white onions, peeled

Brown salt pork; remove from skillet. Remove membrane and large tubes from liver; cut liver into 1-inch cubes. Dredge liver with 1 teaspoon salt, ⅛ teaspoon pepper, and the flour mixed together. Brown on all sides in hot fat. Peel and quarter potatoes. Quarter carrots. Drain mushrooms, reserving liquid. Put tomatoes and 1 cup mushroom liquid (add water to make 1 cup) in skillet; bring to boil. Add remaining salt and pepper. Put liver, salt pork, and vegetables in 1½-quart casserole; pour tomato mixture over top. Cover; bake in hot oven (400° F.) for 1½ hours. Uncover for last 30 minutes. Makes 4 servings.

SAVORY LIVER-AND-SAUSAGE RING

1½ pounds beef liver
1 pound bulk sausage meat
1 egg, slightly beaten
½ cup dry bread crumbs
2 tablespoons ketchup
1 small onion, grated
1 garlic clove, minced
1½ teaspoons salt
½ teaspoon pepper
  Chopped parsley

Pour boiling water over liver; drain; remove heavy membranes and veins. Force liver through food chopper, using fine blade. Mix with remaining ingredients. Pack into 1-quart ring mold. Bake in preheated slow oven (325°F.) for 1 hour. Serve hot or cold. To serve cold, let cool on rack before turning out on platter. Makes 6 servings.

CREOLE LIVER AND LIMAS

1 pound large dried Lima beans
6 cups water
¾ pound beef liver

3 tablespoons margarine
1 medium onion, chopped
½ cup diced celery
2 cups (one 1-pound can) tomatoes
1 can (8 ounces) tomato sauce
¼ teaspoon hot pepper sauce
1½ teaspoons salt

Wash beans and bring to boil in the water. Boil for 2 minutes, turn off heat, and let stand for 1 hour. Cook until tender; drain and put in casserole. Cut liver into small pieces. Brown in margarine with onion and celery. Add remaining ingredients. Pour over Limas. Bake in preheated moderate oven (350° F.) for 45 minutes. Makes 6 servings.

LIVER AND NOODLES, ITALIAN STYLE

1 pound beef liver
2 tablespoons butter
  or margarine
2 cups cooked wide noodles
1 can (10½ ounces)
  tomato purée
  Salt, pepper, and dried basil
4 slices Mozzarella cheese
8 slices bacon

Sauté liver in the butter until cooked through. Cut into 1-inch cubes. Put noodles in shallow 1-quart baking dish. Add liver and tomato purée. Sprinkle with salt, pepper, and basil to taste. Cover with cheese slices. Bake in preheated moderate oven (350°F.) for about 30 minutes. Just before serving, cook bacon until crisp and put on top of dish. Makes 4 servings.

SWISS LIVER

1½ to 2 pounds calf's liver
  Seasoned flour
3 tablespoons each of butter
  and cooking oil
3 tablespoons each of chopped
  onion and parsley
  Salt and pepper to taste
1 cup dairy sour cream

Cut liver into ½-inch slices, then into strips, and dust with seasoned flour. Heat butter and oil. When hot and bubbly, add onion, parsley, and liver strips. Sauté liver quickly, turning strips to brown on all sides. Do not overcook. Strips should be pink in the center. Season with salt and pepper and add sour cream. Heat cream through, but do not let it boil. Serve on fried toast. Makes 4 servings.

LIVER STEAK BÉARNAISE

Cut 8 ounces of calf's liver per serving into slices 1 to 1½ inches thick. Broil over charcoal or in a broiler until crusty brown outside and still pink and rare in center. Brush with mixture of melted butter and oil several times during broiling. Season to taste. If broiling over charcoal, move coals close to meat for last minute to char outside a bit. Sprinkle with chopped parsley and serve with Béarnaise Sauce.

Quick Béarnaise Sauce
1 teaspoon chopped tarragon
2 teaspoons each of chopped green onion and parsley
3 tablespoons wine vinegar
1 tablespoon water
3 egg yolks
2 teaspoons fresh lemon juice
½ teaspoon salt
　Few grains of cayenne
½ cup melted butter or margarine

In small pan cook tarragon, green onion, parsley, wine vinegar, and water. Cook gently until almost a glaze. Put egg yolks in blender with lemon juice, salt, and cayenne. Flick the blender on and off rapidly, just long enough to blend eggs. Melt butter and bring just to boiling point. With blender turned to high, add melted butter steadily until sauce is thoroughly blended and thickened. Add tarragon mixture and beat until well mixed. Makes enough sauce for 6 servings.

DELICATE LIVER DUMPLINGS
¼ pound calf's liver
2 tablespoons butter or margarine
1 small onion, minced
1 egg, beaten
½ cup fine dry bread crumbs (about)
　Salt and pepper
2 tablespoons minced parsley
　Consommé, bouillon, or soup

Remove any skin or tendons from liver and chop liver very fine. Melt butter, add onion and sauté for 2 or 3 minutes. Add liver and cook for 5 minutes. Cool. Add egg and enough bread crumbs to make a stiff mixture. Season with salt and pepper to taste, and add parsley. Shape into ¾-inch balls. Drop into boiling consommé, cover, and simmer for 15 minutes. Makes about 30 dumplings.

LAMB LIVER

SAVORY BAKED LIVER
1 cup fine dry bread crumbs
½ teaspoon poultry seasoning
¼ cup minced parsley
¾ pound lamb liver, sliced thin
　Juice of 1 lemon
1 cup minced onions
⅔ cup minced celery with leaves
1 tablespoon shortening
1 teaspoon salt
　Dash of pepper
1 bouillon cube
¼ cup water
1 tablespoon butter

Mix crumbs, poultry seasoning, and parsley. Put half of mixture in bottom of a well-greased shallow baking dish. Remove membranes and large tubes from liver. Put thin slices of liver on top of crumbs; sprinkle with lemon juice. Cook onions and celery in shortening in

skillet for 5 minutes; spread on liver. Add salt, pepper, and bouillon cube to water; mix well and pour over contents of baking dish. Top with remaining crumb mixture. Dot with butter. Bake in preheated moderate oven (350°F.) for 1 hour. Makes 4 servings.

Note: Pork liver may also be substituted for the lamb liver.

LIVER BALLS AND NOODLES
½ pound lamb liver
1 onion, minced
¼ cup minced parsley
2 cups fine soft bread crumbs
1 egg
1 teaspoon salt
⅛ teaspoon pepper
1 can (10½ ounces) condensed tomato soup
　About 5 cups (10 ounces) noodles, cooked

Cover liver with boiling water; let stand for 2 minutes; remove membrane and cut into pieces; force liver through food chopper twice. Combine with onion, parsley, crumbs, egg, and salt and pepper. Mix well and shape into small balls. Cook a few at a time in 1 quart boiling salted water for 3 minutes; with perforated ladle remove to hot dish. Combine 1 cup of liver-ball cooking liquid with soup; add noodles; heat. Pour over liver balls. Also serve whole-wheat bread and celery and apple salad. Makes 4 servings.

Note: Pork liver may be substituted for the lamb liver in this recipe.

LAMB LIVER, CREOLE
¾ pound sliced lamb liver
2 tablespoons all-purpose flour
1 teaspoon salt
　Dash of cayenne
2 tablespoons shortening
½ bay leaf, crumbled
1 can (8 ounces) tomato sauce
2 tablespoons cider vinegar
½ cup water

Remove membrane from liver and cut liver into thin strips; dip into mixture of flour, salt, and cayenne. Melt fat in skillet, add liver, and brown lightly. Add remaining ingredients; cover and simmer for about 40 minutes. Makes 2 servings.

LAMB-LIVER POT ROAST WITH NOODLES
2 lamb livers (about 2 pounds)
2 cups boiling water
2 tablespoons all-purpose flour
¼ cup bacon fat
3 parsley sprigs
1 bay leaf
⅛ teaspoon ground thyme
1 tablespoon salt
¼ teaspoon pepper
1 onion, sliced
　Hot cooked broad noodles

Wash livers and cover with boiling water. Drain, reserving water. Dry livers and dredge with flour. Brown on all sides in hot fat in heavy saucepan or Dutch oven. Add seasonings, onion, and reserved

water. Cover and simmer for 1½ hours, or until done. Remove livers and slice. Thicken liquid with flour-and-water paste, if desired. Season to taste and serve with liver on hot noodles. Makes 6 servings.

PORK LIVER

DANISH LIVER PÂTÉ
1½ pounds pork liver
6 slices of bacon
1 large onion
⅔ cup milk
⅔ cup light cream
3 tablespoons flour
1 teaspoon pepper
1 tablespoon salt
¼ teaspoon each of ground cloves and allspice
2 eggs, well beaten

Put liver, 4 slices of bacon, and the onion through a food chopper 4 or 5 times, until mixture is as smooth as paste. Beat milk and cream gradually into flour, seasonings, and spices. Cook over low heat, stirring constantly, until smooth and thickened. When mixture has thickened and is still hot, stir it into the beaten eggs. Cool, and mix with meat and onion. Grease a loaf pan (9 x 5 x 3 inches) and pour this batter into it. Lay last 2 slices of bacon across the top. Set the pan in a pan of hot water and bake for 1½ hours in a slow oven (325°F.). Cool; store in the refrigerator. Makes 8 to 10 servings.

Note: This is a softer dish than the usual French pâté, and also makes a good sandwich spread.

PORK LIVER AND VEGETABLES
1½ cups boiling water
1 pork liver (about 2 pounds)
2 tablespoons all-purpose flour
¼ cup bacon fat
3 parsley sprigs
1 bay leaf
⅛ teaspoon ground thyme
2 teaspoons salt
¼ teaspoon pepper
1 onion, sliced
2 cups sliced carrots
1½ cups sliced parsnips
4 potatoes, peeled and cubed

Pour water over liver; drain, reserving water. Remove tough outer membrane from liver; dry meat and dredge with flour. Brown on all sides in fat. Add reserved water and seasonings. Cover and simmer for 1 hour. Add vegetables and simmer for about 30 minutes longer. Makes 6 servings.

PORK LIVER WITH BARBECUE SAUCE
½ pound very thinly sliced pork liver
¼ cup canned tomato purée
2 teaspoons cider vinegar
　Dash of Worcestershire
1 garlic clove, minced
½ teaspoon salt
　Dash of cayenne
¼ cup water

2 tablespoons all-purpose flour
½ teaspoon salt
Dash of pepper
1 tablespoon bacon fat

If liver is not sliced thin, remove membrane, wrap liver in wax paper, and freeze overnight in refrigerator tray. Cut diagonally into thin slices when ready to cook. Prepare barbecue sauce by mixing together tomato purée, vinegar, Worcestershire, garlic, salt, cayenne, and water. Dredge each piece of liver with a mixture of flour, salt, and pepper. Brown quickly in bacon fat. Add barbecue sauce and cook, covered, for about 3 minutes, or just until liver is no longer pink. Do not overcook liver. Add more seasoning to taste and serve very hot. Makes 2 servings.

FRENCH PORK LIVER WITH ONIONS
2 large onions, sliced
¼ cup bacon fat or lard
Salt and pepper
8 thin slices pork liver
All-purpose flour
3 tablespoons vinegar
Chopped parsley

Sauté onions in half of the bacon fat until soft and golden. Season with salt and pepper; keep hot. Season pork liver with salt and pepper, and coat lightly with flour. Sauté in remaining bacon fat for 5 minutes, or until of desired doneness. Put liver on hot serving dish and keep hot. Pour off excess fat from pan in which liver was cooked. Put in hot onions and stir in vinegar. Bring to a quick boil. Spoon onions over liver, and sprinkle with parsley. Makes 4 servings.

SAVORY LIVER AND VEGETABLE PIE
3 slices bacon, diced
1 pound pork liver, diced
2 medium onions, chopped
1 can (3 or 4 ounces)
   sliced mushrooms
¾ cup diced celery and tops
2 medium carrots,
   peeled and diced
1 beef bouillon cube
½ teaspoon salt
2 cups boiling water
½ cup dry sherry
   Dash each of sage, pepper,
   and paprika
½ teaspoon Worcestershire
   Pastry

Cook bacon until browned, and remove from skillet. Cook liver in the fat in skillet until browned and done. Add onion and cook for a few minutes. Mix mushrooms and liquid, celery, carrots, bouillon cube, salt, water, and sherry. Bring to boil, cover, and simmer for 15 minutes, or until carrot is tender. Drain, measure liquid and, if necessary, add enough water to make 2 cups. Add bacon, liver, onion, and remaining seasonings. Bring to boil and put in shallow 1½ quart baking dish. Roll Pastry to fit top of dish. Bake in preheated hot oven (425°F.) for 20 minutes, or until

browned. Makes 6 servings.

Pastry
Sift together 1½ cups all-purpose flour, 1½ teaspoons baking powder, and ½ teaspoon salt. Cut in 1 tablespoon shortening. Add enough milk to make a soft dough that can be rolled (about ½ cup). **Note:** If preferred, 1½ cups biscuit mix may be substituted for the Pastry. Prepare mix as for biscuits.

POULTRY LIVER

Note: Poultry livers can generally be used interchangeably in recipes.

CHICKEN-LIVER PÂTÉ
1 pound chicken livers
1 small onion, halved
¾ cup chicken bouillon
½ teaspoon each of paprika
   and curry powder
1 teaspoon salt
1 tablespoon Worcestershire
¼ teaspoon pepper
¾ cup butter or margarine
   Canned beef consommé (gelatin
   type)

Simmer chicken livers and onion in bouillon for 5 minutes, or until done. Pour all into blender. Add remaining ingredients except butter and consommé; whirl until smooth. Remove cover and add butter, a little at a time, blending until smooth. Put into dishes and chill. When set, pour a thin layer of consommé over top. Refrigerate. Makes 3 cups.

CHOPPED CHICKEN LIVER
1 pound chicken livers
3 hard-cooked eggs
1 small onion
   Salt and pepper
¼ cup cooking oil
   or chicken fat
2 tablespoons mayonnaise

Broil livers until done. Do not overcook. Force through food chopper with eggs and onion. Add salt and pepper to taste, the oil, and mayonnaise. Beat with electric mixer until smooth and fluffy. Chill. Makes 6 servings.

CHOPPED GOOSE LIVER AND GREBEN
1 pound cooked goose liver
1 cup greben*
   Salt and pepper
   Hard-cooked eggs
   Parsley

Force liver and greben through food chopper, using fine blade. Season with salt and pepper to taste. Chill, and serve as a canapé spread with a garnish of wedges of hard-cooked egg and parsley. Makes about 3 cups.
*Greben are cracklings obtained from the rendering of chicken or goose fat.

ITALIAN RICE SOUP WITH CHICKEN LIVERS
½ cup uncooked rice
1 tablespoon butter or margarine

4 cups chicken bouillon
   Salt and pepper
4 chicken livers, cooked
1 egg yolk
   Chopped parsley
   Grated Parmesan cheese

Lightly brown rice in the butter. Add bouillon, bring to boil, and season with salt and pepper. Cover and simmer until rice is done. Meanwhile, chop chicken livers and mix with beaten egg yolk. Remove rice from heat; add liver mixture. Serve in bowls with a sprinkling of parsley and grated cheese. Makes 4 to 6 servings.

SAUTÉED CHICKEN LIVERS AND GREEN BEANS
1 pound chicken livers
¼ cup all-purpose flour
1 teaspoon salt
¼ teaspoon pepper
½ teaspoon poultry seasoning
¼ cup butter or margarine
¾ cup chicken bouillon
1 package (9 ounces) frozen cut
   green beans, cooked

Cut livers into halves and dredge with flour seasoned with salt, pepper, and poultry seasoning. Heat butter in top part of double boiler over direct heat until it begins to brown. Add livers and sauté until lightly browned. Add bouillon and simmer for a few minutes. Put over boiling water; add beans, cover, and heat thoroughly. Makes 4 servings.

CHICKEN LIVERS WITH CARROTS AND PEAS
1 package (10 ounces) frozen peas
   and carrots
1 pound fresh or partially
   thawed chicken livers
   All-purpose flour (about ¼ cup)
10 tablespoons butter or margarine
1 cup milk
¼ teaspoon poultry seasoning
1 chicken bouillon cube

Cook peas and carrots in a little salted water, covered, until tender; drain and put in bottom of a shallow 1-quart casserole. With a kitchen fork prick chicken livers several times to prevent popping. Dredge with a little flour. Fry quickly in ½ cup hot butter in skillet until nicely browned on all sides. Arrange over vegetables. Add 2 tablespoons butter to skillet and stir in 2 tablespoons flour. Gradually stir in milk, poultry seasoning, and bouillon cube. Cook until slightly thickened, stirring constantly. Pour over livers. Bake in preheated moderate oven (350°F.) for 15 minutes. Can be frozen. Makes 4 servings.

CHICKEN-LIVER OMELET
4 eggs
¼ cup water
½ teaspoon salt
⅛ teaspoon pepper
4 tablespoons butter
   or margarine
4 chicken livers, diced

Beat eggs slightly, just enough to blend

whites and yolks. Add water and seasonings. Melt 2 tablespoons butter in small skillet, add livers, and sauté until lightly browned. Heat remaining butter in omelet pan or skillet. When butter sizzles, add egg mixture and reduce heat. As omelet cooks, lift with a spatula, allowing uncooked part to run under. When firm and browned underneath, add half the chicken liver and fold over. Put on a hot platter and top with remaining liver. Makes 2 servings.

CHICKEN LIVERS IN SOUR CREAM
¼ cup chicken fat or butter
2 teaspoons bottled gravy sauce
1 medium onion, thinly sliced
1 pound chicken livers
1½ teaspoons salt
¼ teaspoon pepper
⅛ teaspoon crushed rosemary
1 can (6 ounces) sliced mushrooms
1 tablespoon cornstarch
1 cup dairy sour cream
 Chopped parsley
 Hot cooked rice (optional)

Heat chicken fat, and add gravy sauce and onion. Cook for 5 minutes, stirring frequently. Add chicken livers and sprinkle with salt, pepper, and rosemary. Cook, stirring occasionally, until livers are well browned, about 10 minutes. Drain mushrooms, reserving liquid. Mix cornstarch and liquid, and add to livers. Cook, stirring constantly, until thickened. Add mushrooms and sour cream. Cover and heat for 5 minutes. Sprinkle with parsley, and serve with hot rice, if desired. Makes 4 to 6 servings.

LIVER-AND-BACON SANDWICHES
Cook 8 slices of bacon until crisp. Remove bacon and pour off some of fat. With fork, prick 1 pound chicken livers. Put in fat and cook until browned on both sides. Force through food chopper, using medium blade. Then put bacon and 1 peeled small onion through food chopper. Add 2 tablespoons prepared mustard and enough mayonnaise or salad dressing to moisten. Season to taste with salt and pepper. Spread between 8 slices of bread. Serve with tomato wedges. Makes 4 servings.

CHICKEN-LIVER SAUCE
1 onion, minced
2 garlic cloves, minced
¼ cup olive oil
3½ cups (one 1-pound 13-ounce can) tomatoes
1 can (6 ounces) tomato paste
1¾ cups water
2 teaspoons salt
¼ teaspoon pepper
1 bay leaf
¼ teaspoon poultry seasoning
½ pound chicken livers
1 can (2 ounces) sliced mushrooms, drained
12 ounces spaghetti, cooked

Sauté onion and garlic in 2 tablespoons olive oil until lightly browned. Add to-matoes, tomato paste, water, salt, pepper, bay leaf, and poultry seasoning. Cut chicken livers into pieces and cook in remaining olive oil until browned. Add, with sliced mushrooms, to tomato mixture. Simmer, uncovered, for 2 hours, stirring occasionally. Serve on spaghetti. Makes 6 servings.

LIVERWURST or LIVER SAUSAGE—
A ready-to-eat sausage made of finely ground lean pork and pork liver mixed with spices and seasonings. It must contain at least thirty per cent pork liver. Liverwurst is usually boiled or smoked. The name comes from the German *wurst*, meaning "sausage." The most famous variety is Braunschweiger, a soft and pink liverwurst named after the German town of Braunschweig. Other varieties are darker and firmer.

Availability and Purchasing Guide—Available year round in bulk, in a loaf, and packaged, whole or in slices. The loaf is sometimes called liver cheese and is covered with fresh white pork fat to keep it moist.

Liverwurst is also available canned, as are various spreads, pastes, and pâtés.

Storage—Should be refrigerated in a covered dish or in the original wrapper. Freezing is not recommended.

☐ Canned, kitchen shelf, unopened: 1 year
☐ Refrigerator shelf: 1 week

Nutritive Food Values—An excellent source of iron and vitamin A.

☐ 3½ ounces = 307 calories

MUSHROOM LIVER PÂTÉ
½ pound mushrooms, sliced
1 tablespoon butter
1 pound liverwurst
1 cup dairy sour cream
¼ cup brandy
1 tablespoon chopped scallions
1 teaspoon soy sauce
1 teaspoon sharp prepared mustard
 Parsley
 Melba rounds

Sauté mushrooms in butter until tender. Mash liverwurst and blend with mushrooms and remaining ingredients except last two. Pile in dish and garnish with parsley. Chill. Serve with melba rounds. Makes about 4 cups.

LIVERWURST WITH CREOLE SAUCE
1 large onion, sliced
 Bacon fat or margarine
½ green pepper, chopped
½ teaspoon salt
⅛ teaspoon pepper
4 ripe tomatoes, chopped
¾ pound liverwurst in one piece
½ cup undiluted evaporated milk
⅔ cup cornmeal

To make sauce, cook onion in 2 tablespoons bacon fat for 2 or 3 minutes. Add next 4 ingredients, bring to boil and simmer, uncovered, for 20 minutes. Cut liverwurst in 8 slices. Cut each half and dip in milk, then in cornmeal. Sauté quickly in small amount of bacon fat until delicately browned. Drain on absorbent paper. Serve with the sauce. Makes 4 servings.

LIVERWURST PATTIES
To equal parts of mashed liverwurst, mashed potatoes, and broken bread crusts soaked in milk, add minced onion, salt, pepper, and poultry seasoning to taste; mix well. Drop from spoon onto hot greased skillet; brown on both sides.

LIVERWURST, POTATO, AND EGG SALAD
2 cups diced cooked potatoes
3 hard-cooked eggs, diced
1 cup diced celery
1 tablespoon minced onion
½ cup each of cubed hard salami, liverwurst, and sharp Cheddar cheese
1 cup shredded cabbage
¼ cup olive oil
 Salt and pepper to taste
½ cup mayonnaise
 Salad greens
 Chopped parsley

Mix first 8 ingredients. Add olive oil and salt and pepper. Mix lightly but well. Stir in mayonnaise. Serve salad on greens with a sprinkling of parsley. Makes 4 servings.

LIVERWURST SANDWICHES
½ pound liverwurst
1 package (3 ounces) cream cheese
2 hard-cooked eggs, chopped
 Mayonnaise
⅛ teaspoon onion salt
 Salt and pepper
12 slices rye bread
 Soft butter or margarine

Mash liverwurst, and mix with cream cheese and eggs. Add enough mayonnaise to moisten. Add onion salt, and salt and pepper to taste. Spread bread with butter, then with liverwurst mixture. Put slices together to make 6 sandwiches.

LOBSTER—A member of the family of crustaceans, to which shrimps and crabs also belong. They lack spinal columns and have "crusty" outer skeletons or shells with jointed bodies and limbs.

The familiar American lobster (*Homarus americanus*) closely resembles the European lobster (*H. vulgaris*). The small Cape lobster (*H. capensis*) of southern Africa is also a relation. The Cape lobster, living in many southern waters such as the Gulf of Mexico, is also called spiny lobster or rock lobster. It lacks the huge claws characteristic of the American lobster.

The American lobster, found off the Atlantic coast from North Carolina to Labrador, has five pairs of legs. The first pair is modified into huge claws or pincers, notched on the inside edge, with which the lobster catches and crushes its food. The huge, hinged tail is a powerful lever for swimming. The large claws and tail contain the most meat.

The lobster's eyes are on stalks, and there are two pairs of waving antennae. It is not surprising that an ancestor of the word "lobster" is the Anglo-Saxon *lobbe* or "spider."

Live lobsters are mottled and splotched greenish blue, with touches of orange. The vivid red color, characteristic of lobster, comes out in cooking.

Whole lobsters, boiled, broiled, or baked, or the meat in stews, salads, or casseroles, are delicious eating. In early days when the first English settlers came to America, lobsters were sold for as little as a penny apiece. They were extremely large: it has been reported that six-foot lobsters were caught by the Dutch in New Amsterdam waters.

Lobsters have always been a part of one of the oldest and most cherished of New England customs—the clambake. Buried in a pit with hot stones, often wrapped in seaweed, and served with all sorts of other delicacies, lobsters are as much a part of a clambake as are steamed clams.

Availability—Fresh lobsters are available year round, live, cooked whole, or as cooked meat.

Frozen cooked lobster meat and uncooked rock-lobster tails are available, as is lobster Newburg.

Canned lobster meat and rock-lobster tail meat is available, as is lobster Newburg, lobster Thermidor, bisque, and chowder.

Purchasing Guide—Fresh live lobsters are available in varying sizes: "Jumbo" weighs over 2 pounds, "Large" weighs from 1½ to 2 pounds, "Quarters" weigh 1¼ pounds, "Eighths" weigh 1⅛ pounds, "Chicken" lobsters are the smallest and weigh 1 pound.

Look for live lobsters with tails that curl under the body when they are picked up; this is an indication of freshness. Cooked lobster in the shell should be bright red in color and have an agreeable odor. Cooked meat should be firm and pinkish- or reddish-white.

☐ Two 1-pound lobsters = ½ pound cooked lobster meat

Storage—Fresh, live lobsters should be cooked immediately. Do not attempt to keep lobsters alive by placing in water; they will suffocate. Keep frozen lobster solidly frozen until ready to use.

☐ Fresh, cooked; and canned, opened and covered, refrigerator shelf: 1 to 2 days

☐ Fresh, prepared for freezing; or frozen, refrigerator frozen-food compartment: 1 month

☐ Fresh, prepared for freezing; and frozen, freezer: 6 months

☐ Canned, kitchen shelf: 1 year

Do not refreeze frozen lobster once it has been thawed.

Nutritive Food Values—Lobster is a good source of protein and iron. It is low in fat.

☐ 3½ ounces, cooked and shelled = 95 calories

Basic Preparation

☐ **To Boil**—Fill a large kettle with sufficient water to cover lobsters. Add 1 tablespoon salt for each quart of water. Bring water to a rolling boil. Grab live lobsters, one at a time, at the back of their heads, just beyond the claws. Do not let claws reach you. Plunge lobsters head first into boiling water. Simmer, covered, for 5 minutes for the first pound and 3 more minutes for each additional pound of lobster. (1½-pound lobsters will cook in about 8 to 10 minutes, 2-pound lobsters will take 11 to 12 minutes).

Remove cooked lobster from water. Place it on a board or work table on its back. With a heavy, sharp knife or a mallet or hammer, split lobster in half lengthwise, from head to tail. Remove the stomach and the intestinal tract. Keep the green liver (also called "tomalley") or any reddish deposit. This latter is the roe of the lobster and it is called "coral." Both liver and coral are used in some lobster recipes. Crack claws with a nutcracker and remove meat carefully, in pieces as large as possible.

☐ **To Broil**—Use a sharp knife with a point. Place live lobster on its back with the large claws over its head. Insert the point of the knife just under the mouth and with a quick motion draw the knife down the whole length of the body, splitting the lobster into 2 halves. Open out the body and remove the intestinal vein, liver, roe, and stomach, which is located just under the head. Save liver and roe.

Crack claws.

Brush cut surfaces with a mixture of half melted butter and half fresh lemon juice. Put lobster under broiler at least 6 inches away from the source of heat and broil, without turning, until shell turns red and flesh becomes white and opaque and flecked with brown. Sprinkle with salt and serve with additional hot melted butter mixed with lemon juice. Allow one 1½-pound lobster for each serving.

☐ **To Broil Rock-Lobster Tails**—Put thawed rock-lobster tails on broiler pan and brush with melted butter. Broil under medium heat, brushing occasionally with butter, until done, 8 to 12 minutes.

☐ **To Freeze**—Use only live lobsters for freezing. To freeze in the shell, plunge the lobster into boiling water. Remove as soon as the lobster starts to turn color. Cool as quickly as possible. Wrap in moisture- vapor-proof wrapping, excluding as much air as possible. Seal and freeze.

To freeze lobster meat, plunge lobsters into boiling water and cook. (See directions on To Boil for time.) Cool, and remove meat from shell. Pack meat tightly into a freezer container allowing ½-inch headspace. Seal.

LOBSTER AND ORANGE COCKTAIL

1 pound cooked lobster meat
¼ teaspoon salt
2 large navel oranges
  Lettuce
  Cocktail Sauce
  Ground nutmeg

Cut lobster meat into ½-inch pieces; sprinkle with salt. Peel and section oranges. Combine orange sections and lobster meat. Chill. Arrange lettuce in 6 cocktail glasses. Place lobster mixture on top; cover with Cocktail Sauce. Garnish with nutmeg. Makes 6 servings.

Cocktail Sauce
¼ cup heavy cream, whipped
1 tablespoon mayonnaise or
  salad dressing
2 tablespoons fresh orange juice

Blend whipped cream with mayonnaise and orange juice. Makes 6 servings.

LOBSTER BISQUE

Remove any membrane from 1 can (6½ ounces) lobster. Separate meat into small pieces, put in bowl, and cover with ⅓ cup dry sherry. Let stand for 20 minutes. In top part of double boiler, over simmering water, melt ¼ cup butter or margarine. Blend in 3 tablespoons flour. Gradually add 3 cups milk and cook, stirring, until thickened. Season with 1 teaspoon steak sauce, salt, seasoned salt, and pepper to taste. Add soaked lobster with the sherry; simmer, covered, for 10 minutes. Makes about 4 cups, or 4 servings.

ROCK-LOBSTER CHOWDER

6 frozen rock-lobster tails
   (3 to 5 ounces each)
2 egg yolks, hard-cooked
1 tablespoon butter
1 tablespoon flour
   Grated rind of 1 lemon
   Dash of pepper
4 cups milk
½ cup heavy cream
½ teaspoon salt
½ teaspoon cayenne
1 teaspoon aromatic bitters
1 tablespoon dry
   Spanish sherry (optional)

Thaw rock-lobster tails. Cut away underside membrane and remove meat from shell. Dice lobster meat. Mash egg yolks to paste with fork. Add butter, flour, lemon rind, and pepper and blend thoroughly. Bring milk to boil and gradually stir into paste. Add lobster pieces and simmer over low heat for 5 minutes. Add cream and bring to boil again, stirring constantly. Add salt, cayenne, bitters, and sherry if desired. Serve very hot. Do not boil after adding sherry. Makes 6 servings.

LOBSTER STEW

One 2-pound lobster
   Butter
3 cups milk
1 cup heavy cream
   Salt, pepper, and paprika

Boil lobster and remove meat. Cut into cubes and fry in plenty of butter until lightly browned. Scald milk; add to lobster meat and cook slowly for about 5 minutes. Add cream and bring almost to boil, but do not allow to boil. Add salt and pepper to taste and paprika to heighten color. This dish is even better if it stands for a few hours before you reheat and serve. Makes 3 servings.

STEAMED LOBSTER TAILS

4 frozen rock-lobster tails
   (3 to 5 ounces each)
1 bay leaf
   Salt
½ cup mayonnaise
½ cup dairy sour cream
2 tablespoons prepared horseradish
1 tablespoon capers, drained
   Freshly ground pepper to taste

Cook unthawed lobster tails, covered, in 1 inch of boiling salted water with bay leaf in electric skillet or cooker-fryer for 6 to 10 minutes. Remove from water, split each tail, and loosen meat, but leave in shell to serve. Mix remaining ingredients and serve as sauce with lobster. Makes 4 servings.

FRENCH-FRIED BUTTERFLY LOBSTER

Cut 3 cooked shelled rock-lobster tails into sections 1 inch in length. Make a small cut in center of each scallop or section. Stuff a thin slice of water chestnut into each section. Make a batter of ⅔ cup cornstarch mixed with 2 beaten eggs. Dip lobster pieces into additional plain cornstarch and then into batter. Fry in deep hot fat (370°F. on a frying thermometer) for 3 to 4 minutes, or until golden brown. Serve with soy sauce and mustard, if you wish. Makes 3 servings.

LOBSTER NEWBURG

2 cups cooked or canned lobster
2 tablespoons butter or margarine
¼ teaspoon salt
   Dash of cayenne
3 tablespoons sherry
3 egg yolks
1 cup light cream
   Buttered toast

Heat lobster in butter for a few minutes. Add salt, cayenne, and sherry. Beat egg yolks; slightly mix with cream and add to lobster. Cook over low heat until thickened, but do not boil. Stir constantly. Serve at once on hot toast. Makes 4 servings.

LOBSTER SOUFFLÉ

One 2- to 2½-pound lobster
   Salt, pepper, and paprika
7 tablespoons butter or margarine
2 celery stalks, finely chopped
2 onions, finely chopped
2 carrots, finely chopped
¼ cup brandy
1 cup white wine
1 cup light cream
1½ tablespoons all-purpose flour
3 egg yolks, well beaten
5 egg whites

Split lobster and remove liver, intestines, and coral, if any. Season each half to taste with salt, pepper, and paprika. In a heavy skillet melt 5 tablespoons butter and add chopped vegetables. Place lobster halves on top and cook until shells turn red. Pour brandy over lobster and blaze. Add wine and cook gently for 15 minutes. Remove lobster from pan; when cool enough to handle, take the meat from body and claws, cut into bite-size pieces, and return it to shells. To the broth in the pan add the liver, coral, intestines, and ½ cup cream. Heat through thoroughly and then put through a fine sieve or mix in an electric blender. Arrange lobster meat in the shells in a 2-quart dish. Pour half of sauce over lobster. Make a rich cream sauce with 2 tablespoons butter, the flour, and ½ cup cream. Let cool slightly and add egg yolks. Season to taste. Beat egg whites until stiff but not dry and fold them into the cream sauce. Heap this mixture on top of the two lobster halves. Bake in preheated very hot oven (450°F.) for 15 to 20 minutes, or until puffed and browned on top. Serve with remaining lobster sauce. Makes 3 to 4 servings.

ROCK LOBSTER IN ALMOND SAUCE

6 frozen rock-lobster tails
   (3 to 5 ounces)
   Boiling salted water
1 cup slivered blanched almonds
6 tablespoons butter
3 tablespoons flour
½ teaspoon paprika
   Salt and pepper to taste
2 cups milk

Cook lobster tails in boiling salted water for 6 minutes. Drain and drench with cold water. Remove meat from shells and slice. Brown almonds in butter. Blend in flour and seasonings; add milk and cook, stirring, until thickened. Add lobster, and reheat. Makes 6 servings.

CURRIED ROCK LOBSTER

6 frozen rock-lobster tails
   (3 to 5 ounces)
4 cups boiling water
1 teaspoon salt
1 bay leaf
2 tablespoons minced onion
2 celery stalks, minced
¼ teaspoon ground thyme
2 tablespoons minced parsley
3 tablespoons butter or margarine
3 tablespoons flour
1 bouillon cube
2 or more teaspoons curry powder
1 teaspoon paprika
½ cup heavy cream
   Juice of ½ lemon
   Hot cooked rice

Cook lobster tails in boiling water seasoned with salt and bay leaf for 6 minutes. Remove tails and rinse with cold water. Reserve stock and reduce to 1½ cups by boiling. Discard bay leaf. Remove lobster meat from shells, and dice. Cook next 4 ingredients in butter for 2 or 3 minutes. Blend in flour. Add bouillon cube, curry, and paprika. Stir in reserved stock and cook, stirring, until thickened. Add cream, lemon juice, and lobster; heat. Serve on rice. Makes 6 servings.

LOBSTER AU BRANDY

4 lobsters (1¼ pounds each)
2 tablespoons butter or margarine
½ teaspoon cayenne
1 tablespoon salt
   Freshly ground black pepper to taste
¼ cup minced shallots
½ cup brandy
1 cup clam juice or fish stock
1 bay leaf
½ teaspoon crumbled dried thyme
2 parsley sprigs
2 cups heavy cream
2 tablespoons flour

Plunge lobsters into boiling water. As soon as they turn red, remove claws. Remove tails and cut each tail crosswise into 4 pieces. Split forecarcass and remove coral and liver. Reserve. Heat 1 tablespoon butter in a skillet and add lobster pieces. Add cayenne, salt, and pepper. Cook, stirring, for 5 minutes. Add shallots and ¼ cup brandy. Cover and cook for 7 minutes longer. Add clam juice, bay leaf, thyme, and parsley. Cover and cook for an additional 15 minutes. Add 1 cup cream and cook for 5 minutes more. Remove lobster and remove meat from shells. Add remaining butter to coral and liver. Stir in flour. Gradually stir in remaining cream. Heat liquid in which lobster was cooked and gradually

Lobster Newburg

stir in coral mixture. Cook over low heat, stirring constantly, until smooth and thickened. Sprinkle with remaining brandy and reheat slightly. Serve with rice. Makes 4 to 6 servings.

MOLDED EGG-LOBSTER SALAD
1 envelope unflavored gelatin
2 cups milk
¾ cup mayonnaise or salad dressing
1½ teaspoons seasoned salt
¼ teaspoon pepper
1 teaspoon curry powder
1 tablespoon instant minced onion
1 can (5½ ounces) lobster, diced
1 cup diced celery
  Juice of 1 lemon
6 hard-cooked eggs
  Salad greens

Sprinkle gelatin on 1 cup of the milk; heat, stirring to dissolve gelatin. To remaining milk add mayonnaise and seasonings; beat until blended. Add next 3 ingredients and 4 eggs, diced. Pour into 6-cup mold; chill until firm. Unmold on greens and garnish with remaining eggs, sliced. Makes 4 servings.

CRAB-STUFFED LOBSTER
One 2-pound lobster
  Butter or margarine
2 tablespoons all-purpose flour
2 tablespoons minced parsley
1 tablespoon fresh lemon juice
1 tablespoon prepared mustard
1 teaspoon prepared horseradish
1 teaspoon salt
1 cup milk
1 cup tiny soft bread cubes
1 package (6 ounces) frozen crabmeat, thawed, drained, and flaked
  Fine dry bread crumbs
  Grated Parmesan cheese

Have lobster split down center, cleaned, and claws cracked. Remove liver and coral, and set aside for stuffing. Melt ¼ cup butter in saucepan. Stir in flour, parsley, lemon juice, mustard, horseradish, and salt. Gradually add milk, and cook, stirring constantly, until thickened. Add bread cubes, crab, liver, and coral. Heat and stir only until blended. Pack into and over cavity of lobster. Sprinkle with crumbs and cheese, and dot with butter. Bake in preheated hot oven (400° F.) for 25 to 30 minutes, or until dark golden-brown. Makes 3 to 4 servings.

LOBSTER CASSEROLE À LA COSTA
2 medium onions, chopped
1 garlic clove, minced
¼ cup butter or margarine
1 small bay leaf
½ teaspoon cuminseed, crushed
½ teaspoon monosodium glutamate
½ teaspoon salt
¼ teaspoon pepper
1 can (8 ounces) tomato sauce
2 cups water
1⅓ cups instant rice
2 cups cooked lobster
  or rock-lobster meat, cut
  into bite-size pieces

Cook onions and garlic in 3 tablespoons butter for 5 minutes. Add remaining in-gredients except 1 tablespoon butter and bring to boil. Pour into 1½-quart casserole and dot with remaining butter. Cover. Bake in preheated moderate oven (375°F.) for about 30 minutes. Makes 4 servings.

ROCK LOBSTER AND FILLET OF COD SARAPICO
1 pound frozen rock-lobster tails, thawed
6 pieces fresh cod fillets (about 2¼ pounds)
3 tablespoons butter
3 tablespoons flour
½ teaspoon ground turmeric
¾ teaspoon salt
½ teaspoon pepper
1 cup heavy cream
1 package (3 ounces) cream cheese
½ cup crumbled blue cheese
½ cup dry white wine
⅓ cup each of chopped ripe olives and pimiento
1 lime or lemon, thinly sliced

Put lobster tails in large kettle of boiling salted water. Simmer for 10 minutes; drain. Cut shell; remove meat and cut into large pieces. Poach cod in seasoned water until fish flakes and is done; drain. Melt butter in saucepan; blend in flour, turmeric, salt, and pepper. Add cream and cook until thickened, stirring constantly. Blend in cheeses and wine. Put each piece of cod on a 12-inch square of foil. Put some lobster on each. Sprinkle with olives and pimiento. Pour sauce over. Put slices of lime on each. Wrap foil around fish and pinch edges tightly together to close package. Put in shallow baking pan and bake in preheated hot oven (400°F.) for about 15 minutes, or until heated. Serve 1 package for each person. Makes 6 servings.

JELLIED LOBSTER RING
1 envelope unflavored gelatin
¼ cup cold water
½ cup boiling water
½ cup mayonnaise
¼ cup ketchup
  Juice of 1 lemon
2 cups diced cooked lobster meat
½ cup diced celery
2 tablespoons minced sweet pickles
2 tablespoons chopped pitted green olives
¼ teaspoon salt
  Salad greens
1 package (10 ounces) frozen peas, cooked
2 green onions, chopped
  French Dressing

Soften gelatin in cold water; dissolve in boiling water. Add next 8 ingredients. Pour into 5-cup ring mold and chill until firm. Unmold on greens. Fill center with peas and onions moistened with dressing. Makes 4 to 6 servings.

Jellied Crabmeat Ring
Use recipe for Jellied Lobster Ring, substituting 2 cups flaked cooked crabmeat for the lobster.

Jellied Fish Ring
Use recipe for Jellied Lobster Ring, substituting 2 cups flaked poached flounder for the lobster.

Jellied Shrimp Ring
Use recipe for Jellied Lobster Ring, substituting 2 cups diced cooked shrimps for the lobster.

SOUTH AFRICAN DEVILED ROCK LOBSTER
8 frozen rock-lobster tails (6 ounces each)
½ cup butter or margarine
6 tablespoons all-purpose flour
¼ cup heavy cream
¾ cup milk
3 tablespoons each of finely chopped onion, green pepper, and celery
2 teaspoons powdered mustard
2 tablespoons ketchup
1 tablespoon each of Worcestershire and aromatic bitters
1 teaspoon salt
1 tablespoon each of paprika, chopped parsley, and fresh lemon juice
½ cup toasted bread crumbs

Drop frozen lobster tails into large kettle of boiling salted water. Cook for 5 minutes after water reboils. Drain off water; drench tails with cold water. Cut through underside membrane with kitchen scissors. Remove meat and reserve shells. Flake lobster meat with fork. Melt 6 tablespoons butter in saucepan, blend in flour, stir in cream and milk, and cook until thickened. Sauté onion, pepper, and celery in remaining butter. Add to cream sauce. Stir in mustard, ketchup, Worcestershire, bitters, salt, paprika, parsley, and lemon juice. Add lobster meat. Heat thoroughly. Fill shells with lobster mixture. Sprinkle tops with bread crumbs and dot with additional butter. Put under broiler for a few minutes until bread crumbs are golden-brown. Makes 8 servings.

CHICKEN AND LOBSTER, COSTA BRAVA
3 frozen rock-lobster tails (about 7 ounces each)
1 frying chicken, cut up
½ cup chicken bouillon
¼ cup olive oil
1 carrot, peeled and grated
2 leeks or 6 green onions, minced
¾ cup dry sherry
½ cup brandy
¾ teaspoon salt
  Dash of pepper
1 tablespoon tomato paste or ketchup
½ cup canned beef gravy

Cut away the thin undershell of the lobster tails. Then with shears, cut right through the hard shell so that each tail is in 3 pieces. Wash and dry chicken pieces. Use the back, neck, wing tips, and giblets for making chicken bouillon. Brown chicken on all sides in hot oil. Remove from skillet and add lobster to drippings. Cook until shell is bright red and the white flesh translucent. Remove lobster. Add vegetables and cook for about 1 minute. Add sherry and simmer for 2 minutes. Add brandy and boil for 2 minutes, or until partially evaporated. Add seasonings, tomato paste, bouillon, canned gravy, and chicken. Cover and simmer for 30 minutes, or until chicken is tender. Add lobster, and heat. Makes 4 to 6 servings.

LOBSTER-AVOCADO SANDWICHES

- 2 cups diced cooked lobster meat or 2 cans (5½ ounces each)
  Juice of 1 lime or lemon
- 1 cup dairy sour cream
  Mayonnaise or salad dressing
- 2 tablespoons minced sweet onion
  Salt and pepper
- 1 peeled medium-size ripe avocado, diced
- 4 round hard rolls, split and toasted
  Ripe olives
  Carrot sticks

Sprinkle lobster with lime juice and let stand in refrigerator for 1 hour. Drain. Blend sour cream, ¼ cup mayonnaise, and the onion. Season to taste with salt and pepper. Fold in lobster and avocado. Spread bottom halves of rolls with mayonnaise. Top with filling and cover with roll tops. Serve with a garnish of olives and carrot sticks. Makes 4 sandwiches.

STUFFED ROCK-LOBSTER TAILS

- 12 frozen rock-lobster tails (6 ounces each)
- 3 cans (10½ ounces each) frozen cream-of-shrimp soup
- ⅓ cup cream or sherry
- 2 cans (3 or 4 ounces each) sliced mushrooms, drained
  Buttered fine dry bread crumbs
  Paprika

Cook lobster according to directions on package. Cool. Cut shells down center, remove meat, and cut into chunks; reserve shells. Heat soup; add cream or sherry and mushrooms; mix with lobster. Stuff into shells; sprinkle with crumbs and paprika. Bake in preheated moderate oven (350°F.) for about 25 minutes, or until hot and lightly browned. Makes 12 servings.

LOBSTER RABBIT

- 2 tablespoons chopped green pepper
- ¼ cup butter or margarine
- 2 tablespoons all-purpose flour
- ¼ teaspoon salt
  Dash of cayenne
- ½ teaspoon powdered mustard
- ½ teaspoon Worcestershire
- 1 cup tomato juice
- 1 cup grated sharp Cheddar cheese
- 1 egg, slightly beaten
- ¾ cup milk
- 1 cup diced cooked lobster meat
  Hot toast
  Crisp bacon (optional)

In top part of double boiler over direct heat, cook green pepper in butter for 2 or 3 minutes. Blend in flour and seasonings. Put over boiling water and stir in tomato juice. Cook, stirring until thickened. Add cheese, egg, and milk; cook, stirring, for 3 or 4 minutes. Add lobster and heat.

Serve on toast, with bacon strips on top. Makes 4 servings.

LOBSTER LIGUANEA

- ½ cup soy sauce
  Dash of hot pepper sauce
- 1 cup sherry
  Meat and shells from 2 cooked medium lobsters
- 2 tablespoons cooking oil or melted butter

Mix soy sauce, pepper sauce, and sherry. Cut the lobster meat into bite-size pieces and add to first mixture. Mix well and let stand for 1 hour to marinate. Drain and put on broiler pan. Brush with oil and broil for 10 minutes, basting frequently with the marinade. Put lobster meat in the shells and baste again. Broil for 2 or 3 minutes longer. Serve at once in the shells. Makes 4 servings.

LOGANBERRY—This berry resembles a blackberry in shape but its color is red and, when fully ripe, it takes on a purple tinge. In flavor it resembles the raspberry, but is more acid. Some botanists consider the loganberry a hybrid between a blackberry and a raspberry; others think it may be a distinct species. Loganberries came originally from California.

Availability—Fresh loganberries are at their height in June and July. They are also available canned.

Purchasing Guide—Select bright, fresh, plump berries of uniform color. Good berries should be free from moisture, dirt, leaves, stems, and adhering caps. Caps may indicate immature fruit with undeveloped flavor. Avoid soft, wet berries. Stained containers often indicate over-ripe or damaged berries.

Storage—Pick over berries and remove any that may be spoiled. Do not wash before storing. Use as soon as possible.

☐ Fresh, refrigerator shelf: 3 days

☐ Fresh, refrigerator frozen-food compartment, prepared for freezing: 2 to 3 months

☐ Fresh, freezer, prepared for freezing: 1 year

☐ Canned, kitchen shelf: 1 year

☐ Canned, refrigerator shelf, opened: 4 to 5 days

Caloric Values

☐ Fresh, 3½ ounces = 267 calories

☐ Canned, 3½ ounces, in heavy syrup = 404 calories

Basic Preparation—Wash berries just before using. Place in a sieve and allow water to run gently over them. Do not soak in water. Drain well. Use berries for pies and tarts, jams, preserves, and ices.

☐ **To Freeze**—Use only firm, plump, ripe berries with glossy skins. Remove bruised or green berries, stems, and leaves. Wash in cold water and drain well. Can be frozen in sugar syrup, in a dry pack with or without sugar, or can be puréed.

Sugar Syrup—Put berries in freezer container, leaving 1-inch headspace, and cover with a syrup made of 4 cups water boiled with 7 cups granulated sugar. Cover.

Dry Pack, without Sugar—Spread berries in a single layer on a tray. Put in freezer and freeze until hard. Pour frozen berries into freezer container, leaving ½-inch headspace. Cover.

Dry Pack, with Sugar—Add ¾ cup sugar to each 4 cups berries. Toss berries carefully in sugar until most of sugar is dissolved. Pack in containers, leaving 1-inch headspace. Cover and freeze.

Puréed—Push berries through a strainer or food mill. Add 1 cup sugar to each 1 quart purée. Stir to dissolve sugar. Spoon into freezer containers and cover. Allow 1-inch headspace.

LOGANBERRY-CHEESE TARTS

- ½ cup sugar
  Water
- 1 pint loganberries
- 1 tablespoon cornstarch
- 8 ounces cream cheese
- 3 tablespoons light cream
- 6 baked medium tart shells

Mix sugar and ¼ cup water in saucepan. Bring to a rolling boil and pour over berries. Let stand until cool; drain, reserving syrup. Mix cornstarch and 1 tablespoon water. Add to syrup and cook, stirring, until clear and thickened. Mash cheese and blend with the cream. Spread cheese mixture in tart shells. Top with berries and spoon syrup over top. Makes 6 servings.

LOGANBERRY PIE

- 4 cups fully ripe, juicy loganberries
- 1 cup sugar
- ⅓ cup all-purpose flour
- ½ teaspoon ground cinnamon
  Pastry for 2-crust 9-inch pie, unbaked
- 1½ tablespoons butter or margarine

Pick over and wash loganberries. Mix with next 3 ingredients. Roll out half of pastry and line a 9-inch pie pan. Fill with berry mixture and dot with butter. Roll out rest of pastry; cover pie and crimp edge. Prick top crust. Bake in preheated hot oven (425°F.) for 35 to 45 minutes. Serve cold or slightly warm. Makes 6 to 8 servings.

LOGANBERRY ICE
½ cup light corn syrup
1½ cups sugar
4¼ cups water
1 tablespoon unflavored gelatin
2 quarts loganberries
1 tablespoon fresh lemon juice

Combine corn syrup, sugar, and 4 cups water in saucepan. Bring to a boil and boil for 5 minutes. Soften gelatin in remaining ¼ cup water, add to syrup, and stir until dissolved. Let stand until cold. Meanwhile wash and drain berries; force through food mill. Strain through fine sieve or cheesecloth. Add juices to gelatin mixture; pour into ice-cream container. Adjust dasher. Pack with 1 part rock salt to 6 parts ice; turn rapidly until stiff. Pour off water; repack with ice and salt. Cover freezer with newspapers until serving time. Makes 10 servings.

LOGANBERRY JAM
2 quarts ripe loganberries
6½ cups sugar
½ bottle liquid pectin

Crush berries completely, one layer at a time. (If desired, sieve half of pulp to remove some of the seeds.) Measure 4 cups into a very large saucepan. Add sugar and mix well. Put over high heat, bring to a *full rolling boil and boil hard for 1 minute,* stirring constantly. Remove from heat and at once stir in pectin. Skim off foam with metal spoon. Then stir and skim for 5 minutes to cool slightly and to prevent floating fruit. Ladle into hot sterilized jars, and seal. Makes about seven ½-pint jars.

LOQUAT—A tropical evergreen tree and its fruit that is also known as a "Japa-

nese medlar." The loquat tree is a small, ornamental evergreen tree with broad leaves and fragrant white flowers. The fruit is small, round, downy, and yellow-orange in color, with large black seeds. The flesh is pale yellow to orange, very juicy, with a delicious, slightly acid flavor, not as rich and sweet as most tropical fruit.

The loquat is a native of China, but it is now grown in most tropical and subtropical countries, and in the Mediterranean regions of Europe. In America, loquats are grown in California, Florida, and the Gulf States, both for the decorative value of the tree and the use of its fruit.

The loquat fruit is best eaten fresh, but it is also used in preserves and jellies. It is a delightful fruit when it is very ripe. Loquats are occasionally available in specialty fruit stores throughout the United States, but they are not the best of shippers and should be enjoyed where they are grown.

SPICED LOQUATS
4 pounds partially ripe loquats
1 cup boiling water
1 lemon, sliced
1 cup vinegar
1 tablespoon whole cloves
3 cinnamon sticks
4 cups sugar
½ teaspoon salt

Wash loquats, remove seeds, and measure 2 quarts. Steam in the boiling water for 3 minutes to prevent shriveling. Add remaining ingredients and boil for 10 minutes. Let stand overnight. Bring to boil again, and cook until syrup is thick. Pour into hot sterilized jars, and seal. Makes about five ½-pint jars.

LOQUAT JAM
1 pound partially ripe loquats
1½ cups sugar
1 cup water

Wash fruit. Scald, peel, and remove seeds. Force fruit through food chopper, using coarse blade. Put ground fruit, sugar, and water in saucepan. Bring to boil and boil rapidly until mixture sheets from side of spoon. Pour into hot sterilized jars, and seal. Makes about two ½-pint jars.

LOVAGE (Levisticum officinale)—A perennial herb, also called smellage or smallage, lovage is a member of the carrot family to which parsley and celery also belong. Lovage is a tall plant, growing five to seven feet high with greenish- or whitish-yellow flowers. Its large, heavy, light-green leaves resemble those of celery and the greens have a celerylike flavor. The root is strong in taste and smell. Although celery is shorter and has white flowers, there is so great a resemblance between it and lovage that wild celery is

sometimes sold as lovage and is also called smellage or smallage; and one of the French names for lovage is *céleri bâtard,* or false celery.

Lovage is native to southern Europe and Asia, predominantly in India.

The Greeks and Romans used lovage to a great extent in their cookery, and during the Middle Ages, when the monks cultivated herb gardens, lovage was used in monasteries to season foods. It was cultivated to such an extent in 14th-century England that it is still referred to as "Old English lovage." Astrologers have claimed that it is a sun herb, whose sign is Taurus the bull. "If Saturn offend the throat," lovage is recommended as a cure.

Lovage was grown in America by the early colonists. The dried root was popular as something to chew. It has been suggested that the root was especially useful during the long, long sermons, when children longed for something to do.

Fresh and dried leaves of lovage are used for flavor in cooking; the seeds, in a cheesecloth bag, are often simmered with stews. The root may be blanched and served like celery, or candied. The leaves are also used as a potherb. Add seeds to a salad dressing for a fruit salad, or rub the inside of a salad bowl with a few leaves to give a celery taste.

Dried lovage root, cut into small pieces or powdered, is available in specialty food stores.

LOW-CALORIE WEIGHT CONTROL
—It is just as important in weight control to know how many calories one expends in physical activity as it is to know how many calories there are in one's foods. The best way to lose excess weight is to bring the daily caloric intake below the output, to eat a balanced diet, and to secure adequate exercise. This permits sensible, healthy weight reduction, and avoids the nervousness, headaches, and short temper which usually go with extreme or crash diets. Establishing a total daily caloric intake at about 500 calories below the caloric output is a good working rule. On this basis the average person will lose a pound a week, or fifty pounds a year.

Your calorie output, that is the calories expended, depends on your body size, age, and physical activity. An adult of 100 pounds burns fewer calories than one of 150 pounds, assuming they are living on about the same pattern of physical activity. An average adult of 150 pounds uses up about sixty calories an hour just to live: in heart action, breathing, living function, and the like. This is called his basic metabolism rate. If he (or she) does some sedentary work such as writing, sewing, or reading he will burn up to eighty to 100 calories an hour. Cooking, dusting, ironing, hand-washing, and rapid typewriting take about 110 to 160 calories per hour. Mopping, gardening, carpentry, and walking moderately fast use 170 to 240 calories an hour. Hanging out clothes, heavy scrubbing, waxing floors burn 250 to 350 calories per hour.

Vigorous tennis, swimming, cycling, skiing, and dancing use 400 to 500 calories per hour.

One's daily caloric requirements decrease each year after twenty-five as body processes tend to slow down and one's energy expenditure decreases. Actually, the decrease averages about five per cent for each decade past age twenty-five. Thus, adults of forty-five or fifty years

of age need about ten per cent fewer calories than they did when they were twenty-five or thirty, and they must eat less to avoid overweight.

For most persons past their teens who wish to lose weight, a 1,400 calorie a day diet is recommended as being safe, within the capacity of most of us, and it will provide the energy needed for a normal day's work.

LOW-CALORIE COOK BOOK

APPETIZERS & SOUPS

CRAB-CHEESE DIP

2 cans (6½ to 7 ounces each) crabmeat, or 2 packages (6½ ounces each) frozen crabmeat, thawed
1 box (8 ounces) creamed cottage cheese
2 tablespoons mayonnaise
1 tablespoon prepared mustard
1 tablespoon fresh lemon juice
½ teaspoon salt
Parsley
Twisted lemon slices
A few capers

Drain crabmeat thoroughly. Reserve reddest pieces for garnish (about half). Put remaining half in container of electric blender with cheese, mayonnaise, mustard, lemon juice, and salt. Whirl until blended. Pile on serving dish and garnish with remaining crabmeat, parsley, lemon slices, and capers. Makes 1⅔ cups.

About 27 calories, 0.5 gram carbohydrate, 4 grams protein, and 1 gram fat per tablespoon.

• • • • •

STUFFED MUSHROOMS

2 cans (6 ounces each) mushroom crowns
1 box (8 ounces) skim-milk cottage cheese
2 tablespoons minced chives
Dash of hot pepper sauce
¼ teaspoon Worcestershire
½ teaspoon celery salt
½ teaspoon powdered mustard

Drain mushrooms and hollow out stem sides slightly. Mix remaining ingredients and top each crown with some of the mixture. Makes about 2 dozen.

About 10 calories, 0.5 grams carbohydrate, 2 grams protein, and no fat each.

• • • • •

SLICK CHICK SOUP

1 quart nonfat milk
1 tablespoon instant-type flour
4 chicken bouillon cubes
1 teaspoon instant minced onion
White pepper
Chopped parsley

Bring first 4 ingredients to boil. Season with pepper to taste. Serve with a sprinkling of chopped parsley. Makes 4 cups.

About 100 calories, 15 grams carbohydrate, 9 grams protein, and 0.5 grams fat per cup.

CREOLE VEGETABLE SOUP

2 cups chicken stock
2 cups water
1 chicken bouillon cube
1 teaspoon Creole seasoning
2 cups canned tomatoes
¼ cup cooked corn
½ cup sliced okra
2 tablespoons chopped onion
2 tablespoons uncooked rice
Seasoned salt and pepper

Mix all ingredients, except last 2, in kettle. Bring to boil, cover, and simmer for 20 minutes. Add seasoned salt and pepper to taste. Makes 6 cups.

About 48 calories, 9 grams carbohydrate, 2 grams protein, 0.5 grams fat per cup.

MAIN DISHES

LOW-CALORIE SEASONINGS FOR FISH, MEAT, AND POULTRY

Chicken: *paprika, thyme, sage, bay leaf, marjoram, tarragon, and monosodium glutamate.*
Lamb: *mint, rosemary, garlic, curry, basil, oregano, parsley.*
Fish: *mustard, paprika, curry, bay leaf, lemon juice, hot pepper sauce.*
Veal: *bay leaf, ginger, marjoram, curry, parsley, thyme, tarragon.*
Beef: *curry, chili powder, thyme, poultry seasoning, garlic, onion.*

Note: Mushrooms are fairly low in calories and can be added to any meat for variety and flavor.

SKEWERED SHRIMPS AND VEGETABLES

2 pounds uncooked cleaned shelled shrimps
½ pound fresh mushrooms, washed
2 medium green peppers, cut into 1-inch pieces
1 can (1 pound) onions, drained
⅓ cup soy sauce
½ cup salad oil
½ cup white wine
½ teaspoon celery salt

Put shrimps, mushrooms, green pepper, and onions in bowl. Mix remaining ingredients and pour over contents of bowl. Cover and marinate in refrigerator for several hours. A few minutes before serving, alternate shrimps and vegetables on skewers. Broil over a medium fire or under broiler for 3 to 5 minutes, rotating the skewers as ingredients broil. Makes 6 servings.

About 418 calories, 10 grams carbohydrate, 45 grams protein, and 22 grams fat per serving.

SCALLOPED TUNA

2 cans (7 ounces each) tuna
3 tablespoons all-purpose flour
½ teaspoon salt
¼ teaspoon pepper
¼ teaspoon powdered thyme
1½ cups nonfat milk
½ cup finely diced celery
1 box (9 ounces) frozen cut green beans, cooked

Drain tuna, reserving 2 tablespoons oil. Break tuna into pieces. Heat 2 tablespoons oil, and blend in flour and seasonings. Gradually add milk and cook, stirring, until thickened. Add tuna and vegetables, and mix well. Turn into shallow 1½-quart baking dish and bake in preheated moderate oven (350°F.) for about 30 minutes. Makes 6 servings.

About 253 calories, 7 grams carbohydrate, 18 grams protein, and 17 grams fat per serving.

CREOLE COD FILLETS

2 pounds cod fillets
2 tablespoons instant-type flour
1 small onion, sliced
1 can (1 pound) tomatoes
1 pimiento, chopped
1 bay leaf
¼ teaspoon monosodium glutamate
1 teaspoon salt
Dash of pepper
¼ teaspoon oregano

If fish is frozen, allow to thaw. Cut into serving pieces and put in shallow 2-quart baking dish. Mix remaining ingredients and pour over top. Bake in preheated moderate oven (350°F.) for about 1 hour. Makes 6 servings.

About 133 calories, 7 grams carbohydrate, 24 grams protein, and 1 gram fat per serving.

COTTAGE BEEF AND EGGS

¼ pound dried beef
¼ cup chopped green onions and tops
6 eggs, beaten
½ cup skim-milk cottage cheese
⅛ teaspoon pepper
Salt to taste
Chopped parsley
Paprika

Shred dried beef. Add remaining ingredients, except last 2, and mix well. Pour into shallow 1½-quart baking dish. Sprinkle with parsley and paprika. Bake in preheated moderate oven (350°F.) for 20 minutes, or until puffed and golden-brown. Makes 4 servings.

About 203 calories, 2 grams carbohydrate, 24 grams protein, and 11 grams fat per serving.

BARBECUED BEEF PATTIES

1 pound ground round steak
1 teaspoon salt
¼ teaspoon pepper
½ cup tomato juice or vegetable juice cocktail
⅛ teaspoon non-caloric liquid sweetener
1 teaspoon fresh lemon juice
1 teaspoon powdered mustard
1 teaspoon steak sauce

Mix lightly beef, salt, and pepper. Shape into 8 patties. Brown on both sides in Teflon-coated or lightly greased skillet. Mix remaining ingredients and pour over patties. Bring to boil and simmer for a few minutes. Makes 4 servings.

About 204 calories, 1 gram carbohydrate, 23 grams protein, and 12 grams fat per serving.

CURRIED LAMB MOLD

2 envelopes unflavored gelatin
4 cups water or unsalted stock
4 chicken bouillon cubes
2 teaspoons curry powder
4 cups cooked lean lamb, cut into ½-inch cubes
2 pimientos, cut into pieces
Chicory
1 tomato, cut into wedges
½ unpeeled cucumber, scored and thinly sliced

Soften gelatin in 1 cup water in saucepan. Dissolve bouillon cubes in 1 cup boiling water. Add to gelatin and stir until dissolved. Add 2 cups cold water. Put a small amount of mixture in tall 1½-quart mold. Chill until firm. Add curry powder to remaining mixture and

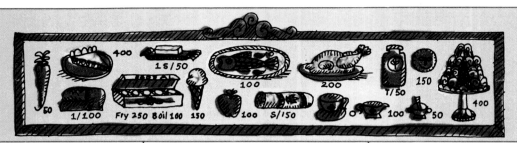

chill until thickened, but not firm. Fold in lamb and pimiento, and spoon lightly onto firm gelatin in mold. Chill several hours, or until firm. Unmold on serving plate and garnish with chicory, tomato wedges, and cucumber slices. Makes 8 servings.

About 183 calories, 3 grams carbohydrate, 18 grams protein, and 11 grams fat per serving.

Note: For variety, you can substitute diced cooked veal or chicken for the lamb.

GLAZED ROAST CHICKEN
4-pound roasting chicken
  Salt
  Monosodium glutamate
1 onion, peeled
1 carrot
1 or 2 celery stalks
1 tablespoon cornstarch
1 cup fresh orange juice
  Pimiento
  Watercress
  Parsley
2-inch pieces of green onion, cooked until slightly wilted

Wash chicken, and rub neck and body cavities lightly with salt and monosodium glutamate. Stuff body cavity with onion, carrot, and celery. Close vent and truss bird. Put in casserole or on rack in shallow roasting pan. Roast in preheated slow oven (325°F.) for about 3 hours. Meanwhile, mix cornstarch with orange juice. Cook, stirring, until smooth and thickened. About 30 minutes before chicken is done, brush with the mixture. Brush again after 15 minutes. Serve in casserole or remove to a hot platter. Garnish with pimiento, watercress, parsley, and green onion. Makes 6 servings.

About 395 calories, 9 grams carbohydrate, 38 grams protein, and 23 grams fat per serving.

SWISS EGGS
4 ounces process American cheese, cut into small thin slices
2 tablespoons butter or margarine
2 tablespoons nonfat dry-milk granules
1 tablespoon prepared mustard
½ teaspoon salt
  Dash of cayenne
⅓ cup water
6 eggs, slightly beaten

Arrange cheese in greased 9-inch pie pan. Dot with half the butter. Mix dry milk, mustard, salt, and cayenne. Add water and beat until smooth. Pour half on cheese. Add eggs and remaining milk mixture. Dot with remaining butter. Bake in preheated moderate oven (350°F.) for 25 minutes, or until golden-brown and puffed. Makes 4 servings.

About 291 calories, 3 grams carbohydrate, 18 grams protein, and 23 grams fat per serving.

CHEESE-TOMATO GRILL
4 ripe medium tomatoes
1 pound creamed cottage cheese
1 cup grated Cheddar cheese
  Salt and pepper

Cut each tomato into 3 thick slices. Broil on one side and turn. Mix cheeses and salt and pepper to taste. Spread generously on tomato slices and broil until golden-brown and bubbly. Makes 6 servings.

About 171 calories, 6 grams carbohydrate, 21 grams protein, and 7 grams fat per serving.

SALADS AND DRESSINGS

JELLIED TUNA SALAD
1 envelope unflavored gelatin
¼ cup cold water
½ teaspoon powdered mustard
½ teaspoon salt
½ teaspoon instant minced onion
2 tablespoons sugar
1 tablespoon fresh lemon juice
1¼ cups buttermilk
  Yellow food coloring (optional)
½ cup diced celery
1 can (3¼ ounces) tuna, drained and broken into small pieces
  Salad greens

Soften gelatin in cold water. Dissolve over hot water. Blend in seasonings and sugar. Add lemon juice, buttermilk, and a few drops coloring, if used. Chill until thickened, but not firm. Fold in celery and tuna. Pour into 4 individual molds and chill until firm. Unmold on salad greens. If desired, serve with Cooked Salad Dressing, page 1086. Makes 4 servings.

About 86 calories, 5 grams carbohydrate, 12 grams protein, and 2 grams fat per serving.

PATIO SALAD
1 cup melon balls or cubes
1 tomato, peeled and cut into wedges
1½ quarts broken salad greens
¼ cup salad oil
1½ tablespoons fresh lemon juice
½ teaspoon instant minced onion
½ teaspoon Worcestershire
¾ teaspoon salt
⅛ teaspoon pepper
½ teaspoon sugar

Combine first 3 ingredients in salad bowl. Put remaining ingredients in small jar, cover, and shake well. Add to first mixture in bowl and toss lightly. Makes 6 servings.

Salad: about 32 calories, 6 grams carbohydrate, 2 grams protein, no fat per serving. Dressing: about 85 calories, 1 gram carbohydrate, no protein, 9 grams fat per serving.

COTTAGE CHEESE AND CUCUMBER SALAD
2 tablespoons white vinegar
2 tablespoons sugar
½ teaspoon each of poppy and celery seed
1½ cups creamed cottage cheese
  Salad greens
20 slices of unpeeled cucumber

Heat vinegar, sugar, and seed to boiling. Pile cheese onto greens and arrange cucumber slices diagonally in the cheese. Pour dressing over top and chill until ready to serve. Makes 4 servings.

About 112 calories, 19 grams carbohydrate, 9 grams protein, and no fat per serving.

GREEN-BEAN AND CARROT SALAD
1 pound whole fresh green beans
  Salt
3 medium carrots
  Piquant Salad Dressing, page 1086

Cook beans in small amount of boiling salted water until tender. Drain and chill. Peel carrots and cut diagonally with waffle cutter. Or, slice or cut julienne, if preferred. Cook in small amount of boiling salted water until tender-crisp. Chill. Arrange vegetables attractively on serving plate. Pass Dressing. Makes 8 servings.

About 32 calories, 6 grams carbohydrate, 2 grams protein, and no fat per serving, exclusive of Dressing.

PANAMA RADISH SALAD

- 4 bunches (1 quart) radishes
- ⅓ cup thin onion rings
- 1 cup diced fresh tomato
- 1¼ teaspoons salt
- ⅛ teaspoon minced garlic
- ⅛ teaspoon pepper
- 1 teaspoon finely chopped fresh mint
- 2 tablespoons fresh lemon juice
- 2 tablespoons salad oil
  Parsley

Wash radishes and slice. Add onion and tomato. Combine the seasonings, lemon juice, and oil. Mix well and pour over the salad. Toss lightly. Garnish with parsley. Makes 6 servings.

About 65 calories, 13 grams carbohydrate, 1 gram protein, and 1 gram fat per serving.

SILHOUETTE SALAD

- 1 envelope unflavored gelatin
- 1 cup cold water
- 1 can cream of chicken soup
- 1 tablespoon fresh lemon juice
  Dash of pepper
- 1 can (5 ounces) chicken, diced
- ½ cup diced celery
- ¼ cup chopped green pepper
- 2 tablespoons chopped pimiento
- 1 teaspoon instant minced onion

Soften gelatin in ½ cup of the water. Dissolve over hot water. Beat soup into remaining water. Stir in gelatin, lemon juice, and pepper. Chill until thickened, but not set. Fold in remaining ingredients. Pour into 1-quart mold and chill until firm. Unmold on greens. Makes 4 servings.

About 139 calories, 8 grams carbohydrate, 11 grams protein, and 7 grams fat per serving.

TOMATO SALAD DRESSING

- 1 package old-fashioned French dressing mix
- 1½ cups tomato juice
- ¼ cup each of malt vinegar and salad oil

Empty contents of package of mix into a screwtop, quart-size jar. Add remaining ingredients, cover, and shake well. Chill. Makes 2 cups.

About 22 calories, 1 gram carbohydrate, no protein, and 2 grams fat per tablespoon.

COOKED SALAD DRESSING

- ½ teaspoon salt
- ¼ teaspoon each of powdered mustard and paprika
  Dash of cayenne
- 2 tablespoons vinegar
- ¼ cup nonfat milk
- 1 egg, beaten
- ¼ teaspoon non-caloric liquid sweetener

Mix all ingredients in top part of small double boiler. Put over hot water and cook, stirring, until thickened. Cool and chill. Makes ½ cup.

About 13 calories, no carbohydrate, 1 gram protein, and 1 gram fat per tablespoon.

PIQUANT SALAD DRESSING

- ½ teaspoon powdered mustard
  Dash of monosodium glutamate
- ¼ teaspoon seasoned salt
- ½ teaspoon celery salt
- 1 tablespoon all-purpose flour
- ½ cup nonfat milk
- 1 egg yolk, beaten
- 3 tablespoons vinegar
  Few drops of non-caloric liquid sweetener

In top part of small double boiler, mix seasonings and flour. Add milk and cook over boiling water, stirring, until thickened. Stir in egg yolk and cook for 1 minute longer, stirring. Remove from heat and stir in vinegar and sweetener. Cool; chill. Makes ⅔ cup.

About 17 calories, 1 gram carbohydrate, 1 gram protein, and 1 gram fat per tablespoon.

CUCUMBER SAUCE

Mix 1 container of plain yogurt with 1 grated small cucumber. Stir in 1 tablespoon chopped fresh dill, and salt to taste. Chill. Stir again before serving. Makes 1½ cups.

About 8 calories, 1 gram carbohydrate, 1 gram protein, no fat per tablespoon.

VEGETABLES

LOW-CALORIE SEASONINGS FOR VEGETABLES

Green Vegetables: *lemon juice is good with all of them, and dill seed is especially good with cabbage.*
Carrots: *parsley, mint, nutmeg.*
Tomatoes: *a combination of onion, bay leaf, and celery.*

CURRIED ONIONS AND CUCUMBER

- 1½ cups water
  Salt
- 3 large onions, cut into eighths
- 1 large cucumber, peeled and diced
- 3 tablespoons all-purpose flour
- ¼ cup nonfat dry-milk granules
- ½ to 1 teaspoon curry powder
- 1 tablespoon butter or margarine
  Pepper

Bring 1 cup of the water to boil in saucepan. Add a little salt, onions, and cucumber. Bring to boil and simmer, covered, for about 5 minutes. Mix flour, dry milk, and curry powder. Blend in remaining water. Stir slowly into vegetable mixture and cook, stirring, until smooth and thickened. Add butter and salt and pepper to taste. Makes 6 servings.

About 54 calories, 8 grams carbohydrate, 1 gram protein, 2 grams fat per serving.

GREEN BEANS, CAPE COD STYLE

- 1 pound green beans
- 2 tablespoons half-and-half (half milk and half light cream)
- 2 teaspoons sugar
- 1 tablespoon butter or margarine
  Salt and pepper to taste

Wash beans and remove stem ends; cut beans into halves lengthwise. Put in saucepan and barely cover with boiling water. Cook, covered, for about 20 minutes, or until just tender. Drain, add remaining ingredients, and toss lightly. Makes 4 servings.

About 75 calories, 9 grams carbohydrate, 3 grams protein, 3 grams fat per serving.

SAUTÉED GREEN PEPPERS

- 6 large green peppers
- 3 tablespoons butter or margarine
  Salt and pepper

Remove seeds from peppers and cut peppers into eighths. Put in skillet, cover with boiling water, and cook, covered, for 3 minutes; drain. Add butter and sauté peppers slowly until lightly browned. Season to taste. Makes 6 servings.

About 70 calories, 4 grams carbohydrate, no protein, and 6 grams fat per serving.

● ● ● ● ●

BRAISED RADISHES
2 tablespoons butter or margarine
2 cups sliced radishes
1 bouillon cube
¼ cup hot water
⅛ teaspoon ground marjoram
Salt

Melt butter in saucepan. Add radishes and cook for 5 minutes, stirring frequently. Dissolve bouillon cube in the hot water, and stir into radishes. Add marjoram and simmer for 3 to 4 minutes. Add salt if necessary, and serve hot as a vegetable. Makes 4 servings.

About 34 calories, 3 grams carbohydrate, 1 gram protein, 2 grams fat per serving.

● ● ● ● ●

SIMMERED TOMATOES AND CABBAGE
4 cups coarsely cut cabbage
4 tomatoes, peeled
1 teaspoon salt
¼ teaspoon pepper
1½ teaspoons caraway seed
2 tablespoons butter or margarine
2 tablespoons all-purpose flour

Put cabbage and tomatoes in saucepan, and bring to boil. Reduce heat and simmer, covered, for about 10 minutes. Add salt, pepper, and caraway seed, and simmer for 5 minutes. Cream butter with flour, and stir into vegetable mixture. Cook, stirring, until thickened. Makes 4 servings.

About 110 calories, 11 grams carbohydrate, 3 grams protein, and 6 grams fat per serving.

DESSERTS

COFFEE SPONGE
1 envelope unflavored gelatin
2 cups nonfat milk
1 tablespoon instant coffee powder
⅛ teaspoon salt
1 teaspoon non-caloric liquid sweetener
1 teaspoon vanilla extract
2 egg whites

Soften gelatin in milk in saucepan. Add coffee and heat, stirring, until gelatin and coffee are dissolved. Add salt and sweetener. Chill until slightly thickened. Add

vanilla and fold in beaten egg whites. Chill until firm. Makes 6 servings.

About 40 calories, 5 grams carbohydrate, 5 grams protein, and no fat per serving.

● ● ● ● ●

LOW-CALORIE PEACH SHERBET
1 cup plain yogurt
2 cups sliced fresh peaches
½ cup honey
½ cup fresh orange juice

In container of electric blender, combine all ingredients in order given. Whirl for 1 minute, or until ingredients are thoroughly blended. Pour into refrigerator tray and freeze until firm around edges. Turn into chilled bowl and beat until smooth and fluffy. Return to tray and freeze until set. Remove from freezer about 15 minutes before serving to soften slightly. Makes 6 servings.

About 145 calories, 32 grams carbohydrate, 2 grams protein, and 1 gram fat per serving.

● ● ● ● ●

STRAWBERRY FLUFF
2 envelopes strawberry-flavor dietary gelatin dessert
1½ cups hot water
1 tablespoon fresh lemon juice
1 package (2 ounces) whipped topping mix
½ cup nonfat milk
6 fresh strawberries

Dissolve gelatin dessert in the hot water. Add lemon juice and chill until thickened, but not firm. Prepare topping mix as directed on the label, using nonfat milk. Reserve ½ cup. Fold remainder into thickened gelatin and pile into 8-inch pie pan. Chill until firm. Decorate with reserved topping and unhulled strawberries. Makes 6 servings.

About 81 calories, 5 grams carbohydrate, 4 grams protein, 5 grams fat per serving.

● ● ● ● ●

BLUEBERRY-TOPPED CHEESECAKE
1 box (10½ ounces) no-bake cheesecake filling
1½ cups nonfat milk
1 cup blueberries

Butter generously an 8-inch pie pan and coat with half the graham-cracker crumbs in box of mix. (Do not add sugar and margarine as directed on label.) Reserve

remaining crumbs for other uses. Prepare filling as directed on the label, using nonfat milk. Pour carefully onto crumbs in pan and chill for 1 hour. Arrange berries on top, and add a few green leaves, if desired. Makes 6 servings.
Note: For a thinner cheesecake to serve 8, substitute a 9-inch pie pan for the 8-inch one.

For 6 servings, about 264 calories, 26 grams carbohydrate, 22 grams protein, and 8 grams fat per serving.

● ● ● ● ●

ORANGE CAKE
2½ teaspoons non-caloric liquid sweetener
⅓ cup butter, melted
2 eggs, beaten
1¼ cups sifted cake flour
¼ teaspoon salt
2 teaspoons baking powder
⅔ cup fresh orange juice

Stir 2 teaspoons sweetener into butter. Add eggs and mix well. Add sifted flour, salt, and baking powder alternately with ⅓ cup orange juice, mixing until blended. Pour into 9-inch layer cake pan, lined on the bottom with wax paper. Bake in preheated moderate oven (375°F.) for about 30 minutes. (Cake layer will be thin.) Remove to serving plate and peel off paper. Just before serving, mix remaining ½ teaspoon sweetener and ⅓ cup orange juice in small saucepan. Bring to boil and simmer for 2 to 3 minutes. Spoon over slightly warm or cold cake. Makes 8 servings.

About 149 calories, 14 grams carbohydrate, 3 grams protein, 9 grams fat per serving.

● ● ● ● ●

BAKED APRICOT WHIP
¾ cup cooked dried apricots, sieved or puréed in blender
4 egg whites, beaten stiff
Dash of salt
3 tablespoons honey

Fold apricot purée into egg whites. Add salt and honey, and mix lightly. Pile lightly into 1-quart casserole and bake in preheated moderate oven (375°F.) for 20 minutes, or until firm. Makes 6 servings.

About 92 calories, 20 grams carbohydrate, 3 grams protein, and no fat per serving.

ANGEL CAKE LEMON DELIGHT
    1 cup sifted cake flour
    1½ cups sugar
    1½ cups egg whites (9 to 10 whites)
    ½ teaspoon salt
    1½ teaspoons cream of tartar
    1 teaspoon vanilla extract
    Lemon Topping
    1 large fresh peach, peeled and sliced
    Mint leaves

Sift flour and ¾ cup sugar. Beat egg whites with salt until foamy; add cream of tartar and beat until stiff, but not dry. Gradually beat in remaining sugar. Sift dry ingredients onto egg-white mixture, a little at a time, and carefully fold in after each addition until well blended. Add vanilla. Spoon into ungreased 10-inch tube pan and run a knife through mixture to break up any large air holes. Bake in preheated slow oven (325°F.) for 1 hour. Invert pan on neck of tall bottle until cold. Remove from pan to serving plate and spread with Lemon Topping, allowing some to run down sides of cake. Arrange peach slices around edge and put a mint leaf between each slice. Makes 10 servings.

Lemon Topping
    2 tablespoons cornstarch
    ¼ teaspoon salt
    1 cup water
    ¼ cup fresh lemon juice
    2 teaspoons non-caloric liquid sweetener
    1 egg yolk, beaten
    1 teaspoon butter
    1 teaspoon grated lemon rind
    Few drops of yellow food coloring (optional)

Mix cornstarch, salt, and water in saucepan. Add lemon juice and sweetener and cook, stirring, for 2 minutes. Remove from heat and stir in remaining ingredients. Cool.

About 185 calories, 40 grams carbohydrate, 4 grams protein, and 1 gram fat per serving.

Note: Calories will be about the same if mix is used to prepare the cake.

FRUIT-COCKTAIL WHIP
    1 can (8¼ ounces) dietetic-pack fruit cocktail, chilled
    1 box (3¾ ounces) vanilla-flavor deluxe dessert mix
    ½ cup cold nonfat milk

Drain fruit cocktail, reserving liquid. Add enough cold water to liquid to make ½ cup. Prepare dessert mix with nonfat milk and liquid as directed on the label, substituting the liquid for the ½ cup cold water called for. Fold in fruit and chill. Makes 6 servings.

About 95 calories, 14 grams carbohydrate, 3 grams protein, and 3 grams fat per serving.

LIME-GRAPE DESSERT
    2 envelopes lime-flavored dietary gelatin dessert
    1 cup boiling water
    ½ cup cold water
    ⅔ cup bottled unsweetened grape juice
    30 seedless green grapes

Dissolve gelatin in boiling water. Remove ½ cup of mixture to small bowl and add the cold water. Chill until slightly thickened. Add grape juice to remaining gelatin and pour into 4 sherbet glasses, filling them about one-half full. Chill until firm. Beat thickened gelatin until frothy and double in bulk. Let stand in bowl of ice and water until mixture holds its shape, stirring occasionally. Fold in grapes and pile lightly onto firm gelatin. Chill until firm. Makes 4 servings.

About 56 calories, 10 grams carbohydrate, 4 grams protein, and no fat per serving.

BEVERAGES

ORANGE-MILK STARTER
Beat together with rotary beater ⅔ cup nonfat milk, ⅓ cup fresh orange juice, 1 raw egg, and dash of salt. Serve in tall glass. Makes 1 serving.

About 170 calories, 17 grams carbohydrate, 12 grams protein, and 6 grams fat.

BANANA SLIM SHAKE
Mash 1 ripe banana. Add 1 cup nonfat milk and dash of vanilla extract. Shake all together until well blended. Makes 1 serving.

About 176 calories, 35 grams carbohydrate, 9 grams protein, and no fat.

LUCULLUS—Lucius Licinius Lucullus (c. 110-56 B.C.) was a Roman general so extravagant in his living habits that his name has become synonymous with luxurious feasting. Gourmet banquets of elaborate proportions are often called "Lucullan feasts."

Lucullus spent much of his life as an army officer, campaigning and governing in Asia Minor. When he retired to Rome with the fortune he had accumulated as the spoils of his eastern campaigns, he was one of the wealthiest Romans. He lived and ate in such style that even the extravagant Romans of his day were staggered. His dining quarters were splendidly appointed, with purple covers on the tables and plates studded with precious stones. It was said that he kept more than 5,000 dishes in his house for his guests.

His extravagance was such that it is reported that a single dinner (for three) cost almost $6,000. It was served in the Apollo Room, one of a number of rooms that Lucullus reserved for elaborate dining.

LUNCH, LUNCHEON—The word lunch is used to denote a light meal in the middle of the day. Lunch may also mean a light meal which can be eaten at any time or any place, such as a picnic lunch.

A luncheon is a midday meal, too, but a more social one. Generally, the word is used when a group of people are being entertained either at home or in a restaurant or club.

SALAD LUNCHEON

PINEAPPLE-STRAWBERRY SALAD
SOUR CREAM
OLIVE AND BACON ROLLS CHEESE SQUARES
CHOCOLATE ALMOND PIE COFFEE

The day before, prepare pineapple; make the dressing; cut bread, and prepare cheese mixture; roll olives in bacon; and make the piecrust and filling.

For 5 or 6 Persons

Pineapple: Pare 1 large fresh pineapple, and cut into 5 or 6 thick slices. Remove cores, and arrange slices on chicory or other salad greens on plates. Wash, and hull 1 quart strawberries; reserve 5 or 6 with caps for garnish. Slice remainder, and arrange petal-fashion on pineapple. Top with a spoonful of dairy sour cream, mixed with a little mayonnaise. Garnish each with a whole berry.

Olive Rolls: Allow 3 per person. Cut slices of bacon into halves. Roll around large stuffed green olives, and secure with toothpicks. Bake on rack in shallow pan in preheated hot oven (400°F.) for 10 minutes, or until bacon is done.

Cheese Squares: Cut crust from loaf of unsliced bread, and cut bread into 2-inch squares, or use dinner rolls. Cream ½ cup margarine. Add ½ pound shredded sharp Cheddar cheese, ½ teaspoon Worcestershire, and dash of cayenne. Mix in 2 stiffly beaten egg whites. Spread a heaping tablespoon of cheese mixture on top of each bread square. Bake in preheated hot oven (400°F.) for 15 minutes, or until puffy.

Pie: To make crust, mix 1½ cups vanilla-wafer crumbs and ¼ cup soft butter. Press into 8-inch pie pan. Bake in preheated moderate oven (350°F.) for about 8 minutes; cool. To make filling, melt 1 chocolate almond bar (1 pound) in top part of double boiler over hot water. Add a dash of salt, and cool. Add 1 teaspoon vanilla extract, and fold in 1 cup heavy cream, whipped. Pile lightly into pie shell, and chill for several hours, or overnight. Top with whipped topping or whipped cream.

BUFFET LUNCHEON

BARBECUED CHICKEN
COLD VEGETABLE PLATTER
FRENCH DRESSING   SOUR CREAM
WATERMELON AND CANTALOUPE PICKLES
BUTTERED CORN BREAD
CHERRY AND APRICOT TARTS   COFFEE

The morning of the buffet, cook vegetables, and refrigerate. Bake tart shells, and prepare filling and toppings. Make corn bread, and barbecue chicken.

For 8 Persons

Barbecued Chicken: Have 2 large fryers cut into quarters. Sprinkle with salt and pepper, and roll in flour. Put in shallow baking pan. On each, put a thick slice of bacon. Cover pan with foil. Bake in preheated hot oven (400°F.) for 40 minutes. Uncover; pour over chicken 2 cans (3 ounces each) sliced mushrooms, undrained. Streak with bottled barbecue sauce. Cover, and bake for 10 minutes longer. Uncover, and broil for 10 minutes, or until lightly browned. (If prepared ahead, reheat in oven just before serving.)

Vegetable Platter: Cook 1 box each of frozen Lima beans and 2 boxes each of broccoli, green and wax beans, according to package directions. Peel, cut, and cook 3 large carrots. Serve with French dressing and dairy sour cream.

Corn Bread: Prepare 2 packages cornbread mix according to the label directions. Cut, and butter.

Tarts: Bake eight 4-inch pastry tart shells. Cool; fill shells two-thirds full with instant vanilla pudding. In saucepan, mix ⅓ cup sugar and 3 tablespoons cornstarch. Drain liquid from 1-pound can of pitted red sour cherries into saucepan. Mix well, and cook, stirring, until clear and thickened. Add cherries, juice of ½ lemon, and a little red food coloring if desired. Cool, and fill half of tarts. On remaining tarts, put a canned whole apricot, and top each with a little apricot jam or preserves. Sprinkle with flaked coconut. Chill until ready to serve.

LYONNAISE—A French culinary expression meaning "in the manner of Lyons," a city renowned throughout France for the richness and excellence of its food. Specifically, "lyonnaise" stands for dishes cooked with onions. *Pommes lyonnaise* are home-fried potatoes cooked with onions; *omelette à la lyonnaise* is an omelet with onions and parsley.

POTATOES LYONNAISE

  6 medium potatoes
  ¼ cup butter or lard
  2 tablespoons cooking oil
  3 medium onions, thinly sliced
    Salt and pepper
  ¼ cup minced parsley

Boil potatoes. Peel and slice thinly while still hot. Heat 2 tablespoons of the butter and the oil in a heavy kettle. Cook potatoes in it until golden; they must not brown. In another skillet heat remaining butter. Over low heat cook onions in it until soft and just barely golden; do not let brown. Combine onions and potatoes. Season with salt and pepper to taste. Cook together over low heat for 3 minutes, stirring occasionally to blend. Sprinkle with parsley. Serve immediately. Makes 4 servings.

Note: The secret of this classic French dish is to cook the potatoes and onions separately and blend them later. The onion slices should be of equal thickness so that they will cook uniformly.

OMELETTE À LA LYONNAISE

  1 medium onion, sliced thin
  4 tablespoons butter or margarine
    Few sprigs of parsley, chopped
  4 eggs
  ¼ cup water
  ½ teaspoon salt
  ⅛ teaspoon pepper
  ½ teaspoon vinegar

Sauté onion in 3 tablespoons of the butter until just lightly browned. Sprinkle with parsley. Beat eggs slightly, just enough to blend yolks and whites. Add water, salt, and pepper. Pour into pan and cook over medium heat. As omelette cooks, lift with a spatula, letting the uncooked part run under. When firm and browned underneath, fold and put on a hot platter. Add remaining butter to skillet and brown. Cool slightly, add vinegar, and pour over omelette. Makes 2 servings.

MACARONI—A food paste made from a mixture of semolina and water, and dried in the form of slender tubes or fancy shapes: elbow macaroni and macaroni shells, for example. The semolina used is the purified middlings (medium-size particles of ground grain) of durum or other hard wheat.

To make macaroni, semolina is mixed with water and kneaded to give a smooth and elastic dough that will pass through dies, which are metal discs full of holes. For macaroni, a steel pin is placed in the center of each hole in the die and the dough is extruded in the hollow rods known as macaroni. (If no pin is used,

the dough comes out in the solid rods known as spaghetti.) For elbow macaroni, a pin with a notch on one side is used. The notch allows the dough to pass through more quickly on one side, causing it to curve slightly. A revolving knife attached to the die cuts the dough at frequent intervals into short lengths.

Long strands of macaroni are collected on racks and taken to drying ovens. Short lengths, such as elbow macaroni and shells, are collected on trays or drawers and placed in drying cabinets.

Macaroni products are not baked. They are dried slowly in the presence of constantly circulating filtered air.

The art of making macaroni is very old. Although most people associate it with Italy and give Naples as its place of origin, the Chinese recorded the eating of macaroni-like products in various forms as early as 5,000 B.C. One of the more popular legends concerns the Chinese maiden who was lured from her breadmaking by her lover, a member of the famous Marco Polo expedition to the Orient. While the maiden neglected her bread dough, the wind blew leaves from an overhanging tree into the batter. In an attempt to help her save the dough from waste, the sailor forced the dough through a wicker basket which served as a sieve. The thin strands of dough dried in the sun and, when the sailor departed, the maiden presented him with the dough in this new shape. He cooked the strands of dried dough on his ship and found the dish so delicious he made it many times thereafter. The food came to be favored by all members of the crew and finally by the great explorer himself, Marco Polo. Whatever the truth of the legend, it is historical fact that by the 14th century, Italy was the only European country in which macaroni was made and that for a full hundred years the method of its manufacture was an Italian secret. An Italian ruler is credited with naming the food. When he was served the delicious dish, he is said to have declared *"Ma caroni"* which means "How very dear!"

Macaroni products are a staple Italian food, and macaroni proper is most popular in southern Italy and especially Naples, where it is served with many different sauces. Like all pasta, macaroni is healthful, nutritious, and inexpensive. It also has the considerable advantage that children love it.

Availability and Purchasing Guide—Macaroni is available packaged in all food stores. Among the fancy shapes available are elbow, shell, ribbon, and twist.

Available canned are macaroni with cheese; macaroni with various tomato, cheese, and mushroom sauces; macaroni with beef; and macaroni and vegetable soup. Macaroni salad is available in jars, and macaroni with cheese and macaroni with beef and tomatoes are available frozen.

Macaroni doubles in volume when cooked.

☐ 1 pound, raw = 4 cups raw = 2 to 2¼ quarts, cooked

☐ 1 cup, raw = 2 to 2¼ cups, cooked

Storage—Store uncooked macaroni in a cool dry place.

☐ Kitchen shelf: 3 to 6 months

☐ Refrigerator shelf, cooked and covered: 4 to 5 days

☐ Refrigerator frozen-food compartment, prepared for freezing: 3 to 4 weeks

☐ Freezer, prepared for freezing: 1 year

Nutritive Food Values—Primarily a source of carbohydrate with small quantities of B vitamins.

☐ Macaroni, 3½ ounces, cooked = 148 calories

☐ Macaroni and cheese, 3½ ounces = 215 calories

Basic Preparation—Macaroni should be cooked in a large quantity of salted water. For the best results follow package directions for amount of water and time required; this varies with the shape

and make of the product. In general, allow 3 quarts water and 1 tablespoon salt to 8 ounces of macaroni. Add the macaroni gradually to rapidly boiling water; the water should continue to boil. Cook, uncovered, until tender. Stir occasionally to prevent sticking. Macaroni is usually cooked *al dente,* which means medium-done or slightly firm. When tender, drain immediately. Rinsing is not necessary. Serve with butter or desired sauce. Macaroni which is to be added to a dish requiring additional cooking should be slightly undercooked.

CRAB AND SHELL CHOWDER

3 cups small shell macaroni
3 tablespoons butter or margarine
½ pound mushrooms, sliced
1 teaspoon onion powder
2 tomatoes, peeled, seeded, and sliced
½ teaspoon salt
2 cans (6 ounces each) crabmeat
¼ teaspoon hot pepper sauce
¼ teaspoon pepper
1 cup light or heavy cream
5 cups milk
2 tablespoons chopped parsley
1 tablespoon chopped chives

Cook and drain seashells. Melt butter. Add mushrooms, onion powder, and tomatoes. Cook over medium heat for 5 minutes. Add salt, crabmeat, hot pepper sauce, pepper, cream, and milk. Cook for 5 minutes, or until thoroughly heated. Stir occasionally. Add parsley and chives. Combine with seashells and mix thoroughly. Heat through again if necessary. Makes 6 servings.

Shrimp and Shell Chowder

For crabmeat in Crab and Shell Chowder, substitute 2 cans (4½ ounces each) small shrimps. Proceed as directed.

Lobster and Shell Chowder

For crabmeat in Crab and Shell Chowder, substitute 2 cans (5 ounces each) lobster meat. Proceed as directed.

SHRIMP-AND-CHEESE MACARONI LOAF

1 envelope unflavored gelatin
1¼ cups milk
1½ cups shredded process American cheese
1 tablespoon grated onion
2 cans (5 ounces each) shrimps, deveined
½ cup minced celery
⅔ cup elbow macaroni, cooked
1 teaspoon sweet garden relish
1 pimiento, chopped
½ cup mayonnaise
½ teaspoon salt
Dash of cayenne
Curry Mayonnaise

Sprinkle gelatin over milk in top part

of double boiler; let stand for 5 minutes. Scald over boiling water, stirring until gelatin is dissolved. Stir in cheese and onion. Cool; then chill until slightly thickened. Cut shrimps into halves lengthwise. Add shrimps and remaining ingredients except mayonnaise to gelatin mixture. Turn into oiled 3½-cup fish mold or loaf pan (9 x 5 x 3 inches). Chill until firm. Unmold; garnish with salad greens, tomatoes, and cucumbers, if desired. Serve with Curry Mayonnaise. (To make, season mayonnaise with a little curry powder.) Makes 6 servings.

CLAM, MACARONI, AND CHEESE CASSEROLE

3 tablespoons butter or margarine
2 tablespoons all-purpose flour
1 cup milk
1 teaspoon salt
⅛ teaspoon pepper
3 cups cooked elbow macaroni
½ pound American cheese, diced
1 can (10½ ounces) minced clams, undrained
2 tablespoons chopped parsley
¼ cup cracker crumbs
Paprika

Melt 2 tablespoons butter in saucepan and stir in flour. Remove from heat and stir in milk gradually. Cook over low heat until slightly thickened, stirring constantly. Add salt and pepper. Combine sauce with macaroni, cheese, clams, and parsley in 1½-quart casserole. Sprinkle with cracker crumbs and paprika and dot with remaining butter. Bake in preheated moderate oven (375°F.) for about 30 minutes. Makes 4 to 6 servings.

COMPANY FISH AND MACARONI CASSEROLE

2 cups boiling salted water
1 small carrot, cut into pieces
1 small onion, cut into quarters
1½ pounds cod or haddock fillets
1 cup elbow macaroni
Butter or margarine
⅓ cup all-purpose flour
1 teaspoon salt
½ teaspoon white pepper
1½ cups fish liquid
½ cup light or heavy cream
1 egg yolk
3 tablespoons white wine
¼ cup grated mild Cheddar or Swiss cheese
¼ cup fine dry bread crumbs

To boiling water, add carrot, onion, and fish. Simmer until fish is barely tender; do not overcook. Drain; reserve liquid. Discard carrot and onion. Cut fish into small pieces. Cook and drain macaroni. Melt 3 tablespoons butter, stir in flour. Cook over low heat until golden, stirring. Season with salt and pepper. Combine fish liquid and cream. Gradually stir into flour mixture. Cook over low heat until slightly thickened, stirring. Remove from heat. Beat in egg yolk and wine, 1 teaspoon at a time. Place a layer of cooked macaroni in buttered 1½- to 2-quart baking dish. Sprinkle with grated cheese and top with a layer of fish and sauce to cover. Repeat layers. The final layer should be macaroni. Sprinkle top with crumbs and any remaining cheese. Dot with 2 tablespoons butter. Bake in preheated hot oven (425°F.) for about 20 minutes. Makes 6 servings.

MACARONI, SHRIMP, AND ORANGE SALAD

Cook, drain, and cool 1¼ cups macaroni shells. Combine with 2 cups cooked, shelled, and deveined shrimps. (If canned shrimps are used, rinse first in cold water and drain.) Add 1 thinly sliced medium onion and 4 medium oranges, peeled free of skin and white membrane and diced. Toss together and chill. At serving time, toss with a dressing made by combining 1 teaspoon sugar, 1½ teaspoons salt, ¼ teaspoon cayenne, 1 teaspoon paprika, ⅓ cup salad oil, and ¼ cup fresh lemon juice. Serve piled on bed of lettuce. Makes 6 servings.

Macaroni, Tuna, and Orange Salad

Follow recipe for Macaroni, Shrimp, and Orange Salad, substituting 2 cans (7 ounces each) tuna, drained, for the shrimps. Proceed as directed.

Macaroni, Lobster, and Orange Salad

Follow recipe for Macaroni, Shrimp, and Orange Salad, substituting 2 cups diced cooked lobster meat for the shrimps. Proceed as directed.

MACARONI, LOBSTER, AND ARTICHOKE SALAD

- 2 cups elbow macaroni
- 1 package (9 ounces) frozen artichoke hearts
- 2 cans (5½ ounces each) lobster meat
- 1 teaspoon crumbled dried basil
- 1 teaspoon salt
- ½ teaspoon pepper
- ½ cup lemon French dressing
- ½ cup mayonnaise
  Lettuce
- ½ cup sliced radishes

Cook and drain macaroni. Cook artichoke hearts according to package directions. Drain. Combine macaroni, artichoke hearts, and next 5 ingredients; chill. Add mayonnaise and pile on lettuce bed. Decorate with radish slices. Makes 6 to 8 servings.

FISH AND MACARONI SALAD

- 2 cups cooked fish or canned salmon, tuna, or bonito
- ¼ cup fresh lemon juice
- 1 cup 1-inch pieces of green beans, cooked
- ¼ cup French dressing
- ¾ cup mayonnaise
- 2 tablespoons pickle relish
- 1 tablespoon prepared mustard
- 2 tablespoons chili sauce
- 2 cups cooked elbow macaroni
  Lettuce

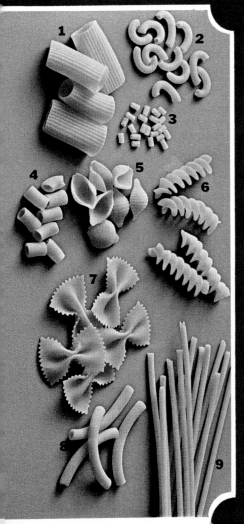

Lamb-Chop and Macaroni Skillet

1—Rigatoni; 2—Elbows; 3—Tubettini; 4—Ditali; 5—Shells; 6—Twist; 7—Bows; 8—Mezzani; 9—Macaronelli;

¼ cup chopped parsley

Flake fish after removing all bones. Sprinkle fish with lemon juice. Chill. Put green beans in a bowl and pour French dressing over them. Chill. Mix mayonnaise with pickle relish, mustard, chili sauce, and macaroni. Add drained marinated green beans to fish. Arrange macaroni around edge of a salad bowl lined with chunks of lettuce. Fill center with fish mixture. Sprinkle top with chopped parsley. Chill until ready to serve. Makes 6 servings.

BACON-TOPPED MACARONI AND CHEESE

2 cups elbow macaroni
1 tablespoon salt
6 cups water
½ pound bacon ends
3 tablespoons flour
1 cup undiluted evaporated milk
  Salt and pepper to taste
1 teaspoon Worcestershire
1 small onion, grated
1½ cups (6 ounces) sharp Cheddar cheese, shredded

Cook macaroni in boiling salted water until tender. Drain and save liquid, adding water to make 2 cups. Fry bacon and remove to absorbent paper to drain. Pour off all but 3 tablespoons fat from skillet; stir in flour. Remove from heat and slowly add evaporated milk and 2 cups macaroni water. Bring to boil, stirring constantly. Season with salt, pepper, Worcestershire, and onion. Add cheese and heat gently until cheese is melted. Add cooked macaroni; mix well. Put in serving dish; crumble bacon on top and serve immediately. Makes 4 servings.

HAM BALLS AND MACARONI SHELLS IN SKILLET

1 pound cooked smoked ham
½ cup fine dry bread crumbs
2 eggs, slightly beaten
¼ teaspoon pepper
¼ cup chopped parsley
⅓ cup butter or margarine

1 medium-size green pepper, diced
  About 2½ cups
  (one 1-pound 4-ounce can)
  pineapple chunks, undrained
2½ cups water
½ cup vinegar
  Salt and pepper to taste
  About 3 cups (8 ounces)
  shell macaroni
¼ cup chopped canned pimientos

Grind ham in meat grinder. Combine ham, bread crumbs, eggs, pepper, and parsley; mix well. Shape into 1½-inch balls. Chill for 30 minutes. Melt butter in 10-inch skillet. Add ham balls and cook over low heat until ham balls are browned on all sides. Remove ham balls; reserve drippings. Add green pepper to drippings and cook for 5 minutes. Drain pineapple; reserve syrup. Add pineapple liquid, water, vinegar, and salt and pepper to green pepper. Heat to boiling point. Gradually add macaroni so that mixture continues to boil. Cook, uncovered, over low heat, stirring occasionally, until shells are almost tender. Add ham balls, pimientos, and pineapple chunks.

Bacon-Topped Macaroni and Cheese

Heat to serving temperature, stirring occasionally. Makes 4 to 6 servings.

HOT HAM AND MACARONI SALAD

    8 ounces elbow macaroni
    1 onion, chopped
    ¼ cup butter or margarine
    1 tablespoon all-purpose flour
    1 teaspoon sugar
    1 teaspoon salt
    ½ teaspoon powdered mustard
    1 cup water
    ¼ cup vinegar
    1 egg, slightly beaten
    1 cup cooked ham in strips
    ½ cup shredded carrot
    1 cup raw-spinach leaves

Cook and drain macaroni. Brown onion lightly in butter. Blend in flour, sugar, salt, and mustard. Gradually add combined water and vinegar and cook, stirring constantly, until slightly thickened. Add a little of the hot mixture to the egg, mix well, and stir into mixture in skillet. Add macaroni, ham, and carrots, and heat gently. Garnish with spinach. Makes 4 servings.

PORK BALLS WITH MACARONI

    3 slices of white bread
    ⅓ cup milk
    1 pound ground pork
    1 small onion, chopped
    1 teaspoon salt
    ¼ teaspoon pepper
      Dash of nutmeg
    1 egg
      Cornstarch
    2 tablespoons butter
      or margarine
    2 chicken bouillon cubes
    1½ cups water
    1 garlic clove, minced
    1 cup uncooked broken
      macaroni or elbows
      Chopped parsley

Soak bread in milk and crumble. Mix well with pork, onion, salt, pepper, nutmeg, and egg. Shape into 12 balls, and roll in cornstarch. Brown on all sides in butter. Add bouillon cubes, water, and garlic. Cover and simmer for 30 minutes. Add macaroni, and cook for 20 minutes longer, adding more water, if necessary. Sprinkle with parsley. Makes 4 servings.

HAMBURGER, MACARONI, AND GREEN-BEAN CASSEROLE

    1 pound ground beef
    1 medium onion, chopped
    3 tablespoons all-purpose flour
    1½ teaspoons salt
    ⅛ teaspoon pepper
    2 cups milk
    2 cups shredded sharp
      Cheddar cheese
    8 ounces elbow macaroni, cooked
    1 box frozen cut green
      beans, cooked

Cook beef and onion, stirring with fork, until meat loses its red color. Blend in flour, salt, and pepper. Add milk and cook until thickened, stirring constantly. Add 1½ cups cheese and stir until melted. Mix with cooked macaroni and beans, and put in 2-quart casserole. Sprinkle with remaining ½ cup cheese. Bake in preheated moderate oven (350°F.) for 35 minutes, or until top is lightly browned. Makes 6 servings.

RED-WINE BEEF WITH MACARONI

    2 pounds lean boneless beef chuck
    2 tablespoons butter or margarine
    1 pound (7 medium) onions,
      cut into chunks
    1 tablespoon paprika
    1 bay leaf, crumbled
    2 teaspoons salt
    ¼ teaspoon pepper
    1 cup dry red wine
    4 ounces shell or ribbon macaroni
    2 cups water
      Chopped parsley
      Dairy sour cream (optional)

Cut beef into 1½-inch pieces. Heat butter in large heavy skillet or Dutch oven. Add meat and cook until lightly browned. Add onion and cook until liquid is evaporated. Sprinkle with paprika and add other seasonings and wine. Bring to boil, cover, and simmer for 2½ hours. Add macaroni and water. Bring again to boil and simmer for 15 to 20 minutes, stirring occasionally. Sprinkle with parsley and serve with sour cream. Makes 6 servings.

MACARONI-FRANKFURTER SKILLET

    2 cans (10½ ounces each)
      condensed beef broth
    1½ cups water
    2 tablespoons butter or margarine
    1 large onion, chopped
    2 cups (8 ounces) elbow macaroni
    1 teaspoon salt
    1 pound sliced frankfurters
    1 can (6 ounces) whole mushrooms
    2 canned pimientos, cut into strips

Combine broth and water; mix well. Melt butter in 10-inch skillet. Add onion and cook over low heat for 5 minutes. Add broth mixture and heat to boiling point. Add macaroni and cook, uncovered, stirring occasionally, until almost tender, about 10 minutes. Add salt, sliced frankfurters, undrained mushrooms, and pimientos. Cook for 10 minutes, or until macaroni is tender, stirring frequently. Makes 4 servings.

LAMB-CHOP AND MACARONI SKILLET

    2 tablespoons butter or margarine
    4 shoulder lamb chops,
      about ½-inch thick
    4 cups water
    1 package (1½ ounces) dehydrated
      onion-soup mix
    1 teaspoon salt
    ¼ teaspoon pepper
      About 3 cups (8 ounces)
      shell macaroni
    1 package (10 ounces) frozen
      mixed vegetables
    ¼ cup dry sherry (optional)

Melt butter in 10-inch skillet. Add lamb and cook over low heat until browned on both sides. Cover and cook over low heat for 30 minutes, or until lamb is tender. Remove lamb; reserve drippings. Add water to lamb drippings and heat to boiling point. Add soup mix and salt and pepper; mix well. Add shell macaroni and mixed vegetables. Cook, uncovered, stirring occasionally, for 10 minutes. Add lamb and sherry. Cook for 5 minutes, stirring frequently, or until macaroni and vegetables are tender. Makes 4 servings.

BAKED CHICKEN-MACARONI SALAD

    2 cups (8 ounces) elbow macaroni
    4 cups diced cooked chicken
    ⅓ cup toasted chopped almonds
    1 tablespoon fresh lemon juice
    1 teaspoon grated lemon rind
    1½ cups grated Swiss cheese
      (about ⅓ pound)
    2 teaspoons celery salt
    ½ teaspoon pepper
    1½ cups mayonnaise
      Parsley

Cook and drain macaroni. Combine with all other ingredients except parsley. Turn into buttered 2-quart baking dish. Bake in preheated moderate oven (350°F.) for 30 minutes. Garnish with parsley. Makes 4 to 6 servings.

MACARONI-MEAT TIMBALE

    3¼ cups elbow macaroni
    2 cups thick white sauce, made
      with half milk, half cream
    4 egg yolks
    ⅓ cup grated Parmesan cheese
      Butter or margarine
      Fine, dry bread crumbs
    ¼ cup minced onion
    1 garlic clove, minced
    1 pound veal and pork mixed,
      ground twice
    ½ pound chicken livers, chopped
    ⅓ cup chopped pimiento
    1½ cups cooked green peas
    ¼ cup tomato paste
    1 teaspoon salt
    1 teaspoon sugar
    ½ teaspoon oregano
    1 teaspoon grated lemon rind
    ¼ teaspoon pepper

Cook and drain macaroni. To white sauce, add egg yolks and grated Parmesan, blending thoroughly. Combine with macaroni and mix thoroughly. Generously butter a 3-quart casserole and sprinkle with fine dry bread crumbs to coat thoroughly. Make filling by melting 2 tablespoons butter in skillet. Add onion and garlic. Cook until onion is soft. Add ground meat and chicken livers. Cook, stirring occasionally, for 15 minutes. Add remaining ingredients. Cook over low heat for about 20 minutes, stirring frequently. Spoon two thirds of macaroni mixture into casserole. Press macaroni firmly against bottom and sides, leaving a well in the middle. Spoon filling into well. Top with remaining macaroni, taking care that meat is completely and thickly covered. Bake in preheated moderate oven (350°F.) for about 30 minutes. Makes 6 to 8 servings.

SOUR-CREAM MACARONI CASSEROLE

1¼ cups elbow macaroni
1 small onion, minced
1 can (3 ounces) chopped
   mushrooms, drained
2 tablespoons chopped
   green pepper
2 tablespoons butter or margarine
2 tablespoons chopped
   stuffed olives
1 cup grated sharp Cheddar cheese
1 cup dairy sour cream
1 teaspoon seasoned salt
¼ teaspoon seasoned pepper
1 can (7½ ounces) tuna
   or 1 cup diced cooked ham,
   chicken, or other meat
¼ cup milk
½ cup buttered soft bread crumbs
   Paprika

Cook and drain macaroni. Cook onion, mushrooms, and green pepper in the butter for 2 or 3 minutes. Add to macaroni with remaining ingredients, except last 2. Mix well and put in shallow 1½ quart baking dish. Sprinkle with crumbs and paprika. Bake in preheated moderate oven (350°F.) for about 30 minutes. Makes 6 servings.

FINNISH MACARONI

1½ cups small elbow macaroni
2 quarts hot milk
1½ teaspoons salt
1 teaspoon sugar
1 tablespoon butter
2 egg yolks
½ cup light cream
   White pepper

Cook macaroni in hot milk in top part of double boiler over boiling water until soft, about 30 minutes. Stir in salt, sugar, and butter. Beat together egg yolks and cream. Add to macaroni. Season with pepper. Makes 4 to 6 servings.

DANISH MACARONI SALAD

1 cup elbow macaroni
1 cup heavy cream
½ teaspoon salt
¼ teaspoon white pepper
1 teaspoon sugar
1 teaspoon white vinegar
1 to 2 tablespoons prepared
   horseradish
   Parsley

Cook macaroni. Drain, rinse in cold water, drain again, and chill. Whip cream until stiff. Add salt, pepper, sugar, and vinegar. Stir in horseradish. Mix with chilled macaroni; garnish with parsley. Makes 4 servings.

SICILIAN MACARONI AND EGGPLANT CASSEROLE

1 eggplant
1 or 2 tablespoons olive oil
½ pound macaroni twists
¾ teaspoon salt
1 teaspoon crumbled
   dried oregano
½ teaspoon crumbled
   dried basil
½ cup pine nuts
½ cup grated Parmesan cheese
2 cups (one 1-pound can)
   Italian-style tomatoes
2 tablespoons butter or margarine

Cut unpeeled eggplant into ¼-inch slices. Heat oil in skillet. Cook eggplant in it until well browned on both sides, adding more oil as necessary. Cook and drain macaroni. Butter a 2-quart casserole. Arrange half of macaroni on bottom. Top with half of eggplant. Sprinkle with half of salt, mixed oregano and basil, pine nuts, and Parmesan. Repeat layers, using the same quantity of ingredients. Top final layer with tomatoes. Dot with butter and bake in preheated moderate oven (350°F.) for 30 minutes. Makes 4 servings.

EGG-MACARONI SALAD

2 cups (8 ounces) elbow macaroni
½ cup chopped celery
¼ cup chopped parsley
3 hard-cooked eggs, quartered
¼ cup sliced scallions
½ cup mayonnaise
2 teaspoons prepared mustard
¾ teaspoon salt
¼ teaspoon pepper
1 medium tomato, cut into wedges

Cook macaroni according to package directions. Drain in colander. Combine macaroni, celery, parsley, eggs, and scallions; toss lightly. Combine mayonnaise, mustard, salt, and pepper; blend. Combine macaroni mixture and mayonnaise mixture; toss lightly, but thoroughly. Top with tomato wedges. Chill. Makes 4 servings.

MACARONI, BEAN, AND EGG SALAD

2 cups elbow macaroni, cooked
½ cup mayonnaise
¼ cup French dressing
   Dash of hot pepper sauce
⅓ cup diced sweet pickles
2 tablespoons vinegar
6 hard-cooked eggs, cubed
2 cups (one 1-pound can)
   red kidney beans, drained
   Salt and pepper to taste
   Watercress

Mix all ingredients except cress. Chill; serve on cress. Makes 6 servings.

MACARONI PARMESAN

1 cup small soft bread cubes
2 tablespoons butter or margarine
⅛ teaspoon garlic salt
8 ounces elbow macaroni
1 cup dairy sour cream
½ cup grated Parmesan cheese
2 egg yolks
½ teaspoon paprika
½ teaspoon salt
¼ teaspoon pepper

Brown bread cubes in butter, add garlic salt and set aside. Cook and drain macaroni. Put in top pan of chafing dish or double boiler over boiling water. Mix remaining ingredients and stir into macaroni. Heat gently and sprinkle with browned bread cubes. Makes 4 servings.

TOSSED MACARONI AND CHEESE

8 ounces macaroni
½ cup butter or margarine
1 garlic clove
½ cup chopped parsley
2 cups grated Parmesan
   or Romano cheese

Cook macaroni in boiling salted water until tender; drain and put on hot platter. Melt butter in saucepan with garlic and simmer for a few minutes. Remove garlic. Pour butter over hot macaroni. Add parsley and 1½ cups grated cheese; toss well. Sprinkle with remaining cheese. Makes 4 to 6 servings.

BAKED MACARONI WITH TOMATOES AND CHEESE

8 ounces macaroni, broken
1 medium onion, chopped
2 tablespoons butter or margarine
   Water
1 medium green pepper,
   cut into pieces
2¼ cups (one 1-pound, 3-ounce can)
   tomatoes
1 can (6 ounces) tomato paste
1 teaspoon salt
¼ teaspoon pepper
¾ pound sharp Cheddar or
   process American cheese

Cook macaroni in boiling salted water until tender; drain and put in shallow 2-quart casserole. Fry onion in butter until brown; add ½ cup water and remaining ingredients except cheese; bring to boil. Pour over macaroni. Cut 9 thin slices of cheese; set aside. Shred remaining cheese. Add to macaroni and stir lightly. Bake in preheated moderate oven (350°F.) for 1 hour. Stir once during baking. Top with sliced cheese. Bake for 5 minutes longer, or until cheese melts. Makes 4 to 6 servings.

MACARONI AND CHEESE SOUFFLÉ

1½ cups elbow macaroni
6 tablespoons butter or margarine
¼ cup flour
1½ teaspoons salt
½ teaspoon paprika
   Dash of cayenne
2 cups milk
½ pound sharp
   Cheddar cheese, grated
6 eggs, separated

Cook macaroni according to package directions; drain. Melt butter; stir in flour, salt, paprika, and cayenne. Add milk and cook, stirring, until thickened. Remove from heat, add cheese, and stir until melted. Beat egg yolks until light and add to cheese sauce. Add macaroni. Beat egg whites until stiff and fold into mixture. Pour into greased 3-quart casserole. Bake in preheated very hot oven (475°F.) for 10 minutes. Reduce heat to hot (400°F.) and bake for 25 minutes longer. Makes 6 to 8 servings. Can be frozen.

MACARONI AND CHEESE SALAD

1 cup elbow macaroni
2 cups (½ pound) Swiss

or sharp Cheddar cheese, cubed
1 cup diced celery
¼ cup chopped walnuts
1 cup mayonnaise
½ teaspoon powdered mustard
½ teaspoon Worcestershire
Salt and pepper
Lettuce and cucumbers

Cook and cool macaroni. Combine with cheese, celery, and walnuts. Blend in mayonnaise, mustard, and Worcestershire. Add salt and pepper to taste. Chill for 1 hour. Serve on lettuce and garnish with cucumber slices. Makes 4 servings.

MACARONI DOUBLE-CHEESE CASSEROLE
2 cups (8 ounces) elbow macaroni
8 ounces sliced
   process Cheddar cheese
1 cup chopped mushrooms
1 teaspoon salt
⅛ teaspoon pepper
¼ cup grated Cheddar cheese

Cook elbow macaroni according to package directions. Drain in colander. Arrange sliced cheese on bottom and sides of greased 1½-quart casserole. Combine macaroni, mushrooms, and salt and pepper; mix well. Turn into casserole over cheese. Sprinkle with grated cheese. Bake in preheated moderate oven (350°F.) for 30 minutes. Makes 4 servings.

MACAROON—A small round, crunchy confection made of almond paste or ground almonds, sugar, and egg whites.

The little cakes are called *macaron* in French and the English have adopted the name. But originally the Italians gave the delicacies their title of *maccarone,* a word of the Neapolitan dialect which also refers to dumplings, small cakes, and macaroni.

The origin of the macaroon is not known. It is thought that they came to France from Italy during the 16th century. In any case macaroons were readily appreciated by the French and subsequently mass produced. The macaroons of the town of Nancy, in northeastern France, enjoyed a great reputation in the 17th century. Even today the delicately flavored pastries of this town are considered the best. They have been made by successive generations of the same family for over 200 years.

Macaroons are easily baked at home. They also can be bought in food and bakery stores.

MACAROONS
8 egg whites
2¼ cups (1 pound)
   granulated sugar
½ teaspoon vanilla extract
1 pound almonds, grated
½ pound whole almonds

Beat egg whites until foamy. Add granulated sugar, 2 tablespoons at a time, and beat for 30 minutes; then add vanilla and grated nuts. Refrigerate for several hours, then drop by teaspoonfuls onto unglazed paper on cookie sheets. Press an almond into center of each cookie. Let stand overnight. Bake in preheated slow oven (300°F.) for approximately 1 hour, or until cookies can be lifted from the paper. Makes about 7 dozen.

COCONUT MACAROONS
2 egg whites
1 teaspoon vanilla extract
½ teaspoon salt
1 cup sugar
2 cups shredded or flaked
   coconut

Beat egg whites until stiff. Gradually beat in vanilla, salt, and sugar, 1 tablespoon at a time. Fold in coconut. Drop by teaspoons onto unglazed brown paper on a cookie sheet. Bake in preheated slow oven (325°F.) for about 20 minutes, or until golden. Makes 30 macaroons.

CHOCOLATE MACAROONS
3 egg whites
¼ teaspoon salt
1 cup sugar
½ cup ground blanched almonds
½ teaspoon vanilla extract
1 cup semisweet chocolate pieces,
   melted and cooled

Beat egg whites and salt until stiff but not dry. Gradually beat in sugar until mixture is thick and glossy and stands in peaks. Fold in remaining ingredients. Drop by teaspoons onto well-buttered cookie sheets and bake in preheated moderate oven (350°F.) for 15 minutes. Makes about 4 dozen.

DANISH MACAROONS
½ pound blanched almonds
2¾ cups confectioners' sugar
7 egg whites
1 teaspoon baking powder

Grind almonds very fine; there should be 2⅔ cups when ground. Sift sugar; mix well with ground almonds. Whip egg whites stiff with the baking powder added. Fold into almond mixture. Beat smooth, or turn out mixture onto marble slab and work smooth with wooden paddle or spoon. The mixture should be stiff enough to hold its shape. Start oven at slow (275°F.). Shape small balls of almond mixture; place 1 inch apart on a greased cookie sheet covered with wax paper. Bake in slow oven for about 20 minutes, until delicately browned. Remove from oven, invert the paper, and wet the back of it with a cloth wrung out of cold water. The macaroons drop off easily. Makes 4 to 6 dozen macaroons.

BRAZIL-NUT MACAROONS
5 egg whites
¼ teaspoon cream of tartar
½ teaspoon salt
1 teaspoon vanilla extract
1¼ cups sugar
1½ cups flaked coconut
1 cup finely chopped Brazil nuts
¼ cup diced candied orange peel
Candied cherries

Beat egg whites until foamy. Add cream of tartar, salt, and vanilla and beat until whites begin to hold their shape. Gradually add sugar and beat until stiff but not dry. Fold in coconut, nuts, and orange peel. Drop from teaspoon onto well-greased cookie sheets. Put a cherry half in center of each. Bake in preheated slow oven (325°F.) for 20 minutes. Makes 4 dozen.

CHERRY-COCONUT MACAROONS
1 egg white
⅛ teaspoon salt
½ teaspoon vanilla extract
½ cup sugar
1 can (3½ ounces) flaked coconut
Candied cherries

Beat egg white until foamy. Add salt and vanilla and beat until white begins to hold its shape. Add sugar, 2 tablespoons at a time, and beat until mixture is very stiff but not dry. Fold in coconut. Drop by teaspoons onto well-greased cookie sheets. Put a cherry half in center of each cookie. Bake in preheated moderate oven (350°F.) for 12 to 15 minutes. Makes 16 cookies.

CORN-FLAKE MACAROONS
2 egg whites
¼ teaspoon salt
1 cup sugar
1 teaspoon vanilla or almond
   extract or grated
   orange rind
3 cups corn flakes

Beat egg whites until foamy. Add salt, then sugar, 2 tablespoons at a time, beating after each addition until sugar is blended. Then continue beating until mixture will stand in peaks. Add flavoring; fold in cereal. Drop by teaspoons onto greased cookie sheets. Bake in preheated moderate oven (350°F.) for about 15 minutes. Makes about 3 dozen.

MACAROON ANGEL PUDDING
4 egg whites
¼ teaspoon salt
1 cup sugar
1 teaspoon vanilla extract
1 cup fine Graham-cracker crumbs
1 teaspoon baking powder
½ cup flaked coconut
½ cup chopped nuts
Whipped cream

Beat egg whites with salt until frothy; gradually beat in sugar and continue beating until mixture holds a peak when beater is lifted. Add vanilla. Mix together crumbs, baking powder, coconut, and nuts; fold into egg-white mixture. Pile into well-buttered deep 9-inch pie pan. Bake in preheated moderate oven (350°F.) for 30 minutes. Cut into wedges and serve warm with cream. Makes 8 servings.

MACAROON CREAM

1 envelope unflavored gelatin
2 tablespoons cold water
4 eggs, separated
¾ cup sugar
⅛ teaspoon salt
2 cups scalded milk
1 teaspoon vanilla extract
¼ teaspoon almond extract
¼ pound almond macaroons,
crumbled (about 1½ cups)

Sprinkle gelatin over water; let stand. Beat egg yolks slightly; combine with sugar and salt. Add milk gradually and cook in top part of double boiler over boiling water, stirring constantly, until mixture coats a spoon. Add gelatin mixture and stir until dissolved. Gradually fold into stiffly beaten whites. Add flavorings. Spread crumbled macaroons in serving dish; top with custard mixture. Chill for several hours before serving. Makes 6 to 8 servings.

MACE—An aromatic spice made from the arillode, or false aril, which covers the seed of the nutmeg. The nutmeg (*Myristica fragrans*), a tropical evergreen tree, bears a golden pear-shape fruit which, when its external covering is removed, reveals a red arillode over its hard kernel (the nutmeg itself). This arillode is dried, becoming yellowish-orange and, either whole (sometimes called a "blade") or powdered, is the mace available for cookery.

Mace has the sweet strong flavor and odor of the nutmeg although it is somewhat more pungent. Mace is used to flavor sauces, soups, poultry, and fish, and in creamed vegetables, custards, soufflés, cakes, and desserts.

The nutmeg is native to the Moluccas, or Spice Islands, in the East Indies, and is now also grown in the West Indies. As early as the 6th century mace was known to the court of Constantinople. By the end of the 12th century mace was found in Denmark and other parts of northern Europe and by the 13th century in England. Arab traders had a monopoly on the spice trade and drove the prices so high that only the rich could afford spices.

Mace was as widely used as its price would allow, flavoring pottage, puddings, tarts, pastries, cakes, and conserves. Like so many other spices, it was used medicinally too. A medieval chest and cough serum called Wine of Tyre had mace as an ingredient. Some herbalists suggested using rosemary flowers steeped in liquid and spices including mace for a mouthwash to sweeten the breath.

SHERRY CRAB SOUP

2 cans (10½ ounces each)
cream-of-celery soup
2½ cups milk
4 hard-cooked eggs
½ teaspoon Worcestershire
¼ teaspoon powdered mace
1 teaspoon curry powder
2 cans (7 ounces each)
crabmeat, cleaned
½ cup sherry
Lemon peel

Mix soup with milk. Remove egg yolks from whites. Chop whites and add to soup. Add Worcestershire, mace, curry powder, and crabmeat; simmer for 10 minutes. Put in individual bowls; crumble egg yolks over top. Pass pitcher of sherry heated with 2 pieces of twisted lemon peel. Makes 4 large servings.

INDIVIDUAL SALMON CASSEROLES

2 pounds salmon fillets, 1½ inches
wide and ½ inch thick
1 cup chopped fresh mushrooms
3 tablespoons butter or margarine
¼ cup all-purpose flour
½ cup light cream or half-and-half
1 teaspoon onion juice
Salt and pepper to taste
Pinch of mace
Buttered bread crumbs
Paprika
Toast rounds

Butter 8 glass custard cups and coil the salmon fillets around to line the sides, saving any scraps left over. Meanwhile, sauté mushrooms in butter until golden-brown, add flour, and stir until smooth. Gradually stir in cream and cook over low heat, stirring constantly, until smooth and thickened. Season with onion juice, salt and pepper, and mace. Divide sauce evenly among the custard cups and top with any scraps of salmon you have left. Bake in preheated moderate oven (375° F.) for 20 minutes. Loosen edges with sharp knife. Turn out upside down on a baking pan, draining off any juice from the salmon which has collected during baking. Sprinkle tops with buttered bread crumbs and paprika and bake for 5 minutes longer. Serve on toast rounds. Makes 8 servings.

CHICKEN, POTATO, AND CELERY SCALLOP

4 cups sliced raw potatoes
1 cup diced celery
3 cups diced cooked chicken
2½ to 3 cups chicken gravy
Salt and pepper to taste
¼ teaspoon powdered mace
Buttered soft bread crumbs

Cook potato and celery in small amount of boiling salted water until tender; drain. Mix with chicken and gravy and season with salt and pepper. Add mace. Pour into 2-quart casserole; top with crumbs. Bake in preheated very hot oven (450°F.) for 20 minutes. Makes 4 to 6 servings.

CAULIFLOWER IN BREAD-CRUMB SAUCE

1 large head cauliflower
Boiling water
1½ teaspoons salt
¼ cup butter or margarine
⅛ teaspoon pepper
¼ teaspoon powdered mace
3 tablespoons fine dry
bread crumbs
1 large hard-cooked egg,
finely chopped

Remove outer leaves from cauliflower, leaving a few young tender leaves attached. Place in a saucepan with 1 inch of boiling water and 1 teaspoon salt. Bring to boiling point, uncovered, and cook for 5 minutes. Cover and cook for 20 minutes, or until cauliflower is tender. Turn head to cook uniformly. Remove cauliflower to serving dish, keeping the head intact. Dot 2 tablespoons butter over hot cauliflower so that butter melts and runs inside flowerets. Sprinkle with ½ teaspoon salt, the pepper, and mace. Cook bread crumbs in remaining butter for ½ minute and sprinkle over the head. Scatter with chopped hard-cooked egg. Makes 6 servings.

MACE CHEESE PUFFS

3 large eggs, separated
Dash of salt
½ teaspoon pepper
⅛ teaspoon powdered mace
1½ cups grated Cheddar cheese
Buttered bread slices or crackers

Beat egg yolks. Add salt, pepper, mace, and cheese. Beat egg whites until they stand in soft stiff peaks. Fold into the mixture. Pile thickly on buttered bread slices. Bake in preheated hot oven (400° F.) until puffed, 12 to 15 minutes. Serve hot for lunch or supper. Makes 6 servings.

CORNISH FRUITED SAFFRON BREAD

½ teaspoon saffron threads
1½ teaspoons brandy
or fresh lemon juice
1 package dry yeast
or 1 cake compressed yeast
¼ cup lukewarm water*
1 egg, well beaten
½ cup melted butter
1 cup lukewarm milk

4 cups sifted all-purpose flour
¾ cup sugar
¾ teaspoon salt
½ teaspoon ground nutmeg
¼ teaspoon powdered mace
¼ cup each of raisins
    and currants
2 tablespoons each of diced
    candied orange and lemon peel
1 tablespoon diced citron
1 egg beaten with 1 tablespoon
    water, for glazing

Soak saffron in brandy for 10 to 15 minutes. Strain. Mix yeast with water and set aside. *Use very warm water (105°F. to 115°F.) for dry yeast; use lukewarm water (80°F. to 90°F.) for compressed. Let stand for a few minutes, then stir until dissolved. Add egg and butter to milk. Sift dry ingredients. Add dried and candied fruits and mix with fingers to coat. Add all liquids, including saffron infusion, to dry ingredients, mixing with hands until well blended. Set aside to rise for 2 hours if you want to make the bread at once. Otherwise, refrigerate in covered bowl overnight. When ready to shape loaf, dump dough onto floured board; roll lightly in flour. Roll about ½ inch thick; dough should be length of a long loaf pan, or divide it into halves for 2 pans (9 x 5 x 3 inches). Roll dough over and over tightly like a jelly roll, fold ends under and place in greased pan or pans with seams on bottom. Press dough to even top. Brush with egg beaten with water. Set in a warm room (about 75°F. to 80°F.) and let rise until dough is light and spongy. Refrigerated dough takes longer to rise; 2 to 3 hours is sufficient. Place loaf in preheated hot oven (400°F.) for 5 minutes. Reduce heat to moderate (375°F.) and bake for 25 minutes. Reduce again to 350°F. and bake for 20 minutes longer. Turn out on cake rack and cool before slicing.

WIGS

1 package active dry yeast or
    1 cake compressed yeast
¼ cup lukewarm water*
1½ cups scalded cooled milk
6 cups sifted all-purpose flour
2 teaspoons salt
1 egg, beaten
½ cup sugar
½ cup butter, melted
¼ teaspoon powdered mace

Dissolve the yeast in the water. *Use very warm water (105°F. to 115°F.) for dry yeast; use lukewarm (80°F. to 90°F.) for compressed. Add milk and stir in the flour that has been sifted with the salt. Add remaining ingredients. Cover and let rise until doubled. Stir down. Add just enough more flour to knead, about 1 cup. Knead well for about 5 minutes. Place in buttered bowl and let rise again. When doubled, make into any shape desired and place on buttered

cookie sheets. Let rise again. When risen, bake in preheated moderate oven (375° F.) for 20 to 25 minutes. Makes about 55 small buns.

Christmas Wig Buns

To the above recipe, add 2 teaspoons grated orange rind, ½ cup raisins, ½ cup mixed candied fruit peels, and ½ cup nuts. Shape into buns. When baked, brush with a mixture of 2 cups confectioners' sugar blended with enough milk or water to make a thin glaze.

SPICED SQUASH PUDDING

¾ cup sugar
1 tablespoon flour
¾ teaspoon salt
1 teaspoon ground ginger
½ teaspoon powdered mace
3 large eggs
1½ cups mashed cooked
    butternut or hubbard squash
1½ cups milk
2 tablespoons light mild molasses
2 tablespoons melted butter
    or margarine
    Whipped cream

Combine sugar, flour, salt, ginger, and mace. Beat in eggs. Stir in squash, milk, molasses, and butter. Mix well. Pour into buttered 1½-quart casserole. Bake in preheated moderate oven (350°F.) for 1¼ hours, or until firm in the center. Serve with whipped cream. Makes 8 servings.

BANANA SOUFFLÉ

3 firm ripe bananas
1½ tablespoons fresh
    lemon juice
⅓ cup sugar
1 tablespoon cornstarch
⅛ teaspoon salt
½ teaspoon powdered mace
¼ teaspoon grated lemon rind
¾ cup milk
3 large eggs, separated
2 tablespoons butter or margarine
1½ teaspoons vanilla extract
    Whipped cream, sweetened to taste

Peel and slice bananas and dip into lemon juice. Mix together in a saucepan sugar, cornstarch, salt, mace, and lemon rind. Add milk and mix well. Stir and cook over medium heat until thickened. Add a little of the hot mixture to beaten egg yolks. Then mix with remaining hot mixture. Stir in butter and sliced bananas. Beat egg whites until they stand in soft stiff peaks. Fold into custard mixture along with vanilla. Turn into 1½-quart soufflé dish. Place in a pan of hot water. Bake in preheated moderate oven (350° F.) for 1 hour, or until firm. Serve as dessert with whipped cream. Makes 6 servings.

BIRD'S-NEST PUDDING

5 to 6 fresh pears
⅔ cup sugar
¼ teaspoon salt
½ teaspoon powdered mace
1 tablespoon cornstarch

Cornish Fruited Saffron Bread

Individual Salmon Casseroles

2 eggs
2 cups milk

Wash, pare, and core pears. Place in 1-quart casserole. Fill centers with sugar, saving ¼ cup for custard. Combine the ¼ cup sugar, the salt, mace, and cornstarch. Beat in eggs. Mix in ¼ cup cold milk. Heat remaining milk, add, and pour over pears. Bake in preheated slow oven (325°F.) for 1½ hours, or until a knife inserted in custard comes out clean and pears are tender. Makes 5 to 6 servings.

FROZEN EGGNOG PIE

2 cups unsalted pretzel crumbs
½ cup melted butter
3 egg yolks, slightly beaten
1 cup sugar
¼ teaspoon salt
½ cup milk
3 tablespoons rum
½ teaspoon powdered mace
3 egg whites
1 cup heavy cream, whipped

Prepare crumbs by crushing pretzels fine in blender or grinder. Mix with butter and press into buttered 9-inch pie pan. Chill. In top part of small double boiler mix egg yolks, ½ cup of the sugar, the salt, and milk. Cook over simmering water, stirring constantly, until slightly thickened. Remove from heat and add rum and mace. Cool. Beat egg white until almost stiff. Gradually beat in remaining sugar. Fold with cream into first mixture. Pile lightly in crumb pie shell, and freeze. Makes 6 to 8 servings.

MACE COFFEECAKES

3 tablespoons shortening
1 egg
1 cup sugar
2 cups sifted all-purpose flour
2 teaspoons baking powder
½ teaspoon salt
½ teaspoon powdered mace
1 cup milk
  Topping
48 pecan halves
2 tablespoons butter or margarine

Cream together shortening, egg, and sugar. Add sifted dry ingredients alternately with milk. Spread thinly in 3 greased and floured 8-inch round pans. Sprinkle with Topping; arrange pecans on cakes and dot with butter. Bake in preheated moderate oven (375°F.) for about 20 minutes. Let cool and remove from pan without turning upside down. Makes three 8-inch cakes. Chopped pecans may be used instead of halves, if preferred.

Topping

2 tablespoons sugar
1½ teaspoons each of ground cinnamon and nutmeg
1 teaspoon powdered mace

Mix all ingredients together.

POPPY-SEED MACE COOKIES

½ cup soft butter or margarine
1 cup firmly packed dark brown sugar
1 egg
1 tablespoon milk
2 cups sifted all-purpose flour
2 teaspoons baking powder
¼ teaspoon salt
½ teaspoon powdered mace
2 tablespoons poppy seeds

Cream butter; add sugar and egg; beat until light. Add all ingredients except seed; mix well. Shape into 1-inch balls; flatten to ¼-inch thickness. Make a thumbprint in center of each. Sprinkle center with seed. Bake in preheated hot oven (400°F.) for 6 to 8 minutes. Makes about 4 dozen. Store in an airtight container.

BANANA-MACE WHIPPED TOPPING

1 egg white, unbeaten
1 large ripe banana
2 tablespoons sugar
⅛ teaspoon salt
½ teaspoon powdered mace

Place all ingredients in a small mixing bowl. Beat with a rotary or electric beater until light and fluffy. Serve as a topping for cakes and puddings. Makes 1⅔ cups.

BUTTERSCOTCH-MACE SUNDAE SAUCE

1 cup firmly packed brown sugar
¼ cup light corn syrup
¼ cup butter or margarine
½ cup water
½ cup light cream
¼ teaspoon powdered mace

Mix sugar, corn syrup, butter, and water in saucepan. Put over low heat and cook until a small amount of mixture forms a very soft ball when dropped in very cold water (232°F. on a candy thermometer). Remove from heat and stir in cream and mace. Makes about 1¾ cups.

MACÉDOINE—A French culinary term which refers to a mixture of raw or cooked fruit or vegetables. The name comes from Macedonia, the homeland of Alexander the Great. This region, located in the south central part of the Balkans, had a population made up of Turks, Greeks, Albanians, Slavs, and other national groups, each with its own language and cultural traditions. Thus the word macédoine, or medley, was adopted from history into culinary language.

A macédoine is either a fruit dessert or a vegetable salad. In French, this is specified, as in *macédoine de fruits* or a *macédoine de légumes*. A proper French *macédoine de fruits* is served in a glass or silver bowl bedded in a bucket of crushed ice to keep it chilled. The fruit in season is sprinkled with sugar or with a sugar syrup, and often flavored with a few spoonfuls of kirsch or other liqueurs. The fruits should be chosen for contrast in color, shape, and texture. Some fruits particularly good are: orange or grapefruit sections; melon balls; seeded white grapes; fresh or canned cherries; strawberries; raspberries; fresh-pineapple wedges; sliced pears, peaches, and nectarines; cubes or slices of avocado.

The *macédoine de légumes* is a combination of fresh vegetables, cooked separately, then warmed together until hot, dressed with butter, and seasoned and served in a vegetable dish.

MACÉDOINE OF VEGETABLES

1 box (10 ounces) frozen peas
1 cucumber, peeled and thinly sliced
4 green onions, minced
½ cup French dressing
1 ripe avocado
  Juice of 1 lemon
  Salt
  Salad greens
1 can (1 pound) sliced pickled beets, drained

Cook peas until barely tender; drain. Cool, and toss with cucumber, green onions, and ¼ cup dressing. Peel and slice avocado. Sprinkle with lemon juice and salt. Arrange avocado slices on greens in a circle around edge of platter. Arrange beet slices next to avocado. Pile pea mixture into center. Pour remaining dressing over avocado and beets. Makes 6 servings.

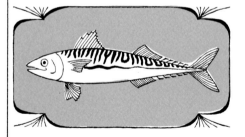

MACKEREL—A long, slender, salt-water fish (*Scomber scombus*) found in the Atlantic Ocean from Labrador to North Carolina and from Norway to Spain. Mackerel run in schools and are caught in nets. In cold weather mackerel migrate to the south and into deeper water; in warm weather they are found near the coast.

The common mackerel averages a length of one foot and a weight of one to two pounds; others weigh six to seven pounds. Mackerel scales are small and smooth, its back steely-blue or greenish, its belly silvery-white. The flesh is firm and fatty, with a distinctive flavor and a savory taste.

Availability and Purchasing Guide—Mackerel is available in food stores all year round. Fresh mackerel is most abundant from April to November. It is sold whole, up to about 16 inches in length, and in fillets.

Also available are frozen fillets and canned mackerel, plain, and in tomato sauce or white wine sauce. Mackerel roe is available canned. Smoked or salted mackerel is available.

When buying fresh fish, look for firm flesh with a steely-blue skin and a fresh odor.

Storage—Fresh fish should be used as soon as possible. Wrap in moisture-proof paper and keep in coldest part of refrigerator.

- [ ] Fresh, raw; and lightly smoked, refrigerator shelf: 1 to 2 days
- [ ] Fresh, cooked; lightly smoked, cooked; and canned, opened and covered, refrigerator shelf: 3 to 4 days
- [ ] Fresh or lightly smoked, prepared for freezing; and frozen, refrigerator frozen-food compartment: 2 to 3 weeks
- [ ] Fresh or smoked, prepared for freezing; and frozen, freezer: 1 year
- [ ] Canned, kitchen shelf: 1 year
- [ ] Heavily smoked, refrigerator shelf: 2 to 3 months
- [ ] Heavily smoked, refrigerator frozen-food compartment, prepared for freezing: 4 to 5 months

Nutritive Food Values—A good source of protein.

- [ ] Fresh mackerel, 3½ ounces, broiled = 236 calories
- [ ] Canned, 3½ ounces, solids and liquid = 180 calories
- [ ] Salted, 3½ ounces = 305 calories
- [ ] Smoked, 3½ ounces = 219 calories

Basic Preparation—Mackerel, a fatty fish with firm flesh, can be broiled, baked with or without stuffing, sautéed, or pan-broiled.

Wash under cold running water but do not soak in water.

Thaw frozen fish in refrigerator, allowing 8 hours for 1 pound of fish.

- [ ] **To Freeze**—Freeze whole or in fillets. Eviscerate; remove head and tail. Wash thoroughly. Dip fish or pieces of fish into a solution of 4 cups cold water and 2 teaspoons ascorbic acid for 20 seconds. Drain and pat dry. Wrap in moisture-vapor-proof wrapping, excluding as much air as possible. Seal.

BROILED MACKEREL WITH MUSTARD SAUCE

- 2 large or 4 small mackerel (about 3 pounds)
- ¼ cup melted butter or margarine
- ½ teaspoon paprika
- 2 teaspoons prepared mustard
  Juice of ½ lemon
- ½ teaspoon salt
- ⅛ teaspoon pepper

Put fish on greased broiler rack. Combine remaining ingredients and brush on fish. Broil under medium heat for 8 to 12 minutes, brushing with sauce several times. Makes 4 servings.

BAKED MACKEREL

Clean a 4-pound mackerel. Oil a large oval baking dish or pan and put the fish in it. Dot with butter, and sprinkle with salt and pepper. Bake in preheated hot oven (425°F.) for about 45 minutes. Baste often with drippings in pan. Serve with hollandaise or tomato sauce. Makes 4 to 6 servings.

BAKED STUFFED MACKEREL

- Split mackerel (about 4 pounds)
- Salt and pepper
- 1 small onion, chopped
- 1 tablespoon chopped parsley
- ¼ pound fresh mushrooms, sliced
- 6 tablespoons vegetable shortening
- 1 cup soft bread crumbs
- 1 teaspoon chopped fresh or dried mint

Sprinkle fish inside and out with salt and pepper. Cook onion, parsley, and mushrooms in 3 tablespoons hot shortening for 5 minutes. Add to crumbs and mint; season to taste with salt and pepper. Stuff fish with mixture and sew openings closed or use toothpicks. Cut several gashes in skin. Put remaining shortening in baking pan and add fish. Bake in preheated moderate oven (350°F.) for 45 to 50 minutes. Makes 4 servings.

SAUTÉED MACKEREL MEUNIÈRE

- 6 mackerel fillets
- Milk
- All-purpose flour
- Butter or margarine
- Salt and pepper to taste
- Chopped parsley

Dip fillets into milk and roll in flour. Sauté in hot butter until browned on both sides. Remove to a hot platter, and sprinkle with salt, pepper, and parsley. Add a little more butter to skillet, melt, and pour over fish. Makes 6 servings.

MACKEREL PIE

- 2 tablespoons margarine
- 2 tablespoons flour
- ¾ cup undiluted evaporated milk
  About 2½ cups (one 1-pound, 4-ounce can) peas, undrained
- ½ teaspoon grated lemon rind
- ⅛ teaspoon pepper
- 1 teaspoon salt
- 1 can (1 pound) mackerel
- 3 cups seasoned mashed potatoes

Melt margarine and blend in flour. Remove from heat and slowly stir in evaporated milk diluted with liquid drained from canned peas. Return to heat and cook slowly until sauce is slightly thickened. Add lemon rind, pepper, salt, and liquid drained from canned mackerel. Put mackerel, coarsely flaked, in 2-quart casserole. Pour sauce over fish. Top with mashed potatoes. Mark top in crisscross design with fork. Bake in preheated hot oven (425°F.) for 20 minutes, or until heated and lightly browned. Makes 4 servings.

TARTARE FISH LOAF WITH CAPER SAUCE

- 1 can (1 pound) mackerel
- 1 pimiento, chopped
- ½ green pepper, minced
- ¼ cup minced sour pickle
- 1 small onion, grated
  Grated rind of ½ lemon
- ½ teaspoon powdered mustard
- ⅓ cup salad dressing
- ¾ cup rolled cracker crumbs
- 1½ tablespoons soft fat

Flake undrained fish and crush bones with fork. Combine all ingredients, mixing well. Shape into oval loaf on oiled ovenproof platter or baking dish. Bake in preheated moderate oven (375°F.) for about 35 minutes. Serve with Caper Sauce. Makes 4 large servings.

Caper Sauce

- ¼ cup butter or margarine
- ¼ cup all-purpose flour
- 1 teaspoon salt
- ⅛ teaspoon white pepper
- 2 cups milk
- ⅓ cup drained capers

Melt butter and blend in flour and seasonings. Add milk gradually and cook, stirring constantly, until sauce is thickened. Add capers. Makes about 2 cups.

SALT MACKEREL BAKED IN CREAM

- 1 salt mackerel, about 1½ pounds
- ½ cup all-purpose flour
- ⅛ teaspoon pepper
  Pinch of paprika
- ½ cup milk
- ¾ cup heavy cream
  Butter or margarine
  Chopped fresh mint

Soak mackerel in cold water for 10 hours, changing water twice. Drain. Season flour with pepper and paprika. Roll mackerel in flour mixture. Put in buttered shallow baking dish. Pour milk and cream over top, and dot with butter. Bake in preheated moderate oven (375°F.) for about 20 minutes. Sprinkle with mint. Makes 6 servings.

PICKLED MACKEREL WITH CUCUMBER SLICES

- 1 can (1 pound) mackerel, drained
- 1 cup cider vinegar
- 1 onion, sliced
- ¾ teaspoon salt
- 1 teaspoon whole mixed pickling spice
- ¼ teaspoon pepper
  Cucumber slices

Put large pieces of mackerel in a shallow dish or on a platter. Put vinegar, onion, and other seasonings in saucepan; bring to boil, cool slightly, and pour over fish. Put in refrigerator to chill. Serve with crisp slices of cucumber. Makes 4 servings.

MADELEINE—A small delicate cake, somewhat like a butter cookie, baked in special shell-shape pans.

MADELEINES

¾ cup butter, clarified*
  and cooled
2 eggs
¾ cup sugar
½ teaspoon grated lemon rind
½ teaspoon vanilla extract
1 cup unsifted all-purpose flour
  Butter

*To clarify butter, put it in a small deep saucepan. Heat slowly until foam disappears from top and there is a light-brown sediment in the bottom of the pan. This takes about 10 minutes. When clear, remove from heat and skim off any brown top. Pour off clear butter, leaving sediment in pan; cool. Put eggs, sugar, and lemon rind in a rather flat bowl and stir until blended. Put over a saucepan containing 1 or 2 inches of hot water. Water should not touch bowl, nor should it boil. Put saucepan with bowl over low heat for 5 to 10 minutes, or until egg mixture is lukewarm. Remove from over hot water and beat with electric mixer at high speed until light, fluffy, and tripled in volume. Add vanilla. Fold in flour and clarified butter. Do not beat. Generously butter 2¾-inch madeleine pans. Fill two thirds full with batter. Bake in preheated very hot oven (450° F.) for 7 or 8 minutes, or until golden-brown. Let stand for 1 to 2 minutes before removing from pans. Butter pans again, refill with batter, and bake. Repeat until all of batter is used. Makes about 42.

MADRILENE—A name usually given to a clear soup which is flavored with tomato juice and served cold or chilled. The name also applies to various other dishes which are flavored with tomato juice.

The word comes from the French, and means "in the manner of Madrid." Possibly the reason for the term is that tomatoes are so much used in Spanish cookery.

Madrilene soup may be served hot as well as cold. Jellied madrilene, sold in cans, is a favorite American hot-weather soup excellent when garnished with a wedge of fresh lemon.

JELLIED CONSOMMÉ MADRILENE

2 envelopes unflavored gelatin
1 can vegetable juice cocktail
2 cans condensed consommé
1 slice of onion
1 bay leaf
  Lemon slices
  Paprika

Soften gelatin in vegetable juice cocktail in saucepan. Add consommé, onion, and bay leaf. Heat to boiling. Strain into bowl and chill until firm. Beat with fork to break up mixture slightly. Put in bouillon cups and garnish with lemon slices sprinkled with paprika. Makes 4 servings.

HOT CONSOMMÉ MADRILENE

2 cans condensed consommé
1 can vegetable juice cocktail
1 slice of onion
1 small bay leaf
  Minced parsley

Heat consommé and vegetable juice cocktail with onion and bay leaf. Strain into hot bouillon cups. Sprinkle with parsley. Makes 4 servings.

MAIZE—A cereal grain which is also known as Indian corn and corn. The plant is of American origin and was probably first cultivated in Mexico. In the United States the word maize is synonymous with corn and the words are used interchangeably.

Zea mays is the botanical name for maize. It is the only native American cereal grain of major importance. The Indians of New Mexico grew it as long as 2,000 years ago, and grains of maize have been found in the tombs of the Incas of Peru. By the time Columbus reached America, maize was a staple food from the Great Lakes to Argentina. Since it grows easily, with large yields, and makes an extremely palatable cereal, maize is grown wherever climatic conditions permit.

The early settlers called maize "Indian corn" which is natural since the word "corn" was used to describe any grain. It is known as Turkish corn in Italy and Latin corn in Germany, as durra in Egypt and mealies in South Africa.

MALT, MALTED—Malt is a substance made by sprouting or germinating grains, generally barley, but occasionally corn, rye, and oats. After sprouting, the grains are dried and ground. During the process various enzymes, among them diastase, are formed, partially converting the starch to sugar and changing proteins to amino acids. This makes the formerly hard, raw grain into a mellow, crisp, sweet-tasting malt. When grain is malted, it contributes carbohydrates and proteins to the diet. Malt is used in brewing, distilling, yeast-making, vinegar-making, and as an additive for milk.

Malted-milk powder, plain and chocolate-flavored, and malt vinegar are widely available, as is corn syrup, which is a combination of dextri-maltose and cornstarch. Maltose or malt-sugar, a sugar containing both ordinary sugar and milk sugar; malt syrup, consisting essentially of maltose and dextrin; and malt extract are all available in drugstores and health-food stores and are used for baby formulas and special diets because they offer sugar in an easily digested form.

MANGO—A tropical fruit of the mango tree. The fruit is oblong in shape and about the size of a large pear. It is green in color, turning orange-yellow when ripe, and has a delicious, pleasantly acid pulp. The mango tree is of East Indian origin. It is cultivated in the East Indies, China, Malaya, Cayenne, and in southern Florida and California in the United States.

The mango has been cultivated for centuries in Southeast Asia and mangoes are closely connected with the religion and folklore of the East. The tree is considered sacred in India where mangoes are a staple Indian food, and a basic ingredient of chutney. Wealthy Indian gardeners often collect mango trees; some gardens are said to grow hundreds of varieties.

Portuguese traders first carried the mango to Africa from the Far East. From there it was introduced into South America, and so came north to the West Indies in the second half of the 18th century. By the early 19th century the mango had arrived in Mexico, and in 1833 a Florida horticulturalist planted the first trees south of Miami. They were lost after his death, and mangoes were reintroduced in the United States around 1860.

Mangoes are eaten fresh, may be made into jams or jellies, or such desserts as ice cream. Green mangoes are used in making chutney and pickles.

Availability and Purchasing Guide—Mangoes are in season from May to September. They vary in size from a few ounces to 3 or 4 pounds. Mangoes are

Sliced mango   **Spiced Mango Chutney**   **Fresh mangoes**

also available canned, and as nectar. Mango chutney is available.

The flesh of a ripe mango yields slightly when pressed with the finger. The green skin turns to orange-yellow.

Storage—Wrap in wax paper and refrigerate.

☐ Refrigerator shelf, raw or cooked: 1 week

☐ Refrigerator frozen-food compartment, prepared for freezing: 2 to 3 months

☐ Freezer, prepared for freezing: 1 year

Nutritive Food Values—Mangoes are rich in vitamins A, C, and D.

☐ 3½ ounces, raw = 66 calories

Basic Preparation—With a sharp knife, mark a broad band in skin down one side. Peel skin back slightly. The pulp may then be eaten with a spoon, turning the skin back as necessary. Or peel, slice, and use as desired.

☐ **To Freeze**—Mango can only be frozen

puréed. For each 6 cups purée, add 1½ to 2 cups sugar. Freeze in freezer jars, leaving 1 inch headspace.

STEWED MANGOES

1 cup sugar
1 cup water
1 teaspoon vanilla extract
4 small ripe mangoes

Bring first 3 ingredients to boil, and simmer for 5 minutes. Peel and slice mangoes, and add to sugar syrup. Simmer gently for 10 minutes, or until tender. Cool in the syrup. Serve plain or with custard sauce or whipped cream if desired. Makes 4 servings.

MANGO PIE

3½ cups sliced, peeled
    ripe mangoes
2 tablespoons quick-cooking
    tapioca
¾ cup sugar
¼ teaspoon salt
1 tablespoon butter
    or margarine, melted
    Pastry for two-crust 9-inch pie

Combine first 5 ingredients. Let stand for 15 minutes, or while pastry is being made. Roll out half of pastry very thin (less than ⅛ inch thick). Line a 9-inch pie pan and trim pastry at edge of rim. Roll out remaining pastry very thin. Cut several 2-inch slits near center. Fill shell with fruit mixture and moisten edge of crust. Center the top crust on filling and open slits with a knife. Trim top crust, letting it extend ½ inch over rim. To seal, press top and bottom crusts together on rim. Then fold edge of top crust under bottom crust, and flute. Bake in preheated hot oven (425°F.) for 50 to 60 minutes, or until top is well browned. Serve slightly warm or cold.

MANGO TARTS

4 mangoes
1 cup sugar
    Water
1 teaspoon cornstarch
2 egg yolks, beaten

2 tablespoons butter
1 teaspoon ground cinnamon
8 pastry tart shells, baked
   Whipped cream

Peel mangoes and slice thinly into sauce-pan; add sugar and ½ cup water. Cook over low heat for 10 minutes, stirring occasionally. Mix cornstarch with 2 tea-spoons water and gradually beat into egg yolks. Gradually stir hot fruit into egg-yolk mixture. Return to heat. Con-tinue to cook, stirring constantly, or until thick and smooth. Stir in butter and cinnamon; cool. Fill pastry tart shells and decorate with a border of whipped cream. Makes 8 medium-size tarts.

MANGO ICE CREAM

To each quart of softened vanilla ice cream, add 2 cups ripe mango pulp. Mix well and freeze again.

MANGO RUM SUNDAE

1 large ripe mango
¼ cup fine granulated sugar
⅓ cup rum
   Vanilla ice cream

Peel mango and slice into ¼-inch slices. Put in shallow dish and sprinkle with the sugar and rum. Chill for 1 hour. Put ice cream in 4 serving dishes and top with mango slices and the liquid. Makes 4 servings.

MANGO JAM

5 large ripe mangoes
2 tablespoons fresh lemon juice
7½ cups sugar
1 bottle liquid pectin

Peel and remove seeds from mangoes. Crush fruit thoroughly or force through food chopper. Measure 4 cups prepared fruit into a very large saucepan. Add lemon juice and sugar, and mix well. Put over high heat; bring to a *full rolling boil and boil hard for 1 minute*, stirring con-stantly. Remove from heat and at once stir in pectin. Skim off foam with metal spoon. Then stir and skim for 5 minutes to cool slightly and prevent floating fruit. Ladle into hot sterilized jars, and seal. Makes about nine 8-ounce jars.

SPICY MANGO CHUTNEY

4 pounds mature green mangoes
1 large onion
8 ounces green gingerroot, peeled
2 garlic cloves
3 pounds brown sugar
2 ounces yellow chilies
3 teaspoons salt
4 cups vinegar
2 pounds currants
2 pounds raisins

Force mangoes, onion, gingerroot, and garlic through food chopper, using coarse blade. Add remaining ingredients and let stand overnight. Bring to boil and boil rapidly until thick. Pour into hot steril-ized pint jars, and seal. Makes about 8 pints.

MANICOTTO—A noodle shaped like a tube, about one inch in diameter and four inches long. The plural of this Italian word is *manicotti*. Manicotti are boiled until tender, then stuffed with a cheese mixture and baked with a tomato or other sauce.

Homemade *manicotti* are made like crêpes, then filled, rolled up, and baked. These pancakes can be prepared ahead and frozen until ready to use. *Manicotti* noodles are available packaged and filled *manicotti* are available frozen.

Caloric Value

☐ *Manicotti* noodles, 3½ ounces, cooked = 67 calories.

MANICOTTI

1 cup all-purpose flour
1 cup water
   Salt
7 eggs
   Cooking oil
2 pounds Ricotta cheese
¾ cup grated Parmesan
   or Romano cheese
¼ teaspoon pepper
½ pound Mozzarella cheese,
   cut into 12 to 14 strips
3 cans (8 ounces each) tomato sauce

To make pancakes: Combine flour, water, and ¼ teaspoon salt. Beat until smooth. Beat in 4 eggs, one at a time. Heat a 5- to 6-inch skillet, and grease with a few drops of oil. Put about 3 tablespoons batter in hot skillet and roll pan around to distribute evenly. Cook over low heat until firm (do not brown). Turn and cook lightly on other side. Continue making pancakes until all of batter is used. (Do not grease skillet a second time.) This amount will make 12 to 14 pancakes.
To make filling: Mix ½ teaspoon salt, 3 eggs, the Ricotta, ¼ cup grated cheese, and the pepper. Put about 2 tablespoons filling and a strip of Mozzarella on each pancake and roll up. Pour 1 can tomato sauce into large shallow baking dish. Put pancakes, seam side down, in sauce. Cover with remaining sauce and sprinkle with remaining grated cheese. Bake in preheated moderate oven (350°F.) for 45 minutes. Makes 6 generous servings.

BAKED MANICOTTI WITH MEAT SAUCE

2 pounds Ricotta or creamed
   cottage cheese
½ pound Mozzarella cheese, diced
2 eggs, well beaten
2 tablespoons chopped parsley
½ teaspoon pepper
¼ teaspoon ground nutmeg
½ cup slivered blanched almonds
   Salt
1½ cups grated Parmesan cheese
1 pound ground beef
3 cans (10¼ ounces each) mushroom
   or meat sauce
16 manicotti noodles, cooked

Make filling by mixing first 7 ingredients, 1 teaspoon salt, and 1 cup Parmesan.

Blend thoroughly. Cook meat until lightly browned, breaking up with fork. Sprinkle with salt. Add mushroom sauce and bring to boil. Spread one third of mixture in large shallow baking dish. Stuff manicotti with cheese filling and arrange in dish. Cover with remaining sauce and sprinkle with remaining Parmesan. Bake in pre-heated moderate oven (350°F.) for 20 minutes. Makes 6 to 8 servings.

Manicotti à la Béchamel

Follow recipe for Baked Manicotti with Meat Sauce, omitting beef and mush-room sauce. Prepare 3½ cups medium white sauce with half light cream and half milk. Season with instant minced onion. Use as sauce; proceed as directed.

Meat-Filled Manicotti

Follow recipe for Baked Manicotti with Meat Sauce, omitting beef from sauce. Heat 1 tablespoon butter. Add ½ pound each of ground beef, veal, and pork; cook until browned, stirring. Add 2 teaspoons instant minced onion, 1 teaspoon grated lemon rind, ½ teaspoon dried oregano, ⅛ teaspoon hot pepper sauce, 1 teaspoon salt, ½ teaspoon pepper, 2 beaten eggs, and ½ pound Mozzarella cheese, diced. Use to stuff manicotti.

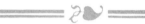

MANIOC—A tropical plant, also known as cassava, mandioc, or yucca, whose roots yield a tuber which is a staple food in Central and South America. The word comes from the language of the Tupi and Guarani, South American Indian tribes.

The manioc or cassava plant is a shrubby perennial that grows to a height of nine feet, with large parted leaves and roots that end in very large tubers. The tubers produce a flour with an extremely high starch content, which varies from fifteen to thirty per cent in contrast to fifteen to twenty per cent for potatoes. The flour, which has very little taste, is used in place of wheat flour. It is either made into nonsweet, thin cakes used like wheat bread, or sprinkled over rice and beans to make them more filling.

There are many varieties of manioc, but the two most widely grown for their starchy content are the bitter manioc (*Manioc utilissima* or *esculenta*) and the sweet (*Manioc dulcis*, variety *Aipi*). The first is more widely used due to its higher starch content, although it contains a poison related to prussic acid. The poison is removed and the manioc prepared in the following way: The root is dug by hand, peeled, washed, and grated or ground. The pulp is put in a bag or in a press and squeezed out, then dried and sifted, and slightly toasted. The juice extracted, which is milky, is poisonous before it is cooked down to a thick consistency to make *cassareep,* or West Indian pepper pot, which is the basis of many sauces.

Tapioca is made from properly treated manioc flour. After the juice has been extracted from the pulp, the pulp is heated over a slow fire until it forms grains which harden in cooking.

The roots of the sweet manioc contain no poisonous juices. They are usually roasted under hot ashes and eaten plain or with butter. Their flavor resembles that of a chestnut and they, too, are very high in starch.

Sweet manioc is available fresh, usually called cassava, in Spanish food stores.

CASSAVA CHICKEN PIE

1 stewing chicken, about
  4 pounds, cut up
1 bay leaf
  Salt
1 onion, peeled
  Few celery leaves
  Water
4 pounds cassava
1 tablespoon each of butter
  and lard
3 eggs, slightly beaten
  Dash each of pepper, cayenne,
  and nutmeg
3 tablespoons all-purpose flour

Put chicken in kettle and add bay leaf, 1 teaspoon salt, onion, celery leaves, and water to cover chicken. Bring to boil, cover, and simmer until chicken is tender, about 3 hours. Remove chicken from broth; reserve 1½ cups broth. Remove chicken meat from bones. Peel cassava and grate on grater, or force through food chopper, using medium blade. Squeeze through a thick cloth to remove liquid. Mix cassava with butter, lard, eggs, ¾ teaspoon salt, the pepper, cayenne, and nutmeg. Press half this mixture into a shallow baking dish (1½ quart). Blend flour with a little cold water. Stir into reserved chicken broth. Cook, stirring constantly, until thickened. Put chicken and gravy in lined dish. Top with remaining cassava mixture. Bake in preheated moderate oven (350°F.) for about 1½ hours. Makes 6 to 8 servings.

MAPLE—A tree native to the north temperate zone, of the genus *Acer*. There are thirteen species of maple native to the American continent; nine of them are found east of the great plains, two in the Rocky Mountain region, and two on the Pacific Coast. The sugar, or rock, maple (*A. saccharum*) highly valued as a timber and shade tree, and the chief source of maple sugar, grows from Newfoundland to South Dakota, and southward to South Carolina and Texas. It sometimes attains a height of 120 feet and a trunk diameter of four feet.

Maples are hardy ornamental trees; their foliage, which turns red and yellow in the fall, is one of the glories of the American countryside. All maples have a sweet sap, but only the sugar maple and the black maple are tapped to make maple syrup. The sugar maple has a light gray bark; the black maple a black bark.

Maple syrup is made by boiling the sap down to a syrup. When the syrup is boiled to the density of strained honey, it is called *maple honey. Maple cream* or *maple butter* is syrup boiled to the soft-sugar stage, cooled, and then stirred smooth. *Maple sugar* is syrup boiled to the hard-sugar stage and then stirred to prevent the individual crystals of sugar from hardening together.

When the colonists came to America they found the Indians making good use of maple syrup and sugar: they used both to sweeten their corn dishes. The colonists learned the art of tapping the trees from their Indian neighbors.

In February, or about the time of the wild goose migration north, the settlers went into the sugar bush, or grove of maples. A hole was tapped into the tree about three feet above the ground and a spout was inserted. On the spout hung a bucket to gather the precious sap. Thawing days, when the sap ran freely, were the most productive.

As the sap from each tree was collected it was poured into huge kettles and kept boiling over large fires. At night the kettles were taken into the sugarhouse (a special building reserved for this purpose) to finish boiling. The boiling off took a long time, for thirty-five or more gallons of sap yield only one gallon of syrup. After the sap had been boiled down it had to be strained through cloth or blankets to remove impurities.

Before being stored for use during the year, some syrup would be poured onto the snow or cracked ice, where it would quickly harden into a sort of sugar, or "jack wax," of a consistency like taffy. A sugaring-off party at the end of the sap run was held every season and hot biscuits dipped into the fresh syrup served as refreshments.

Maple-sugar candy was made in decorative wooden molds in various shapes. Maple syrup was used to flavor many dishes: it was poured over pancakes and biscuits, toast, and desserts. It was used to flavor puddings and cakes and hot and cold drinks. And, in the early days, baked beans were flavored with sweet syrup.

Maple syrup can be used on hot cereals, pancakes, waffles, and other quick breads; to sweeten milk, custards, bread pudding, and applesauce and other fruits.

Availability and Purchasing Guide—Sold as maple syrup and maple sugar.

Maple syrup may be bought pure, 100 per cent maple syrup, or blended with cane syrup or butter.

Maple sugar is sold in shaped candies such as maple leaves and small fruits.

Storage

☐ Maple sugar, kitchen shelf, tightly covered: 1 year
☐ Maple syrup, kitchen shelf, unopened: 1 year
☐ Maple syrup, refrigerator, opened and tightly covered: 1 to 2 months

Nutritive Food Values—A good source of sucrose with some invert sugar and ash.

☐ Maple sugar, 3½ ounces = 348 calories
☐ Maple syrup, 3½ ounces = 252 calories

Basic Preparation

☐ **To Make Maple Cream** (also called Maple Butter or Maple Spread)—Heat maple syrup to 232°F. on a candy thermometer. (At this point it can be poured over snow or cracked ice for the chewy sweet called "jack wax.") Pour syrup into a flat dish, cool rapidly to room temperature, and then stir rapidly for 15 to 20 minutes.

☐ **To Make Maple Sugar**—Heat maple syrup to 240°F. to 242°F. on a candy thermometer. Stir syrup as soon as it has reached this temperature. Pack mixture into molds or leave in bowl and crumble sugar when it has cooled completely.

Maple sugar can be shaved and used as you would brown sugar.

☐ **To Candy Carrots or Sweet Potatoes**—Put cooked small sweet potatoes or cooked whole carrots in a shallow casserole. Cover with maple sugar or syrup. Dot top with butter. Bake in preheated moderate oven (350°F.) for 30 minutes, turning potatoes or carrots in syrup occasionally.

☐ **To Glaze Ham**—Thirty minutes before ham is removed from oven, pour maple syrup over the ham. Spoon pan drippings over ham several times during cooking.

MAPLE DATE-NUT BREAD

1 cup boiling water
1 cup chopped dates
1 egg
½ cup maple or brown sugar
1 cup sifted cake flour
1 teaspoon baking powder
½ teaspoon baking soda
1 teaspoon salt
1 cup whole-wheat flour
1 tablespoon melted butter
½ cup chopped nuts
2 tablespoons maple syrup

Maple Sugar

Sugaring-Off Pie

Maple-Syrup Cake

Maple Syrup

Maple Date-Nut Bread

Baked Apple with Maple Syrup

Pour boiling water over dates; cool. Add egg and sugar. Sift cake flour, baking powder, baking soda, and salt together; combine with whole-wheat flour and add to first mixture. Fold in butter and nuts. Mix only until ingredients are blended. Pour into greased loaf pan (about 9½ x 5½ x 2¾ inches). Bake in preheated moderate oven (350°F.) for 50 to 60 minutes. Remove bread from pan. While hot, brush top with maple syrup.

MAPLE COTTAGE PUDDING

 1 cup maple-flavored pancake syrup
 1 cup sifted all-purpose flour
 1 teaspoon baking powder
 ¼ teaspoon salt
 3 tablespoons sugar
 ½ cup milk
 2 tablespoons melted shortening
 1 egg

Bring syrup to a boil. Pour into greased 1½-quart baking dish. Sift dry ingredients together into a bowl. Add milk, shortening, and egg and beat smooth. Pour cake batter into syrup and bake in moderate oven (375°F.) for about 25 minutes, or until cake is done. Makes 4 servings.

MAPLE PINEAPPLE SAUCE

Combine ½ cup maple syrup and about 1 cup (one 9-ounce can) crushed pineapple, drained. Heat to boiling. Serve on pancakes or waffles. Make 1½ cups.

MAPLE GELATIN

 1¼ teaspoons unflavored gelatin
 ⅓ cup water
 1 cup maple syrup, heated
 1 cup heavy cream, whipped

Soften gelatin in cold water. Let stand for 5 minutes. Add to hot maple syrup and stir until completely dissolved. Chill until slightly set, to the consistency of unbeaten egg whites. Fold in cream. Chill for 2 hours. Makes 4 servings.

FROZEN MAPLE-GRAHAM CREAM

 3 egg yolks
 ¾ cup maple syrup
 1 cup heavy cream
 ½ cup graham-cracker crumbs
 2 egg whites

Beat egg yolks until light and lemon-colored; add syrup and ¼ cup cream; cook, stirring constantly, in top part of double boiler over hot water until thick; cool. Add ¼ cup crumbs; mix well. Beat egg whites until stiff but not dry; fold into custard mixture; pour into refrigerator tray; freeze. When almost frozen, remove from tray and beat with rotary beater until smooth but not completely thawed. Whip cream until stiff. Fold remaining cream and ¼ cup crumbs into partially frozen mixture. Return to tray; freeze. Makes 4 to 6 servings.

BAKED APPLE WITH MAPLE SYRUP

Prepare apples by peeling halfway and coring. Place apples in a shallow dish and fill centers with maple syrup. Add water to cover the bottom. Bake in preheated moderate oven (350°F.) for 30 to 40 minutes, until apples are tender. Spoon pan juices over apples several times during cooking.

MAPLE PARFAIT

    6 egg yolks
    ⅔ cup maple syrup
    ⅛ teaspoon salt
    2 cups heavy cream, whipped

Turn refrigerator control to coldest setting. In top part of small double boiler beat egg yolks and syrup. Add salt and cook over simmering water until slightly thickened, stirring constantly. Cool. Fold in whipped cream. Pour into refrigerator tray and freeze until firm. Makes 6 servings.

MAPLE FREEZE

    ½ cup maple syrup
    2 egg whites
    1 cup undiluted evaporated milk, well chilled

Set refrigerator control for fast freezing. Cook syrup to soft-ball stage (238°F. on a candy thermometer). Beat egg whites until stiff but not dry. Add syrup slowly, beating constantly until all syrup is added and mixture is cool. Whip milk until thick and fold egg-white and syrup mixture into it. Pour into refrigerator tray and freeze until firm. Then turn cold control back to normal. Makes 8 servings.

SUGARING-OFF PIE

Crust:

    1 cup crushed bite-size
        shredded rice biscuits
    ¼ cup sugar
    ¼ cup finely chopped
        salted peanuts
    ¼ cup soft butter or margarine
    2 teaspoons hot water

Filling:

    ⅔ cup sugar
    ¼ cup cornstarch
    ½ teaspoon salt
    2 cups milk
    1 cup maple-flavored syrup
    3 egg yolks, beaten
    1 tablespoon butter or margarine
    ½ teaspoon maple extract

Butter 9-inch pie plate. Combine crumbs, sugar, and peanuts. Add butter and water. Blend until uniform. With back of teaspoon pack crumbs firmly and evenly onto bottom and sides of pie plate. Form an edge around top of crust, not on rim of plate. Bake in preheated moderate oven (350°F.) for 10 minutes. Cool.

To make filling: Combine sugar, cornstarch, and salt in saucepan. Gradually stir in milk and syrup. Cook over medium heat, stirring constantly, until mixture thickens and boils. Gradually beat hot mixture into egg yolks. Replace on heat. Cook and stir over low heat until mixture is very thick. Stir in butter and maple extract. Cool slightly. Pour into baked pie shell. Chill until firm. To serve, garnish with whipped cream and additional peanuts.

MAPLE-SYRUP CAKE

    ⅓ cup shortening
    ½ cup sugar
    ¾ cup maple syrup
    2¼ cups sifted cake flour
    1 tablespoon baking powder
    ¼ teaspoon salt
    ½ cup milk
    3 egg whites
        Maple Icing
    ¾ cup chopped butternuts
        or walnuts

Cream shortening and sugar; stir in maple syrup. Add sifted dry ingredients alternately with milk. Beat egg whites until stiff but not dry. Fold into mixture. Turn into greased 9-inch square pan lined with wax paper. Bake in preheated moderate oven (350°F.) for 45 to 50 minutes. Turn out on rack; remove paper; cool. Spread top and sides of cake with Maple Icing; sprinkle with chopped butternuts.

Maple Icing

    2 cups maple syrup
        Pinch of salt
    2 egg whites

Boil maple syrup until it spins a thread (232°F. on candy thermometer). Pour slowly over stiffly beaten salted egg whites, beating constantly with rotary beater or wire whisk. Continue beating until mixture is stiff enough to stand up in soft peaks.

MAPLE LACE WAFERS

    ½ cup maple syrup
    ¼ cup butter or margarine
    ½ cup sifted all-purpose flour
    ⅛ teaspoon baking soda
    ¼ teaspoon baking powder
        Few grains of salt

Combine syrup and butter in a saucepan; bring to a boil, stirring constantly, and boil hard for ½ minute. Sift remaining ingredients together and add all at once to syrup mixture, stirring briskly. Batter will be slightly lumpy. Drop by half-teaspoons 5 inches apart on greased cookie sheets. Bake in preheated moderate oven (350°F.) for 6 to 8 minutes. Allow to cool for about 1 minute. Remove each wafer carefully from cookie sheet and roll around handle of a wooden spoon. Place on rack to cool. Do not bake more than 6 at a time. If wafers harden too much to handle before removing from cookie sheet, return to oven for a minute. Store in airtight container. Makes about 30.

MARASCHINO—A sweet cherry which is bleached, pitted, and steeped in a syrup made of sugar, water, a touch of oil of bitter almonds, and food coloring. Sweet Royal Ann cherries are the variety most commonly used. The history of this delicacy goes back some three hundred years to Italy, where a white sweet cherry was soaked in a cordial called "maraschino," which was made from still another cherry, the marasca. The name was derived from the Latin *amarus,* meaning "bitter." Later the French created another version: cherries soaked in a sugar syrup. They named their version a maraschino cherry. Once imported to this country maraschino cherries became very popular, and in time homegrown cherries and syrup were developed to produce an all-American product.

Maraschino cherries are used in candies, cookies, cakes, sauces, as well as in fruit cups and fruit salad, and alcoholic beverages.

Maraschino is also the name of a liqueur distilled from cherries.

Availability — Maraschino cherries are available in the red variety flavored with almond and packed with or without stems, or the green-colored, flavored with mint and packed only without stems. Cherries packed without stems will cost less than those with stems. Candied or glacéed maraschino cherries are also available in both red and green, generally for holiday cooking at Christmas and Easter.

MARASCHINO-ALMOND PARFAIT PIE

    1 box (3 ounces)
        lemon-flavored gelatin
    1¼ cups hot water
    1 pint vanilla ice cream
    ¼ cup toasted slivered almonds
    2 tablespoons chopped
        maraschino cherries
    1 baked pie shell (8-inch), cooled

Dissolve gelatin in hot water in a saucepan. Add ice cream by tablespoonfuls, stirring until melted. Then chill until thickened but not set, 15 to 25 minutes. Fold in the almonds and cherries. Pour into the pie shell. Chill until firm, 20 to 30 minutes. Top with additional chopped cherries, if desired.

MARASCHINO SAUCE

    ½ cup sugar
    2 tablespoons cornstarch
        Dash of salt
    1 cup boiling water
    ½ cup maraschino syrup
    2 tablespoons butter
        or margarine
    ¼ cup halved maraschino
        cherries

In saucepan mix sugar, cornstarch, and salt. Gradually stir in boiling water. Add syrup. Bring to boil and cook, stirring constantly, until smooth and thickened. Remove from heat and add butter and cherries. Serve warm on plain cake or vanilla pudding. Makes about 1½ cups.

CREAMY STRAWBERRIES MARASCHINO

    3 cups fresh strawberries
    2 cups heavy cream
    ½ cup confectioners' sugar
    ¼ cup maraschino liqueur

Wash, hull, and drain berries. Beat cream until stiff with sugar and maraschino. Fold in berries. Chill for a few minutes before serving. Makes 6 servings.

CHERRY COCONUT SQUARES

- 1¼ cups unsifted all-purpose flour
- ½ cup soft butter or margarine
- 3 tablespoons confectioners' sugar
- 2 eggs, beaten
- ½ cup granulated sugar
- ½ teaspoon baking powder
- ¼ teaspoon salt
- 1 teaspoon vanilla extract
- ¾ cup chopped nuts
- ½ cup flaked coconut
- ½ cup diced well-drained maraschino cherries

With hands, mix 1 cup flour, butter, and confectioners' sugar until well blended. Spread in greased 8-inch square pan. Bake in preheated moderate oven (350° F.) for about 20 minutes. Mix ¼ cup flour and remaining ingredients. Spread carefully over baked mixture. Bake for about 25 minutes. Cool, and cut into squares. Makes 16.

MARGARINE—A smooth-textured fat used as a spread and in cooking. It may be prepared from animal or vegetable fats or a combination of them in amounts specified by law. The fats may or may not be hydrogenated. The fat ingredients are mixed with pasteurized cream, milk, skim milk, or nonfat dry milk, or any combination of these. When the fat source is vegetable, the fat may be mixed with ground soy beans and water. Optional ingredients such as coloring, flavoring, preservatives, vitamins A and D, emulsifiers, butter, and salt may be added. Differences in ingredients affect the flavor, texture, color, spreadability, baking quality, and nutritive value of the finished product. For specific information regarding ingredients, it is necessary to consult package labels.

Availability and Purchasing Guide—Margarine is available colored yellow, salted and unsalted. Whipped margarine is also available.

- ☐ 1 stick margarine (¼ pound) = ½ cup = 8 tablespoons
- ☐ 1 stick whipped margarine = 2⅔ ounces = ⅓ cup = 5⅓ tablespoons

Whipped margarine must be used by weight since air increases volume.

Storage—Store margarine as butter, tightly wrapped or covered, and in the refrigerator. Margarine may also be frozen in the same manner as butter.

- ☐ Refrigerator shelf, wrapped: 7 to 30 days
- ☐ Refrigerator frozen-food compartment, prepared for freezing: 2 to 3 months
- ☐ Freezer, prepared for freezing: 6 to 8 months

Nutritive Food Values—Margarine contributes calories and vitamins A and D.

- ☐ 3½ ounces = 720 calories

MARINATE, MARINADE, MACERATE—To marinate foods is to steep them in a seasoned liquid, or "marinade," before or after cooking in order that they absorb flavor and/or become more tender. The term "to marinate" is used for meats, venison, fish, and vegetables; for fruits, the term "to macerate" is used.

Marinades began as simple brines for preserving fish. (The word marinade stems from the same root as the word maritime.) In modern usage, a marinade consists of a cooking oil, an acid (vinegar and/or lemon juice and/or wine), and spices. As the food stands in the mixture, the acid and the oil impart the savory flavors of the spices to the food. The acid also has a tenderizing action. Because of this action, marinating is most often associated with tougher, less expensive cuts of meat. However, since such delicious flavor is gained from marinating, foods which need no tenderizing may be marinated for flavor reasons only.

The kind and amount of ingredients used to marinate a meat, fish, or vegetable should not be left to chance. Length of marinating time differs also. Sauerbraten, for example, is marinated in a highly seasoned mixture and requires two days to develop its characteristic flavor. Meats in general can take a marinade containing pepper and the more potent herbs such as bay and thyme, or the stronger spices such as cloves and caraway. With fish or vegetables, the emphasis is on the gentler herbs: basil, marjoram, parsley, etc. Most marinades include the flavor of onion or garlic. Wine is not usually used in vegetable marinades, but either wine or vinegar (or both) may be used in marinades for meats, poultry, or seafood. Lemon juice is good in any marinade.

Marinades are of two types: cooked or uncooked. Cooked marinades are made by first cooking the spices, usually whole, and then cooling before adding the food. They are used with large cuts of meat and to shorten the marinating time. Whole spices, such as peppercorns, cloves, or mustard seed can be used only in cooked marinades since heat is needed to extract their flavor.

Uncooked marinades are combined without heating and usually contain ground spices and/or whole-leaf herbs such as bay, thyme, and marjoram which readily release their flavors without pulverizing or heating.

Since marinades usually contain an acid, they and the foods they serve should be kept in dishes that are either glass, stainless steel, or stainless enamel. Never use aluminum or porous containers such as some pottery for marinating. Preferably use a wooden spoon for stirring and turning.

Marinate foods in containers just large enough to contain the food with marinade to cover. The marinade will be better absorbed. Turn the food several times while marinating.

Keep marinating foods well covered and under refrigeration if they are to steep for more than 1 hour. Higher temperatures hasten marinating, but they also increase bacterial action.

Marinades are powerful. Do not use overly seasoned marinades, or marinate foods too long, or you may kill the food's own flavor.

The length of time for marinating foods varies. Two hours is a good rule of thumb for chicken, fish, and seafood. As a general rule, if the meat is cubed, steep it for three to five hours; if in one piece, overnight.

Cooking with a Marinade

■ After a food has been marinated, it should be drained and dried on paper towels to remove excess marinade. Keep marinade since it may be used later in the cooking.

■ Often a dish is also cooked or finished with the marinade it was steeped in. Stews and pot roasts and dishes requiring a cooking liquid are sometimes prepared in this manner. Depending on the strength of the marinade, and to prevent too much of a good thing, it may be advisable to dilute it with water or broth before adding the liquid to the meat.

■ Part of the marinade may also be used to baste a marinated meat cooked by roasting or broiling, or in making the gravy or sauce.

COOKED MARINADE FOR MEATS AND GAME

- ¼ cup cooking oil
- 1 cup chopped onions
- ½ cup chopped celery
- ½ cup chopped carrot
- ½ cup chopped parsley
- 4 garlic cloves, crushed
- 8 cups cider vinegar or 4 cups cider vinegar and 4 cups dry red or white wine
- 4 cups water
- 4 bay leaves
- 1 tablespoon dried thyme
- ½ tablespoon crushed dried rosemary
- 1 tablespoon peppercorns
- 10 whole cloves
- 10 whole juniper berries, crushed

Heat oil in deep saucepan. Over medium heat cook onions, celery, carrot, parsley, and garlic in oil for 5 minutes, or until onions are soft but still white. Do not brown. Add remaining ingredients. Simmer, covered, over low heat for 45 minutes to 1 hour, stirring occasionally. Strain and cool before using. Makes 8 to 9 cups marinade, or enough for about 12 pounds meat.

Note: The marinade may be strained after use, brought to a boil, cooled, and used again.

UNCOOKED MARINADE FOR SHRIMPS OR LOBSTER

¾ cup brandy, dry sherry,
  or dry white wine
½ teaspoon salt
½ teaspoon pepper
½ teaspoon crushed dried rosemary,
  basil, or thyme

Combine all ingredients and put in deep bowl. Marinate seafood in mixture for 1 to 3 hours. Makes about ¾ cup, or enough for 30 shrimps or one 2-pound lobster.

UNCOOKED MARINADE FOR SMALL PORTIONS OF CHICKEN, MEAT, FISH, OR SEAFOOD

Season food with salt and pepper. Place in deep dish. Sprinkle with minced onion, garlic, chopped parsley, thyme, or any preferred herb. Cover with olive oil and lemon juice to taste.

UNCOOKED MARINADE FOR MEATS

1 cup water
1 cup wine
6 peppercorns
1 bay leaf
8 whole cloves
1 medium onion, thinly sliced
1 teaspoon crushed dried
  rosemary, thyme, or marjoram

Combine all ingredients. Makes 2 cups, or enough for 5 pounds meat.

Note: Dry white wine will give a more delicate flavor, but for red meats and game or venison dry red wine is preferable.

BEER MARINADE FOR BEEF, GAME, OR SHRIMPS

1½ cups beer
½ cup salad oil
1 small onion, thinly sliced
1 garlic clove, mashed
2 tablespoons fresh lemon juice
1 teaspoon salt
½ teaspoon pepper
1 teaspoon powdered mustard

Combine all ingredients and blend thoroughly. Makes about 2 cups, or enough for 2 to 3 pounds meat or shrimps.

MARINADE FOR VEGETABLES

1 cup highly seasoned
  French dressing
2 tablespoons chopped chives
1 garlic clove
  Few sprigs of parsley, chopped
2 teaspoons mixed dried herbs
  (mint, tarragon, basil)

Mix all ingredients, cover, and store in the refrigerator. Remove garlic. Use as a marinade for tomatoes, green beans, broccoli, asparagus, or other vegetables. Makes 1 cup.

MARINADE FOR FRUITS

⅓ cup sweet vermouth
¾ cup olive oil
¼ teaspoon salt
1 tablespoon light corn syrup
1 teaspoon minced fresh tarragon
  or ¼ teaspoon dried tarragon
  Freshly ground pepper to taste

Combine all ingredients and shake well in a jar. Makes about 1 cup.

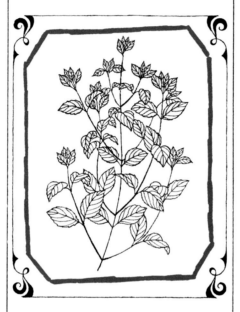

MARJORAM (Majorana hortensis)—This culinary herb, a member of the mint family, is more exactly known as sweet marjoram or knotted marjoram. Its downy light-green oval leaves, up to one inch long, have a mild sagelike flavor, although less strong than sage. The plant grows over one foot tall and has tiny pinkish or lilac flowers. Another variety of marjoram, *M. onites,* is similar to *M. hortensis,* except that it is a smaller plant with a milder flavor. Pot marjoram is another name for sweet marjoram.

Sweet majoram is traditionally associated with happiness after death. Planted on a grave, the Greeks believed that it symbolized the happiness of the loved one. Greeks and Romans put it in their funeral wreaths. Marjoram was also associated with happiness during life. Young Greek and Roman couples wore marjoram crowns at their weddings.

Marjoram has also been used for medicinal purposes. Hippocrates, the Greek physician of the 5th and 4th centuries B.C., recommended its use for eliminating excess bile. The Middle Ages found it effective for the curing of burns and headaches.

Sweet marjoram has always been a beloved herb, partly because of its delightful fragrance. It is among the "herbs for stewing:" mentioned by the Elizabethan writer, Tusser, in 1577. Another writer claimed that "our daintiest women doe put it to still among their sweet herbs." These Elizabethans were carrying on a Greek and Roman tradition of using sweet marjoram in "nosegays" and for strewing it on floors to sweeten and freshen the air.

Sweet marjoram also added its flavor to Elizabethan salads, as we know from Shakespeare. "We may pick a thousand salads ere we light on such another herb," says a character in *All's Well That Ends Well.* The Clown replies: "Indeed, sir, she was the sweet marjoram of the salad, or rather, the herb of grace." This "herb of grace" is so much a part of English history that it is used in heraldry.

In early colonial America sweet marjoram added its flavor to dishes prepared from native ingredients. The English had brought the herb to the colonies along with pennyroyal, sage, and savory. The housewife grew her own herbs, then dried and stored them. The drying was done in a "tin kitchen," a reflector oven that was placed in front of the big fireplace that was the living center of early New England homes. After the herbs were dried they were hung in cupboards close to the fireplace to keep dry and not become moldy in the damp New England winters.

The Shakers, whose communities flourished during the 19th century in Massachusetts, Pennsylvania, and New York, were expert and famous herb growers. The women grew the seasonings, then dried and packaged them, and the men sold them. Shaker seeds were renowned for their quality. Housewives who had neither the time nor the talent to grow their own herbs could buy the packaged seeds from the Shakers who traveled throughout the country selling their wares.

Marjoram can be bought fresh in season. Most marjoram, however, is packaged ground or as dried leaves.

MARJORAM VEAL CHOPS

½ cup olive oil
2 tablespoons fresh lemon juice
1 teaspoon instant minced onion
1½ teaspoons ground marjoram
4 loin veal chops, 1 inch thick
1 cup fine dried bread crumbs
1 teaspoon grated lemon rind
½ teaspoon salt
¼ teaspoon cayenne
  or other pepper
  Butter for frying (3 tablespoons)

Combine olive oil, lemon juice, onion, and 1 teaspoon marjoram in large shallow dish. Place chops in mixture and stand in cool place for 4 hours. Combine bread crumbs, lemon rind, ½ teaspoon marjoram, and salt and pepper. Dip marinated chops into mixture. Heat butter in heavy skillet. Over high heat, brown chops quickly on both sides. Lower heat and cook for 5 to 7 minutes on each side. Makes 4 servings.

PORK FILLET IN SOUR CREAM
- 1½- pound pork fillet
- 2 tablespoons all-purpose flour
- 1 teaspoon salt
- 1 teaspoon ground marjoram
- ½ teaspoon pepper
- 2 tablespoons shortening
- ½ cup hot water
- ½ cup dairy sour cream

Trim excess fat from pork. Cut into 2-inch cubes. Blend flour, salt, marjoram, and pepper. Mix with pork. Brown on all sides in hot shortening. Add hot water. Cook, covered, over low heat for 1 hour, adding more water if necessary. Add sour cream. Heat through thoroughly but do not boil. Serve with mashed potatoes or boiled rice. Makes 4 servings.

POTATOES BOULANGÈRE
- 2 onions, thinly sliced
- 2 tablespoons butter
- 4 medium potatoes, thinly sliced
- 1 cup (one 8-ounce can) consommé
- ½ teaspoon salt
- ¼ teaspoon pepper
- ¾ teaspoon ground marjoram
- ¼ cup minced parsley

Cook onions in butter for 5 minutes, or until soft and golden. Add potatoes, consommé, salt, pepper, and marjoram. Cook, covered, over lowest possible heat for 25 to 30 minutes, or until potatoes are tender. Sprinkle with parsley. Makes 4 servings.

MARMALADE—A preserve of fruit, usually citrus fruit. The fruits are cut into thin slices with the peel, and cooked in water until tender. Sugar is then added and the mixture is cooked again until the solids are suspended in a clear jellylike mixture.

The word marmalade comes from the Portuguese *marmelada*, derived from the Latin *melimelum* meaning "honey apple," which, in its turn, can be traced to the Greek *melimelon,* from *meli,* "honey," and *melon,* "apple."

Marmalade is differently made and defined in different countries. In Great Britain it is made from bitter or Seville oranges, and is an indispensable accompaniment to the breakfast toast. In America, marmalade is also made from oranges, but usually sweet ones, and

from other fruits. In most of the European countries, marmalade is equivalent to jam and it is made from any fruit. In Spain and Portugal marmalade is made from quinces.

In addition to its use as a spread, marmalade is used in cooking for glazes, fillings, toppings, and sauces. Marmalade can be made at home, and a wide variety of commercial marmalades are available.

VALENCIA-ORANGE MARMALADE
- 2 large Valencia oranges
- 2 large lemons
- 11 cups water
- 8 cups sugar

Wash oranges and lemons. Cut fruit into quarters and remove seeds. Put fruit in the water and let soak for 24 hours. Remove fruit, and with a sharp knife remove skin. Remove white part of skin. Cut skin and pulp into thin slivers. Put fruit in water in which it was soaked. Bring to a boil and boil, uncovered, for 1 hour. Add sugar and continue to boil until 2 drops sheet as one from the edge of a spoon, or until 220°F. on a candy thermometer is reached. Pour mixture into hot sterilized glasses. Seal with paraffin or with an airtight sterilized lid. Cool, and store. Makes about 8 jelly glasses.

SEVILLE-ORANGE MARMALADE
- 6 Seville oranges
- 1 lemon
- Water
- 6¾ cups sugar
- ½ teaspoon salt

Wash oranges and lemon, and using a vegetable slicer shred the peel from all unspotted surfaces. Cover peel with cold water and boil until tender. Change water twice during cooking. Remove white skin from oranges and chop pulp. Add 8 cups water, bring to boil, and cook until soft. Put through food mill or strainer. Drain peel and put in large saucepan. Add sieved fruit mixture, sugar, and salt. Bring to boil and boil rapidly until thickened and mixture sheets from side of metal spoon. Cool slightly, stirring several times. Pour into hot sterilized jars, and seal. Makes about ten ½-pint jars.

PEACH MARMALADE
- 1 orange
- 2 lemons
- 1 cup water
- 2 pounds ripe peaches
- 7 cups sugar
- ½ bottle liquid pectin

Cut orange and 1 lemon into quarters. Remove seeds. Grind, chop fine, or cut crosswise into wafer-thin slices. Squeeze the juice from the second lemon. Put these fruits and 2 tablespoons of lemon juice into saucepan. Add water, bring to boil, and simmer, covered, for 20 minutes.

Peel and pit peaches. Chop very fine or grind. Combine peaches and citrus fruit and measure 4½ cups into very large saucepan. Add sugar and mix well. Put over high heat, bring to a *full rolling boil, and boil hard for 1 minute,* stirring constantly. Remove from heat and at once stir in pectin. Skim off foam with metal spoon. Then stir and skim for 7 minutes to cool slightly and prevent floating fruit. Ladle into hot sterilized jars, and seal. Makes about eight ½-pint jars.

QUINCE MARMALADE
Peel and core quinces. Slice fruit and put in large saucepan. Barely cover with water, bring to boil, and simmer, covered, until tender, stirring occasionally. Without draining, mash fruit and beat to a pulp. Measure fruit and put in saucepan. Add ⅔ cup sugar for each cup quince pulp. Bring to boil and cook until thickened and mixture sheets from the side of a metal spoon. Pour into hot sterilized jars, and seal.

CRANBERRY MARMALADE
- 2 oranges
- 1 lemon
- 1½ cups water
- ⅛ teaspoon baking soda
- 1 pound ripe cranberries
- 6½ cups sugar
- ½ bottle liquid pectin

Cut oranges and lemon into quarters, and remove seeds. Grind the fruit, chop fine, or cut crosswise into wafer-thin slices. Add water and soda. Bring to boil and simmer, covered, for 20 minutes, stirring occasionally. Add cranberries and simmer, covered, for 10 minutes. Measure 5 cups fruit into very large saucepan. Add sugar and mix well. Put over high heat, bring to a *full rolling boil and boil hard for 1 minute,* stirring constantly. Remove from heat and at once stir in pectin. Skim off foam with metal spoon. Then stir and skim for 7 minutes to cool slightly and to prevent floating fruit. Ladle into hot sterilized jars, and seal. Makes about eight ½-pint jars.

BLUEBERRY MARMALADE
- 1 medium orange
- 1 medium lemon
- 1 cup water
- ⅛ teaspoon baking soda
- 3 cups blueberries, washed and drained
- 5 cups sugar
- 1 bottle (6 ounces) liquid pectin

Remove peel in quarters from orange and lemon. Lay quarters flat and remove about half of white part. With scissors, cut remaining peel into fine shreds. Put in kettle; add water and soda. Bring to boil and simmer, covered, for 10 minutes. Remove pulp from membrane; add with juice to peel. Cover; simmer for 15 minutes, adding more water if necessary and blueberries and sugar; bring to boil;

simmer for 5 minutes. Remove from heat and stir in liquid pectin. Stir and skim by turns for 5 minutes. Pour into hot sterilized jars, and seal. Makes about six ½-pint jars.

LEMON MARMALADE
See page 1057.

MARRON—A French word describing a species of cultivated chestnut whose fruit contains only a single large nut. Marrons are imported from France and Italy, packaged in cans. The varieties include a purée and whole nuts, in sweetened and unsweetened form, or preserved in vanilla syrup. *Marrons glacés,* cooked chestnuts covered with a thin sugar icing, are a French delicacy. They are imported in rich handsome containers. Their price is high because chestnuts are fragile and there is much breakage when they are being shelled and sugared. *Marrons glacés* are the top grade chestnuts, big, juicy, and perfectly shaped.

MARRON PURÉE
1 pound marrons
½ cup hot milk
1 tablespoon butter
Salt and pepper

With a sharp knife cut a gash in the flat side of marrons. Put nuts in saucepan and cover with cold water. Bring to a boil. Cook for 15 to 20 minutes. Keep marrons in hot water. Remove a few at a time and peel off outer and inner skins. Force marrons through a food mill. Add milk and butter, and season with salt and pepper to taste. Reheat; take care that marrons don't burn. Makes 4 to 6 servings.

Note: The French serve it, instead of potatoes, with pork or turkey.

MARRON COUPE
1 can (7 ounces) marrons glacés
4 ounces brandy
1 quart vanilla ice cream
1 cup heavy cream, whipped

Marinate marrons in brandy for about 30 minutes. Then drain and chop marrons coarsely, reserving brandy syrup. Line bottom of a sherbet dish with part of chopped marrons. Place a generous portion of vanilla ice cream on top and sprinkle remaining marrons on ice cream. Pour brandy syrup on each portion and top with whipped cream. Chill. Makes 8 to 10 servings.

MARRON SOUFFLÉ
2 tablespoons butter
2 tablespoons flour
1 cup milk
1 cup marron purée, unsweetened
½ cup sugar
2 ounces (2 squares) unsweetened chocolate, melted
4 eggs, separated

1 teaspoon vanilla extract

Melt butter in a saucepan. Stir in flour. With a rotary beater beat milk with marron purée and sugar until smooth and well blended. Gradually stir marron mixture into butter and flour. Cook over low heat, stirring constantly, until thickened. Melt chocolate and stir into marron mixture. Beat egg yolks. Gradually stir hot sauce into egg yolks. Cool. Beat egg whites until stiff. Fold egg whites and vanilla into marron mixture. Pour mixture into a heavily buttered 1½-quart mold that has been sprinkled with granulated sugar. Put soufflé dish in a pan of hot water in preheated moderate oven (375°F.) for 40 to 45 minutes. Serve at once. Makes 6 to 8 servings.

MERINGUE WITH MARRON FILLING
4 egg whites, at room temperature
1⅓ cups sugar
½ teaspoon cream of tartar
1 cup canned marron purée, unsweetened
½ cup sugar
½ cup grated semisweet chocolate
2 teaspoons finely grated orange rind
1 package (10 ounces) frozen raspberries

Beat egg whites until stiff. Gradually beat in sugar and cream of tartar, 1 tablespoon at a time. Beat until smooth and glossy and sugar is completely dissolved. With a pastry bag or a spoon, shape 16 mounds on brown paper placed on a cookie sheet. Bake in preheated very slow oven (275°F.) for 35 to 40 minutes, or until pale brown. Turn off heat and let stand in oven until cold. Remove from paper. Blend marron purée with sugar, chocolate, and orange rind. Spread filling thickly on the bottoms of 8 meringues. Top with remaining meringues. Defrost raspberries and press through a sieve. Place filled meringues on serving dishes. Serve puréed raspberries over the top. Makes 8 servings.

MARROW, BEEF—The fatty filling of beef bones, which is prized for its rich and delicate taste and which is also one of the lightest and most digestible of fats. Marrow is used to enrich dishes, or by itself as a spread, or baked or broiled in the bone.

Marrow is popular in England, where it is eaten as a savory, the nonsweet dish that follows the dessert. A savory is said to clear the palate for the port or other wines that may be drunk after dinner. Marrow has been used in England since the Middle Ages when, interestingly, it was used to enrich sweet puddings. Later it became a nonsweet dish. In the 18th century marrow bones were wrapped in

paste to avoid evaporation and baked in the oven. Then they were sent to the table in long narrow bowls covered by a napkin, to be eaten with salt, pepper, and dry toast. Special long-handled spoons were used to scoop out the marrow. Queen Victoria was very fond of marrow toast, a dish made with baked or steamed marrow piled on freshly made hot toast.

Availability and Purchasing Guide—Beef marrow is available wherever fresh meat is sold.

Ask butcher to extract marrow from marrow bone if possible. If not, have him cut marrow bones into 1½-inch lengths.

Storage—Use as soon as possible since the large fat content causes spoilage.
☐ Refrigerator shelf: 1 to 2 days
☐ Refrigerator frozen-food compartment, uncooked: 1 week
☐ Freezer, uncooked: 1 month

Nutritive Food Values—Marrow is very rich in fat with very small amounts of protein. It has the same caloric value as beef fat.
☐ 1 tablespoon, cooked = about 100 calories

Basic Preparation—If not extracted by butcher, use a sharp knife to remove bone marrow from bones. Cut marrow into ½-inch slices and heat in top part of double boiler. Or bones can be simmered in water to cover. Remove marrow carefully from bones and use as directed in recipe.

☐ **To Poach**—Remove marrow from marrow bones which have been cut into 1½-inch pieces. Cut marrow into ½-inch rounds. Bring beef bouillon to boil. Carefully drop marrow slices into bouillon and poach for 3 or 4 minutes. Drain.

☐ **To Roast**—Have butcher split marrow bones and cut them into 4-inch lengths. Put in shallow roasting pan and roast in preheated slow oven (300°F.) for 1 hour. Remove marrow and slice.

MARROW TOAST
Poach or roast marrow. Put hot sliced marrow on crisp toast. Sprinkle with a little minced parsley and fresh lemon juice. Serve at once.

MARROWBONE SOUP
1 beef shinbone, cracked
3 quarts water
1 cup chopped cabbage
4 cups diced mixed vegetables (potato, onion, carrots, turnips, rutabagas, parsnips, etc.)
½ cup pearl barley
Salt and pepper
Few sprigs of parsley, chopped

Have butcher crack the shinbone. Put bone and water in kettle, bring to boil and simmer, covered, for 2 to 3 hours, or until meat separates from bone and marrow is dissolved. Remove bone and take off meat. Add meat to broth. Add vegetables, barley, and salt and pepper. Simmer, covered, until vegetables are tender. Add more salt and pepper to taste. Serve with a garnish of parsley. Makes 6 servings.

MARROW DUMPLINGS (Marrow Balls)
1 egg, slightly beaten
½ cup fine dry bread crumbs
½ cup hot mashed potatoes
  Few sprigs of parsley, chopped
½ cup cooked beef marrow
  Salt and pepper to taste

Mix all ingredients well. Shape into balls the size of walnuts and drop into rapidly boiling salted water. Cook for 7 minutes, or until done. Skim out and serve with clear soup. Or, cook in the soup, if preferred. Makes 4 servings.

MARROW SAUCE
2 cups hot beef bouillon
½ cup beef marrow, cut into ½-inch dice
2 tablespoons all-purpose flour
2 tablespoons butter or margarine
¼ teaspoon paprika
¼ teaspoon grated onion
  Few sprigs of parsley, chopped
1 tablespoon fresh lemon juice
1 tablespoon sherry

Pour 1 cup hot bouillon over marrow and keep hot. Brown flour lightly in the butter. Add remaining bouillon, paprika, onion, and parsley. Bring to boil and cook, stirring, until thickened. Add lemon juice, sherry, and strain into marrow mixture. Stir well and serve hot on beef or veal. Makes 2 cups.

MARROW, VEGETABLE—A squashlike edible gourd shaped like a long egg. These gourds can grow to a very large size and it is the smaller marrows which are best for eating. They are peeled, cut into halves, and seeds removed from the center; they are cooked as any firm squash is cooked. Marrow is similar to squash in food and caloric value.

Vegetable marrow, like squash, can be boiled, mashed, fried, stuffed, and made into jam. This vegetable must be well seasoned and is usually combined with richly flavored foods. The golden flowers of the vegetable marrow can be dipped into batter and made into fritters.

Vegetable marrows are available in specialty vegetable stores during the summer months.

COOKED VEGETABLE MARROW
Peel marrow, remove seeds, and cut marrow into cubes or slices. Cook, covered, in small amount of boiling water for 15 to 20 minutes. Drain, if necessary.

Add butter and season with salt and pepper to taste.

STUFFED VEGETABLE MARROW
1 large vegetable marrow
1½ cups chopped cooked beef or other meat
½ cup soft bread crumbs
1 teaspoon instant minced onion
2 tablespoons ketchup
  Salt and pepper to taste

Cut marrow into halves crosswise. Remove seeds. Mix remaining ingredients and pack into marrow halves. Put halves together and fasten with toothpicks. Bake in preheated moderate oven (350°F.) for 30 minutes, or until tender. Cut into slices. Makes 6 servings.

MARSHMALLOW—An American confection made of sugar, unflavored gelatin, corn syrup, and flavoring. The mixture is whipped until very light, poured into a pan lined with sugar and cornstarch, and allowed to stand until firm. Then the marshmallows are cut into squares and rolled in additional sugar and cornstarch.

Marshmallows can be colored and flavored and rolled in colored sugar and coconut or chocolate sprinkles. They can be dipped into melted bittersweet chocolate or used to prepare many desserts. Some marshmallows are made with the addition of egg whites to make them lighter and puffier.

Marshmallows can be bought in regular one-inch round puffs, white or colored, covered with coconut or chocolate, or in a miniature size the shape and size of an after-dinner mint. Marshmallows are also made in the form of a thick cream and sold in jars.

Toasted, held on a skewer over the fire, marshmallows make a light, sweet treat at the end of a party or picnic.

Caloric Value
☐ 3½ ounces = 315 calories

MARSHMALLOWS
1 envelope unflavored gelatin
⅓ cup cold water
½ cup sugar
⅔ cup light corn syrup
½ teaspoon vanilla extract
  Equal parts of cornstarch and sugar

Soften gelatin in cold water and dissolve over low heat. Add sugar and stir until dissolved. Put in large mixer bowl with corn syrup and vanilla extract. Beat at high speed for 15 minutes, or until mixture is very thick and of marshmallow consistency. Cover bottom of pan (9 x 9 x 2 inches) with equal parts sugar and cornstarch. Pour in mixture and smooth top. Let stand in cool place 1 hour, or until set. Loosen from pan and

turn out on board sprinkled with mixture of equal parts cornstarch and sugar. Cut into squares with knife wet with cold water. Roll in cornstarch and sugar. Makes 1 pound.

CRISPY MARSHMALLOW STICKS
¼ cup butter or margarine
½ pound marshmallows
½ teaspoon vanilla extract
5 cups crisp rice cereal
½ cup semisweet chocolate pieces

Put butter and marshmallows in top part of double boiler. Heat over boiling water until melted and blended, stirring frequently. Add vanilla; beat. Combine with cereal and chocolate pieces in large greased bowl. Mix well. Press into buttered pan (13 x 9 x 2 inches). Cool and cut into sticks 1 x 3 inches.

COCOA MARSHMALLOW PUDDING
Scald 2 cups milk in top part of double boiler; combine 1½ tablespoons cocoa, 2 tablespoons each of cornstarch and sugar, ¼ teaspoon salt; add mixed dry ingredients to milk. Cook until thickened, stirring occasionally. Add 1 cup marshmallows. When they begin to melt, pour pudding into dishes to cool.

PEACH MARLOW
16 marshmallows (¼ pound)
½ cup peach nectar
¼ teaspoon almond extract
⅛ teaspoon salt
1 cup undiluted evaporated milk
2 tablespoons fresh lemon juice
  Few drops each of red and yellow food coloring, if desired

Set refrigerator control for fast freezing. Melt marshmallows in top part of double boiler over boiling water. Add peach nectar and cook until smooth and blended, stirring constantly. Remove from heat; add extract and salt; cool. Pour evaporated milk into refrigerator tray and freeze until mushy. Whip until stiff. Add lemon juice. Fold in marshmallow mixture, blending well. Add food coloring to tint a delicate peach color. Put in refrigerator tray and freeze until firm. Makes 6 servings.

FLUFFY MARSHMALLOW DESSERT
1 pound marshmallows
1 cup fresh milk
1 cup chilled undiluted evaporated milk
½ cup dry skim milk
  Juice of 2 lemons
2 teaspoons vanilla extract
  Red food coloring

Combine marshmallows and fresh milk in top part of double boiler and cook over hot water until marshmallows are melted. Remove from heat and cool. Whip evaporated milk until stiff; add dry skim milk; continue beating until well blended. Stir in lemon juice and vanilla and fold into marshmallow mixture. Divide into two parts; color one part

Marzipan and molds

red. Pour alternate layers into an oiled loaf pan. Chill; slice and serve. Makes 8 to 10 servings.

BLACK-AND-WHITE MARSHMALLOW DELIGHT
1 cup diced cooked prunes
2 bananas, sliced
12 large marshmallows, cut into quarters
1 tablespoon fresh lemon juice
1 cup heavy cream, whipped
2 tablespoons sugar

Mix prunes, bananas, and marshmallows; sprinkle with lemon juice. Lightly fold in cream and sugar. Pile in sherbet glasses. Makes 6 servings.

MARZIPAN—A confectionery paste made of ground blanched almonds, sugar, and egg whites. The paste should be as malleable as clay and can be colored and flavored as desired. It can be shaped into fruits, animals, and other fancy shapes with the fingers. It can be rolled into thin layers between sheets of wax paper and used to cover entire cakes; it can be cut with scissors or a sharp knife into roses and other flowers, letters, bows, and decorations, limited only by the skill of the fingers and the imagination of the decorator.

Marzipan is a very ancient confection and it may have come from the Near East, where both sugar and almonds were plentiful. Persian princes enjoyed sweet almond paste for centuries and tradition says that the Crusaders brought it back to Europe in the shape of a coin, called the "marchpane," a word derived from Arabic. In any case, the confection became very popular and confectioners in such cities as Venice in Italy, Lübeck in Germany, and in Paris did a flourishing business. Later marzipan was traded all over Europe, enchanting people with its richness. It became one of the traditional Christmas sweets, shaped into fruits and flowers. In Denmark where marzipan is immensely popular, as it is in all Scandinavian countries, a sweet marzipan pig is given at Christmas for good luck.

A century ago, no American Christmas would have been complete without exquisitely shaped and tinted marzipan fruits, vegetables, flowers, figures, and classical Christmas tree ornaments, either formed by hand or in special mahogany and cherry molds. Today ornate marzipan can be bought in shops and in fancy candy stores.

Marzipan can be prepared ahead and stored in an airtight container in the refrigerator for several weeks. Almonds can be ground in an electric blender or in a nut grinder until very fine.

MARZIPAN
1 cup blanched almonds
1 teaspoon almond extract
2 cups sifted confectioners' sugar
2 egg whites, slightly beaten

Grind almonds in electric blender or four times in nut grinder. They must be ground extremely fine. Combine ground almonds, almond extract, and confectioners' sugar. Add egg whites, 1 teaspoon at a time, beating vigorously with a spoon. Continue to add egg whites until mixture looks moist. Knead with the hands until smooth and plastic. Makes about 1¼ cups.

MASK—To mask a food is to cover it completely before serving with an appropriate sauce. This is done to give the food a festive appearance and flavor.

VEAL WITH MAYONNAISE MASK
1 breast of veal (4½ to 5 pounds)
1 large onion, sliced
2 teaspoons salt
½ teaspoon pepper
1 celery stalk
6 cups boiling water
1 envelope unflavored gelatin
3 tablespoons cold water
1 cup mayonnaise
  Stuffed olives
  Watercress

Put veal, onion, salt, pepper, celery, and boiling water in large kettle. Bring to boil. Cover and simmer gently for 2½ hours, or until meat is tender. Drain, reserving liquid. Remove meat from bones and cut into coarse pieces. Strain liquid and reduce to ½ cup by boiling uncovered. Pack meat in small mixing bowl and add liquid. Let stand until cold. Cover with wax paper and chill overnight under heavy weight. Turn out on flat plate. Soak gelatin in cold water for 5 minutes. Dissolve over boiling water. Add slowly to mayonnaise, stirring constantly. Pour mixture over veal, spreading with spatula to coat meat on all sides. Garnish with slices of stuffed olives and watercress. Chill until serving time. Cut into wedges. Makes 6 to 8 servings.

MASKED TOMATO SALAD
4 large tomatoes
  Salt and pepper
1 cup cheese, meat, or fish salad stuffing
1 envelope unflavored gelatin
1 tablespoon cider vinegar
1 tablespoon water
  Dash of Worcestershire
1 teaspoon prepared mustard
  Dash of cayenne
1 cup salad dressing
  Lettuce
1 hard-cooked egg
2 stuffed olives

Cut off stem end of tomatoes and remove part of center pulp. Drain tomatoes and sprinkle with salt and pepper; fill with stuffing; chill. Soak gelatin in vinegar, water, and seasonings. Melt over hot water, stirring constantly. Remove from heat and add salad dressing gradually. Dip cold tomatoes into dressing mixture, turn upside down, and put in refrigerator to set. If coating is too thin, a second coating may be given. Serve on lettuce; garnish with sliced egg and olives. Makes 4 servings.

MATÉ—A beverage made from the leaves of various species of holly, chiefly *Ilex paraguariensis,* which is also known as yerba maté or Paraguay tea. The plant is an evergreen shrub or small tree. Maté grows wild in southern Brazil, Paraguay, and Argentina, and is also cultivated. It is a relatively inexpensive drink and is popularly used in most South American countries.

Maté is greenish in color, has an agreeable aroma, and a slightly bitter taste, which is different from that of tea and less astringent. Maté is a stimulant, containing up to five per cent caffeine. It also has valuable restorative properties. It was used long before the white man arrived in this hemisphere.

To make maté the leaves of the plant, which resemble tea leaves and are four to five inches in length, are dried in ovens. Then they are threshed and sifted. To brew maté in the traditional manner, the leaves are put in a gourd, covered with boiling water, and allowed to simmer for at least ten minutes. The tea is sucked through a *bombilla,* a hollow tube of straw, brass, or silver with a perforated bowl which acts as a strainer. The *bombilla* can be an object of pride and value, and it is sometimes chased and embossed. On the pampas, the South American range country, it is customary to see the *gauchos* sitting around the campfire at night, passing the maté gourd from hand to hand, each taking a drink with his own *bombilla.* The *gauchos* are famous for their endurance in the saddle, which they attribute to a diet that consists almost exclusively of meat and maté.

Maté is usually drunk as is, but it can be flavored in any way: with lemon juice, rum, or kirsch, for example. It can be bought in specialty and health-food stores, and prepared and served like tea.

MAYONNAISE—A cold sauce of French origin made with egg yolks, oil, and seasonings, which are blended into an emulsion. It is used as a spread, a sauce for fish, meat, and vegetables, and as a salad dressing.

The origin of the word mayonnaise is disputed. It is said that the Duke of Richelieu, a French statesman (1696-1788), invented the sauce after the victorious battle of Mahón, on the Mediterranean island of Minorca, and named it *mahonnaise* in honor of his victory. Other culinary historians maintain that the word mayonnaise is derived from *moyeu,* the Old French word for "egg yolk," meaning something made from the yolks of eggs.

In French culinary language, a *mayonnaise* is also a dish bound with mayonnaise sauce, such as lobster mayonnaise, chicken mayonnaise, etc.

Availability and Purchasing Guide—Mayonnaise is available in food stores throughout the country. It must contain salad oil, at least 65 per cent by weight; acid ingredients such as vinegar or lemon juice; and an emulsifier such as egg, gelatin, starch paste, or gums. It may also contain salt, certain sweetening ingredients, monosodium glutamate, and a variety of other seasonings so long as they do not impart the color of egg yolk. If a binding agent other than egg is used, the product is then called salad dressing.

Storage—Once opened, mayonnaise should be covered and stored in refrigerator.
☐ Kitchen shelf: 3 months
☐ Refrigerator shelf, opened and covered: up to 6 months

Caloric Values
☐ 3½ ounces = 718 calories
☐ 1 tablespoon = 110 calories

MAYONNAISE (Basic Recipe)
Have all ingredients at room temperature.

2 egg yolks or 1 whole egg
1 teaspoon sugar
1 teaspoon powdered mustard
1 teaspoon salt
2 tablespoons vinegar
2 cups olive oil
2 tablespoons fresh lemon juice

Put egg yolks and seasonings in cold, small deep bowl. Beat with rotary beater or electric mixer until thoroughly blended. Add vinegar very slowly, beating constantly. Add 1 cup oil, 1 drop at a time, until ¼ cup has been added. Then add remaining oil, 1 tablespoon at a time, alternating with a small amount of lemon juice, beating constantly. When all ingredients have been added and mixture is completely blended, refrigerate without stirring. Makes 2 cups.
Note: If mayonnaise curdles, beat 1 egg yolk with 1 tablespoon combined water and vinegar and slowly add the curdled mixture, beating vigorously.

Blue-Cheese Dressing
Add 2 tablespoons crumbled blue cheese,

a few drops of Worcestershire, 1 tablespoon French dressing, and 1 tablespoon chopped chives to 1 cup Mayonnaise. Good on salad greens and cooked vegetables.

Caper Dressing

Add ⅓ cup well-drained chopped capers to 1 cup Mayonnaise. Good on fish and meat salads.

Chili Mayonnaise

Add 1 to 2 teaspoons chili powder to 1 cup Mayonnaise. Good on fish and meat salads.

Chutney Dressing

Add 2 tablespoons chopped chutney to 1 cup Mayonnaise. Good on salad greens, cooked vegetables, meat, fish, and egg salads.

Cumberland Dressing

Add 2 tablespoons mashed currant jelly and ½ teaspoon grated lemon rind to 1 cup Mayonnaise. Good on fruit salads.

Curry Mayonnaise

Add 1 to 3 teaspoons curry powder to 1 cup Mayonnaise. Good with fruit, vegetable, potato, and macaroni salads, seafood, poultry, and eggs.

Fruit-Salad Dressing

To ¾ cup Mayonnaise add ⅓ cup heavy sweet cream, whipped, or ½ cup dairy sour cream, ¼ cup chopped salted almonds, and ¼ cup mashed currant jelly. Good with fruit salads.

Mixed-Herb Mayonnaise

Mix 1 cup Mayonnaise with 1 teaspoon each of minced chives; dried or fresh marjoram; and fresh basil, mint, or thyme leaves. Good with vegetables, macaroni salad, seafood, meat, poultry, and eggs.

Russian Dressing

To ½ cup Mayonnaise add ¼ cup chili sauce and 2 tablespoons pickle relish. Good on greens, meat, poultry, and eggs.

Sharp-Cheddar Dressing

Finely shred ½ pound sharp Cheddar cheese; soften at room temperature. Add 1 cup Mayonnaise, 2 tablespoons vinegar, 1 minced garlic clove, ½ teaspoon salt, dash of cayenne, and 2 teaspoons Worcestershire. Beat until blended. Makes about 2 cups. Good on fruit, vegetable, macaroni, and potato salads.

Tartare Sauce

Add 2 tablespoons minced onion; 3 tablespoons minced pickles; and 1 tablespoon each of minced green olives, capers, and parsley to 1 cup Mayonnaise. Good with fish.

Thousand Island Dressing

Mix 1 cup Mayonnaise, ½ cup chili sauce, 2 tablespoons minced green pepper, 3 tablespoons chopped stuffed olives, 1 minced pimiento, and 1 teaspoon grated onion or 2 teaspoons chopped chives. Makes about 2 cups. Good with seafood, greens, hard-cooked eggs, and vegetables.

BLENDER MAYONNAISE

    1 egg
    ½ teaspoon powdered mustard
    ½ teaspoon salt
    2 tablespoons vinegar
    1 cup salad oil

Combine egg, mustard, salt, and vinegar in blender container. Add ¼ cup oil. Cover and turn motor on low speed. Immediately uncover and pour in remaining oil in a steady stream. Makes 1¼ cups.

MAYONNAISE WITH COOKED BASE

Combine ¼ cup cornstarch with 1 cup cold water in saucepan. Cook until thick and clear. In a deep bowl put 1 unbeaten egg, 1 tablespoon sugar, 1 teaspoon salt, 1 tablespoon prepared mustard, dash of cayenne, ¼ cup cider vinegar, and ¾ cup salad oil. Add hot cornstarch mixture and beat vigorously with rotary beater. Cool and keep in refrigerator. Makes about 2¼ cups. Good on slaw, fruit, cooked or raw vegetables, seafood, and potato or macaroni salads.

GELATIN MAYONNAISE

    2 teaspoons unflavored gelatin
    2 tablespoons cold water
    1 cup mayonnaise

Soak gelatin in cold water for 5 minutes. Put mixture over low heat and stir until gelatin is dissolved. Beat warm gelatin into mayonnaise. Spread mixture on well-chilled dry foods. Press mixture through a pastry tube to make rosettes and other decorations. Chill until mayonnaise is set. Use mixture to coat aspics, cold fish, meat, or fowl. Makes about 1 cup.

MEAD—An ancient drink made of water and honey, fermented with malt, yeast, and other ingredients. The word is connected with the Greek *methy,* "wine," and the Sanskrit *madhu,* "sweet," "honey," or "mead."

Perhaps mead's most famous association is with the early Teutonic tribes who called it the "heavenly drink" of their gods. In one of the earliest pieces of English literature, *Beowulf,* the hero's victory over Grendel the monster was celebrated with the drinking of mead in jeweled cups. Other early drinking vessels were horns and even skulls. The Norsemen drank mead at ritual feasts. A 17th-century Englishman later described the feasts thus: "The Druids and Old British Bards were wont to carouse thereof before they entered into speculations."

During the Middle Ages mead, or metheglin, a later name for the beverage, was drunk throughout Europe. In France, each village had its own special recipe. On the occasion of a wedding, mead was drunk for a month after the actual ceremony. This time was then called the "honey moon."

The drink was not limited to European nations. In East Africa certain of the tribes had special rituals during the brewing of honey wine. In South America where honey was one of the most important foods, the "honey Mother," or the honey goddess was worshiped.

The early American settlers, accustomed to mead in their homelands, brought the custom with them. Other ingredients were used as a substitute for honey. Yankee mead often contained brown sugar, molasses, and cream of tartar, flavored with checkerberry and sassafras. Some localities flavored their mead with bruised walnut leaves.

MEAL—The food, or foods, and drink eaten at a particular, and usually fixed, time to satisfy hunger or appetite.

The word meal is also used to describe the ground seeds of cereal grasses or legumes, especially when coarsely ground and unbolted, i.e.: cornmeal and oatmeal.

MEASURE—In cookery, "to measure" means to calculate accurate amounts of required ingredients. The recipes in this Encyclopedia are based upon accurate, standard measurements. For consistently successful results in cooking and baking it is necessary to have standard measuring equipment and to measure ingredients for each recipe accurately.

EQUIPMENT

■ **Standard Measuring Cups**—Two standard measuring cups are necessary, one for dry ingredients, the other for liquids. A standard measuring cup holds 8 fluid ounces. It should be marked on one side to show ¼, ½, and ¾ cup and on the other to show ⅓ and ⅔ cup. A set of graduated measuring cups is convenient for measuring and leveling part-cup amounts. These hold exactly 1, ½, ⅓, and ¼ cup.

The liquid measuring cup extends above the 1-cup level so that you can measure without spilling. These cups also have lips for pouring. A cup made of glass is preferable because it enables you to see that the liquid is exactly on the line marking the amount you want. Other convenient cups for liquids are the 2-cup and 4-cup measures.

■ **Standard Measuring Spoons**—A set includes 1 tablespoon, 1 teaspoon, ½ teaspoon, and ¼ teaspoon. The tablespoon is used for measuring amounts of less than ¼ cup.

■ **Other Helpful Items**—A spatula or straight-edge knife for leveling measurements, a large spoon for spooning ingredients into cup, a rubber scraper for scraping out measuring cup or spoon, and a washable ruler for measuring rolled dough and unmarked pans.

TO MEASURE FLOUR

Cake flour should be sifted before using it in baking. First sift flour onto a square of wax paper, a paper plate, or into a bowl. Then lift the sifted flour with a spoon into a measuring cup set on a level surface until the cup is heaping full. Now level off by drawing the edge of a spatula or straight knife across the top. Use the edge, not the flat surface of spatula, to avoid packing the flour. Do not tap or shake the cup. And do not sift directly into cup; this gives an undermeasurement. All-purpose flours may or may not be sifted, depending on the individual recipe. However, measuring should be done in the same way as for cake flour. Instant-type flours do not require sifting. They are simply stirred with the leavening, salt, etc. (In this Encyclopedia the measurements given for all flours are based upon the flours having been sifted before measuring unless otherwise specified.)

TO MEASURE BAKING POWDER, SALT, ETC.

Dip dry measuring spoon of correct size into container and remove it heaping full. Level off with spatula or straight-edge knife. Or use the convenient leveler cut from the paper seal inside some baking powder cans. To measure ⅛ teaspoon, first measure ¼ level teaspoon, then divide in half with spatula or knife.

TO MEASURE SUGAR

Spoon granulated white sugar lightly into measuring cup and level off with the straight edge of spatula or knife. (Do not tap or shake cup.) To measure regular brown sugar, pack it firmly into the cup, using back of spoon. When turned out, sugar should hold the shape of the cup. Measure granulated brown sugar in the same way white granulated is measured. Confectioners' sugar may or may not be sifted before measuring, depending on the individual recipe. Spoon lightly into cup and level off.

TO MEASURE SHORTENING

If shortening is soft and pliable, simply spoon it from can or package and press it firmly to proper line of measuring cup. Or into spoon, then level off. Butter or margarine need not be measured into a cup. A ¼-pound stick equals ½ cup. Smaller measurements are indicated on the wrapping in most cases.

TO MEASURE LIQUIDS

Set glass cup on a level surface. Fill until liquid reaches and fills the correct measure in the cup. Be sure to fill level with the mark; it's easy to undermeasure. Flavorings, thick liquids, and syrups like molasses, corn syrup, or honey can be poured from the container into the measuring spoon or cup. If cup has been used to measure shortening or water, the syrup will flow out easily. Use rubber scraper to get the last drop.

TO MEASURE PANS

The recipes in this Encyclopedia have indicated the right size baking pan to use. For successful results it is necessary to use the correct size. Many manufacturers stamp the inch size or cup capacity of their baking utensils either on the utensil itself or on a sticker attached to it. If you are in doubt as to the size, you can measure the pan with a ruler. For diameter, width, or length, measure across the top of the pan from one inside edge to the other. For depth, measure down the inside. In baking cakes, if you are doubtful of the size pan, fill pan only half full with batter. (Bake any extra batter in cupcake pans.) The cakes can then rise fully without going over the tops of the pans.

EQUIVALENT MEASURES

3 teaspoons	= 1 tablespoon
2 tablespoons	= 1 liquid ounce
4 tablespoons	= ¼ cup
5 tablespoons plus 1 teaspoon	= ⅓ cup
8 tablespoons	= ½ cup
16 tablespoons	= 1 cup
1 cup	= 8 fluid ounces
2 cups	= 1 pint
4 cups	= 1 quart
4 quarts	= 1 gallon
8 quarts	= 1 peck (dry)
16 ounces	= 1 pound

✴ EQUIVALENT AMOUNTS ✴

Apples	1 pound = 3 medium (3 cups sliced)
Bananas	1 pound = 3 medium (2½ cups sliced)
Bread	1-pound loaf = 12 to 16 slices
Butter or margarine	¼-pound stick = ½ cup
	1 pound = 2 cups
Cheese, American	1 pound = 4 cups grated
Cottage	1 pound = 2 cups
Chocolate, unsweetened	1 square = 3 tablespoons cocoa plus 1 tablespoon butter
Eggs	2 large = 3 small
Whites	8 to 11 = 1 cup
Yolks	12 to 14 = 1 cup
Flour, all-purpose	1 pound = 4 cups sifted
cake	1 pound = 4¾ to 5 cups sifted
whole-wheat	1 pound = about 3½ cups unsifted
Leavening, per cup flour use	1¼ teaspoons baking powder, or ½ teaspoon baking soda with 2 tablespoons vinegar
Lemon juice	1 medium lemon yields 3 tablespoons juice
Lemon rind	1 medium lemon yields 1 tablespoon grated rind
Milk, evaporated	1 can (14½-ounce) = 1⅔ cups or 3⅓ cups milk
	1 can (6-ounce) = ¾ cup or 1½ cups milk
Nuts in shell, almonds	1¼ pounds = 1 to 1¾ cups nut meats
peanuts	1 pound = 2 cups nut meats
pecans	1 pound = 2¼ cups nut meats
walnuts	1 pound = 1⅔ cups chopped
Nuts, shelled, almonds	1 pound, 2 ounces = 4 cups
pecan meats	1 pound = 4 cups
walnut meats	1 pound = 4 cups
Orange juice	1 medium orange yields ⅓ cup juice
Orange rind	1 medium orange yields 2 tablespoons grated rind
Pasta, macaroni & spaghetti	1 cup = 2 cups cooked
noodles	1 cup = 1 cup cooked
Potatoes, white	1 pound = 3 medium (2⅓ cups sliced)
sweet	1 pound = 3 medium (3 cups sliced)
Raisins	15-ounce package = 3 cups not packed
Shortening	1 pound = 2½ cups
Sugar, brown	1 pound = 2¼ to 2½ cups packed
confectioners'	1 pound = 4 to 4½ cups sifted·
granulated	1 pound = 2¼ cups
Thickening	1 tablespoon quick-cooking tapioca = 1 tablespoon cornstarch or 1⅓ to 1½ tablespoons flour
Tomatoes	1 pound = 3 medium

MEAT *by* ***James A. Beard***—To be correct, one must define meat in the most general of terms: simply as food, or the edible portion of any food. Indeed, John Russell had a broad concept of the word when he wrote The Boke of Nurture, in which he instructed his readers:

> *Of alle maner metes ye must*
> *   thus know and fele,*
> *The fumosities of fysch, flesche*
> *   and fowles dyners and feele,*
> *And alle maner of sawces for*
> *   fische and flesche to preserve*
> *   your lord in heale;*
> *To you it belongyth to know*
> *   alle these euery deale.*

However, in modern usage the word has gradually come to mean the flesh of domesticated animals. We still speak of the firm-meated fish or sweetmeats or nutmeats, but generally the word is reserved for the animal world. Even this refinement has boiled down to the very few varieties of flesh used in our eating habits of today.

The most favored meat, by all odds, is the flesh of the steer or cow, called beef. Strangely enough, it has been the Anglo-Saxons who have made this meat so popular. Three kings of England (Henry VIII, James I, and Charles II) are credited with knighting the loin of beef, whence comes "sirloin," and early French gastronomers who wrote about beefsteak acknowledged that England had really introduced it to them. As a matter of fact, rump steak, the wonderful English cut, is still known in France by its English name and was so listed by Dumas in his *Dictionnaire de Cuisine*. It has remained for Americans to age beef and fatten it with corn and other additives to the point where American beef, and especially the New York type of beef, with its characteristic aging and fattening, has become more famous than the English.

Second in popularity to beef, or possibly its equal, is pork. It is the most versatile of animals, for practically everything but the grunt of a pig is edible and delicious. Pork, when cured and smoked, presents the main meat supply of millions of people and in this form was for long periods of time in history the only meat, save game, that many regions knew. It is interesting to observe the various ways in which pork is prepared around the world. Each country has its own version of sausage, its way of curing and smoking, and its way of using the offal in certain mixtures; each has its own type of head cheese or brawn and its own way of using the feet or trotters and the tails. Without doubt, it would require a separate and special encyclopedia to list all the preparations of pork known to man.

No meat is so universally enjoyed.

Lamb and mutton are third in popularity. The Near Eastern and European countries all savor lamb and use it in an astonishing number of ways. In the south of France, Greece, and Italy, as well as in Spain and Portugal, one of the great dishes is young lamb. Also, the North Africans and the nomadic tribes of the desert countries have countless preparations for making lamb delicious. It is only in these United States that lamb has had a struggle for popularity. Certainly one of the reasons for such slow acceptance is that most lamb is marketed too old; second, it is usually cooked badly, and almost always overcooked in the average American home, a point that many food propagandists will not admit.

If veal were sold as it is in Europe—white-fleshed young veal that has been milk fed—it, too, would be used more widely in this country. As it is, the many hundreds of delicious veal dishes so dear to the hearts of Italians, Swiss, and French never show up on our menus. Fortunately, there is a small industry rising in the United States that is adopting a process perfected in Holland of feeding milk solids and vitamins to calves and not allowing them to wander in pastures. This method is producing fine, tender white veal, something heretofore rarely seen in our markets.

Meat is by far the most important element in our diet. It has often been said that the United States is a "meat and potato" country. This is true in many sections, but the improvement in our marketing system has altered the pattern greatly, and "fysch" as well as "flesche" can be enjoyed in the most inland regions.

Nutritive Values

Meat ranks as high nutritionally as it does in popularity. It forms the basis for one of the four food groups required for a balanced diet (the others are the milk, bread-cereal, and vegetable-fruit groups), and is the major factor in the planning and preparation of nutritious meals for the family. Meat is essentially protein and the word, appropriately enough, comes from the Greek word meaning "first" or "of primary importance." Meat is rich, too, in the B vitamins so necessary to good health: thiamine, riboflavin, and niacin. Provided in meat, too, are vitamins A, C, D, E, and K, as well as the minerals calcium, phosphorus, iron, sodium, potassium, magnesium, copper, cobalt, manganese, zinc, and aluminum.

Meat from all animals is almost completely utilized by the body: the protein being at least 97 per cent digested and the fats at least 96 per cent. The old

wives' tale that pork is hard to digest has long since been disproved.

MEAT SELECTION

There are enough cuts and kinds of meat available in the retail markets of the United States for a homemaker to prepare a different meat dish for her family every day for an entire year. While all of these cuts and kinds would probably not be available in any one store, the typical meat retailer does offer a much wider selection of meat products than would be available anywhere else in the world. Therefore, regardless of the area, it is possible to keep variety in the menu.

In choosing a meat, it helps to remember that there are seven basic retail cuts of meat which apply to all animals: blade cuts (shoulder), rib cuts, loin cuts (backbone), sirloin cuts (hipbone), arm cuts (arm bone), breast cuts, and leg cuts. Fortunately, one need not be an expert to select quality meat. Reliable brands and Federal stamping insure a satisfactory selection.

Three major factors are concerned with the judging and grading of meat carcasses and cuts.

1. *Conformation*—This refers to the general build, form, shape, contour or outline of the carcass, side, or cut. Superior conformation implies short necks and shanks, thick backs with full loins, deep plump rounds, well-fleshed ribs, and thick shoulders. The most desirable cuts, including the loin, rib, round (or leg), and chuck (shoulder), have full muscles and a large proportion of edible meat to fat and bone.

2. *Maturity*—This is related to the age of the animal. In grading unribbed carcasses of beef, the degree of maturity is determined primarily by characteristics of the skeleton, particularly the ossification of the cartilages on the ends of the chine (lower part of backbone) bones. The color and texture of the lean are also considered in determining maturity in ribbed carcasses.

3. *Quality*—This is closely associated with maturity. The color and texture of the lean are key factors in determining quality. In grading unribbed carcasses of beef, the character of the fat is also considered. Best quality is associated with youth for tenderness, with lean meat that is well marbled (intermingling of fat with lean), and with color typical of the meat being judged. The lean of beef should be bright red, firm, and velvety to the touch. It is well marbled with little veins of fat and has a thick white or creamy white, firm fat covering. The lean of quality pork should be firm and tender with a pinkish cast and some marbling.

Outside fat should be firm and snowy white. The lean of good lamb should be pinkish to deep red in color, firm and fine-textured, with an even covering of clear, white brittle fat and a great deal of marbling. Veal should have grayish-pink flesh and very little exterior fat. What fat there is should be firm and creamy white. It has no marbling.

Meat must be government graded if it is to be shipped from state to state. Each carcass is stamped with a purple stamp with the legend "U.S. Insp'd & P'S'D." Grades of meat include:

Prime (beef, lamb, and veal)—Thick, velvety well-marbled flesh with a smooth waxy white coating of fat. Limited quantity usually sold to better restaurants and hotels.

Choice (beef, lamb, and veal)—Well-marbled meat with a smaller amount of covering fat. Best retail buy since smaller amount of fat means less waste and more meat for the money with no loss of quality in the meat.

Good (beef, lamb, and veal)—Thinner fat covering which is softer and more oily, slight amount of marbling. Good buy for a budget-minded consumer.

Standard (beef and veal)—Very thin fat covering, smaller amount of meat which has little or no marbling. Meat is tough and poorly flavored when cooked.

The grading stamp is usually run down the length of the carcass after inspection. However most markets which sell precut and prepackaged meat state the grade of the meat on the price label.

Hogs are graded by yield and quality of meat. Most meat cuts come from barrows and gilts under 1 year old when killed. Grades are choice, medium, and cull. Choice meat is grayish pink in color with reddish bones and firm white fat. The trend today is toward breeding butcher-type hogs with less fat. There is no grade identification on the carcass. It may be graded, however, by the packer on a quality and weight basis. Many cuts carry packer brands.

Prepared meats include sausages, cured hams, cured bacon, dried beef, corned beef, and canned meats of various kinds. In addition, there are other edible parts called "variety meats." These include the brain, tongue, liver, heart, and kidneys from the animals listed above; the thymus glands or sweetbreads of calves; oxtail and tripe.

MEAT STORAGE

Fresh Meats

■ Unwrap meat and remove market paper. Do not wash meat.

■ Loosely wrap each meat in wax paper or foil, leaving ends open. Prepackaged meat can be refrigerated in the original wrapper if it is to be used within one to two days.

■ Store in meat compartment or coldest part of food compartment of refrigerator.

■ Variety meats or ground meat should be cooked within one to two days or wrapped for freezing and frozen.

■ Cured and smoked meats should be refrigerated at once in their original wrapper. Canned hams that must be refrigerated (the label so states) should be stored promptly.

■ Large cuts of meat should be kept frozen at 0°F. or lower.

Smaller pieces of meat such as ground meat patties, chops, and small steaks can be kept frozen satisfactorily in a refrigerator frozen-food compartment for several weeks. Longer storage requires a deep freeze.

Some meats are freeze dried and can be stored at room temperature. The meat is not shrunken in appearance and is lightweight, ideal for campers. The meat is generally sealed in an airtight container made of foil, or in a can. It can be found in camping supply stores.

Cooked Meats

■ Cooked meats should be cooled quickly, uncovered, then covered or wrapped, and stored promptly in the refrigerator. Do not allow meats to stand at room temperature longer than two hours. Meat cooked in liquid may be cooled quickly in the liquid by putting the pan containing the meat where there is a good circulation of cool air. Or it can be cooled by setting the pan in cold or running water.

FREEZING MEAT

Most meats freeze satisfactorily if properly wrapped, frozen quickly, and kept at 0°F. or below. (Cured meats should not be frozen for any length of time as the salt in these meats causes development of rancidity.) To insure good quality remember the following:

■ Freeze meat while it is fresh and in top condition. Meat will not improve in the freezer.

■ Select proper wrapping materials. Choose a moisture- vapor-proof wrap so that air will be sealed out and moisture locked in. Pliable wraps such as freezer foil, transparent moisture- vapor-proof wraps and certain types of plastic bags are good for wrapping bulky, irregularly shaped meats, since these wraps can be molded to the meat. Freezer papers and cartons coated with cellophane, polyethylene, or wax; laminated freezer paper; plastic bags and certain types of

waxed cartons are suitable for some cuts of meat. Casserole dishes containing meat sometimes are frozen in the dish in which they will be reheated or baked.

■ Prepare meat for freezing before wrapping: Trim off excess fat and remove bones when practical to conserve freezer space. Meat should not be salted as salt shortens freezer life. Wrap in "family-size" packages. Place double thickness of wrap between chops and patties for easier separation.

■ Wrap tightly, pressing out as much air as possible. Roasting-size pieces of meat or large pot roasts should have exposed bones well padded with freezer or wax paper so they will not pierce wrapping.

■ Label properly. Indicate name of cut and date on package.

■ Freeze at once at −10°F. or lower, if possible. Allow space for air between packages during initial freezing time. Try to avoid freezing such a large quantity of meat at one time that the freezer is overloaded and temperature therefore raised undesirably.

■ Maintain freezer temperature at 0°F. or lower during freezer storage. Higher temperatures and fluctuations above that temperature impair quality.

■ Refreezing of defrosted meat is not recommended except in emergencies. There is some loss of juices during defrosting and the possibility of deterioration of the meat between the time of defrosting and refreezing.

Basic Preparation—It is generally best to use a low temperature for cooking meat as this causes less shrinkage and results in juicier meat with more flavor and less drippings. Two methods are used in meat cookery: *Dry heat*, which includes oven-roasting, oven-broiling, panbroiling, and panfrying, is used for more tender cuts; *moist heat*, which includes braising, pot-roasting, and cooking in liquid, is used for less tender cuts.

☐ **To Oven-Roast**—Charts can only give an approximate idea of when meat is done to the degree desired since this depends on the contour of the meat and the amount of bone and fat. A meat thermometer inserted into the thickest part of the meat without touching a bone can tell accurately when a piece of meat is ready. Place meat, fat side up, on a rack in a shallow pan. Add no water and do not cover. Lard or season meat as desired. Insert meat thermometer. Roast in preheated slow oven (325°F.). If a browner roast is desired, raise the oven temperature to extremely hot (500°F.) for the last 5 to 10 minutes of cooking time.

The searing method of roasting re-

quires that meat is roasted until brown, about 20 minutes, in an extremely hot oven (500°F.). Heat is then reduced to slow (300°F.) and meat is roasted to the desired degree of doneness. A large amount of drippings results.

☐ **To Oven-Broil**—Preheat broiler. Grease broiler rack to prevent meat from sticking. Cut meat into 1- to 2-inch thickness. Slash edges of meat to prevent curling during broiling. Place meat about 3 inches away from the source of heat. If thick, sear meat and then cook at a lower temperature to degree of doneness desired. If meat is cut thin, broil at moderate temperature during the entire cooking process. Season meat after cooking and use tongs to turn meat to avoid piercing and loss of meat juices.

For all steaks over 2 inches thick, sear each side; then lower broiler rack and broil for 20 minutes per side, longer if necessary.

☐ **To Panbroil**—Rub a heavy skillet very lightly with fat. Keep pan over high heat. Brown meat on one side, turn, and brown meat on the other side. Lower heat and continue cooking until meat is done. Use no cover or water and season meat after cooking.

☐ **To Panfry**—This method is generally used for thin cuts of meat or liver. Cook the meat in a small amount of fat in a skillet.

☐ **To Braise and to Pot-Roast**—Season meat. Dredge with flour and brown in hot fat or shortening in a heavy Dutch oven. Add a small amount of liquid, cover tightly, and simmer slowly for a long period of time. Add more small amounts of liquid if necessary to prevent sticking. Meat can also be baked in a preheated moderate oven (350°F.), covered, for the same length of time.

☐ **To Cook in Liquid**—Meat may be dredged with flour and browned before cooking, but this is not necessary. Add enough water or stock, some say cold, some say boiling, to cover and *simmer* (do not boil), covered. With some meats such as corned beef or tongue it may be necessary to change water after it starts to boil and replace it with fresh boiling water.

☐ **To Cook Frozen Meat**—Thaw meat in the refrigerator, allowing 5 to 8 hours per pound. Thawing can be shortened by placing wrapped meat under running cold water, allowing 2 to 6 hours. Meat can be cooked from the frozen state but requires different cooking times:

Roasting from frozen state requires ⅓ to ½ as much more time than that allowed for roasting from unfrozen state. Insert meat thermometer after meat has been cooked halfway. When broiling from frozen state, place meat at least 4 inches below source of heat and allow from ¼ of the time to twice as long as the regular broiling time. If the rack cannot be lowered, broil meat at a lower temperature. To panbroil allow ¼ to ½ as much more time as you would for unfrozen meat.

When they are braised or cooked in liquid, frozen meats need only a little more time than fresh meats to cook. Substantially longer cooking times are required only for the larger cuts of meat.

☐ **To Tenderize Meat**—Pounding and marinating are two methods used to tenderize meat. Artificial meat tenderizers are made from enzymes extracted from papaya, pineapple, and lemon and are sold seasoned and unseasoned. Follow manufacturers' directions for using.

Marinades are also used to tenderize and flavor meat. Meat can be marinated in a liquid usually containing some kind of acid for several hours at room temperature or in the refrigerator. Packaged marinades are available. Pork is marinated for flavor rather than for tenderness; the high percentage of fat makes pork naturally more tender. See page 1109 for Marinade recipes.

☐ **To Lard Meat**—This is generally done to meats which require additional fat because there is no marbling in the meat to provide fat. Larding is usually accomplished by threading slivers of salt pork or bacon into the meat. Small pockets may be cut into the meat and stuffed with cubes of salt pork or bacon. Some meats may also be completely covered with thin sheets of suet or pork fat which are tied in place. This is called barding. When cooking game it is necessary to use larding or barding since game is lacking in fat.

MEATBALL—A dish made of ground meat shaped into a ball before cooking. The meat can be purchased already ground, or it can be ground at home. Meatballs can be made from any kind of meat, of any size; they can be fried, boiled, stewed, or cooked with other foods. They can be served by themselves as a meat course, or as an accompaniment, such as in spaghetti sauce with meatballs. They are often stretched and bound with other foods such as cereals, bread, eggs, cheese, and vegetables.

Meatballs are a favorite dish in most countries and are prepared and served differently in different lands. Among the most popular meatballs are those of Sweden, *köttbullar*, and Denmark, *frikadeller*.

SPICY SAUSAGE-BALL APPETIZERS
2 pounds highly seasoned
    sausage meat
One 5-ounce can water chestnuts,
    drained and chopped

Combine sausage meat and water chestnuts. Shape into 1-inch balls. Bake in preheated slow oven (325°F.) for 45 minutes, or until browned. Makes 12 servings.

BARLEY-ONION SOUP WITH BEEF BALLS
½ cup uncooked barley
4 cups water
2 quarts bouillon or water
1 pound ground beef
6 large onions
  Dash of Worcestershire
  Salt and pepper

Soak washed barley in water overnight; do not drain; add bouillon and bring to boil; cook until barley is tender, about 1½ hours. Shape ground beef into small balls; brown in skillet; remove from pan. Cook chopped onions in meat drippings until tender and lightly browned. Add meatballs and onions to soup mixture; simmer for 30 minutes. Season to taste. Makes 8 servings.

LIMA-BEAN SOUP WITH SAUSAGE BALLS
½ cup dried Lima beans, washed
5 cups water
¾ pound bulk sausage meat
1 onion, chopped
¼ cup chopped celery
1 cup cubed potatoes
1 teaspoon salt
¼ teaspoon pepper
6 soda crackers
1 tablespoon minced parsley
1 egg
1½ cups milk

Soak Lima beans in water overnight; do not drain. Cook until tender. Cook sausage meat very slowly in heavy kettle until about ⅓ cup fat has been collected, but do not brown sausages. Remove sausage meat; keep 1 tablespoon fat in kettle and save remainder for other purposes. Brown onion, celery, and potatoes lightly in fat in kettle; add salt, pepper, cooked Lima beans, and liquid; cook until potatoes are tender, about 30 minutes. Roll crackers into fine crumbs and mix thoroughly with parsley, egg, and partially cooked sausage meat; shape into about 20 small balls and drop into soup 20 minutes before it is done. Just before serving, add milk; season with more salt and pepper and heat to boiling point but no longer. Makes 4 large servings.

WHITE SOUP WITH MEATBALLS
6 cups water
1½ pounds veal bone and meat
1 medium onion, chopped
  Salt
1 tablespoon flour
1 cup milk
  Pepper
  Dash of ground nutmeg
  Meatballs

Add water to veal, onion, and 2 tea-spoons salt; simmer for 2 hours. Skim, remove veal; slip meat from bones and chop fine; reserve 1 cup for meatballs. Add remaining meat to broth. Add flour stirred to a smooth paste with milk. Season to taste with salt, pepper, and nutmeg. Bring to a boil and serve at once over meatballs. Makes 1 quart or 4 servings.

Meatballs
1 cup chopped cooked veal
½ cup soft bread crumbs
1 egg
½ teaspoon poultry seasoning
¼ cup undiluted evaporated milk
¼ cup seasoned all-purpose flour
2 tablespoons fat drippings

Combine veal, crumbs, beaten egg, and poultry seasoning. Shape into marble-size balls. Roll in evaporated milk, then in flour; brown in drippings.

BUTTERMILK BEEF BALLS
1 pound ground beef
1 cup buttermilk
¼ teaspoon Worcestershire
1¼ teaspoons salt
  Dash each of ground ginger and
    pepper
1 tablespoon grated onion
  Shortening

Combine all ingredients, except shortening; beat until light and fluffy. Drop by heaping teaspoons into hot deep fat (300° F. on a frying thermometer); fry for 2 to 3 minutes. Drain, and serve hot. Makes 2 dozen.

SPICY BEEF BALLS IN MILK GRAVY
¾ pound ground beef
1 cup grated raw potatoes
1½ teaspoons salt
¼ teaspoon each of ground
    nutmeg and mace
⅛ teaspoon pepper
  All-purpose flour
1 tablespoon butter
1 cup water
1 cup milk
  Paprika

Mix together meat, potatoes, and seasonings. Shape into 16 small balls. Roll each in flour until well coated. Brown slowly in hot butter in heavy skillet; pour off fat drippings. Add water; cover and cook slowly for 30 minutes, adding more water if necessary to prevent sticking. Add milk mixed with 1 tablespoon flour; cook only long enough for gravy to thicken slightly; season to taste. Sprinkle generously with paprika. Makes 4 servings.

KIEK MET BALLEKENS (Flemish Fricasseed Chicken with Meatballs)
1 roasting chicken (4 to 5 pounds) and
  giblets (no liver)
2 celery stalks
1 onion
1 bay leaf
1 parsley sprig
⅛ teaspoon each of ground
    nutmeg and thyme
1 pound ground veal

4 slices of white bread,
  crusts trimmed
2 eggs, beaten
¼ cup milk
  Pepper, salt, and nutmeg
  to taste
3 egg yolks
¼ cup cornstarch
1 cup heavy cream
  Dusting of cayenne and ground
  nutmeg (optional)
  Hot cooked rice

Place chicken and giblets in a soup pot with vegetables and seasoning. Barely cover with water. Bring to a boil. Reduce heat, cover, and poach for 50 minutes, or until done, depending on size of chicken. Remove some of the cooking broth to smaller pot and reserve for meatballs.

Mix veal with crumbled white bread. Add eggs, milk, and seasonings, and blend well. Roll mixture into balls the size of marbles. Simmer meatballs in reserved cooking broth for 7 minutes. Meanwhile remove skin from chicken. Carve and disjoint chicken and place in a deep serving platter along with meatballs. Cover with foil and keep in a warm oven.

Strain broth and bring to a full boil. Mix together egg yolks, cornstarch, and heavy cream. Gradually pour 4 cups of the hot broth into egg mixture, stirring rapidly with a wire whisk. Replace over low heat. Cook, stirring constantly, until smooth and thick. Taste and correct seasoning, adding cayenne and nutmeg if desired. Pour sauce over chicken and meatballs. Arrange rice around platter. Makes 8 servings.

Note: This dish is often served with green peas cooked with mushrooms.

BEEF AND KIDNEY-BEAN BALLS
½ cup dried kidney beans, washed
1 small onion, minced
1 egg
½ pound ground beef
½ cup coarse cracker crumbs
½ teaspoon salt
⅛ teaspoon pepper
3 teaspoons shortening
  Chili sauce

Cover beans with water and soak overnight; do not drain. Cook until tender; drain. Mash beans, using a fork. Add remaining ingredients except shortening and chili sauce. Cool, and shape into 12 balls. Panfry slowly in shortening until well browned on all sides, about 15 minutes. Serve hot with chili sauce. Makes 4 servings.

PORCUPINES WITH VEGETABLE-CHEESE SAUCE
1 onion, chopped
1 pound ground beef
½ cup cooked rice
1 tablespoon chopped parsley
1 egg
2 teaspoons salt

¼ teaspoon pepper
2 tablespoons butter or margarine
3 tablespoons flour
1½ cups milk
½ cup shredded sharp cheese
2¼ to 2½ cups (one 1-pound, 4-ounce
  can) peas and carrots, drained

Mix onion, ground beef, rice, parsley, egg, 1 teaspoon salt, and the pepper; form into 24 small balls. Drop into heavy kettle containing 4 cups boiling water. Simmer for 35 minutes, turning occasionally. To make sauce, melt butter, stir in flour, add milk, and cook until thickened; add cheese and 1 teaspoon salt; cook until cheese melts. Add peas and carrots; pour over meat. Heat thoroughly. Makes 6 servings.

Note: One package (10 ounces) frozen peas and carrots, cooked, or 2 cups diced fresh carrots and peas may be used.

LAMB BALLS WITH TOMATO CURRY
1½ pounds ground raw lamb
1 onion, minced
¾ cup soft stale-bread crumbs
1½ cups milk
2 teaspoons salt
¼ teaspoon pepper
  Cooking oil
  Tomato Curry

Mix all ingredients except oil and curry. Shape into small balls and brown on all sides in hot oil. Reduce heat and cook, covered, until done. Serve with Tomato Curry. Makes 6 servings.

Tomato Curry
3¼ to 3½ cups (one 1-pound, 13-ounce
  can) tomatoes
1 teaspoon each of salt, sugar, instant
  minced onion, and curry powder
¼ teaspoon pepper
¼ cup soft stale-bread crumbs

Simmer all ingredients for 15 minutes. Makes about 3 cups.

BARBECUED CORN AND MEATBALLS
4 ears of corn
1 pound ground beef
  Salt and pepper to taste
  Barbecue sauce

Husk corn and remove silk. Wash and dry; break each ear into halves. Season beef with salt and pepper and form into 8 balls. Alternate corn and meatballs on long skewers, putting 2 pieces of corn and 2 meatballs on each skewer. Put on broiler pan and broil for 10 minutes under medium heat, turning once. Brush meat and corn with barbecue sauce and continue broiling for about 8 minutes longer, turning once and brushing with sauce. Makes 4 servings.

SWEDISH MEATBALLS
¼ pound fresh pork
1 egg, slightly beaten
1 cup milk
½ cup fine dry bread crumbs
2 tablespoons minced onion
3 tablespoons butter or margarine
1¼ pounds ground beef

1½ teaspoons salt
½ teaspoon pepper
  Dash of mace
2 tablespoons all-purpose flour
1 cup hot water
¾ cup light cream

Have butcher grind pork, or force through food chopper 3 or 4 times, using medium blade. Combine egg, milk, and bread crumbs; let stand for a few minutes. Brown onion in 1 tablespoon of the butter. Combine with soaked crumbs, meats, seasonings, mace. Mix with spoon until smooth. Shape into 3 dozen balls about 1 inch in diameter. Brown in remaining butter. Pour off most of fat. Sprinkle meatballs with flour, and shake pan. Add hot water. Cover, and simmer for 35 to 40 minutes. Add cream, and heat. Serve meat with the pan gravy. Makes 6 servings.

DANISH MEATBALLS
1 pound beef round, ground
½ pound lean pork, ground
¼ cup flour
1 teaspoon salt
½ teaspoon pepper
1 onion, grated
2 eggs
1 cup milk
¼ cup butter or margarine

Mix meats in bowl with flour, salt, pepper, and grated onion. Add eggs, one at a time, then the milk. Form into 8 to 10 patties. Fry in butter in a skillet over medium heat for 45 minutes, turning often. Makes 6 servings.

MEATBALLS, POLISH STYLE
1 pound ground beef
1 egg
½ cup fine dry bread crumbs
1 teaspoon salt
½ teaspoon pepper
2 tablespoons minced parsley
½ cup rye-bread crumbs
2 cups (one 1-pound can) tomatoes
  Juice of 1 lemon

Combine beef, egg, dry bread crumbs, salt, pepper, and parsley; mix well. Shape into small balls and brown in greased skillet; pour off fat. Sprinkle meatballs with rye-bread crumbs; add tomatoes and lemon juice. Cover and simmer for 45 minutes, adding water if necessary. Makes 4 servings.

SWEET-AND-SOUR MEATBALLS
¼ cup fine dry bread crumbs
1 teaspoon instant minced onion
1 teaspoon salt
  Dash of pepper
2 cups water
1 pound lean beef, ground
1 egg, well beaten
2 tablespoons cooking oil
1 cup sliced celery
1 red and 1 green pepper, each
  seeded and cut into wedges
⅓ cup cider vinegar
⅓ cup firmly packed light
  brown sugar
2 tablespoons soy sauce

Ham Loaf made in a ring mold and Meat Loaf with a Potato Frosting

2 tablespoons cornstarch
4 pineapple slices,
  cut into halves
8 small pieces of pickled
  cauliflower

Mix bread crumbs, onion, salt, pepper, and ½ cup water. Add beef and egg. Shape into 16 balls. Brown slowly in oil in large skillet. Remove. Cook celery and peppers in skillet for 5 minutes. Add remaining water, vinegar, brown sugar, and soy sauce. Add cornstarch mixed with a little water. Cook for 3 minutes. Add meatballs, pineapple slices, and pickled cauliflower. Heat. Makes 4 servings.

SWEET-AND-SOUR BEEF AND PORK MEATBALLS

1 can (3 ounces) chopped mushrooms
1 pound ground beef
½ pound ground lean pork
1 tablespoon sherry
1 teaspoon instant minced onion
  Soy sauce
1 tablespoon cooking oil
1 beef bouillon cube
1 small onion, thinly sliced
1 medium green pepper, slivered
1⅔ cups drained pineapple chunks
¼ cup sugar
¼ cup cider vinegar
3 tablespoons cornstarch
  Hot cooked rice

Drain mushrooms, reserving liquid. Add enough water to liquid to make 1 cup and set aside. Mix meats, mushrooms, sherry, instant onion, and 2 tablespoons soy sauce. Shape into 12 to 16 balls and brown on all sides in hot oil. Drain off fat. Add 1 cup reserved liquid and bouillon cube. Cover and simmer for 30 minutes. Add next 3 ingredients. Blend 2 teaspoons soy sauce and remaining ingredients except rice. Stir gradually into hot mixture. Cover and cook for 10 minutes, stirring frequently. Serve on rice. Makes 4 to 6 servings.

How to Cook Superbly: Meat Loaves

by Helen Evans Brown

There's nothing lowly about a meat loaf if it's carefully seasoned, baked to the just-right degree, and served with an appropriate sauce. In fact, it then becomes an Epicurean delight. It can be further glamorized by baking it in a ring or other fancy mold, packing it with hidden surprises, or masking it with a beautiful crust of mashed potatoes or rich flaky pastry. Meat loaves are inexpensive, too. They can be made ahead and baked at the last minute, served hot or cold, and they are so easy that even a brand-new cook can make them superbly!

EQUIPMENT

You will need no special equipment for most meat loaves. A loaf pan, the kind used for bread and measuring 9 x 5 x 3 inches, is nice to have but not necessary. If you want to bake your loaf in the form of a ring or any other special shape, you will need the proper mold, of course, and in a couple of the recipes given below (the chicken loaf and the liver loaf) you will need a food chopper unless you can wheedle your butcher into grinding the meat for you. Otherwise you'll just need your ordinary kitchen measures and utensils.

BASIC MEAT LOAF

2 pounds lean beef, ground
2 teaspoons salt
¼ teaspoon pepper
2 eggs
½ cup soft bread crumbs
½ cup milk or other liquid
¼ cup chopped onion
1 teaspoon fresh chopped or ¼ teaspoon dried herbs (basil, marjoram, rosemary, sage, savory)
3 or 4 slices of bacon or salt pork (optional)

Mix all ingredients except bacon together thoroughly, using your hands or a heavy-duty electric mixer. (If you prefer to use a spoon, beat eggs slightly before adding.) Pack into a lightly greased loaf pan, or form into a loaf on a baking sheet; top with bacon and bake in preheated moderate oven (350°F.) for 1 hour, or until the loaf shrinks slightly from the sides of the pan. If you have not covered the top with bacon, it is a good idea to baste it occasionally with equal amounts of melted butter and wine, water, or bouillon. Serve with or without a sauce such as mushroom, tomato, or sour cream. Makes 6 to 8 servings.

VARIATIONS ON BASIC MEAT LOAF

☐ **Crustier Loaves**—If you want a crustier loaf, either pack the meat into a loaf pan lined with wax paper, then turn out in a shallow baking dish; or form into a loaf using your hands, score top with diamond shapes using the back of a knife, and cover with bacon or baste as above. (It is easier to make a pan gravy when the loaf is baked this way. Remove loaf to a warm platter; pour fat from the baking dish, leaving the brownings. Return 2 tablespoons of fat to the dish, add 2 tablespoons of flour, and stir well together. Add 1½ cups of hot water or bouillon and stir until the brownings have dissolved. Cook gently, stirring, until smooth and thickened. If the pan isn't flameproof, transfer to a saucepan. Correct seasoning with salt and pepper and whatever other seasoning you wish and serve sauce with the meat loaf.)

☐ **Ring or Other Molds**—Measure the mold you are planning to use with water, and for each 2 cups allow 1 pound of meat. Bake the loaf as above, in the mold, but for a ring mold or any shallower shaped mold, allow less time for baking. A ring mold holding 6 cups bakes in 45 minutes.

☐ **Other Meats**—Instead of all beef, the meat may be a combination of beef, veal, and pork. A good mixture is 1 pound beef to ½ pound each of veal and pork. (For other meats see recipes on page 1128.)

☐ **Other Liquids**—Instead of milk the liquid may be wine (red or white, or even dry sherry), evaporated milk, sour cream, canned tomato sauce, cream sauce, gravy, or almost any canned soup.

☐ **Other Crumbs**—In place of bread crumbs, cooked rice, ready-to-eat cereals, uncooked rolled oats, or cracker crumbs may be used. If ingredient is dry, increase the liquid by ¼ cup.

☐ **Other Seasonings**—Any favorite seasoning may be added, such as a dash of hot pepper sauce, some lemon juice, or Worcestershire, gravy seasoning, or other liquid seasoning. Herbs may be increased and spices such as nutmeg, cloves, or allspice can be used. And if you like a special mixed seasoning, try it by all means. Other ways to change the seasoning are to increase the amount of onion, or add any of the following to the mixture: a puréed garlic clove, ½ to 1 cup shredded cheese, ½ cup minced green or ripe olives, ½ to 1 cup sautéed sliced or chopped mushrooms, ¼ to ½ cup chopped green pepper, pimiento, celery, nuts, or parsley.

☐ **Other Variations**—A row of hard-cooked eggs (4 small ones or 3 large) may be put in the middle of the loaf. To do this, fill the loaf pan ¼ full of meat mixture, lay shelled hard-cooked eggs down the middle, and carefully pack remaining meat around and over them. Bake as above. Or add rows of stuffed olives, pitted ripe olives, or a layer of whole nuts.

☐ **Potato Frosting**—To cover a meat loaf with mashed potatoes, bake it as usual, turn out of pan onto a baking dish or heatproof platter, and spread with well-seasoned mashed potatoes. You will need

2 cups (4 medium-size potatoes). If you want to get extra fancy, allow an extra cup of mashed potatoes and pipe it on top in a design, using a pastry bag and rose tube. Brush with butter or sprinkle lightly with grated cheese and return to the hot oven (400°F.) for 20 minutes, or until brown.

☐ **Pastry Crust**—Make pastry for a 2-crust pie. Roll into a rectangle about 10 x 14 inches. Put cooled meat loaf, top side down, in the middle of the pastry. Fold pastry completely around the loaf, sealing the edges with water. Turn right side up on a baking sheet and brush crust with 1 egg slightly mixed with 1 tablespoon milk or water. If you want added glamour, cut little designs from pastry and stick them on with some of the egg. Glaze them, too. Bake in preheated hot oven (425°F.) until nicely browned.

VEAL LOAF

    2 pounds ground veal
    3 ounces pork fat, ground
    ½ cup cracker crumbs
    2 teaspoons salt
    ¼ teaspoon pepper
    ½ cup minced onion
    ¼ cup heavy cream or undiluted
        evaporated milk
    ½ teaspoon grated nutmeg or 1
        teaspoon chopped fresh tarragon or
        basil or ¼ teaspoon crumbled dried
        tarragon or basil
    2 eggs
    ¼ cup butter or margarine
    ¼ cup water
        Herb Sauce

Combine all ingredients except last three. Mix thoroughly and pack into a loaf pan, ring mold, or other mold. Bake in preheated moderate oven (350°F.) for 1 to 1¼ hours, basting occasionally with butter and water mixed together. The veal loaf is done if the juices run clear when pierced with a skewer and if meat shrinks slightly from the sides of the pan. Serve with Herb Sauce or a mushroom or tomato sauce, if desired. Makes 6 servings.

Herb Sauce

Mix 1 tablespoon minced parsley, 1 tablespoon minced chives, and 1 teaspoon of the herb used in the loaf with 1 cup thin white sauce. The juices of the veal loaf may be poured from the mold and added to the sauce, too. Makes 1 cup.

LIVER LOAF

  1½ pounds calf's or beef liver
    ½ cup dry bread crumbs
    4 anchovy fillets
    ½ cup finely chopped onion
    ¾ pound pork sausage
  1½ teaspoons salt
    ¼ teaspoon pepper
    1 to 2 teaspoons mixed fresh or ¼ to
        ½ teaspoon crushed dried herbs
        (basil, marjoram, rosemary, sage,
        savory) or ½ teaspoon ground ginger
        (optional)

    ⅓ cup heavy cream or undiluted
        evaporated milk
    4 slices of bacon

Cut raw liver into strips; coat with crumbs, then put through the food chopper; grind anchovies. Combine with remaining ingredients except bacon, mix well, and pack into a loaf pan. Cut bacon slices into halves and cover top. Bake in preheated moderate oven (350°F.) for about 1 hour. This needs no sauce, although it can be served with tomato sauce. It's as delicious cold as it is hot. Makes 8 servings.

LAYERED BEEF-AND-ONION LOAF

  1½ pounds ground beef
    3 tablespoons flour
    2 teaspoons Worcestershire
    ½ teaspoon pepper
  1½ teaspoons salt
    1 small onion, grated
        Pinch each of ground marjoram and
        thyme
    ¾ cup undiluted evaporated milk
    ¾ cup water
    1 tablespoon margarine
    2 cups sliced onions

Put meat in large bowl; add all except last 4 ingredients. Whip mixture with large spoon or electric mixer. Add milk and the water slowly, beating constantly, until liquid has been absorbed. Cover and chill. Melt margarine in skillet; add sliced onions; cook until just tender. Spread layer of meat mixture in round shallow baking dish. Add sliced onions and top with remaining meat mixture. Score top in 6 wedge-shape pieces. Bake in preheated moderate oven (350°F.) for about 1 hour. Serve in wedges. Makes 6 servings.

PRESSED LAMB LOAF

    4- pound shoulder of lamb
        Water
    1 tablespoon salt
    ½ teaspoon each ground marjoram,
        thyme, and caraway seed
    1 medium onion, sliced
        Salt
        Pepper

Put meat in deep kettle and add water to cover. Add salt, marjoram, thyme, caraway seed, and onion. Simmer, covered, for 3 to 4 hours, or until very tender. Drain; reserve broth and chill. Remove meat from bones and chop very fine. Remove fat from chilled broth and measure 2 cups. Moisten meat with broth. Season with salt and pepper to taste. Oil a loaf pan (9 x 5 x 3 inches). Pack meat into pan. Cover with waxed paper; weigh down with a heavy object, such as a large can of fruit. Chill overnight. Unmold before serving. Makes 4 to 6 servings.

HAM LOAF

    2 pounds ground ham
    ½ cup soft bread crumbs
    ½ green pepper, minced
    1 teaspoon prepared mustard
        Salt (if needed)

    1 teaspoon chopped fresh or ¼
        teaspoon crushed dried oregano
    2 eggs
    ½ cup milk
        Dash of hot pepper sauce

Combine all ingredients, pack in a loaf pan, and bake in preheated moderate oven (350°F.) for 1 hour. Serve with a thin white sauce or mushroom sauce, if desired. Makes 6 servings.

INDIVIDUAL HAM LOAVES

    1 pound ground ham
  1½ pounds ground pork
    2 eggs, well beaten
    1 cup cracker crumbs
    1 cup milk
    1 teaspoon powdered mustard
    ¼ cup prepared horseradish
    1 small onion, grated
    ¼ teaspoon salt
    ¼ teaspoon pepper
        Sweet-and-Sour Mustard Sauce

Mix all ingredients except sauce. Pack into sections of 3-inch muffin pan. Put on shallow baking pan and bake in preheated moderate oven (350°F.) for about 1 hour. Serve hot with sauce. Makes 12 loaves.

Sweet-and-Sour Mustard Sauce

Combine 1 cup water, ½ cup brown sugar, ¼ cup vinegar, 2 teaspoons powdered mustard, ¼ teaspoon salt, and dash each of pepper and cayenne. Bring to boil and thicken with 3 tablespoons cornstarch mixed with cold water.

MANILA MEAT LOAF

    1 pound chopped beef
    2 teaspoons meat extract
        Monosodium glutamate
    1 cup soft bread crumbs
    ½ pound each of ham and pork
        shoulder, ground
    ¼ cup grated Swiss cheese
    2 tablespoons each of chopped ripe
        olives and sweet pickles
    1 raw egg
        Salt, pepper, and cayenne
    3 hard-cooked eggs, shelled
    ½ cup canned tomato sauce
    1 teaspoon soy sauce
    2 teaspoons fresh lemon juice
    1 onion, sliced
        Pinch of sugar

Mix together beef, meat extract, ½ teaspoon monosodium glutamate, and bread crumbs. For the filling, toss together ham and pork, cheese, olives, pickles, raw egg, a pinch of monosodium glutamate, and salt, pepper, and cayenne to taste. Oil a loaf pan well. Make a layer of half of beef mixture, then cover with half of ham filling. Press hard-cooked eggs halfway into meat, then cover with the balance of ham and, finally, the rest of beef. Tap the pan smartly a few times, then invert over a greased shallow baking pan and turn out loaf. Combine tomato sauce with soy sauce and lemon juice. Pour into baking dish and add onion sliced into rings, pinch of sugar, and salt and pepper to taste. Bake in preheated moderate oven (350°F.) for 1½ hours, basting occasionally and adding water to sauce, if necessary. Makes 6 servings.

CHICKEN LOAF

- 1 roasting chicken (5 to 5½ pounds) or 2 frying chickens (2½ to 3 pounds each)
- ¼ cup heavy cream
- 2 ounces soft bread crumbs (4 thin slices)
- 2 teaspoons salt
- 2 tablespoons soft butter or margarine
- 1 egg
- ⅛ teaspoon pepper
- 1 teaspoon mixed fresh or ¼ teaspoon dried herbs: basil, marjoram, thyme, rosemary, sage, savory (optional)

The hardest part of making this meat loaf is grinding the meat. Remove skin from chicken and cut and scrape meat from bones; discard sinews. Put meat through a food chopper, using the fine blade. You should have about 4 cups of ground meat. Mix with the other ingredients and pack into a loaf pan. Bake in preheated moderate oven (350°F.) for about 1 hour. Do not overcook, as this loaf should be juicy. Serve hot with a mushroom sauce, if desired, or cold without sauce. Makes 6 servings.

Note: Add 1 teaspoon curry powder to the chicken-loaf mixture before baking and serve cold, with chutney, for an exciting buffet dish.

MELON—The fruit of a number of annual trailing plants which grow from seed and belong to the gourd family, *Cucurbitaceae.* The word melon comes from the Greek *meleopepon,* a combination of *melon,* meaning "apple" and *pepon,* a kind of edible gourd.

The two best-known groups of edible melons are *Cucumis melo,* the muskmelons, and *Citrullus vulgaris,* the watermelon. Muskmelons are, in their turn, divided into two principal varieties: the net-skinned, *C. melo cantalupensis,* of which cantaloupes and Persian melons are perhaps the most familiar; and the smooth-skinned, *C. melo inodorus,* to which group honeydews and casabas belong. There are many variations of these two types of muskmelons, including Crenshaw, honeyball, and Santa Claus or Christmas melons.

Muskmelons originated in southern Asia from whence they moved to the Near East and into Europe. The watermelon is a native of tropical and southern Africa and was known to the Egyptians in the days of the pyramid builders.

The ancient Greeks, centuries before Christ, are said to have put melon seeds in jars filled with rose leaves and then sowed them. They insisted that the grown melon would smell of roses, and, accord-ing to Alexis Soyer, 19th-century English chef and writer, claimed that "its flavor called to mind its sweet and delicious abode with the Queen of flowers."

The Roman Emperor Tiberius enjoyed melons so much that he wanted to keep them all year round. A greenhouse, the first of its kind, was prepared for his use so that the sun-loving fruits could flourish during the winter.

By the end of the 17th century, when English essayist John Evelyn wrote his *Acetaria, or Discourse of Sallets,* melons were considered to be of "transcendent delicacy and flavor, cooling and exhilarating Nature . . . Paragon with the noblest Production of the Garden." This judgment is of the muskmelon, but the watermelon is not neglected. It is called a Winter Melon and Evelyn records it to be "exceedingly cooling."

Melons have been popular in America since early colonial days. They arrived in the New World a few years after Columbus, brought over, it is thought, by his friends. In 1588 when the Englishman Hariot published his *A Briefe & True Report of the New Found Land in Virginia,* watermelons and other melons (both known as "mellions") were being planted by the Indians.

Availability and Purchasing Guide

Cantaloupe—Small, oval shape. Rind is coarse and heavily netted; grayish with light background. Flesh is salmon color. Pungent aroma and sweet taste. When ripe, there is a softening at blossom end and a lightening of rind color. Available May to October.

Casaba—Large, almost globular; may be pointed at blossom end. Rough furrowed rind with no netting; yellow. Flesh is creamy white. Little aroma; sweet and juicy. When ripe, rind color deepens. Available August to November.

Crenshaw—Large with round base and pointed stem end. Rind is smooth; green and gold color. Flesh is salmon color. Juicy with spicy taste. When ripe, there is a softening at blossom end; rind color deepens. Available July to October.

Honeyball—Round. Rind smooth or slightly netted; yellow-gold with pink tinges. Flesh is pink. Pleasant aroma; very sweet taste. When ripe, rind yields to slight pressure. Available June to November.

Honeydew—Large, oval to oblong shape. Rind is velvety smooth and may be slightly netted; whitish-green to creamy yellow. Flesh is light green. Faint fragrance; very sweet and juicy. When ripe there is a softening at blossom end; rind turns creamy yellow. Available June to October.

Persian—Similar in shape to cantaloupe, but larger. Rind has even, fine netting over deep-green background. Flesh is orange-pink. Pleasant aroma; mildly sweet taste. When ripe there is a softening at blossom end and rind color lightens. Available July to October.

Santa Claus (Christmas or Winter Casaba)—Large, oblong shape. Rind is green-gold with trace of netting. Flesh is yellowish-green. Juicy and sweet taste. When ripe there is a softening at blossom end and yellowing of rind. Available in December.

Watermelon—Very large, oblong, and symmetrical. Rind is smooth; deep green to greenish-gray, yellowish on underside. Flesh is pink or red; avoid melons with a hard white streak in flesh. Very juicy and sweet. When ripe, it is symmetrical with good color and bloom over surface; thumping the melon should produce a good hollow sound. Available May to September.

A combination of cantaloupe and honeydew balls is available frozen.

Storage—Keep unripe fruit at room temperature. Ripe fruit should be kept in a cool place. Chill just before serving. Unused melon should be covered and stored in refrigerator. Ripe melons, wrapped in plastic or foil, can be kept in the refrigerator for a week but after that, when the fruit is removed, the tissue breaks down rapidly at room temperature.

Caloric Values

- ☐ Cantaloupe, 3½ ounces = 30 calories
- ☐ Casaba, 3½ ounces = 27 calories
- ☐ Honeydew, 3½ ounces = 33 calories
- ☐ Watermelon, 3½ ounces = 26 calories
- ☐ Melon balls (cantaloupe and honeydew), 3½ ounces, in syrup = 62 calories

Basic Preparation—Cut small melons into halves, larger ones into sections. Discard seeds and stringy part. Use lemon or lime as garnish.

Can be cubed and used in salads, sherbet; can be pickled and spiced.

Fill melon halves with fruit or ice cream. Combine different kinds of melon balls in a fruit cup; top with mint. The rind of larger melons can be used as a fruit cup or punch bowl.

☐ **To Make Melon Balls**—Use a ball cutter or a measuring teaspoon; cut into melon with a circular motion.

☐ **To Freeze**—Melons are not recommended for freezing alone but can be frozen in combination with other fruits. The best varieties to freeze are honeydew and cantaloupe.

Use ripe melons; peel, cut into halves, and remove seeds. Cut melon into cubes or balls.

Melons—beautiful, cooling, succulent:
1—Honeydew; 2—Casaba; 3, 4, 5—Crenshaw;
6, 9—Cantaloupe; 7—Persian;
8—Dark-skinned cannonball watermelon;
10—Muskmelon; 11—Watermelon

Sugar Pack—Sprinkle 2 cups sugar over each 3 quarts melon. Stir until sugar is dissolved. Pack into containers, leaving 1-inch headspace. Cover.

Syrup Pack—Pack melon into containers and add syrup to cover. Boil 4 cups water with 3 cups sugar for syrup. Cool, and then pour over melon. Allow 1-inch headspace. Cover.

MELON SIMPLICITY

Serve halves or wedges of any chilled melon with a shaker of dried grated orange rind and another of ground ginger.

MELON INDIA RELISH

1½ pounds (4 cups) prepared melon rind
4 cups cold water
   Salt
2 sweet red peppers
2 green peppers
2½ pounds green cabbage
3 Spanish onions
4 cups cider vinegar
2 cups firmly packed light brown sugar
2 teaspoons each of ground cinnamon and mace
2 teaspoons each of paprika and powdered mustard
1 teaspoon curry powder
2 tablespoons mustard seeds
1 tablespoon celery seeds

Use watermelon, cantaloupe, or honeydew melon rind. To prepare rind, peel off green skin and remove soft portion from melon rind; cut rind into pieces and soak in water with 3 tablespoons salt in refrigerator overnight. Chop vegetables fine or force through medium blade of food chopper. Mix in ⅓ cup salt and let stand in refrigerator overnight. In morning, rinse and drain rind and chop fine. Drain vegetables and add to rind. Add remaining ingredients, bring to boil, and simmer for about 45 minutes, stirring occasionally. Pack at once in hot sterilized jars; seal. Makes about 5 pints. **Note:** If red peppers are not available, additional green can be substituted, but relish will not be as colorful.

WESTERN MELON CONSERVE

2 cups any diced peeled melon
2 cups diced peeled fresh peaches
3 cups sugar
   Grated rind and juice of 2 lemons
⅔ cup chopped California walnuts

In large saucepan mix all ingredients except nuts. Cook over low heat, stirring occasionally, for 1¼ hours, or until thick and clear. Add nuts and pour at once into hot sterilized jars and seal. Makes 1½ pints.

HOT MELON CHUTNEY

2 cups cider vinegar
1½ cups firmly packed light brown sugar
1 cinnamon stick
2 cardamom seeds
½ teaspoon each of aniseed, coriander, and mustard seed
2 tablespoons salt
⅛ teaspoon each of cayenne and ground mace

2 garlic cloves, minced
2 or 3 canned hot green peppers, sliced
2 cups seedless raisins
¼ pound dried apricots, sliced
½ cup sliced preserved gingerroot
1 cup water
1½ pounds underripe melon

Mix vinegar and sugar in kettle. Add next 5 ingredients tied in cheesecloth bag. Add salt, cayenne, mace, and garlic. Boil, uncovered, for 15 minutes. Add next 5 ingredients and simmer, covered, for 30 minutes. Peel melon, discard seeds and stringy portion; slice thin; measure 3 cups. Add to first mixture and simmer, uncovered, for 45 minutes longer, stirring occasionally. Remove spice bag. Ladle chutney at once into 5 hot sterilized ½-pint jars and seal.

MELT—In culinary language, "to melt" is to change a solid substance into a liquid one by heating. This is done to make it more assimilable with other foods, such as melting butter for sautéing, melting chocolate to incorporate it into a cake batter, etc. Generally speaking, it is best to melt foods slowly over low heat.

MENU—The bill of fare or list of dishes to be served at a given meal, written in the order in which they are to be served. At elegant private dinners it is customary to have a menu at each place so that the diners will know what is to come and can pace their eating accordingly. These cards may be elaborately decorated and written in ornate script. In restaurants, the menu lists all of the dishes available from which individual selections can be made for a meal.

In French *menu* means "small or detailed," from the Latin word *minutus,* or "small." The French originally called the bill of fare the *escriteau,* which means "written out." The menu was not for the use of the guests, however, but was a working menu for the chef. In a banquet of fifty-two dishes, such as the one given in 1571 for a wedding party, the chef would certainly need some reminder of the dishes to be served and in what order they should arrive at the table.

The individual menu came into use during the 19th century, probably making its first appearance at the great restaurants of Paris, and then being adapted for private dinners.

HOW TO COMPOSE MENUS

by Helen Evans Brown

Meal planning is no problem for some people; others face it with daily dread. A menu, to be good, must follow a few simple rules—rules that are instinctive to some while others have to learn them. If you're the I-hate-to-plan-meals type, memorize the fundamentals so the job will be fun. Here are some do's and don't's that apply to both family and guest meals, plus a few special suggestions for party menus.

DO'S

■ *Do keep within your budget,* but make the food allowance weekly rather than daily.

■ *Do make use of seasonal foods.* They are not only the best buys but are at their best when plentiful.

■ *Do plan ahead* so that you won't have to go marketing every day. This also saves preparation time, as you can cook extra amounts to be used at a later date.

■ *Do make a shopping list* so that you won't go in for impulse buying, but make it flexible enough to allow for special bargains that you may find.

■ *Do plan to use leftovers* and use them imaginatively; either freeze and use at a future date, or plan a special dish around them to give variety to the week's menu.

■ *Do plan your meal around one dish* and not necessarily the main one. If, for instance, the dessert is going to be a filling one—say strawberry shortcake—you may want the rest of the meal to be fairly light. Likewise, if the soup is rich, the entrée should be sparing; if the *pièce de résistance* is highly spiced, the flavor of its accompaniments and the other courses should be fairly bland. I won't go into the esoteric idea of planning your menu to harmonize with the wine you are serving, but I mention it just to emphasize that everything in the meal should be considered in order to have a perfect whole.

■ *Do keep meals simple.* In this day and year two courses, at least for a family meal, are usually sufficient, although some people prefer three. A first course such as soup, fruit, seafood cocktail, or salad (as in the Far West), and a main course, or a main course and salad or dessert, are the most popular everyday dinners.

■ *Do try a one-course meal on occasion,* particularly if it's a family favorite. A hearty soup like *minestrone* or fish chowder, when served with a homemade hot bread, or boiled lobsters with side dishes of celery and ripe olives, will usually please everyone.

■ *Do try new dishes.* Lest meals become monotonous, try at least one new recipe a week, but not more than one a meal. Also try new foods, or foods that are new to your family, such as a variety meat, fish, or vegetable that you've never served before. If the experiments prove successful, repeat them; if not, try other new dishes.

■ *Do consider nutrition.* Doctors agree that if meals are well balanced nutritionally, there is no need for a healthy person to have extra vitamins or other food supplements. Remember to serve the seven basic foods every day. Provide at least one quart of milk per person—part may be foods cooked with milk, or cheese; three servings of cereals including bread and foods made with flour or other grains; two servings of fruit (one should be citrus); three servings of vegetables (one should be raw); two servings of meat, fish, or poultry; one egg (may be used in cooking); two servings of fats and butter. If there is a member of your family who is dieting or has allergies, that will have to be taken into consideration, perhaps by substituting special dishes for that person.

■ *Do vary methods of preparation.* For the sake of contrast, don't have everything boiled, fried, baked, or broiled, although there are obvious exceptions to this rule, such as a New England boiled dinner, a mixed grill (broiled), or *fritto misto* (frittered). In this case you can have another course that is contrasting. (I'd pick apple brown Betty with the first, floating island with the second, and a mixed green salad for the third.)

■ *Do serve hot things hot, and cold things cold,* but don't overdo it. Certainly you want warm plates for hot foods, but don't have them so hot that they will burn fingers or further cook meats, fish, or other foods that are already done to your liking. Have cold plates for cold food, but don't ice everything that isn't hot. Like wines, many fruits, vegetables, desserts, and other "cold" dishes are best at room tempera-

ture. Excessive icing ruins their flavors.

■ *Do have meals attractive looking.* Eye appeal greatly influences appetite. Contrasts in color and texture add interest as do attractive arrangement and garnishes, although the latter should not be overdone. And remember that portions that are too large, or plates that are crowded, are definitely unappealing to many people.

■ *Do vary textures.* The Chinese do this to perfection, not only varying the textures of the different dishes in a meal, but having several textures in one dish. Their extensive use of water chestnuts, bamboo shoots, and nuts helps greatly, as do their crisply cooked vegetables. We can accomplish this by having some foods crisp, some firm, some soft, and some chewy. Sometimes crisp raw celery, or a few toasted almonds are all that is needed to spark a meal.

DON'T'S

■ *Don't repeat ingredients in a menu.* For instance, don't serve tomato soup and tomato sauce at the same meal; or cheese appetizers, potatoes au gratin, and cheese and fruit; or cream of mushroom soup, creamed sweetbreads, and ice cream. On the other hand, don't go into a tizzy if you had planned brown rice with filberts in the main course and discover that the petits fours you ordered are decorated with nuts; or if your husband asks for sherry in the consommé when you had already made a Bordelaise (wine) sauce for the meat.

■ *Don't repeat colors.* Everyone knows this rule, and a strange thing about it is that not only do one-color meals look unappetizing, they usually taste the same way. Take, for instance, steamed white fish, mashed potatoes, and cauliflower. Even if you were eating blindfolded, it wouldn't be appetizing. But substitute brown shoestring potatoes and bright green beans for the vegetables, and all is well. If you can't get color contrast any other way, you can do it with a garnish: a sprig of watercress, a broiled mushroom cap, a slice of tomato or pickled beet, or even a dash of paprika or minced parsley. And remember that the color of the plates and platters should be harmonious, too, which is why it is smart to choose white or natural china, unless you plan to acquire several sets.

GUEST MEALS

Although most of the rules above also apply to meals where there are to be guests, there are a few special do's and don't's that shouldn't be overlooked.

DO'S FOR GUEST MEALS

■ *Do consider* the occasion, the season, the size of your dining facilities, and the amount of help available. These will all help you to decide whether to have a formal or informal meal, indoors or out, sit-down or buffet, and what the menu shall be.

■ *Do keep a file for guests.* Write down the menu, the guests, the occasion, and the success of the party. If there were flaws, note them. If everything was perfect, repeat the menu for other guests. A cross file of your friends is a good idea, too. In it you can note their likes, dislikes, and allergies, and the dates when they were entertained.

■ *Do write the menu* before you start to cook, and refer to it as you go along. Many a hostess, including me, has found some special little extra, perhaps one that took hours to fix, still in the refrigerator the next day. Of course, it wasn't missed, which just goes to prove that we often plan more food than we need.

■ *Do prepare food ahead.* If you don't have kitchen help (and who does?), prepare as much as possible ahead and freeze it. Prepare other dishes the day before, and keep anything that needs last-minute preparation to a minimum. Be sure that you do not have to leave your guests for more than a few minutes at a time. Make it appear as if you were producing a meal by magic.

■ *Do make guests comfortable.* If you are having a sit-down dinner, don't have too many guests for the size of your table. It's miserable to knock elbows. If it's to be a buffet, provide tables and chairs, or at least small nested tables, so that no one will have to eat standing up, or from his lap. Even if it's a cocktail party, have enough seats so that at least half the guests can be seated at one time.

■ *Do try parties two days running.* If you can take it, that is. It has lots of advantages. Your house and silver will still be shining the second day, the flowers will still be fresh, and you can serve exactly the same menu. The only thing that won't be the same will be the guests.

DON'T'S FOR GUEST MEALS

■ *Don't be ostentatious.* If your budget is a modest one, don't serve guests luxury items that you would never dream of having for your own family. Of course, you will want one or two dishes to be especially nice, but to have a meal that runs from fresh caviar to beef Wellington to a flaming bombe is apt to be pretentious. You don't have to compete with an elegant restaurant to make your guests happy.

■ *Don't have everything elaborate.* Remember that at guest meals, as well as those for the family, it is not necessary to have every dish garnished and sauced, or cooked with wine or herbs, or squiggled with a pastry tube. A fancy dish or two will be enjoyed much more if its accompaniments are simply prepared, even downright plain, like a well-boiled potato.

■ *Don't serve too much.* Many people think that their menu must be longer if their guest list is large. If three courses are enough for four guests, they are also enough for forty; you just increase the quantity. Even if you are serving a buffet, the number of dishes need not be larger than for a sit-down meal. The table won't look skimpy if it has a flower or fruit arrangement and the tableware and napery are attractively displayed.

■ *Don't try out new recipes on guests.* It's far better to serve a dish that you know you do well, than to try a new one that sounds exciting. It could be a flop, either because the recipe has a flaw or because your technique is wrong. Or even if it's well cooked, you may not like it.

■ *Don't serve exotic controversial foods* unless you are sure your guests will like them. While some would be overjoyed at a supper featuring tripes *à la mode de Caen,* others might be revolted. Lots of people are (or pretend to be) allergic to seafood. If you don't know for sure, play it safe and have beef, ham, veal, or poultry.

MERINGUE—A meringue is a mixture of beaten egg whites and granulated sugar. It may be served as a topping for pies, cakes, and puddings, or used as a pastry shell.

Meringues are a dessert of great elegance with universal appeal. They are said to have been invented in 1720 by a Swiss pastry cook who made them in Meyringen, a small town in Germany that gave them their name. Whatever their origin, meringues became a fashionable dessert. Marie Antoinette, according to court lore, made them herself with her own royal hands at the Trianon.

Meringue as a topping is far more popular in the United States than in Europe. On the other hand, the meringue shell filled with cream or ice cream is probably Europe's top dessert. In Switzerland, meringues are of an awe-inspiring opulence, consisting of an alpine cluster of snowy shells filled with billowing swirls of the most delicious freshly whipped cream.

There are two types of meringues, soft and hard, depending on the amount of sugar added to the egg whites during beating. The success of a meringue depends on the proper beating of the egg whites and the proper addition of the sugar to keep the meringue light and puffy. It is also most important to bake meringues at low temperatures.

HOW TO MAKE PERFECT MERINGUES

■ Separate eggs while they are cold.

■ Allow egg whites to warm to room temperature since at this temperature they can be beaten to incorporate more air.

■ Use a small deep bowl and a beater free from grease since fat interferes with the proper beating of egg whites. The egg whites will increase 2½ to 4 times their original volume. A rotary hand beater can be used in making a soft meringue but it will be necessary to use an electric mixer to prepare a hard meringue.

■ When egg whites are beaten to the foamy stage, add salt and cream of tartar (1 teaspoon to each 1 cup unbeaten egg whites). Cream of tartar (it is the best even though lemon juice or vinegar may also be added in its stead) is an acid salt added to make it easier to beat the egg whites to maximum volume; it also increases the stability of the egg-white foam. It produces a meringue that is more tender.

■ The addition of sugar determines the type of meringue produced. Two tablespoons granulated sugar per egg white results in a soft meringue which is the type used for toppings. Four to 5 tablespoons sugar per egg white are added for hard meringues, the type used for shells. Beat in the sugar gradually, 1 tablespoon at a time, and until no grains of sugar can be felt when a small amount is rubbed between the fingers. The sugar is added when the egg whites have been beaten until they hold soft peaks. If the sugar is added before this time, maximum volume cannot be reached.

■ When spreading a meringue on a pie or cake be sure to spread it over the entire surface so that the filling is completely covered and meringue is attached to the edge of the dish. This prevents shrinkage of the meringue during baking. It makes no difference if the filling is hot or cold.

■ When preparing a hard meringue, spoon or pipe it onto unglazed brown paper for easier removal when done.

■ To prevent "weeping meringues," bake them properly: Bake a soft meringue in preheated moderate oven (350°F.) for 12 to 15 minutes depending on the thickness of the meringue, or until it is golden-brown. Cool the meringue at room temperature and it will not bead. When completely cold it can then be refrigerated. Bake an individual hard meringue (tart-size) in preheated very slow oven (275° F.) for 45 minutes, then reduce heat to 250°F. and bake another 15 minutes, or until very lightly golden and hard to the touch. Bake larger hard meringues (pie-size) in preheated very slow oven (275° F.) for 1 hour. The oven temperature should be low in order to dry the meringues and make them crisp instead of gummy.

■ A meringue mixture can also be poached in milk and used to top a soft custard.

■ Allow meringues to cool in the oven.

QUICK MERINGUE TOPPING FOR PIES OR PUDDINGS

Beat egg whites until foamy throughout. Add ¼ teaspoon salt for 3 egg whites, scant ¼ teaspoon for 2 whites. Add sugar, 2 tablespoons at a time (use 2 tablespoons for each egg white), beating after each addition until blended. Continue beating until mixture stands in stiff peaks. If desired, flavor meringue, using ¼ to ½ teaspoon vanilla, almond, or other extract. Spread on pie or pudding and bake in preheated moderate oven (350°F.) for 12 to 15 minutes depending on the thickness of the meringue.

NEVER-FAIL MERINGUE PIE TOPPING

1 tablespoon cornstarch
2 tablespoons cold water
½ cup boiling water
3 egg whites
  Dash of salt
6 tablespoons sugar
1 teaspoon vanilla extract

In saucepan blend cornstarch and cold water. Add boiling water and cook, stirring constantly, until clear and thickened. Cool completely. Beat egg whites until foamy. Add salt. Gradually add sugar, beating at high speed until stiff. Turn mixer to low speed. Add vanilla. Gradually beat in cold cornstarch mixture. Turn mixer again to high speed and beat well. Spread on 9-inch lemon meringue or other meringue pie. Bake in preheated moderate oven (350°F.) for 12 to 15 minutes.

INDIVIDUAL MERINGUE SHELLS

⅛ teaspoon salt
½ teaspoon cream of tartar
2 egg whites
½ cup sugar
½ teaspoon vanilla extract

Add salt and cream of tartar to egg whites and beat with rotary beater until foamy; add sugar gradually and continue beating until very stiff. Add vanilla. Spoon onto lightly buttered unglazed brown paper on cookie sheet and flatten to make a thin base about 1½ inches in diameter. With a pastry tube or spoon, surround base with meringue to height of 2 inches, leaving center unfilled. Bake in preheated very slow oven (275°F.) for 45 minutes, then reduce heat to 250°F. and bake another 15 minutes, or until very lightly golden and hard to the touch. Transfer paper to a damp board and remove meringue with a spatula. When cold, fill with any flavor of ice cream or fruit and top with whipped cream or other sauce. Makes 4 meringue shells.

Meringue Pie Shell

Use recipe above. Spread mixture on bottom and up side just to rim of well-greased 8-inch pie pan. Bake in preheated very slow oven (275°F.) for about 1 hour, or until light brown and hard to the touch. For a thicker, more generous meringue, double ingredients in above recipe and bake in a 9-inch pie pan for the same length of time.

FRUIT MERINGUES

½ cup each of pitted dates, dried apricots, and shredded coconut
¼ cup each of glazed cherries and nuts
Rind of ½ orange
Pinch of salt
½ teaspoon vanilla extract
2 egg whites
⅔ cup confectioners' sugar

Put fruits, nuts, coconut, and orange rind through food chopper, using coarse blade. Mix well and form into 1-inch balls. Add salt and vanilla to egg whites; beat until stiff. Add sugar gradually, beating well after each addition. Dip fruit balls into meringue and place on greased cookie sheets. Bake in preheated slow oven (300°F.) for about 35 minutes. Cool. Makes about 3½ dozen.

RICH ALMOND MERINGUES

1 cup soft butter
½ cup almond paste
½ cup firmly packed light brown sugar
1 egg
2 cups sifted all-purpose flour
¾ cup raspberry jam
3 egg whites
¾ cup granulated sugar
½ cup flaked coconut
½ cup slivered almonds

Cream butter with almond paste; gradually beat in brown sugar and egg. Blend in flour. Pat into lightly buttered pan (13 x 9 x 2 inches). Bake in preheated slow oven (325°F.) for 20 minutes. Spread with jam. Beat egg whites until frothy. Gradually add granulated sugar, and beat until stiff meringue is formed. Fold in coconut and nuts; spread on top of jam. Return to oven for about 20 minutes. Cool in pan. Cut into 1½-inch squares. Store airtight. Makes about 4½ dozen cookies.

ALMOND MERINGUE COOKIES

1¼ cups soft butter or margarine

2 cups sugar
½ teaspoon each vanilla and almond extracts
2 eggs
4 cups sifted all-purpose flour
½ teaspoon salt
Topping

Cream butter and sugar. Add extracts and eggs, one at a time, beating well after each addition. Add sifted dry ingredients and mix well. Shape into 2 rolls 2 inches in diameter. Wrap in wax paper and chill for several hours or overnight. Cut into ⅛-inch slices and arrange on ungreased cookie sheet. Spread with Topping and bake in preheated moderate oven (375°F.) for 8 to 10 minutes. Makes about 8 dozen cookies.

Topping

Beat 3 egg whites slightly; add ¼ teaspoon salt, ½ cup sugar, 1 tablespoon ground cinnamon, and ¾ cup ground unblanched almonds; mix.

WALNUT MERINGUES

2 cups walnut meats
2½ cups (1 pound) pitted dates
1 to 2 teaspoons grated lemon rind
3 egg whites
⅔ cup sugar
Candied cherries
Gold dragées

Grind walnuts and dates together; add lemon rind. Beat egg whites until stiff but not dry; add sugar gradually, beating until meringue stands in peaks. Shape walnut-date mixture into tiny balls, pick up with tongs, and roll in meringue mixture. Bake on greased cookie sheets in preheated slow oven (250°F.) for about 30 minutes. Decorate tops with bits of candied cherries and gold dragées. Makes about 50 tiny walnut-meringue confections.

MERINGUE WITH ORANGE SAUCE

6 egg whites
¼ teaspoon cream of tartar
½ teaspoon salt
1 cup sugar
¼ teaspoon orange extract
Orange Sauce
Toasted almond slivers

Beat egg whites until frothy; sprinkle over cream of tartar and salt; beat until stiff but not dry. Gradually beat in sugar and add extract. Pour into a buttered loaf pan (9 x 5 x 3 inches) and put in pan of hot water. Bake in preheated moderate oven (350°F.) for 1 hour. Place pan on cake rack to cool. At serving time, remove from pan to oblong platter. Spoon Orange Sauce over meringue and sprinkle with toasted almond slivers. Makes 8 servings.

Orange Sauce

1 cup sugar
5 tablespoons flour
⅛ teaspoon salt
Grated rind of 1 orange
Juice of ½ lemon

½ cup fresh orange juice
3 egg yolks
1 teaspoon butter
1 cup heavy cream, whipped

In a heavy saucepan mix together sugar, flour, and salt. Add orange rind, fruit juices, and egg yolks. Cook over low heat, stirring, until thickened and smooth; add butter, and cool; fold in whipped cream.

CHRISTMAS MERINGUES

2 egg whites
⅛ teaspoon salt
1 cup sugar
1 tablespoon fresh lemon juice
1½ cups ground Brazil nuts
Maraschino cherries

Beat egg whites until stiff but not dry. Add salt and gradually beat in sugar and lemon juice. Continue beating until very stiff. Measure ⅓ cup and reserve. Fold nuts into remainder. Drop by tablespoons onto brown-paper-covered cookie sheets. Top each with small amount of reserved meringue and a bit of cherry. Bake in preheated slow oven (275°F.) for about 35 minutes. Remove cookies to rack while warm. Makes 3½ dozen.
Note: Store airtight.

FLORIDA MERINGUE ORANGE PUDDING

6 large oranges
¾ cup granulated sugar
2 cups milk
3 tablespoons cornstarch
¼ teaspoon salt
3 eggs, separated
6 tablespoons confectioners' sugar

Grate half of rind from 1 orange and set aside. Peel and section oranges; place in 1½-quart casserole; sprinkle with ¼ cup granulated sugar. Scald 1½ cups milk in top part of double boiler. Mix remaining granulated sugar with cornstarch and salt; stir in remaining milk. Add slightly beaten egg yolks, pour slowly into scalded milk, and cook until thickened, stirring constantly. Cool; pour over oranges. Make meringue by beating salted egg whites until stiff but not dry; beat in confectioners' sugar and grated rind. Pile lightly on pudding. Bake in preheated moderate oven (350°F.) for 10 minutes, or until delicately browned. Cool and chill in refrigerator for several hours before serving. Makes 6 servings.

METTWURST—This very popular German sausage is made from pork, seasoned with salt, white pepper, and ground coriander. The meat is ground to a pasty consistency, stuffed into casings, cured, and smoked. It is eaten without further cooking, as a spread for sandwiches.

Thanks to its soft consistency and good spreading quality, mettwurst is also known in German as *Schmierwurst*, that is, a sausage that is smeared or spread on.

Mexican Cookery

by Helen Evans Brown

Mexican food is a fascinating combination of both Spanish and Indian influences, making much use of such native American staples as corn, beans, and tomatoes and Spanish favorites like rice, olives, and almonds.

Mexican food is a fascinating combination of Spanish and Aztec, and makes use of many foods native to America: beans, corn, tomatoes, avocados, and pumpkins. Rice, olives, and almonds are also used extensively, as they are in Spain, and many Spanish chicken, fish, and seafood dishes are popular. But the most typical dishes of all, the native Mexican ones, are made with *masa*, which is corn kernels soaked in lime water, then ground to a meal. These include *tortillas, tamales, tacos, enchiladas, tostadas,* and many others. The names of these differ in different parts of Mexico so that even Mexicans disagree as to just exactly what constitutes a *tostada,* an *enchilada,* and the like.

Sometimes all these native Mexican dishes are grouped together under the term *antojitos,* "little whims." In Mexico, there are two kinds of soup, liquid, *aguada,* and dry, *sopa seca.* The dry soups are like our casseroles and include such dishes as *arroz Mexicano, sopa de fideos,* and *sopa seca de tortilla.*

Mexicans like a salad of mixed greens, just as we do, although they also have many compound salads such as potato with sardines, squash with onions, asparagus and eggs, garbanzos (chick-peas) and beets. Mexicans have a very sweet tooth and their puddings are apt to use more sugar than we normally like.

However, they also have many fruits for desserts, especially mangoes, papayas, and pineapples, which grow luxuriantly below the border.

 Notes on Some Typical
Mexican Ingredients

CHILES (Chili Peppers)—Dried Mexican chilies are hard to find except where there is a large Mexican population. Canned green chilies are more generally available, but if they can't be found, green peppers or even canned pimientos can be substituted.

CILANTRO (Coriander)--This is coriander; it is used fresh, like parsley. It is the same thing as Chinese parsley so if you can't find it in a Mexican or Spanish store, you may be able to in a Chinese one. Or if you have the time, plant some coriander seeds, the kind in your spice cabinet. The pungent flavor is characteristically Mexican and adds much to *salsa fría* and other dishes.

JACK CHEESE—This cheese, much used in Mexican cookery, is available in many parts of the country. Where not, substitute a mild Cheddar.

ANTOJITOS

TORTILLAS
(Mexican Bread)

In Spain, a *tortilla* is an omelet; in Mexico, it is the staff of life, a pancake-like bread usually made of corn treated with lime water *(masa),* although flour *tortillas (tortillas de harina)* are preferred by some Mexicans, especially in Sonora. In the Southwest and far West, *tortillas* are readily available, but in other parts of the United States they are found only in specialty food stores, usually canned. However, *masa harina,* tortilla flour, is available, and directions for making *tortillas de maíz* (corn) are on every package. A *tortilla* press is also available although the prepared *masa* may be rolled between sheets of plastic to any size or thickness. Mexicans, of course, pat them into thin cakes between their palms.

TORTILLAS DE MAÍZ
(Corn Tortillas)

Mix 2 cups *masa harina* with 1½ cups warm water, then form into balls about 1¾ inches in diameter (3 tablespoons), and roll between sheets of plastic or oiled wax paper into round thin pancakes 6 inches in diameter. Cook on a moderately hot, dry, or very lightly greased griddle, turning frequently until dry and very lightly flecked with brown. *Tortillas* may be reheated on the griddle.

TORTILLAS DE HARINA
(Flour Tortillas)

These are made in different sizes, although usually larger than the corn kind. It is still possible to find some Mexican women who make them by hand, patting out such huge ones that they extend all the way up the arm as she pats and pulls them into shape.

    4 cups all-purpose flour
    2 teaspoons salt
    ⅓ cup lard
    1 cup (or more) warm water

Sift flour and salt together, work lard into it with the fingertips, then stir in enough water to form into a firm ball.

Knead very well and form into egg-size balls. Cover and let stand for 20 minutes; then roll out until they are 7 or 8 inches in diameter. (If the large flour *tortillas* are desired, use a much bigger ball of dough, and roll and pull until round and thin, thinner than the regular ones, and about 18 inches in diameter.) Cook these like the corn *tortillas,* on a medium-hot griddle, for 2 minutes on one side, 1 on the other. These, hot and served with butter, are delicious, and are first cousins to the Chinese *doily* and the Indian *chapati.* The extra-large and thin flour *tortillas* are sensational when crisped in a very hot oven for about 3 minutes, and served brushed with melted butter. They are even good cold!

TOSTADAS

Tostadas were originally *tortillas* that were fried or toasted until crisp. Now the word means a number of different things, depending upon which part of Mexico you are in. Usually they are whole *tortillas,* fried until crisp and covered with various meats, cheeses, and vegetables, a sort of Mexican sandwich. When the *tortillas* are cut into quarters or eighths and fried crisp, they are usually called *tostaditas,* although, again, they are sometimes *tostadas* or *totopos.* This way they are good with dips.

TOSTADITAS AL ESTILO DE POTOSÍ
(Little Toasts, Potosi Style)

Cut *Tortillas de Maíz* into quarters and fry in deep fat until crisp. Drain. On each piece spread *Frijoles Refritos* (page 1141), a little finely chopped lettuce, a slice of radish, a slice of avocado. Sprinkle with salt and top with a little shredded Jack cheese and either *Salsa de Chile Colorado* or *Salsa de Chili Verde* (page 1142).

TOSTADAS COMPUESTAS
(Mexican Sandwiches)

For each serving fry a *Tortilla* crisp, put it on a plate, spread it with fried beans, sprinkle with cooked crumbled *Chorizo* (page 1140) and grated cheese; broil until cheese is melted. Cover with chopped lettuce, sprinkle with a little French dressing and some grated Parmesan, and garnish with ripe olives and radishes.

GUADALAJARA TOSTADAS
(Guadalajara Toasts)

Fry *Tortillas* until crisp and top with fried beans, chopped lettuce, chopped pickled pigs' feet, and grated cheese. Serve with *Salsa Rapida de Chili* (page 1142).

TOTOPOS
(Bean and Cheese Appetizers)

Another appetizer using *tostadas* is made by spreading them with *Frijoles Refritos* (page 1141), sprinkling with shredded cheese, and slipping under the broiler until the cheese melts.

CARNITAS AL ESTILO DE ELENA
(Meat Crisps, Elena's Style)

Cut 1½ pounds lean boneless pork into 1-inch cubes, sprinkle with salt and pepper, and bake in slow oven (300°F.) for 2 hours, stirring occasionally and draining off the fat. They should be brown, tender, and crisp, but not dry. Serve with *Tostaditas*.

GUACAMOLE
(Avocado Paste)

To make this dish, mash 2 very ripe avocados until smooth, add 2 tablespoons finely minced onion, 1 teaspoon salt, lemon juice to taste, and either 2 teaspoons chili powder or 1 chopped peeled green chili. Keep covered closely until serving time. Serve with *Tostadas,* or as a sauce. Makes about 2 cups.

ENCHILADAS
(Stuffed Tortillas)

There are many different *enchiladas*. In fact, *tortillas* can be filled with any left-over meat, poultry, seafood, or cheese, so they are very economical. They are usually rolled but sometimes folded.

    Lard or shortening
    Tortillas
    Enchilada sauce or Salsa Rapida
      de Chile (page 1142)
    Cooked Chorizo (page 1140)
    Sautéed chopped onion
    Salt and pepper
    Grated Cheddar cheese

Heat lard, dip *tortillas* into it to make them hot and pliable, then dip into heated sauce. Put about ¼ cup sausage mixed with some onion and salt and pepper to taste in a strip on the *tortilla,* and roll. Pour on more sauce, sprinkle with grated cheese, and serve. Sometimes the *enchiladas* are slipped under the broiler to melt the cheese, sometimes reheated in the oven before the sauce and cheese are added.

ENCHILADAS DE POLLO
(Chicken Enchiladas)

    Lard or cooking oil
12 or more tortillas
 2 cups light cream
 1 cup very rich chicken bouillon
 ½ cup chopped onion
 2 tablespoons butter or margarine
 2 cups chopped cooked chicken
 1 cup Salsa Rapida de Chile (page
      1142)

 1 cup dairy sour cream
    Salt to taste
1½ cups grated Jack cheese

Heat lard and cook *tortillas* for a few seconds; then dip into cream and bouillon which have been combined. Reserve remaining liquid. Make the filling by sautéing onion in butter and adding remaining ingredients, except the cheese. Spread filling on *tortillas,* roll, and place seam side down on a baking dish. Pour reserved liquid over top, sprinkle with cheese, and bake in preheated moderate oven (350°F.) until hot and cheese is melted, about 25 minutes. Makes 6 servings.

TACOS
(Fried Filled Tortillas)

Tacos, like *tostadas,* are a form of Mexican sandwich. They are *tortillas* that are filled with a variety of things, then folded or rolled, and fried until crisp. Or the *tortillas* are put into hot fat and as soon as they become limp they are folded and held with tongs that way until crisp. They are then filled. The filling may be fried beans mixed with *Chorizo* (page 1140) or cheese; or chopped cooked beef, chicken, or pork; shredded lettuce, chopped raw onion, and sometimes sliced avocado are put on top of the filling, and bottled *taco* sauce or *Salsa de Chile Colorado* or *Verde* (page 1142), is sprinkled over all. Like an American sandwich, you can make up your own.

TACOS DE JOCOQUI
(Sour-Cream Tacos)

12 tortillas
    Hot lard or oil
 1 pound shredded Jack cheese
 1 can (4 ounces) peeled
      green chilies
    Salt and pepper to taste
1½ cups tomato sauce or Salsa Rapida
      de Chile (page 1142)
 ½ cup cream sauce
2½ cups dairy sour cream

Dip *tortillas* into hot lard. On each one put about ¼ cup cheese, ⅓ chili in a strip, salt and pepper, and 2 tablespoons tomato sauce. Roll and put in a baking dish, seam side down. Mix cream sauce and sour cream, pour over all, and bake in preheated moderate oven (350°F.) for 30 minutes. Makes 6 generous servings.

TAMALES

Tamales are made of a cornmeal dough which is spread on corn husks. This in turn is spread with a filling, then rolled and steamed.

TAMALES DE MAÍZ
CON CHILE Y QUESO
(Green Corn Husk Tamales)

When corn is in season a great treat is *tamales* made with the green corn husks rather than the dried ones. Sometimes no *masa* is used, just the corn ground to a paste; sometimes the *tamales* are sweet,

sometimes a trifle hot. But this way, with cheese and chilies, is especially good and delicious served with grilled or roasted meats.

1¾ cups tortilla flour
 1 cup warm water
 ½ teaspoon salt
 ¼ cup lard
    Fresh corn husks
 1 cup grated fresh corn
 ½ cup diced Cheddar cheese
 2 canned green chili peppers, chopped
 ½ teaspoon salt

Mix together first 4 ingredients and beat until very creamy and smooth. Trim thick bottom part from corn husks and wash well, removing any silk. For each *tamale* take 2 corn husks, pointed part at top, and paste together at one side with some of the *masa* mixture. This makes the husk wider. Now spread another tablespoon of the mixture on the inside, about 1 inch from bottom and extending about 2 inches up the husk. Top with 2 teaspoons corn-cheese filling made by combining the last 4 ingredients. Fold husk around filling, paste with a little more *masa,* then fold bottom toward top so that the pointed arms extend a little above the bottom or trimmed end. Stand open side up in a steamer and steam for 1 hour. These may be frozen and reheated over steam. Makes about 1 dozen.

SOUPS

SOPA DE AGUACATE
(Avocado Soup)

 2 canned green chilies
 2 ripe avocados
 ½ teaspoon salt
 1 tablespoon minced cilantro or 1
      tablespoon minced onion
 6 cups hot chicken bouillon

Rinse seeds from chilies and press chilies through a sieve. Peel and pit avocados and also press through a sieve, or whirl together in a blender. Add salt and *cilantro,* and divide mixture among 6 soup dishes. Pour over hot seasoned bouillon and serve at once with *Tostadas.* Makes 6 servings.

CALDO DE PESCADO
(Fish Soup)

 4 cups chopped onions
 ¼ cup oil, preferably olive
 2 pounds tomatoes, peeled and chopped
    Herb bouquet (parsley, bay,
      marjoram)
 ½ cup white wine
 1 chili pepper or 1 tablespoon chili
      powder
 ¼ cup flour
 6 cups water
    Salt
 6 slices of fish (4 or 5 ounces each)
 6 slices of toast

Cook onions in oil until lightly browned; add tomatoes, herb bouquet, wine, and chili, and simmer until almost dry. Dis-

Polvorónes

Frijoles

Ensalada
de Naranjas

Chile con Carne   Colache

card bouquet, add flour and water (or fish stock made from bones), and salt to taste. Bring to a boil, turn low to simmer, add fish, and cook until fish flakes easily with a fork. Arrange toast in soup dishes and carefully put a slice of fish on each piece of toast. Divide soup among dishes and serve. Makes 6 servings.

FISH

SEVICHE
(Pickled Raw Fish)

Acapulco is famous for this dish of pickled raw fish. It is delicious for a first course. Shred any raw white fish, or cut sea scallops into small pieces. For 1 pound fish, cover with the juice of 4 lemons and allow to stand for 4 hours, stirring occasionally. Drain and combine with 2 peeled and cubed tomatoes, 2 chopped canned or fresh green chilies, 3 tablespoons olive oil, ½ teaspoon oregano, 1 teaspoon salt, some freshly ground black pepper, and if you have it and like it, fresh *cilantro*. Garnish with sliced avocado and raw onions. Makes 4 servings. Or try it as a filling for a tomato or a half avocado!

BACALAO VERACRUZANO
(Codfish in Spicy Tomato Sauce)

1 pound salt codfish
  Herb bouquet (bay, parsley, thyme)
1 large garlic clove
¼ cup olive oil
1 onion, chopped
1 tablespoon butter
1 cup tomato purée
2 pimientos, chopped
1 can green chilies, chopped
¼ cup chopped green olives
1 tablespoon capers

Freshen codfish by soaking in cold water for 3 to 4 hours. Drain and cook in fresh water to cover, to which herb bouquet has been added. When tender, drain, but reserve stock. Crush garlic with the flat of a knife and cook in olive oil until golden. Remove garlic. Cut codfish into pieces, removing any bone, and lightly brown in

garlic oil. In the meantime, cook onion in butter until wilted, add tomato purée, 1 cup of fish stock, the pimientos, chilies, and olives. Simmer for 10 minutes; then add capers and combine with the codfish. Serve with crusty bread. Makes 6 servings.

MEAT AND POULTRY

CHILE CON CARNE
(Chili with Meat)

When beans are added to this dish, it becomes *chile con carne con frijoles.*

3 large garlic cloves, crushed
1 cup chopped onions
2 tablespoons lard or bacon fat
1 pound beef
1 pound pork
2½ cups (one 1-pound, 13-ounce can)
  tomato purée
2 teaspoons salt
¼ cup chili powder
2 teaspoons dried oregano
½ teaspoon ground cuminseed
½ cup or more pitted ripe olives
  (optional)

Cook garlic and onions in shortening until wilted. Cut meat into ½-inch cubes and add. Brown meat; add all ingredients except olives and simmer until meat is tender. Add the olives just long enough to heat. Garnish with additional chopped onion if desired. Makes 6 servings.

MENUDO
(Tripe Stew)

In Sonora they specialize in *Menudo,* but all Mexico adores it, especially on Christmas or New Year's Eve. *Menudo* actually means "minced" or "cut into small pieces," and the word for tripe is *tripa.* This dish, however, is known simply as *Menudo.*

5 pounds tripe
1 large veal knuckle
4 garlic cloves, cut
3 teaspoons salt
2 cups chopped onions
1 teaspoon ground coriander
1 tablespoon chili powder (or more) or
  1 can peeled green chilies, chopped
2 quarts water

2½ cups (one 1-pound, 13-ounce can)
  whole hominy
  Juice of 1 lemon

Cut tripe into strips ¾ inch wide. Put all ingredients except hominy and lemon juice in a large pot and simmer for 6 hours, or until tripe is tender, adding more water if necessary. Add hominy, and heat. Add lemon juice and serve in soup dishes, with chopped green onions if desired, and if possible chopped *cilantro.* Makes 6 to 8 servings.

CHORIZO
(Mexican Sausage)

Chorizo, or Mexican sausage, is used in many Mexican dishes: in *Frijoles Refritos, tacos* or *tostadas,* and with eggs. It is available in some places, but if not in your territory, try this.

Mash 2 garlic cloves in 1 teaspoon salt. Add 1 tablespoon vinegar, 1 tablespoon tequila or brandy, 1½ tablespoons chili powder, 1½ teaspoons salt, and 1½ pounds ground pork. Mix these ingredients together, fry until brown, break up with a fork, and use as directed.

MOCHOMAS
(Minced Pork)

This Chihuahuan dish is reminiscent of French *rillettes.*

2 pounds pork, not too lean
  Water
1 garlic clove
2 teaspoons salt
1 small dried chili pepper or a dash
  of hot pepper sauce

Cut pork into pieces and add just enough water to cover. Crush garlic in salt and add, along with chili. Simmer until pork is tender and water absorbed. Pour off fat and reserve. Shred meat with a fork, discard chili, add reserved fat, and cook, stirring occasionally, until meat is crisp. Serve with *Tostadas* (page 1137), *Guacamole* (page 1138), and sliced tomato. Makes 6 servings as a luncheon dish, 12 as an appetizer or a snack.

PASTEL DE MAÍZ CON GALLINA
(Chicken Pie with Corn Crust)

Grate the kernels from 12 large ears of

raw corn. Season with 2 tablespoons melted butter, 1 teaspoon salt, and a little freshly ground pepper. Have a 4-pound roasting chicken cut up. Put in a heavy pot with 1 sliced onion, an herb bouquet, 2 cups water, and 1 teaspoon salt. Cover and simmer until tender, adding a little water if there is danger of sticking. Cool slightly and remove bones; cut meat into fairly large pieces. Put half of corn mixture in a buttered 2-quart casserole, add chicken in a layer, and cover with remaining corn. Sprinkle with 1 tablespoon melted butter and bake in preheated moderate oven (350°F.) for about 45 minutes. Makes 6 servings.

CHEESE AND EGGS

CHILES RELLENOS CON QUESO
(Chilies Stuffed with Cheese)

    2 cans (4 ounces each) peeled green
      chilies
    ½ pound shredded Jack cheese
    2 eggs
    1 tablespoon all-purpose flour
    ⅛ teaspoon salt
      Cooking oil for frying

Rinse seeds from chilies, divide large chilies into thirds, smaller ones into halves, and drain on paper towels. Press cheese into little "sausages," using 2 tablespoons for each one, then wrap in a chili strip. Beat eggs until thick and light; fold in flour and salt. Have ready about 2 inches of hot oil in a deep skillet. Put stuffed chilies, one at a time, in the batter, spoon some over them, and take up in a spoon so that some of the batter is included. Slip into hot oil and turn almost at once, so both sides are covered with hot oil. Add another chili until the pan is full but not crowded. Cook until golden on both sides and serve at once, or reheat in 2 cups *Salsa Rapida de Chile* (page 1142) mixed with 2 cups chicken bouillon. They will puff up again in the sauce. Makes 6 servings.

HUEVOS RANCHEROS
(Ranch-Style Eggs)

There are many ways to prepare this favorite egg dish. The sauce may be poured over fried or poached eggs that have been placed on crisply fried *Tostadas,* or the sauce may be put in a baking dish, the raw eggs dropped on top, and the whole baked in preheated hot oven (400°F.) until set, about 15 minutes.

Salsa

    2 tablespoons chopped onion
    2 tablespoons olive oil
    1 garlic clove, minced
    3 canned green chilies, chopped
    1 teaspoon dried oregano
    1 pound (3 medium) ripe tomatoes,
      peeled and chopped
    1 teaspoon salt
    6 eggs
    6 Tostadas (page 1137)

Cook onion in oil until wilted; add other ingredients except eggs and *Tostadas* and simmer for 10 minutes. Use as above. Makes 6 servings.

VEGETABLES

FRIJOLES
(Mexican Beans)

Mexican beans are as important as *tortillas* and, like them, are served morning, noon, and night. They freeze well, so keep a batch on hand.

    1 pound Mexican pink or pinto beans
    6 cups water
    ½ teaspoon ground cuminseed
      (optional)
    2 garlic cloves (optional)
    2 teaspoons salt
    2 tablespoons bacon fat or lard

Cover beans with water, add cuminseed and garlic, or not, as you wish, and simmer over very low heat for 1½ hours. Add salt and bacon fat and continue cooking until beans are tender. Top with a little chopped red pepper if desired. Makes 6 servings.

FRIJOLES FRITOS
(Fried Beans)

Heat ¼ cup bacon fat or lard in a heavy pot. Add 4 cups cooked beans, a few at a time, and mash them into the fat. Add bean liquid and more beans until all are added and mashed. Cook, stirring occasionally, until beans are a thick mush. Makes 4 servings.

FRIJOLES REFRITOS
(Crisp Fried Beans)

Use additional lard or bacon fat, the more the better, and cook *Frijoles Fritos* until they are crispy around the edges. These sometimes have cubed Jack cheese or fried *Chorizo* (page 1140) added. Makes 4 servings.

COLACHE
(Vegetable Medley)

A favorite vegetable dish, this recipe goes back to Aztec days

    1 onion, chopped
    1 tablespoon butter
    1 cup cut green beans
    1 green pepper, chopped
    6 summer squash or zucchini, cut
      into pieces
    2 large tomatoes, cut into sixths
    3 ears of corn, cut into 1-inch pieces
      Salt and pepper to taste

Cook onions in butter until golden. Add beans and ½ cup water, cover, and cook for 10 minutes. Add next 4 ingredients and cook, covered, until vegetables are tender. Season. Makes 6 to 8 servings.

ARROZ MEXICANO
(Mexican Rice)

    1 onion, chopped
    1 garlic clove, minced
    3 tablespoons lard or cooking oil
    1 cup uncooked rice
    2 cups bouillon, or more
    1 cup tomato purée
    1 tablespoon minced parsley
      Salt and pepper to taste

Cook onion and garlic in lard until golden. Add rice and cook until colored, then add remaining ingredients and cook, covered, over low heat. After 12 minutes, check and add more bouillon if necessary. Re-cover and cook until rice is tender and liquid is absorbed. Makes 4 to 6 servings.

Note: This may be served with grated cheese or sliced cooked *Chorizo* (page 1140), or mushrooms may be added.

SALADS

ENSALADA DE AGUACATE Y MAÍZ
(Avocado and Corn Salad)

3 ripe avocados
Lettuce
¾ cup cooked corn
1 canned green chili, chopped
Salt
1 cup dairy sour cream
1 tablespoon sweet cream

Cut avocados into halves, remove pits, then peel off skin. Arrange on lettuce. Combine corn and chili, fill avocado cavities, sprinkle with salt, and pour sour cream mixed with sweet cream over all. Makes 6 servings.

ENSALADA DE COLIFLOR CON AGUACATE
(Cauliflower Salad with Ham and Avocado)

1 cauliflower
3 tablespoons olive oil
1 tablespoon wine vinegar
1 teaspoon salt
Pepper
1 cup chopped cooked ham
¼ cup minced parsley
½ cup mayonnaise
2 tablespoons light cream
1 teaspoon fresh lemon juice
1 avocado

Break cauliflower into flowerets and cook in salted water until just tender; drain. Mix oil, vinegar, salt, and a few grindings of pepper and pour over cauliflower; chill. Mix together next 5 ingredients and pour over. Garnish with sliced avocado. Makes 6 servings.

ENSALADA DE NARANJAS
(Orange, Cucumber, and Pepper Salad)

4 oranges
1 cucumber
1 sweet onion
1 green pepper
Lettuce
French dressing

Peel and slice oranges, discarding seeds. Peel and slice cucumber; chop onion and green pepper. Arrange lettuce on a flat dish and put oranges and cucumber on top, alternating slices. Sprinkle with onion and green pepper and serve very cold with a simple dressing made with olive oil, wine vinegar, and salt and pepper to taste. Makes 6 servings.

ENSALADA DE NOCHE BUENA
(Christmas Eve Salad)

This is a traditional salad for the night before Christmas. In Mexico it used to be served only with sugar, but now many prefer French dressing or mayonnaise.

1 head lettuce, shredded
3 beets, cooked and sliced
3 red apples, cored and sliced
3 pineapple slices, quartered
2 oranges, peeled and sliced
2 bananas, sliced
½ cup roasted peanuts
½ cup pomegranate seeds

Spread lettuce on a large plate, then arrange beets and fruits in as symmetrical a manner as possible, with colors contrasting. Sprinkle with nuts and pomegranate seeds; serve dressing separately. Makes 8 servings.

SAUCES

SALSA DE CHILE VERDE
(Green Chili Sauce)

2 cans (4 ounces each) peeled green chilies or 8 fresh green chilies
1 pound green tomatoes
1 garlic clove
1 cup minced onions
2 cups chicken bouillon
½ teaspoon salt

If canned chilies are used, rinse off seeds and chop. Toast fresh ones over a gas flame or under a broiler until blistered all over, then wrap in a cloth and in several layers of newspaper to steam. Scrape off skins, discard stems and seeds, and chop fine. Peel and chop tomatoes and mash garlic. Simmer all ingredients for 10 minutes. Makes about 4 cups.

SALSA RAPIDA DE CHILE
(Quick Chili Sauce)

This is a quick all-purpose chili sauce that is different from the old type in that it uses chili powder and tomato.

½ cup chopped onion
1 large garlic clove, mashed
2 tablespoons lard or olive oil
1 tablespoon all-purpose flour
¼ cup chili powder
½ teaspoon dried oregano
¼ teaspoon ground cuminseed
1 teaspoon salt
1 cup tomato purée
1 cup water or bouillon

Cook onion and garlic in lard until wilted. Add flour, cook for 1 minute, then add other ingredients. Simmer for 10 minutes before serving hot. Makes about 2 cups.

SALSA DE CHILE COLORADO
(Red Chili Sauce)

6 dried red chili peppers (chiles colorados)
2 cups water
1 pound ripe tomatoes or 2 cups canned tomatoes
2 large garlic cloves
3 tablespoons olive oil
¼ teaspoon ground cuminseed
½ teaspoon dried oregano

Using tongs, hold chilies over a gas flame to toast, or put under a broiler. Do not burn. Remove stems, shake out seeds, cover with water, and bring to a boil. Let stand for 20 minutes. Put in a blender with the water and whirl until smooth; or grind chilies and press through a strainer, then combine with water. Whirl tomatoes in blender or press through a strainer. Mash garlic and combine all ingredients. Simmer for 15 to 20 minutes. This sauce may be thickened slightly with 1½ tablespoons each of butter and flour. Makes about 3½ cups.

SALSA CRUDA
(Spiced Tomato Sauce)

2 pounds ripe tomatoes
1 large onion

1 can (4 ounces) peeled green chilies
1 teaspoon cilantro (fresh coriander),
   if available
1 can tomatillos (optional)*
1 garlic clove, minced
1 teaspoon dried oregano
¼ teaspoon ground cuminseed
2 tablespoons olive oil
2 tablespoons wine vinegar
   Salt and pepper to taste

Peel and chop tomatoes and onion; rinse chilies of seeds and chop; mince *cilantro;* mash undrained *tomatillos* if used; combine all ingredients. Serve cold on broiled steak or hamburger. Makes about 2 cups.

Tomatillos are small green Mexican tomatoes, with a distinctive flavor.

PANCAKES

GORDITAS
(Fat Pancakes)

3 cups masa harina
2 cups warm water
½ teaspoon salt
½ pound shredded Jack or Cheddar
   cheese
3 ripe avocados
   Salt and pepper to taste
   Salsa de Chili Verde (page 1142)
   or Salsa Cruda (above)

Mix *masa harina,* water, and salt, adding a little more water if too dry. Divide into 6 parts and form into round cakes ½ inch thick. Cook slowly on a medium-hot griddle until lightly browned on both sides. Split open and sprinkle with cheese. Top with sliced avocado, season with salt and pepper, and sprinkle with a little *Salsa.* Makes 6 servings.

DESSERTS AND CAKES

GUAYABAS RELLENAS
(Stuffed Guavas)

Guava shells are available in cans in specialty shops. Simply drain, saving the syrup, and stuff with *queso fresco* (Mexican fresh cheese) or cream cheese. Sprinkle chopped nuts on top, arrange in a shallow dish, pour syrup over, and serve. One can of guava shells and ½ pound cheese will make 6 servings.

CHURROS
(Mexican Crullers)

This dessert came to Mexico from Spain, where it is served at all fiestas and fairs, and often for breakfast. It is made with *choux* paste, just like cream puffs; a cream-puff mix can be used.

1 cup water
½ cup butter
1 cup unsifted all-purpose flour
   Dash of salt
3 or 4 eggs
   Fat for deep frying
   Confectioners' sugar

Put water in a saucepan and bring to a boil. Add butter and as soon as it's melted, dump in flour and salt. Stir over heat until mixture forms a mass. Cool slightly and beat in eggs, one at a time, until smooth. Put in a pastry bag with a star tube (or into a *churros* gun, called a *churrero*) and squeeze in a continuous spiral into deep fat heated to 370°F. When brown, drain; sprinkle with confectioners' sugar. Makes about 2 dozen.

EMPANADAS DE DULCE
(Sweet Turnovers)

Empanadas are Mexican turnovers, either baked or fried in deep fat. Any plain pie pastry can be used. Roll it thin and cut into 3-inch circles; for sweet or dessert *empanadas,* fill with a spoonful of any of the fillings below. Moisten edges with water, fold over, and press edges firmly with a fork to seal. Either fry in deep fat (390°F. on a frying thermometer) until brown, or bake in preheated hot oven (400°F.) for 15 to 18 minutes, or until brown. Dust with confectioners'

sugar or ground cinnamon and sugar while still hot.

Fillings

● 1 cup drained crushed pineapple mixed with ½ cup grated coconut.

● 1 cup thick applesauce mixed with ¼ cup chopped nuts.

● ½ cup mashed cooked yams mixed with ½ cup grated coconut and ½ cup crushed pineapple.

● 1 cup chopped raisins or dates mixed with ½ cup chopped nuts and held together with a little jelly or corn syrup. Or use mincemeat or any fruit preserve.

POLVORÓNES
(Teacakes)

1 cup butter or margarine
   Confectioners' sugar
2¼ cups unsifted all-purpose flour
½ teaspoon salt
1 teaspoon vanilla extract

Mix butter, ½ cup sugar, and remaining ingredients until smooth. Chill for 2 hours. Form into 1-inch balls and bake on ungreased cookie sheets in preheated moderate oven (375°F.) until very lightly browned, 16 to 20 minutes. Remove from pan and roll at once in more confectioners' sugar. Makes 4 to 5 dozen.

CHOCOLATE MEXICANO
(Mexican Chocolate)

Another food native to America makes a popular beverage in Mexico. There they make it from a sweetened chocolate that is spiced with cinnamon, and foam it at the table in a picturesque earthen jug, using a *molinillo,* or little wooden mill, that is twirled rapidly between the palms of the hands. Here we can use an eggbeater. Use ½ ounce (½ square) unsweetened chocolate, 2 teaspoons sugar, and ¼ teaspoon ground cinnamon for each 1 cup milk. Heat in top part of a double boiler until chocolate is melted. Then whip vigorously until a good foam forms on the top.

From the land of plenty pours wholesome, good food:
grains and the meats fed on them, sweet-water fish,
fruits and vegetables. And this abundant wealth of
raw material is still further enriched by the varied culinary
traditions of the peoples who settled this section.

MIDWESTERN COOKERY

by Paul Engle

There is far more variety in the landscape of the Midwest, and in its kinds of foods and ways of preparing them, than tradition believes. From the once heavily wooded land of Ohio, full of streams, to the rolling long-grass prairies of Illinois and Iowa, to the flatter short-grass plains of Nebraska, Kansas, and the Dakotas, with the lake-abundant forests of Michigan, Minnesota, and Wisconsin to the north, this area produces so much food that, for the first time in the hungry world's history, there is simply too much.

The Midwest believes with the old poet: "We may live without poetry, pictures or books,/ But civilized man cannot live without cooks." This has been true of the Midwest from the beginning. One look at those fat, black soils, and the first settlers knew they were created to make fat, red meat. In the 1850's a visitor described this combination of eating food and producing it: "Business before soup—it is the first course of the dinner and the last. Between fish and pudding he will sell a prairie. With every mouthful of bread he will engage to deliver ten thousand bushels of wheat. . . . If he sees his neighbor prefers mutton, he at once offers to sell him sheep by the thousand; if he dines on pork, he will invite him into a speculation on hogs. . . . Your plate is brought to you heaped up with roast beef. Every third man has his pudding. The waiters hand about the ice cream in slices, which suggest the resemblance of small prairies. And, finally, the dinner goes off, like the finale of a display of fire works, with 'Jenny Lind cake,' 'vanities,' 'cookeys,' 'lady fingers,' 'jelly snips,' and 'pecans.' "

There are two large aspects of food in the Midwest. One is the vast accumulation of grain, and of the meats which are fed with it. The other is the smaller, traditional serving of foods prepared in the national ways of the countries from which the original settlers came. These survive in a surprising profusion.

Save for small Indian gardens which hardly scratched the surface, the Midwest had been nothing but trees and grass forever. Now the great crops go on forever, over the continually rising and falling slopes which run from eastern Ohio to western Nebraska. The windmill (and later the gasoline and electric engines) allowed man to live away from streams for the first time, so that they could settle in the midst of the riverless hills and not perish of thirst. The original prairie grasses, which had rotted for thousands of years to make a dense loam, were torn up and planted to the greatest single crop raised anywhere in the world: corn, itself a developed grass. With wheat in the westernmost states, and soy beans, and oats, the Midwest turns its earth, rains, and labor into grain. This is in turn eaten by cattle and hogs (almost no lamb or veal is eaten here) who are, in turn, eaten by the rest of the country and the world.

Fat pigs are plentiful in the Midwest and a fat pig is just corn in another shape, to which a tough hide of bristles has been added for the outside and a grunt inside.

The midmost part of the Midwest is the "Corn Belt," Illinois, Indiana, Iowa. Hardly ten per cent of the whole country, it produces two thirds of its corn. Three times as many bushels of corn are raised as of wheat, and eighty-five per cent of it is fed to livestock. The bacon and ham you eat are succulent because of the rich corn eaten to make them. The cow gets not only the kernel, but the cut-up stalks as well, to which molasses may have been added in the silo. That Thanksgiving turkey is stuffed first with corn before the cook adds her own stuffing.

Corn saturates the Midwest as no other single food dominates any other area of the world, unless it may be rice in some portions of Asia, and even that is grown on a far smaller scale. Thus, flying over or driving through the Midwest, you see the effect of food-raising on the landscape everywhere. Those long, wide fields, edged with fences or trees, represent the corn and wheat, the pastures and gardens which will nourish much of this country and, indeed, the whole earth. To be in the constant presence of food produces a different attitude. Instead of just possessing it, we are possessed by it in the Midwest, for food is our way of life.

All of our holiday celebrations turn finally into a celebration of food. We praise the Fourth of July, in the country's pride, for making us free of England. Then we settle down to the picnic or the massive dinner, both of which prove that we have attained another sort of independence, a freedom from hunger, and an access to abundance, no other country has known. The Midwest is the middle of that exuberance of food.

In the Dakotas, there will be the Scandinavian rye bread, dark and firm, the sort of loaf you can heft in the hand, as distinct from those airy white loaves which a farmer could squeeze down to the thickness of a sandwich if he leaned on it. There will be pies of every sort. Concord grape pie in Ohio, washed down with some of that smooth wine from the islands in Lake Erie, will turn any tired blood youthful. A wide platter of whole strawberries covered with sugar and mosquito netting and left in the sun will offer a richness and sweetness not to be found in any candy store. Cornmeal mush in winter, dripping with syrup, is like sweet corn in summer, a solid delicacy.

Nor must it be forgotten that there is actually some water in the Midwest. The Great Lakes provide a whitefish of a firm sweetness. The rivers have bass and crappie in ever-decreasing numbers, but the typical fish of the region is that ancient survivor, the catfish, with a boneless meat which has more resemblance to chicken than to the usual fish. This gray-backed swimmer, the color of the earthy rivers through which he slowly wavers, has a skin rather than scales, and the fierce expression of a monster beyond time, but he tastes as sweet as corn, which he loves to eat if he is ever lucky enough to swim into a flooded cornfield.

There are pheasants to be had in many of the Midwest states, growing plump on spilled grain in the autumn. Unlike many wild fowl, the pheasant, and the duck, who glean in the grain fields, get fat and mild in flavor. The Dakotas swarm with the gaily colored pheasants, and so do those counties of Iowa and Illinois with enough cover to protect the young but enough cornfields to leave ample feed. Oddly enough, the progress of mechanical cornpicking has increased the amount of grain left in the field. The rollers tear off the ears quickly, acres faster in a day than a man, but they also crush many, while the individual farmer picked each ear neatly and without loss. The birds benefit, and can live for weeks on the scattered kernels.

Probably there are two great gravies of the Midwest, aside from the natural juice of beef roast itself. One is the giblet gravy of chicken and turkey, savory with the butter which has been used for basting, and the other is the gravy made from the drippings of chicken roasted with cream. In an age of diet-watching, when most diners do not come to the table after a long afternoon in the open air, these rich additions to food are losing favor, but their flavor cannot be replaced by any other food.

If you have access to corncobs, and a

lot of them, try grilling steaks over them. Since the beef will have been fattened on corn, it is only proper that it should be cooked over the cob, which will give a clean, glowing bed of even heat.

This impressive plenty is expressed in celebrations all over the Midwest: Sauerkraut Day among the Germans; Kolache Day with the Czechs in Iowa; Cheese Day (with a Cheese Queen!) in Wisconsin, thirty nationalities serving their own unique foods at the Festival of Nations in St. Paul, Watermelon Day, Sweet Corn Day, in Illinois. Besides these, Chicago is full of Polish foods like *kielbasa*, a coarse sausage wtih pork, garlic, and caraway seeds. Milwaukee has bratwurst (a firm sausage of veal and pork) and bockwurst, a more perishable sausage of veal, eggs, chives, and seasonings. There is also a Norwegian *Lefse* Day (*lefse* is a thin, flavory potato bread).

Many of the same people who raise the great quantities of similar beef, corn, and wheat keep these national foods alive, as if in protest against the mass production in which they are engaged. The Dutch still make *oliebollen* fritters, the Swedes their light pancakes and tiny meatballs, the Welsh their pasties, the Danes their kringles (a sweet bread), the Germans their tortes.

There are many local tricks, such as frequently adding a little sugar to vegetables, cooking goose with enough vinegar to make it slightly delicately sour, mixing unexpected bits of smoked fish in salad, adding a ham hock or a little bacon to vegetables, mashing potatoes with cream for fluffiness, serving chili sauce (if homemade, savory and sweet), cooking chicken and pork chops in milk, making beautifully dark rye bread. These happen elsewhere, but are especially native to the Midwest.

Here sweet corn husked more than a minute before putting in the kettle, or picked a day before eaten, is looked on with contempt, in the belief its sugar turns to starch. Here squaw corn in Wisconsin will fill any known stomach (and probably all four of the cow's), with its onions and green peppers fried in bacon drippings and mixed with corn, creamed, or, in the old manner, dried. Head cheese, stuffed into a stomach lining, with peppers, garlic, spices, and then smoked, is a German and Czech delicacy (the latter call it *jelita),* and *jaternice,* a garlic bologna, is also offered. The *kolache* is a pastry filled with poppy seed, plum, any fruit, or cheese.

Perhaps the greatest single Midwest food is beef, as steak or as roast. The "finishing" of a young steer, from its rough condition off the western range, is the noblest agricultural art. The animal

must not simply gain weight, he must carry the little flecks and lines of fat, from the rich corn kernels, through the red meat and not only on the edge. This distinguishes Midwest beef from that of grass-fed steers. Kansas City and Omaha, Sioux City and Denver offer every cut of beef prepared in every known way, even buried in a pit and barbecued, and often the best restaurants are near the packing yards and the customer enters the door with the smell of manure dense in the air; once inside, it is the rich tang of cooking beef. This closeness to the source of food and the cooking of it is another Midwestern characteristic.

Where but in the Midwest, having so much green food, would a cook deliberately wilt lettuce leaves and serve them warm, with sugar, vinegar, and bacon bits? With so much food, imagination now must go not into ways of getting it, but in ways of preparing and serving it. Between the Alleghenies and the Rockies, the foods, and their ways, vary as the look of the landscape varies.

Here, at last, the melting pot has merged with the cooking pot. We are grateful for both.

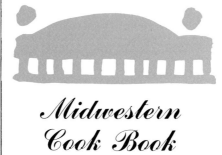

Midwestern Cook Book

by Ethel Keating

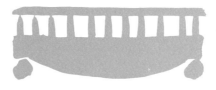

APPETIZERS AND SOUPS

CAVIAR
Most people think of caviar as Russian, although much of it comes from Denmark, Norway, Sweden, Iran, the western United States, and from Wisconsin. There at the turn of the century, the enterprising wife of a commercial fisherman believed whitefish roe the equal of the famed Russian product. She set out to prove it. By trial and error in her kitchen she at last hit upon a satisfactory recipe, and ever since Great Lakes whitefish

caviar has been competitive. Its flavor makes it enjoyable on many occasions and the price of a 4-ounce jar is modest.

CAVIAR BOWL
1½ cups dairy sour cream
  1 cup (8 ounces) whitefish caviar
  1 tablespoon mayonnaise
  1 tablespoon finely minced green onion
  1 tablespoon finely minced parsley
    Pumpernickel

Spoon sour cream into a footed glass bowl, or form into a ring on a serving plate. Make a depression in the center. Fill with a mixture of the caviar, mayonnaise, and green onion. Sprinkle the parsley to form a ring on the sour cream. Serve with pumpernickel bread cut into small squares. Makes 8 to 10 servings.

HERRING IN SOUR CREAM
  2 pound jar of herring in wine sauce
  1 cup dairy sour cream
  1 tablespoon mayonnaise
  1 Bermuda onion, thinly sliced
  1 carrot, grated

Drain herring and discard the onion from the jar. Add remaining ingredients to herring and refrigerate for several hours. Makes 8 to 10 servings.

HOT SWISS-CHEESE APPETIZERS
Sprinkle 1-inch fingers of Gruyère cheese with salt and freshly ground pepper. Wrap tightly in flaky piecrust. Refrigerate for at least 1 hour. Fry in deep hot fat (375°F. on a frying thermometer) until nicely browned. Serve at once.

KANSAS CORN CHOWDER
  ½ cup diced salt pork or bacon
  3 to 4 medium-size potatoes
  ½ onion
  2 cups water
2¼ to 2½ cups (one 1-pound, 4-ounce can) cream-style corn
  2 teaspoons salt
    Pepper to taste
  2 cups light cream, scalded

Sauté salt pork until brown and crisp; add potatoes and onion that have been put through a food chopper. Add water, corn, and seasonings; simmer, covered, for 15 minutes. Stir in the cream. Reheat but do not boil. Makes about 1½ quarts or 4 servings.

BEEF BROTH WITH DUMPLINGS
All persons of Central European origin appreciate clear soups, beef or chicken, because they are the perfect foils for interesting additions such as liver dumplings, farina dumplings, matzo balls, devil balls, noodles, etc.

Beef Broth
  1 pound lean beef, ground
  1 beef shank, cracked
  1 carrot, diced
  1 onion, ½ peeled and ½ unpeeled
  1 to 2 leeks
  2 celery stalks and tops
  ½ cup tomato purée
  ½ cup diced celery root
  4 egg whites and shells

6 to 8 peppercorns
2 teaspoons salt
1 garlic clove, crushed
3 quarts ice and water

Mix all ingredients, adding ice and water gradually, blending carefully. Bring slowly to the boiling point. Simmer slowly for 2 hours. Do not stir. Strain through several thicknesses of cheesecloth. Chill. Remove fat before using as broth for following recipes. Makes 3½ quarts.

Devil Balls

1 can (3 ounces) deviled ham
1 egg
½ cup sifted cracker crumbs
    Pepper to taste
1 tablespoon minced parsley

Mix all ingredients. Shape into small balls. Drop into boiling soup. Cover and cook for 2 minutes. Makes 16 small balls.

Farina Dumplings

1 cup milk
1 teaspoon sugar
¼ teaspoon salt
¼ teaspoon butter
¼ cup farina
1 egg
¼ cup minced parsley

Let milk, sugar, salt, and butter come to a boil; add farina and stir over heat until farina no longer sticks to the sides of the pan. Beat in egg and parsley. Drop by teaspoonfuls into boiling clear soup. Cook until dumplings rise to the surface, about 2 minutes. Makes about 20 small dumplings.

Liver Dumplings

2 eggs, separated
1 cup cracker crumbs
¼ cup melted butter or margarine
1 cup ground raw liver (freeze liver
    and grind when frozen)
1 onion, grated
1 teaspoon salt
    Pepper to taste
    Few gratings of nutmeg

Mix together beaten egg yolks, cracker crumbs, melted butter, liver, onion, and seasonings. Fold in stiffly beaten egg whites. Form into 24 rounded dumplings and cook in boiling soup for 5 to 6 minutes. Makes 2 dozen.

Matzo Balls

2 eggs
2 tablespoons cold water
½ cup matzo meal
1 tablespoon minced parsley
¼ teaspoon salt

Beat eggs with the cold water; add enough matzo meal to make a soft dough, the parsley, and salt. Chill for several hours. Shape into small balls; drop into boiling water, cover, and simmer for 20 minutes. Drain and serve in hot soup. Makes 12 small balls.

FISH AND SHELLFISH

GREAT LAKES FISH BOIL

Nothing could be easier to prepare or more delectable than an outdoor Great Lakes fish boil. At Sturgeon Bay, Wisconsin, in the summertime, hundreds come to the community feasts put on by local organizations. Serve it with cabbage salad, garden-ripe tomatoes, and oven-fresh homemade bread.

In a large covered kettle of salted water gently boil for 20 minutes well-scrubbed, medium-size new potatoes. Place a slotted tray over potatoes, or cover with cheesecloth that extends over the sides of the kettle. This is to facilitate the removal of the fish. Now add 2-inch thick whitefish or trout steaks (or fish may be filleted) and simmer gently for another 10 minutes, or until fish is tender. Lift fish to a big serving tray, surround with the potatoes in their jackets, and serve with plenty of melted butter.

SMELTS

When the temperature of the streams flowing into the Great Lakes reaches 36°F. the great smelt run is on. Amateur and professional fishermen—men and women, young and old—join in the sport of smelt dipping.

Leaving the lakes, smelts throng in unbelievable numbers into tributary streams to spawn. And hundreds of people, in festive spirits and with much hoopla, line the banks to scoop up the glittering smelts that literally darken the waters by their numbers. The run lasts for several days and the dipping continues throughout the night; bonfires and lanterns gaily illuminate the scene.

Ten to twelve to the pound, these ocean-water fish caught in fresh-water streams are delectable.

SAUTÉED SMELTS

2 pounds cleaned smelts
    Beer
½ cup sifted all-purpose flour
¼ cup finely ground
    blanched almonds
2 teaspoons salt
½ teaspoon pepper
    Butter, bacon fat, or cooking oil
    Lemon wedges, tartare sauce

Cover smelts with beer and refrigerate for several hours. Dry on absorbent paper, then shake, one at a time, in a paper bag containing the flour, almonds, salt, and pepper. Have fat ⅛ inch deep in skillet. When hot but not smoking, open fish and place, slit side down, in fat. When crisp, turn and brown skin sides. Cooking time is 5 to 8 minutes, depending upon size. Place on heated platter. Serve with lemon wedges and tartare sauce. Makes 4 servings.

SMELTS WITH LOBSTER OR CRABMEAT STUFFING

1 can (6½ ounces) lobster or crabmeat
1 green onion, minced
1 tablespoon minced parsley
    Salt and pepper to taste
1 teaspoon Worcestershire
    Mayonnaise
20 to 24 smelts
2 eggs, slightly beaten
    Fine cracker crumbs
    Melted butter
    Dry white wine

Mix together lobster, onion, parsley, and seasonings; add enough mayonnaise to make a paste. Stuff smelts; sew the openings. Brush with slightly beaten egg and roll in cracker crumbs. Place side by side in well-buttered baking dish. Bake in preheated moderate oven (350°F.) for 20 to 25 minutes, basting every 5 minutes with equal parts of melted butter and wine. Makes 4 servings.

BUTTER-STUFFED LAKE MICHIGAN TROUT

One 4-pound lake trout, boned
    Sherry
¾ cup butter
1 green onion, minced
2 tablespoons minced parsley
½ cup finely chopped mushrooms
1 garlic clove mashed
    in 1 teaspoon salt
1 cup dry white wine
1 cup heavy cream
2 egg yolks
    Salt and pepper
¼ cup heated brandy

Brush inside of boned fish with sherry; refrigerate for 2 hours. Cream butter and add onion, parsley, mushrooms, and garlic. Place fish in open baking pan; spread ¾ of butter mixture inside of fish and remainder on outside. Pour wine over the fish and bake in preheated moderate oven (375°F.) for 45 minutes, basting often. Carefully lift fish to a heatproof platter. Strain liquid remaining in pan; simmer until reduced to half. Mix cream with slightly beaten egg yolks. Gradually beat hot sauce into egg-yolk mixture. Reheat over low heat for 2 or 3 minutes, stirring constantly. Season to taste with salt and pepper. Pour heated brandy over the fish; ignite and baste over fish until flames are extinguished. Pour sauce over and serve at once. Makes 4 servings.

LAKE SUPERIOR WHITEFISH

Most of the whitefish caught in Lake Superior's icy waters are shipped directly to large city markets, for example, Chicago. It is elegant when baked or broiled on a one- to two-inch seasoned oak plank. In the Middle West, the vogue for planking fish and steaks started in the gay 90's when a Chicago department store offered planks for sale at fifteen cents each.

PLANKED LAKE SUPERIOR WHITEFISH

4-pound boned whitefish
    Salt and pepper to taste
    Sherry

1 *Planked Lake Superior Whitefish and tomatoes stuffed with baby Lima beans*

2 *Broiled Porterhouse Steak*

3 *Kolaches*

4 *Pineapple Blue-Cheese Salad Ring*

5 *Polish Sausage with Red Cabbage*

6 *Kansas Corn Chowder*

7 *Polish Babka*

8 *Light Pumpernickel Bread*

Fresh lemon juice
Coarse salt
Paprika
Duchesse Potatoes
Vegetables
Parsley
Lemon wedges

Season the cleaned and boned whitefish with salt and pepper. Place on a buttered plank; brush with sherry and lemon juice. Refrigerate for at least 2 hours. Cover the exposed parts of the plank with salt to protect it from burning. Sprinkle fish with paprika and broil 4 inches from source of heat until nicely browned, about 15 minutes. Brush salt from plank. Pipe Duchesse Potatoes around edge of plank and fill in exposed areas with vegetables such as whole tomatoes stuffed with baby Lima beans, stalks of white asparagus, glazed whole onions, etc. Place under broiler until potatoes are lightly browned. Decorate with parsley and lemon wedges. Makes 4 to 6 servings.

Duchesse Potatoes

Put 6 hot freshly cooked medium potatoes through a ricer. Add 2 tablespoons butter, 1 teaspoon salt, freshly ground pepper to taste, and 1 egg plus 2 egg yolks. Beat until mixture is fluffy.

BAKED LAKE SUPERIOR WHITEFISH WITH SAVORY DRESSING AND LOBSTER SAUCE

4- to 5-pound whitefish, boned
    Lime juice
4 slices of bacon, diced
¼ cup chopped green onion
¼ cup minced parsley
½ cup chopped celery
3 cups bread cubes
    Milk
1 teaspoon salt
1 tablespoon fresh lemon juice
1 teaspoon dried summer savory
1 egg, well beaten
2 tablespoons drained capers
    Parsley
    Lobster Sauce

Place fish, skin side down, in a well-buttered shallow baking pan. Sprinkle with lime juice and refrigerate for several hours. Sauté bacon and vegetables in skillet for 5 minutes; remove from heat. Moisten bread cubes with a little milk and add to sautéed vegetables along with remaining ingredients, except parsley and Lobster Sauce. Put dressing on top of fish and bake in preheated moderate oven (375°F.) for 45 minutes. Remove fish to a heated serving tray. Garnish with parsley. Serve with Lobster Sauce. Makes 4 to 6 servings.

Lobster Sauce

2 tablespoons butter
1 tablespoon flour
    Salt and pepper to taste
¾ cup milk
1 cup cooked or canned lobster
2 egg yolks
½ cup light cream
1 tablespoon sherry

Melt butter and blend in flour and seasonings; add milk and stir until thickened and smooth. Add lobster and heat thoroughly. Just before serving gradually add some of hot sauce to the egg yolks, beaten slightly with the cream. Add mixture to remaining sauce. Reheat but do not allow to boil. Flavor with sherry.

FROGS' LEGS

The first white men in Michigan were the French-Canadian missionaries sent to convert the Chippewas. Then came the French-Canadian trappers, in search of beaver, otter, and other fur-bearing animals. One of the things that endeared the land to them were the frogs that abounded in the marshy bogs. Frogs' legs, the French gourmet dish they loved so much at home, could be enjoyed here in the Michigan wilderness. And frogs' legs are still a Michigan specialty.

1 dozen medium-size frogs' legs
    Salt and pepper
½ cup butter or margarine
2 garlic cloves, crushed
    Juice of ½ lemon
2 tablespoons each of chopped chives, parsley, and fresh tarragon
2 tablespoons brandy
¼ cup dry white wine

Wash frogs' legs in cold water; dry well. Season with salt and pepper. Heat butter in a large skillet until foamy; add garlic, lemon juice, and frogs' legs. Sauté over moderately high heat until golden-brown on both sides; add chives, parsley, and tarragon and cook for 1 minute. Pour brandy over and flame. Add wine and cook for another minute. Serve with parsley-buttered potatoes, tossed salad, and chilled white wine. Makes 6 servings.

MEAT, POULTRY, AND GAME

RIB ROAST OF BEEF ON A SPIT

Bone 3 or 4 ribs of beef and roll or tie well. Have meat at room temperature. Put on spit and test for balance. Crush 3 garlic cloves in 2 tablespoons salt; add 1 teaspoon freshly ground pepper and 1 tablespoon ground ginger; rub well into meat. Insert meat thermometer. Bank grayed coals to back of grill. In front of coals put a pan of foil larger than the roast to catch the drippings. Roast for 2½ to 3 hours on constantly turning rotisserie according to your preference of doneness, gauged by meat thermometer (140°F. for rare, 160°F. for medium, 170°F. for well done). Remove and let stand for 20 minutes before serving. Put on heated serving platter. Makes 6 to 8 servings.

STEAK TARTARE

1 pound sirloin or tenderloin

steak, freshly ground twice
½ cup chopped onion or green onion
1 tablespoon ice water
    Butter
    Pumpernickel or rye bread
    Egg yolks
    Salt and freshly ground pepper to taste
    Garnishes: chopped onion, capers, freshly grated horseradish, and chopped parsley

Lightly mix the steak with the chopped onion and ice water. (The ice water makes it fluffy.) Pile lightly on buttered slices of bread. Make an indentation in the center of the meat and slip in a raw egg yolk. Sprinkle with salt and freshly ground pepper. Serve on individual plates with a garnish of onion, capers, horseradish, and chopped parsley. Makes 4 servings.

TONGUE WITH RAISIN SAUCE

Scrub a fresh tongue with warm water; cover with cold water and add 2 sliced carrots, 1 small onion, 2 celery stalks, 6 peppercorns, small piece of bay leaf, and 1 teaspoon salt. Simmer for 2 to 4 hours, depending upon size. Drain; plunge into cold water, peel off skin, and trim. Slice thin; arrange on a heated serving platter. Pour Raisin Sauce over tongue and top with toasted almond halves. Garnish with lemon wedges and watercress. Makes 6 servings.

Raisin Sauce

2 tablespoons butter
2 tablespoons all-purpose flour
1 cup beef bouillon
1 cup dry white wine
½ cup raisins
½ teaspoon grated lemon peel
6 whole cloves
4 gingersnaps
¼ cup firmly packed dark brown sugar

Melt butter and add flour; stir until blended. Add bouillon and wine; cook, stirring constantly, until thickened and smooth. Add remaining ingredients. Cover and simmer until raisins are plumped. Makes about 2½ cups.

ROAST FRESH HAM WITH SOUR CREAM GRAVY

1 fresh ham or leg of pork (6 to 7 pounds)
    Salt and pepper
    Garlic slivers
    Crumbled dried rosemary and sage
2 each of onions, carrots, celery stalks, and parsley sprigs, coarsely chopped
½ cup white wine
    Parsley and cinnamon apple slices (optional)
1 cup dairy sour cream

Score skin side of the fresh ham and season well with salt and freshly ground pepper. With a sharp knife cut slits in the meat and stuff with slivers of garlic and a combination of rosemary and sage. Place in a shallow roasting pan on a bed of the chopped vegetables. Pour wine over all. Roast in preheated moderate oven (350°F.) for about 35 minutes per pound (internal temperature 185°F.), or until meat is tender and skin is crisp and brown. Baste often. Add another ½ cup wine if necessary. Place roast on a heated platter; garnish with parsley and cinnamon apple slices if desired.

Strain pan juices into a bowl. Let fat rise to top. Skim all fat, reserving ¼ cup for the sauce. Add water to remaining liquid in bowl to make 2 cups. Heat ¼ cup fat. Stir in ¼ cup flour. Gradually stir in the 2 cups juice and water. Cook over low heat until thick and smooth, stirring constantly. Stir in sour cream and heat but do not boil. Serve gravy with the roast. Makes 8 to 10 servings.

ROAST HAM WITH BEER GLAZE

In an uncovered roasting pan place a precooked ham and pour 1 cup beer over it. Roast in preheated moderate oven (350°F.) for 1 hour; baste every 15 minutes with drippings. Remove from oven; score the fat diagonally in two directions to form diamonds; stud with whole cloves. Spread ham with Beer Glaze and roast for 30 minutes longer, or until well glazed; baste often with drippings. Place on heated serving platter; garnish with crisp watercress and crabapple pickles.

Beer Glaze

Combine 1 cup brown sugar, 1 tablespoon all-purpose flour, 1 teaspoon powdered mustard, and 2 tablespoons wine vinegar with enough beer to make a smooth paste.

PARTY PORK CHOPS

8 pork chops, 1½ inches thick
  Salt, pepper, and paprika
  All-purpose flour
  Butter
1 can (14½ ounces) evaporated milk, undiluted
1 cup sliced fresh mushrooms
1 can (10½ ounces) mushroom soup
½ cup chopped walnuts or cashews
  Minced parsley

Season pork chops to taste with salt, pepper, and paprika; dredge with flour. Brown quickly in a small amount of butter. Place chops in shallow baking pan and pour evaporated milk over. Bake in preheated slow oven (325°F.) for 1 hour. Add mushrooms and the mushroom soup, and bake for 30 minutes longer. Sprinkle with walnuts which have been browned lightly in butter and with minced parsley. Makes 8 servings.

HAM BALLS

¾ pound smoked ham, ground
½ pound raw lean pork, ground
½ cup milk
½ cup cracker crumbs
  Brown-Sugar Sauce

Mix together ham and pork; add milk and cracker crumbs. Form into 12 balls 2 inches in diameter. Place in a shallow baking pan. Pour Brown-Sugar Sauce over meatballs. Bake in preheated slow oven (325°F.) for 2 hours. Makes 4 servings.

Brown-Sugar Sauce

Bring to boil ¾ cup brown sugar, ½ cup cider vinegar, ½ cup water, 6 whole cloves, and 1 tablespoon powdered mustard.

SPARERIBS AND SAUERKRAUT

3 to 4 pounds meaty spareribs
1 tablespoon butter
1 quart sauerkraut
1 carrot, grated
1 teaspoon caraway seed
  Freshly ground pepper to taste
2 onions, thinly sliced
3 large tart apples, cored and cut into rings
1½ cups white wine or water

Quickly brown spareribs in butter in hot skillet. Rinse sauerkraut and mix with the carrot, caraway seed, and pepper; put half in roasting pan. Cover with half the onion and apple rings and top with the browned spareribs. Spoon remaining sauerkraut over top. Add remaining onion and apple rings. Pour wine over top. Cover and bake in preheated moderate oven (350°F.) for 1½ hours. Good with mashed potatoes, pumpernickel, and cold beer. Makes 4 servings.

■ **Variation**—Substitute browned smoked pork chops and weisswurst for the spareribs in the above recipe. Proceed as directed. (Weisswurst are the famous white-meat sausages of Munich; made of veal and pork, they are delicate both in taste and color.)

BAKED CANADIAN BACON WITH PORT-WINE SAUCE

1½ cups firmly packed light brown sugar
1 tablespoon wine vinegar
1 tablespoon prepared mustard
  Whole Canadian bacon (2 to 3 pounds)
1 cup white wine
  Port-Wine Sauce

Make a paste of brown sugar, vinegar, and mustard. Remove casing from bacon and spread with the paste. Let stand overnight. Place in baking dish with the wine. Cover and bake in preheated moderate oven (350°F.) for 1½ hours; uncover and bake for 30 minutes longer in hot oven (400°F.). Remove from oven and let stand for 30 minutes to "set the fat." Slice and serve with hot Port-Wine Sauce. Makes 10 to 12 servings.

Port-Wine Sauce

Heat together 1 cup currant jelly, 1 cup port, and 1 tablespoon butter. Do not allow to boil. Makes about 1½ cups.

POLISH SAUSAGE WITH RED CABBAGE

1 medium-size head red cabbage
  Boiling water
¼ cup fresh lemon juice
2 tablespoons butter or margarine
½ cup red wine
¼ cup sugar
  Salt and pepper
2 apples, peeled, cored, and sliced
1 pound Polish sausage

Shred cabbage, scald with boiling water, and drain. Pour lemon juice over cabbage. Melt butter; add cabbage and the next 5 ingredients. Cover and simmer for 30 minutes. Top with sausage and continue cooking for 15 minutes longer. Makes 4 servings.

LAMB PATTIES WITH CRANBERRY MINT SAUCE

1 garlic clove
1 teaspoon salt
¼ teaspoon pepper
1½ pounds ground lamb
⅓ cup minced parsley
1 egg
½ cup pine nuts
  Watercress
  Cranberry Mint Sauce

In mixing bowl crush garlic in salt; add pepper, lamb, parsley, and egg. Mix lightly until well blended. Stir in pine nuts. Form into 8 patties 1 inch thick. Broil over coals or under broiler until nicely browned on each side but pink inside. Place on heated serving platter; garnish with watercress. Serve with Cranberry Mint Sauce. Makes 4 servings.

Cranberry Mint Sauce

Bring to boil 2 cups whole-berry cranberry sauce; add 3 drops spearmint or peppermint flavoring. Serve hot. Makes 2 cups.

CHICKEN PIE

A characteristic of "downstate" Illinois chicken pie is that it never contains vegetables. And it is always topped with light fluffy baking-powder biscuit dough.

1 roasting chicken (4 to 5 pounds)
1 cup chicken bouillon
3 cups water
1 celery stalk
1 parsley sprig
1 green onion
2 teaspoons salt
  Creamy Gravy
  Biscuit Dough

Disjoint chicken and place in large kettle; add next 6 ingredients. Bring to the boiling point and skim. Cover and simmer until chicken is tender, 2 to 2½ hours. Let chicken cool in broth. Remove chicken from broth; reserve broth for gravy; discard skin and remove meat from bones. Place meat in 2½-quart shallow baking dish. Pour Creamy Gravy over and top with Biscuit Dough. Bake in preheated hot oven (425°F.) for 15 to 20 minutes. Makes 6 servings.

Creamy Gravy

In saucepan melt ¼ cup chicken fat or butter and add ¼ cup flour; cook until bubbly. Add 3 cups strained chicken broth; cook until thickened and smooth. Just before pouring over chicken, add 2 egg yolks mixed with ½ cup light cream.

Biscuit Dough

2 cups sifted all-purpose flour
3 teaspoons baking powder
½ teaspoon salt
½ cup butter
½ to ⅔ cup dairy sour cream

Sift flour, measure, and sift with baking powder and salt; blend in butter. Add sour cream. Toss on a floured board; knead several times. Pat out to the size of the casserole and fit on top of chicken. With a sharp knife cut the crust into diamonds. Or drop dough by tablespoons on top of chicken. Or bake biscuits and lay on top of heated casserole.

CHICKEN LOAF WITH ALMOND AND MUSHROOM SAUCE

¾ cup chicken bouillon
3 tablespoons bread crumbs
4 eggs, well beaten
3 cups chopped cooked chicken
2 tablespoons melted butter
2 tablespoons chopped parsley
    Almond and Mushroom Sauce

Heat bouillon; add bread crumbs and mix well. Add remaining ingredients except Almond and Mushroom Sauce. Pour into a buttered loaf pan (9 x 5 x 3 inches). Bake in preheated moderate oven (350°F.) for 30 to 35 minutes. Unmold. Slice and serve with Almond and Mushroom Sauce.

Almond and Mushroom Sauce

3 tablespoons butter or margarine
½ pound fresh mushrooms
¼ cup flour
2 cups chicken bouillon
1 teaspoon fresh lemon juice
1 teaspoon salt
    Pepper to taste
½ cup shredded blanched almonds

Melt butter; add mushrooms and sauté until pale golden. Sprinkle with flour and blend well. Gradually stir in bouillon. Cook, stirring constantly, until thickened and smooth. Add lemon juice, seasonings, and almonds. Serve hot. Makes 6 servings.

VENISON

Venison is plentiful in northern Michigan. The meat is lean and somewhat dry. Because the fat has a strong flavor, it should be trimmed away completely and replaced with salt pork. This can be done with a larding needle, or by piercing the meat with a sharp knife and pushing in strips of chilled larding pork, or by wrapping meat with thin slices of larding pork and securing it with a string.

ROAST VENISON

Lard a leg or loin of venison and sprinkle with garlic salt, pepper, and flour. Place in a shallow roasting pan and bake in preheated slow oven (325°F.) for 20 to 25 minutes per pound. For the best flavor, venison should be served rare or medium rare. Serve with Wine Sauce, buttered noodles, and hot prunes stuffed with pâté de foie gras.

Wine Sauce

1 cup currant jelly
2 tablespoons prepared mustard
⅛ teaspoon ground ginger
    Grated peel of 1 orange
    Grated peel of 1 lemon
½ cup port
2 tablespoons fresh lemon juice

Combine all ingredients and heat until well blended. Serve hot or cold. Makes about 1¼ cups.

ROAST WILD DUCK

Most people agree that the dark-meat wild duck is more flavorful when cooked rare enough to allow the rich, red juices to follow the blade of the carving knife. If cooked longer, take care not to overcook.

Clean and dress ducks; wipe inside and out with salt. Stuff with ½ onion, section of apple, several pieces of celery, and a parsley sprig. Truss and place on rack in an uncovered shallow pan. Roast in preheated very hot oven (475°F.) for 20 to 25 minutes per pound for medium rare. Baste every 10 minutes with a mixture of butter or olive oil and Italian vermouth. Remove to a heated platter; surround with small tart shells filled with puréed chestnuts. Garnish with watercress.

APPLE GRAVY FOR PORK OR BOILED BEEF

1 cup chopped peeled tart apples
2 tablespoons butter
1 tablespoon flour
1 cup thin white sauce (1 tablespoon butter, 1 tablespoon flour, and 1 cup milk)
¼ teaspoon ground nutmeg
½ cup dairy sour cream

Cook apples in hot butter for about 2 minutes, or until soft and golden. Sprinkle with flour and cook for 2 minutes longer. Stir in white sauce and nutmeg. Cook for 3 to 5 minutes. Remove from heat and stir in sour cream. Makes 1⅔ cups.

STEWED APPLES

2 pounds well-flavored apples
3 tablespoons butter
½ cup sugar
½ cup water
½ cup dry white wine
    Grated rind of 1 lemon

Peel and core apples. Cut into thick circles. Heat butter in heavy skillet. Sauté apples for 3 minutes, turning once with a spatula. Sprinkle with sugar. Add water, wine, and lemon rind. Simmer, covered, over very low heat for 10 to 15 minutes, or until apples are tender. Makes 6 servings.

Note: Serve as an accompaniment for roast goose, duck, game, or pork.

VEGETABLES AND SALADS

ROASTED CORN-ON-THE-COB

Open the outer covering of corn to remove the silk. Replace husks and place in a large pan of ice water. Wrap corn in foil; cook on grill or in coals for 25 to 30 minutes, turning occasionally.

CORN PUDDING

2 cups fresh corn, scraped off the cob
4 eggs, separated
1 cup heavy cream
1 tablespoon flour
½ tablespoon sugar
1 teaspoon salt
½ teaspoon white pepper
¼ teaspoon ground mace

Thinly slice off the top of the kernels, then scrape cobs with back of knife or corn scraper. Corn should have a creamy milky consistency. Beat egg yolks until thick and lemon-colored. Stir in cream, flour, sugar, salt, pepper, and mace. Add corn. Beat egg whites until stiff; fold into mixture. Pour into greased 3-quart baking dish. Bake in preheated moderate oven (350°F.) for 30 minutes, or until set. Makes 6 servings.

MICHIGAN BAKED BEANS

2 pounds Great Northern beans
½ pound salt pork, sliced
1 whole onion, peeled
½ cup sorghum or molasses
½ teaspoon salt
½ teaspoon pepper
1 small bottle ketchup
1 tablespoon prepared mustard
1 tablespoon Worcestershire

Wash beans and discard imperfect ones; cover with cold water and soak overnight. Drain and cover with fresh water. Cook slowly until tender or until skins burst when a few on end of spoon are blown upon. Drain; reserve liquid. Pour boiling water over salt pork; let stand for 10 minutes, then drain. Put beans in bean pot in layers with the salt pork. Bury whole onion in center of pot. Mix 2 cups of the water drained from the beans with the sorghum, salt, pepper, ketchup, mustard, and Worcestershire; pour over beans and add enough more water to cover beans. Cover pot. Bake in preheated slow oven (300°F.) for 4 to 5 hours. Add water as needed to keep beans moist. Uncover during last hour of baking. Makes 12 servings.

SUMMER-SQUASH CASSEROLE

3 tablespoons butter
⅓ cup green onions, chopped with green tops
¾ cup diced celery
3 cups sliced small yellow summer squash
1½ cups cherry tomatoes, halved, or
2 large tomatoes (cut large ones into eighths)

1 teaspoon salt
Pepper to taste
1 teaspoon chopped fresh sweet basil
or ¼ teaspoon ground dried basil

Melt butter. Add onions and celery and cook until onion is transparent. Add squash and blend. Pour into a shallow casserole. Cover with a layer of cherry tomatoes. Mix salt, pepper, and basil and sprinkle over tomatoes. Cover and bake in preheated slow oven (300°F.) for 30 minutes. Makes 4 servings.

WILD RICE CASSEROLE

1 cup wild rice
¼ cup butter
3 tablespoons chopped onion
3 tablespoons chopped green pepper
½ cup slivered blanched almonds
3 cups hot chicken broth

Wash rice and drain well. Melt butter in skillet; add onion, green pepper, rice, and almonds. Sauté over low heat, stirring constantly, until rice begins to turn light yellow. Turn into a casserole; add hot chicken broth. Cover and bake in preheated slow oven (325°F.) for 1½ hours, or until rice is tender and all liquid is absorbed. Makes 4 servings.

PINEAPPLE BLUE-CHEESE SALAD RING

2½ cups (one 1-pound, 4-ounce can) crushed pineapple, undrained
1 box (3 ounces) lime-flavored gelatin
1 package (3 ounces) cream cheese
¼ pound blue cheese
1 cup heavy cream, whipped
Watercress
Slices of avocado and persimmon

Drain juice from pineapple into saucepan; add sufficient water to the juice to make 1½ cups; bring to the boiling point. Pour over gelatin and stir until dissolved. Using an electric beater at low speed, beat in the cream cheese and blue cheese. Cool. Chill. When mixture starts to congeal, fold in drained pineapple and whipped cream. Pour into a 5-cup mold that has been rinsed with cold water. Refrigerate for at least 4 hours. Unmold on a bed of watercress. Garnish with slices of avocado and persimmon. Makes 8 servings.

HOT TOMATO SLICES
Indiana boasts, and rightly so, that they grow some of the finest-flavored tomatoes to be sent to market, whether as fresh tomatoes, ketchup, canned tomatoes, or tomato soup.

6 ripe tomatoes, cut into halves crosswise
1 cup fresh bread crumbs
¼ cup ground filberts
2 teaspoons salt
2 teaspoons sugar
¼ teaspoon ground rosemary
Pepper to taste
¼ cup soft butter or margarine
2 tablespoons minced parsley

Place tomato halves in buttered shallow baking pan. Mix together remaining in-gredients; lightly pile on tomato halves. Bake in preheated slow oven (325°F.) for 15 to 20 minutes. Makes 6 servings.

BREADS

LIGHT PUMPERNICKEL BREAD

2 packages active dry yeast or 2 cakes compressed yeast
1½ cups warm water*
½ cup dark molasses
2 tablespoons caraway seeds
1 tablespoon salt
2 cups rye meal
4 cups sifted all-purpose flour
3 tablespoons soft butter

Sprinkle dry yeast or crumble cake yeast into warm water. *Use very warm water (105°F. to 115°F.) for dry yeast; use lukewarm water (80°F. to 90°F.) for compressed. Let stand for a few minutes, then stir until dissolved. Mix together the dissolved yeast, molasses, caraway seeds, and salt. Mix well. Add rye meal and about 2 cups of the flour; beat well. Add butter and beat well. Add remaining flour gradually and knead until smooth and satiny. Place in a buttered bowl; cover and allow to rise in a warm place until doubled in bulk, about 2 hours, or until dent remains when finger is pressed deep into side of dough. Turn out on lightly floured board; divide into 2 equal parts; cover and allow to rest for 10 minutes. Mold each part into a loaf and place each in a buttered pan (9 x 5 x 3 inches). Cover and allow to rise in a warm place until doubled in bulk, about 50 minutes. Bake in preheated very hot oven (450°F.) for 10 minutes; reduce temperature to moderate (350°F.) and bake for 35 minutes longer. Turn out on a rack to cool. Makes 2 loaves.

HICKORY-NUT GRAHAM BREAD
Many an evening during pioneer days in Wisconsin was spent with an upturned flatiron between the knees. This was the ideal base for cracking hickory nuts. Shagbark hickory trees grew in profusion throughout the Midwest and their fruit added a richness to many dishes.

2 packages active dry yeast or 2 cakes compressed yeast
1½ cups lukewarm water*
1 teaspoon granulated sugar
1½ teaspoons salt
About 2 cups sifted all-purpose flour
½ cup firmly packed brown sugar
¼ cup butter
½ cup boiling water
About 4 cups graham or whole-wheat flour
1½ cups coarsely broken hickory nuts

Sprinkle dry yeast or crumble cake yeast into warm water. *Use very warm water (105°F. to 115°F.) for dry yeast; use lukewarm water (80°F. to 90°F.) for compressed. Let stand for a few minutes, then stir until dissolved. Add granulated sugar. Let stand for 5 minutes. Beat in the salt and all-purpose flour; let rise in a warm place until light and bubbly. Dissolve brown sugar and butter in the boiling water; cool to lukewarm and add to the sponge. Stir in graham flour and nuts. Toss on lightly floured board and knead until smooth and elastic to the touch, about 10 minutes. Cover with a damp cloth and allow to rise in a warm place until doubled in bulk. Turn out on lightly floured board; divide into 2 parts; cover and allow to rest for 10 minutes. Mold each part into a loaf and place each in a buttered pan (8½ x 4½ x 2½ inches). Cover and let rise until doubled in bulk, about 50 minutes. Bake in preheated moderate oven (350°F.) for 50 minutes. Remove from pans and cool on a rack. Makes 2 loaves.

APPLE BREAD

½ cup shortening
1 cup plus 2 tablespoons sugar
1 tablespoon buttermilk
2 eggs, beaten
1 teaspoon vanilla extract
2 cups sifted all-purpose flour
1 teaspoon baking soda
¼ teaspoon salt
1 teaspoon grated lemon rind
1½ cups chopped peeled tart apples
1 teaspoon ground cinnamon

Cream shortening with 1 cup sugar until fluffy. Stir in buttermilk, eggs, and vanilla extract. Sift in flour, baking soda, and salt. Mix well. Add lemon rind and apples. Pour into greased loaf pan (9½ x 5¼ x 2¾ inches). Sprinkle with remaining sugar and the cinnamon. Bake in preheated moderate oven (350°F.) for about 1 hour.

NEBRASKA SPOON BREAD

2½ cups milk, scalded
1 cup yellow cornmeal
1½ teaspoons salt
1½ tablespoons melted butter
4 eggs, separated
1 teaspoon baking powder

Add scalded milk to cornmeal, stirring until smooth. Add salt and cook over boiling water, stirring constantly, until thick. Stir in butter. Cool. Add egg yolks, one at a time, beating well after each addition. Fold in baking powder and stiffly beaten egg whites. Turn into a hot buttered 1½-quart casserole. Bake in preheated moderate oven (375°F.) for about 45 minutes, or until bread is firm and crust is brown. Makes 4 to 6 servings.

CRULLERS
Pioneer Scandinavian women brought to South Dakota the custom of midmorning and midafternoon coffee. If their men were working in the fields, they trudged out to them with cans of hot coffee and a snack such as hot raised crullers rolled in sugar.

1 package active dry yeast or 1 cake
   compressed yeast
¼ cup lukewarm water*
¾ cup scalded milk, cooled to lukewarm
4 cups sifted all-purpose flour
10 tablespoons granulated sugar
½ cup butter or margarine
1 egg
2 egg yolks
1 teaspoon salt
½ teaspoon ground nutmeg
   Confectioners' sugar

Sprinkle dry yeast or crumble cake yeast into warm water. *Use very warm water (105°F. to 115°F.) for dry yeast; use lukewarm water (80°F. to 90°F.) for compressed. Let stand for a few minutes, then stir until dissolved. Add dissolved yeast to milk, 1 cup flour, and 2 tablespoons granulated sugar; beat well. Set aside in a warm place until light and bubbly, about 45 minutes. Cream butter until light and fluffy. Gradually beat in ½ cup granulated sugar. Beat in the egg and egg yolks, one at a time, beating well after each addition. Beat into yeast mixture along with salt, nutmeg, and 3 cups flour. Place in buttered bowl, cover, and let rise until double in bulk. Turn out on lightly floured board; roll out or pat to ½-inch thickness. Cut into strips ½ x 8 inches. Fold each strip in half lengthwise; twist several times and pinch ends together. Cover and let rise until light. Fry in deep hot fat (370°F. on a frying thermometer). Drain on absorbent paper. Dust with confectioners' sugar. Makes 32 crullers.

CHERRY MUFFINS

¼ cup sugar
½ teaspoon salt
1 tablespoon baking powder
2 cups sifted all-purpose flour
1 cup pitted fresh cherries or drained
   frozen cherries
1 egg
¾ cup milk
¼ cup melted butter or margarine

Sift together sugar, salt, baking powder, and flour; add cherries and blend well. Beat egg until thick and lemon-colored; add milk and melted butter; quickly stir into first mixture. Pour into buttered muffin tins. Bake in preheated moderate oven (375°F.) for 25 to 30 minutes. Makes about 1 dozen.

 DESSERTS

CHERRIES IN CURRANT JELLY

4 cups currant juice
8 cups sugar

Mrs. Van's Dutch Apple Cake

1 quart stemmed and pitted red sour cherries

Bring currant juice to a quick boil. Add sugar and bring back to the boiling point; skim. Add cherries and cook slowly for 15 minutes. Pour into hot sterilized jars and seal. Makes about nine ½-pint jars.

PEACH SLICES

2 cups sifted all-purpose flour
¾ cup butter or margarine
1 cup sugar
1 egg yolk
3 tablespoons milk
½ teaspoon grated lemon rind
1 quart sliced fresh peaches
¼ teaspoon ground cinnamon
¼ cup dried currants
Egg white
Confectioners' sugar

Sift flour into a bowl. Blend butter into flour until mixture resembles coarse cornmeal. Add ¼ cup sugar, egg yolk, milk, and lemon rind. Mix well and shape into a ball. Divide pastry into 2 equal parts and refrigerate for 15 minutes. Knead a little on lightly floured board and roll out into 2 equal-size rectangles 9 x 13 inches. Place one sheet of pastry on a pan (9 x 13 inches) with sides; cover with peaches tossed with ¾ cup sugar, the cinnamon, and currants. Adjust the other pastry sheet over peaches and prick lightly with a fork; brush with egg white. Bake in preheated moderate oven (375° F.) for 35 minutes. Cut into slices when cold and dust with confectioners' sugar. Makes 1 dozen 3-inch squares.

CRANBERRY PUDDING

1¼ cups sifted all-purpose flour
2 teaspoons baking soda
½ cup sorghum or molasses
⅓ cup hot water
2 cups raw whole cranberries
Hot Butter Sauce

Sift flour with soda; stir in sorghum. Pour hot water into mixture and when blended stir in cranberries. Pour into buttered 8-inch square pan. Bake in preheated moderate oven (350°F.) for 30 minutes. Cut into squares and place on individual serving plates. Top with whipped cream, a few gratings of orange rind, and chopped pistachio nuts, if desired. Serve with Hot Butter Sauce. Makes 6 to 8 servings.

Hot Butter Sauce
Cook until thoroughly dissolved and hot 1 cup sugar, ½ cup butter, and ½ cup light cream. Makes about 1 cup.

APPLE DUMPLINGS

Apple trees, Jonathan, Delicious, Winesaps, and Grimes Golden, grow luxuriantly on the banks of the Missouri and Lower Platte rivers. So apple desserts have long been favorites.

1 cup sifted all-purpose flour
1 package (3 ounces) cream cheese
Butter or margarine
⅛ teaspoon salt
4 apples, peeled and cored
½ cup sugar
1 teaspoon ground cinnamon
Cinnamon Syrup

Sift flour and blend in cream cheese, ½ cup butter, and salt. Chill. Roll to a rectangle about 9 x 14 inches on lightly floured board. Cover with coarsely grated apples; sprinkle with a mixture of sugar and cinnamon and dot with butter. Roll as for jelly roll. Cut into 1½-inch slices; place, cut side up, 1 inch apart, in buttered shallow baking dish (8 x 14 inches) or unbuttered individual custard cups. Cover with Cinnamon Syrup. Bake in preheated hot oven (400°F.) for 10 minutes; reduce temperature to slow (325°F.) and bake for 45 minutes longer. Makes 8 or 9 dumplings.

Cinnamon Syrup
Cook together until thickened and clear ⅓ cup firmly packed dark brown sugar, 2 tablespoons all-purpose flour, 1 cup water, 1 tablespoon butter, and ¼ cup brandy. Add ¼ teaspoon ground allspice, 1 teaspoon ground cinnamon, and ½ teaspoon ground nutmeg. Pour over dumplings.

RED-CURRANT COBBLER
¾ cup granulated sugar
¾ cup firmly packed light brown sugar
¼ cup butter or margarine, cut into small pieces
1 quart red currants, washed and stemmed
1 cup sifted all-purpose flour
2 teaspoons baking powder

1 egg
⅔ cup light cream or milk

Combine granulated sugar, brown sugar, butter, and red currants. Put in greased 2-quart baking dish. Sift together flour and baking powder. Beat in egg and cream. Sprinkle over currant mixture. Bake in preheated hot oven (400°F.) for about 35 minutes, or until top is crisp. Serve warm, with heavy cream if desired. Makes 6 servings.

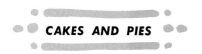

CAKES AND PIES

MRS. VAN'S DUTCH APPLE CAKE
1¼ cups sifted all-purpose flour
½ teaspoon salt
1 teaspoon sugar
1 teaspoon baking powder
½ cup butter or margarine
1 egg yolk
2 tablespoons brandy or milk
Apples and dried currants
Cinnamon Topping

Sift together dry ingredients; blend in butter. Add egg yolk and brandy. Press dough with the fingers into a 9-inch layer-cake pan. Cover with apples that have been peeled, cored, and cut into eighths. Sprinkle with a few currants. Cover with Cinnamon Topping. Bake in preheated moderate oven (350°F.) for 45 minutes. Makes 6 to 8 servings.

Cinnamon Topping
Blend together ¾ cup sugar, 1½ tablespoons all-purpose flour, 2 tablespoons butter, and ½ teaspoon ground cinnamon.

BLUEBERRY TORTE
Crust:
1½ cups graham-cracker crumbs
¼ cup melted butter
2 tablespoons confectioners' sugar

Blend all ingredients together and pat into a 9-inch springform pan. Refrigerate while preparing filling.

Blueberry Filling:
½ cup butter
1½ cups confectioners' sugar
4 egg yolks
2 tablespoons brandy
5 cups (two 1-pound, 4-ounce cans) blueberries
1 cup heavy cream, whipped and sweetened

Cream butter; gradually beat in sugar. Add egg yolks, one at a time, beating well after each addition. Add brandy. Carefully spread over crumbs. Refrigerate overnight. Pour blueberries into a sieve over a bowl and let drain for several hours. Just before serving, spread over butter mixture. Top with sweetened whipped cream.

STRAWBERRY SCHAUMTORTE
6 egg whites
2 cups sugar
1 teaspoon vinegar
1 teaspoon vanilla extract
Fresh sliced strawberries
Whipped cream

Beat egg whites until stiff enough to hold a peak when beater is removed; gradually beat in sugar, 1 tablespoon at a time. Add vinegar and vanilla. Pile evenly in buttered 9-inch springform. Bake in preheated very hot oven (450°F.) for just 7 minutes; turn off heat and leave torte in oven without opening door for at least 4 hours. Pile with fresh sliced strawberries and top with sweetened whipped cream. Makes 6 to 8 servings.

POLISH BABKA
1 cup scalded milk
½ cup sugar
2 teaspoons salt
½ cup butter or margarine
2 packages active dry yeast or 2 cakes compressed yeast
½ cup lukewarm water*
4 eggs, well beaten
6 to 6½ cups sifted all-purpose flour
1 tablespoon each of grated orange and lemon rind
½ cup blanched chopped almonds
1 cup raisins or dried currants
1 teaspoon vanilla extract
½ teaspoon almond extract
Orange Glaze

Scald milk and pour into large mixer bowl with sugar, salt, and butter; cool to lukewarm. Sprinkle dry yeast or crumble cake yeast into warm water. *Use very warm water (105° to 115°F.) for dry yeast; use lukewarm water (80° to 90° F.) for compressed. Let stand for a few minutes, then stir until dissolved. Add dissolved yeast, eggs, and half of flour to butter mixture. Beat for 2 minutes with an electric mixer. Stop the mixer and add more flour, a little at a time, along with grated rinds, nuts, raisins, and extracts. Mix first with a spoon, then with the hand, until dough pulls away from the sides of bowl, but is still quite soft. Turn out on lightly floured board; butter the fingers and knead for 100 strokes, until little bubbles can be seen beneath the surface. Place in a greased bowl; turn once to grease the top. Cover and let rise in a warm place for 1½ hours, or until doubled in bulk. Punch dough down; turn over in bowl, and let rest for 15 minutes. Shape dough into a smooth ring and place in well-buttered 10-inch tube pan. Cover and let rise in a warm place for 45 minutes, or until dough comes within 1 inch of the top of the pan. Bake in preheated moderate oven (350°F.) for 50 minutes. Place a piece of unglazed brown paper over the Babka after first 10 minutes of baking so top will not get too brown. Remove Babka from pan after cooling for 10 minutes. Spread with Orange Glaze while still warm. Makes 10-inch Babka.

Orange Glaze
Moisten 2 cups confectioners' sugar with 2 to 4 tablespoons fresh orange juice until of spreading consistency. Keep brushing sides and top of cake until glaze is set and all is used. Makes about 1 cup.

BUNDKUCHEN
1 package active dry yeast or 1 cake compressed yeast
¼ cup water*
¾ cup milk, scalded and cooled to lukewarm
1 cup and 1 tablespoon sugar
3½ cups sifted all-purpose flour
1 cup butter
4 eggs
Slivered almonds

Sprinkle dry yeast or crumble cake yeast into warm water. *Use very warm water (105° to 115°F.) for dry yeast; use lukewarm water (80° to 90°F.) for compressed. Let stand for a few minutes, then stir until dissolved; add lukewarm milk, 1 tablespoon sugar, and 1 cup flour. Beat well; let stand in a warm place until light and bubbly. Cream butter; gradually beat in 1 cup sugar. Add eggs, one at a time, beating well after each addition. Add yeast mixture and remaining flour; beat for 15 minutes. Butter a fluted tube pan or 2-quart bund pan and sprinkle with almonds. Carefully spoon in the batter. Allow to rise in a warm place until doubled in bulk. Bake in preheated very slow oven (275°F.) for 60 to 65 minutes. Makes 1 loaf.

SWEDISH TEA RING
1 package active dry yeast or 1 cake compressed yeast
¼ cup warm water*
3 cups sifted all-purpose flour
¾ cup sugar
1 teaspoon salt
¾ cup butter or margarine
1 cup light cream
3 egg yolks
Grated rind of ½ lemon
¼ cup melted butter or margarine
2 tablespoons ground cinnamon
½ cup yellow raisins
½ cup diced citron
1 egg white, slightly beaten
Chopped blanched almonds
Confectioners' Icing

Sprinkle dry yeast or crumble cake yeast into warm water. *Use very warm water (105° to 115°F.) for dry yeast; use lukewarm water (80° to 90°F.) for compressed. Let stand for a few minutes, then stir until dissolved. Sift flour, measure, and sift with ¼ cup sugar and the salt; add butter and blend, as for piecrust, until mixture resembles coarse cornmeal. Add yeast, cream, egg yolks, and lemon rind. Beat hard. Refrigerate overnight. Turn out on lightly floured board and roll out to a rectangle 16 x 12 inches. Spread with melted butter; sprinkle with ½ cup sugar and the cinnamon; add raisins and citron. Roll up; place on a buttered cookie sheet, joining ends to form a ring. With scissors cut through ring from edge to center about ¾ of the way, making a cut every 1½ inches. Lift each division slightly upward and place on its side, turning every other one in the opposite direction to form a heart-shape section. Press entire ring flat to make dough an even height. Cover and allow to rise until doubled in bulk. Brush with egg white and sprinkle with almonds. Bake in preheated moderate oven (350°F.) for 30 minutes. When cold, spread with Confectioners' Icing. Makes 1 ring.

Confectioners' Icing

Add 1 tablespoon boiling water to ½ teaspoon fresh lemon juice; stir into ¾ cup sifted confectioners' sugar. Makes ⅓ cup.

BLACK-WALNUT CHOCOLATE DROPS

The mahogany stain on their hands did not come off easily, the pioneers learned, as they shucked black walnuts prior to spreading them out to be "cured" by the sun and frost. Later, they would be stored with the butternuts and hickory nuts. And after that they would lend their wonderful flavor to cakes, cookies, breads, and candy.

- ½ cup butter or margarine
- 1 cup sugar
- 1 egg
- 1 egg yolk
- 3 ounces (3 squares) unsweetened chocolate, melted
- 1 teaspoon vanilla extract
- 1¾ cups sifted all-purpose flour
- ½ teaspoon each of baking soda and baking powder
- ¼ teaspoon salt
- ½ cup milk
- 1 cup raisins
- 1 cup coarsely chopped black walnuts
- Chocolate Frosting

Cream butter until light and fluffy. Gradually beat in sugar. Add egg and egg yolk and beat well. Add chocolate and vanilla. Sift flour with baking soda, baking powder, and salt and add alternately with milk to butter mixture. Stir in raisins and nuts. Drop by teaspoonfuls onto buttered cookie sheets. Bake in preheated moderate oven (350°F.) for 12 to 14 minutes. When cold, spread with Chocolate Frosting. Store in airtight container. Makes 4 dozen.

Chocolate Frosting

Combine 1½ ounces (1½ squares) unsweetened chocolate, melted, 1 egg yolk, and 3 tablespoons light cream. Add 1¼ cups sifted confectioners' sugar and mix well. Makes about ¾ cup.

DANISH KRINGLE

- 1 tablespoon sugar
- 1 teaspoon salt
- 2 cups sifted all-purpose flour
- ½ cup butter or margarine
- 1 package active dry yeast or 1 cake compressed yeast
- ¼ cup warm water*
- 1 egg
- ¼ cup cold milk
- Filling
- Cut dates, chopped pecans, or almond paste
- Confectioners' Icing (triple recipe at left)

Sift together sugar, salt, and flour; cut in butter until mixture resembles coarse cornmeal. *Sprinkle dry yeast or crumble cake yeast into warm water. Use very warm water (105°F. to 115°F.) for dry yeast; use lukewarm (80°F. to 90°F.) for compressed. Let stand for a few minutes, then stir until dissolved. Beat egg until thick and lemon-colored; using a fork, stir egg, milk, and yeast mixture lightly into flour mixture. Refrigerate overnight. Turn out on lightly floured board. Divide into thirds. Cover and let stand for 10 minutes. Roll each part into a rectangle 9 inches wide and as long as it will roll without breaking; it should be thin.

Spread one third of Filling mixture down the center of each rectangle of dough. Top this with a thin layer of dates, prunes, chopped pecans, or almond paste. Fold one edge of dough over the filling and top this with the other. Seal all edges well. Place on buttered cookie sheet in form of an oval or horseshoe. Let rise in a warm place for 1 hour. Bake in preheated moderate oven (375°F.) for 20 to 25 minutes. Frost with Confectioners' Icing while hot. Makes 3 Kringles.

Filling

Cream together ½ cup butter or margarine, ¾ cup sugar, and 1 teaspoon ground cinnamon.

PRUNE KOLACHE

- 1 package active dry yeast or 1 cake compressed yeast
- 2 tablespoons water*
- 4 cups sifted all-purpose flour
- ¼ cup sugar
- 1 teaspoon salt
- 1 teaspoon grated lemon rind
- ¾ cup butter
- 3 egg yolks
- 1 cup heavy cream
- Prune Filling or jam
- Confectioners' Icing (double recipe, at left)

*Use very warm water (105°F. to 115°F.) for dry yeast; use lukewarm (80°F.

to 90°F.) for compressed. Sprinkle dry yeast or crumble cake into water. Let stand for a few minutes; then stir until dissolved. Sift flour with sugar and salt. Add grated lemon rind and yeast; blend in butter. Beat egg yolks and add cream; combine with flour mixture. Blend well. Cover bowl tightly. Refrigerate overnight. Knead several times and roll on lightly floured board to ¼-inch thickness. Cut with 2-inch cutter and place rounds on ungreased cookie sheets. Cover and let rise in warm place until double in bulk, about 1 hour. Using fingertips, make a depression in the center of each Kolache. Fill with Prune Filling. Bake in preheated moderate oven (375°F.) for about 10 minutes. While warm, frost with Confectioners' Icing. Makes 4 to 5 dozen.

Prune Filling

Soak 1½ cups prunes in water overnight. Simmer, covered, until tender; drain. Pit prunes and mash with fork. Add ¼ cup sugar and ½ teaspoon ground cinnamon.

SOUR-CREAM PEACH PIE

- 1 unbaked 9-inch pie shell and pastry strips
- 7 or 8 peaches, peeled and sliced
- ⅓ cup all-purpose flour
- Sugar
- ¼ teaspoon salt
- 1 cup dairy sour cream
- ¼ teaspoon cinnamon

Fill pie shell with sliced peaches. Blend together the flour, 1 cup sugar, and the salt. Stir in the sour cream and pour over the peaches. Arrange strips of pastry over the peaches, lattice-fashion. Sprinkle generously with a mixture of 2 tablespoons sugar and cinnamon. Bake in preheated hot oven (425°F.) for 15 minutes. Reduce heat to 350°F. and bake for 40 minutes longer.

CONCORD GRAPE PIE

- 5 cups Concord grapes
- Sugar
- 1 tablespoon fresh lemon juice
- ¼ cup all-purpose flour
- ⅛ teaspoon salt
- Pastry for 2-crust pie
- Heavy cream

Remove skins from washed grapes by pinching at end opposite the stem. Reserve the skins. Bring pulp to a boil; simmer for 3 or 4 minutes or until pulp is soft. Put through sieve to remove pits. Mix strained pulp with grape skins, 1 to 1¼ cups sugar (depending upon sweetness of grapes), lemon juice, flour, and salt. Pour into 9-inch pastry-lined pie pan. Adjust top crust; flute edges and cut vents in crust. Brush pie top with cream, and sprinkle with sugar. Bake in preheated hot oven (400°F.) for 35 to 40 minutes.

MILK—An opaque white, yellowish, or bluish liquid secreted by the mammary glands of female mammals for the nourishment of their young. Milk is a complete and adequate diet for the very young of its own species, although lacking, perhaps, some of the nutritive needs of adults, and some needs of the young of another species, i.e.: cow's milk does not have enough vitamin C for human infants.

Examined under the microscope, milk is seen as a transparent fluid containing great numbers of minute fat globules suspended together with casein (protein), sugar, and water. Cow's milk, which is the animal milk almost exclusively drunk in the United States, varies in composition from eighty-four to ninety per cent water and sixteen to ten per cent solids. These solids include two to seven per cent fat, two-and-a-half to four-and-a-half per cent casein, two to six per cent sugar, a small amount of albumin, large amounts of calcium and potassium, appreciable amounts of vitamins A, C, D, and the B vitamins thiamine and riboflavin. Almost all the fluid milk sold in the United States has some vitamin D added to it.

The major by-products of milk include butter, sweet cream, dairy sour cream, cheese, yogurt, and various frozen desserts.

Other milk-like liquids known as "milk," are plant latex, coconut juice, and the contents of an unripe kernel of grain. The Indians of America, for instance, drank "milks" made from corn, chestnuts, or hickory nuts.

Milk has been highly regarded from the earliest times. The Sumerians, who flourished some 5,000 years ago in what is now Iraq, were one of the first dairy people. Isis, the principal goddess of ancient Egypt and patroness of agriculture, has been represented in the form of a woman with the horns of a cow, an animal sacred to her. At least 3,500 years ago, hymns in Sanskrit, the ancient language of India, praised the cow. In the Bible, God speaks to Moses of the promised land: "And I am come down to deliver them out of the hand of the Egyptians, . . . unto a land flowing with milk and honey" (Exodus 3.8).

The Greeks and Romans used milk for the making of cheese. The Vikings took cows with them on their voyages to provide daily nourishment. In the Middle Ages and the Renaissance period in Europe, towns had communal cows which provided milk for all the inhabitants. This practice was carried over to the New World by the colonists, who used to pasture their cows together. The Boston Commons, a beautiful historic park

in Massachusetts, was originally a commons for grazing cows.

The first group of American colonists who arrived in Virginia in 1607 brought no cattle with them and the years that followed were hard ones. But in June of 1610 the new Governor of Virginia, Lord Delaware, arrived, bringing, among other things, some cows. This was the saving of the colony and more than 100 cattle were brought in the next year.

In 1619, John Pory, the first secretary of Virginia reported: "Three things there bee which in fewe years may bring this Colony to perfection; the English plough, Vineyards, and Cattle. For cattle they do mightily increase here . . . and are much greater in stature, than the race of them first brought out of England." By 1649 there were 20,000 cattle in Virginia. Today there are more than 15,500,000 milk cows in the United States, and American methods of modern dairy farming are highly specialized. They have resulted in the milk from American cows being the best in the world.

People of other lands drink milk from animals other than cows. The Egyptians use their water buffaloes for milk as well as for work. In Iraq the camel serves as a combination desert car and milk producer. This beast can travel for days without food or water and still provide milk every day. In Peru the llamas flourish in the steep mountain crags and supplement the milk from the few Peruvian cows. Goats are raised in Italy and Greece, where lush pasturage for cows is scarce. Other animals which have been milked since early times are sheep, mares, asses, and zebras.

Some cultures depend upon milk as practically their only food. Various tribes in Africa, the European Lapps, some pastoral groups in Central Asia, and the Todas of India are completely dependent on milk. In India and Africa milk is surrounded with ceremony.

There are also cultures which look askance on milk, and consider it unfit for human consumption. The Chinese, for instance, do not include milk in their diets. They consider it revolting and unclean. The Western world, however, is solidly in favor of milk in all its forms and in America milk is the favorite beverage of young and old, greatly to their advantage.

Availability and Purchasing Guide—There are several types of milk, all of them widely available: whole milk, skim milk, canned milk, and dried milk.

☐ **Whole Milk**—Fresh whole milk is available pasteurized, homogenized, fortified, and with chocolate flavoring added.

Pasteurized Milk: Milk which has been heated to kill any harmful bacteria and

then cooled immediately to 50°F. or lower. In rural areas some raw (unpasteurized) milk is available but it may not be safe, and pasteurization preceding the sale of milk is required in most areas of the United States.

Homogenized Milk: Pasteurized milk in which the particles have been broken up and evenly distributed throughout the milk by a mechanical process. In homogenized milk the cream does not rise to the top of the container as it does in nonhomogenized milk. Homogenized milk forms a softer curd in the stomach and is more easily digested.

Fortified Milk: Pasteurized milk containing added amounts of one or more of the essential nutrients present in milk. The most common addition is vitamin D. *Low-sodium milk,* used for special diets, is available in fluid form in very limited areas, generally on the West Coast. It is milk from which 90 per cent of the sodium has been removed and replaced with potassium. Part of the B vitamins and calcium are lost in the process. Low-sodium milk in powdered form is available at drugstores.

Chocolate Milk: Pasteurized milk to which chocolate syrup or cocoa is added. Vanilla, salt, sugar, and a stabilizer may also be added to keep the drink well mixed.

Whole milk is also available canned, either as evaporated milk or as condensed milk.

Evaporated Milk: Homogenized whole milk from which about 60 per cent of the water has been removed by heating. Vitamin D is added to provide 400 International Units per pint of evaporated milk. When diluted with an equal amount of water, it has about the same food value as fresh whole milk.

Condensed Milk: Milk made by evaporating a mixture of whole milk and sugar. It differs from the unsweetened evaporated milk only in the addition of the sugar which accounts for 40 to 45 per cent of the final product.

In limited quantities, whole dry milk from which the water has been removed is available in powdered form. It requires refrigeration.

☐ **Skim Milk**—Fresh milk from which some fat has been removed is available as fluid skim milk, buttermilk, fortified skim milk, and flavored milk drinks.

Fluid Skim Milk: Made of whole milk from which some fat has been removed. The milk fat remaining usually varies from 1 to 2 per cent.

Buttermilk: Milk to which a lactic-acid-producing culture is added. (Generally the milk used is skim, although buttermilk may occasionally be produced from whole milk, concentrated fluid milk, or reconstituted nonfat dry milk.) Butter granules may be added to enhance the flavor. *Acidophilus milk* is a form of buttermilk used for special diets and available in fluid form in very limited quantities. In powdered form it can be obtained at drugstores.

Fortified Skim Milk: Skim milk to which vitamins, including vitamin C, and minerals are added. Each quart usually contains the minimum daily vitamin and mineral requirements for adults.

Flavored Milk Drinks: Skim or partly skimmed milk to which cocoa and sugar or chocolate syrup has been added. Available in liquid form and also as a dry instant powder. The butterfat content is frequently about 2.2 per cent, otherwise these products are similar to flavored milk.

Skim milk is also available as nonfat dry milk particles. It is made by removing water and fat from fresh fluid whole milk and is reconstituted as skim milk by the addition of water.

☐ **Infant Formulas**—Many infant formulas may include cow's milk, goat's milk, or human milk, depending on the type of diet recommended for the infant and the infant's general state of health. Some formulas come canned and need only to be mixed with water and poured into sterilized bottles. Human milk is available frozen for special infant diets.

Storage—Fresh milk should be stored in the refrigerator immediately. Once canned milk has been opened, it should be refrigerated. When using dry milks, reseal the package, or store in an airtight container.

☐ Milk, refrigerator shelf: 3 to 4 days
☐ Cultured milk products, refrigerator shelf: 10 to 14 days
☐ Canned milk products, kitchen shelf: 1 year
☐ Canned milk products, refrigerator shelf, opened: 10 days

Nutritive Food Values—Milk is an excellent source of protein, calcium, phosphorus, riboflavin, and a fair source of thiamine and vitamin A (if whole milk). It

FOOD	SIZE OF PORTION	CALORIES
Milk, whole	1 glass (8 ounces)	165
Milk, skim or buttermilk	1 glass (8 ounces)	90
Milk, chocolate drink	1 glass (8 ounces)	190
Milk, chocolate	1 glass (8 ounces)	205
Milk, dried whole milk, granules	1 cup	515
Milk, dried whole milk, reconstituted	1 cup	139
Milk, dried nonfat, granules	1 cup	290
Milk, dried nonfat, reconstituted	1 cup	81
Milk, evaporated	1 cup	345
Milk, evaporated, reconstituted	1 cup	173
Milk, sweetened condensed	1 cup	985
Milk, skimmed fortified products	1 glass (8 ounces)	105

is considered an almost perfect food, lacking only vitamin C, iron, and bulk. Milk proteins are essential for growth and repair and are a good supplement to the incomplete proteins of grains.

Since the fat in milk is emulsified, it is easily digested and milk sugar (lactose) increases calcium absorption by the intestines and does not ferment within the colon.

Basic Preparation

☐ **To Cook Milk**—Even, moderate temperatures are recommended for cooking milk.

Skin formation may occur during the heating of milk and may be prevented by covering the pan, diluting the milk, or by the presence of fat floating on the surface. High temperatures cause production of a tough skin.

Milk scorches easily when heated. This may be prevented by stirring over low heat or by heating over hot water.

☐ **To Coagulate Milk**—Milk may be soured by the addition of acid: 1 tablespoon vinegar per cup milk.

Milk may also be coagulated by the addition of rennin (as in making junket). Boiling the milk before adding rennin prevents formation of a firm clot. Excessive stirring after adding the rennin to the milk also breaks the clot. Such desserts should be made in individual molds or dishes since cutting after the clot has formed causes syneresis, or separation of the watery portion of the milk.

☐ **To Use Evaporated Milk**—One half cup evaporated milk plus ½ cup water = 1 cup whole milk. After dilution, evaporated milk may be substituted for whole milk in recipes. Some recipes are especially designed to use undiluted evaporated milk.

Undiluted evaporated milk lends the richness of cream and double the food value of milk to sauces, custards, and cream pie fillings. It produces a firmer custard, however, and it may be desirable to reduce other thickening agents, such as egg or flour.

Undiluted evaporated milk may be used as a binding agent in meat loaves or to coat croquettes and other foods to be breaded.

Evaporated milk may be used in yeast breads without being scalded. Breads with a higher percentage of milk solids remain moist and fresh longer, and also brown more during baking.

Evaporated milk may be whipped and substituted for whipped cream in some recipes. It triples in volume when whipped: Measure the amount desired and pour into ice-cube tray. Place in freezing compartment to chill until fine

ice crystals form around edge. Chill bowl and beater at same time. Never dilute evaporated milk to be whipped. Turn chilled evaporated milk into cold bowl and whip rapidly with cold beater (electric mixer is easier) until it is stiff and will hold a peak. Use immediately.

The whipped milk will stand up longer with the addition of 2 tablespoons lemon juice for each cup evaporated milk used (measured before whipping). Add fresh lemon juice after whipping and whip just until blended in. For an even more stable whip (i.e., toppings), soften ½ teaspoon unflavored gelatin in 2 teaspoons cold water and dissolve in 1 cup scalded evaporated milk. Chill as above and whip. Add ¼ cup sugar and whip only until blended.

☐ **To Use Condensed Milk**—Condensed milk is used mainly in desserts, candies, and frostings. For good results, use recipes specifically developed for condensed milk.

☐ **To Use Dried Milk**—Once dried milk is reconstituted, refrigerate and use as fresh skim milk.

Reconstitute according to package directions.

Instant nonfat dry milk may be used to replace whole-milk solids or to enrich a recipe with additional nonfat milk solids. The instant nonfat dry milk may be blended into the dry ingredients or added to liquid ingredients in both instances. Follow recipe directions for reliable results. As with evaporated milk, enriching baked goods with additional milk solids in the form of instant nonfat dry milk produces better browning and longer keeping qualities.

In hamburgers, meat loaves, and croquettes, instant nonfat dry milk adds tenderness and flavor (and food value) by absorbing and holding meat and juices.

Instant nonfat dry milk may be whipped and used for toppings, frozen and chiffon desserts, and salads and fluffy salad dressings. Follow package directions to prepare whipped instant nonfat dry milk. Any cool, thickened mixture, such as partially set gelatin, fruit sauce, or cooked custard, may be folded into the whipped milk. Or the instant nonfat dry milk may be sprinkled over partially set gelatin and whipped together until stiff peaks form; this mixture will about triple in volume and may be used as a base for Bavarians, parfaits, etc.

☐ **To Use Buttermilk**—When buttermilk is substituted for fresh milk in a recipe using baking powder, ¼ teaspoon baking soda plus ½ cup buttermilk = 1 teaspoon baking powder plus ½ cup fresh milk.

Strawberry Frosted

MILK SHAKE—A drink in which milk is shaken or blended together with such other ingredients as ice cream, fruit, or flavorings. Although a thick mixture, milk shakes are sipped, often through a straw. They should be frothy and made quickly from chilled ingredients.

A milk shake is called a "frosted" when made with ice cream which has been completely blended into the milk and a "float" when the ice cream is not blended but is floating in the milk.

Milk shakes are of American origin, served at sweet shops, lunch counters, and drugstore counters. They are a convenient way of absorbing nourishment in an easy and appetizing manner. They can be fortified with malt, eggs, and substantial fruit like bananas.

Using an electric blender is the easiest way to make a milk shake. An electric mixer is also helpful. Milk shakes can be made by pouring the milk and flavoring from one container into another to blend them, or by using a hand beater.

VANILLA MILK SHAKE

Add ¼ teaspoon vanilla extract to 1 cup whole milk; mix well. Makes 1 serving.

SPICED FRUIT MILK SHAKE

Put 3 tablespoons strained canned baby fruit in a tall glass. Add ½ teaspoon sugar and a dash of ground cinnamon, and fill with chilled milk. Shake well.

MOCHA CREAM SHAKE

    4 teaspoons sugar
    2 tablespoons instant coffee powder
    ½ cup chocolate syrup
    2 scoops chocolate ice cream
    3 cups cold milk

Combine sugar, coffee, syrup, and ice cream in blender container. Cover and whirl at high speed. Remove cover (only if blender is type with no opening in lid) and, with motor on, gradually add milk. Pour into tall glasses. Makes 4 servings. **Note:** Only a large blender can be used for this amount. In a smaller blender prepare only half of recipe at one time.

PRUNE SHAKE

    2 cups milk
    8 pitted cooked prunes
    ½ cup prune juice
    2 tablespoons sherry
    2 teaspoons honey

Combine ingredients in blender container. Cover and whirl at high speed until smooth. Pour into 4-ounce glasses. Makes 4 servings.

CHOCOLATE FROSTED

With rotary beater, beat together 4 cups chocolate milk and 1 cup chocolate or vanilla ice cream. Serve in tall glasses with a sprinkling of grated unsweetened chocolate. Makes 4 servings.

BANANA FROSTED

Sieve 2 ripe bananas, beat until smooth

or whirl in blender. Add 1 cup vanilla ice cream and 4 cups whole milk. Beat or whirl in blender until smooth. Serve in tall glasses. Makes 4 servings.

STRAWBERRY FROSTED

1 pint fresh strawberries
⅓ to ½ cup sugar, as desired
2 cups whole milk
1 cup vanilla or strawberry ice cream
  Whipped cream

Clean berries, reserving 4 for decoration. Force remaining berries through a sieve. Add sugar and chill. Add milk and ice cream and stir until ice cream is partially melted. Pour into glasses, and top each serving with whipped cream and a whole berry. Makes 4 servings.

POLKA-DOT PUNCH FLOAT

¼ cup honey
3 cups cold milk
1 teaspoon ground cinnamon
¼ teaspoon each of ground ginger
  and nutmeg
1½ cups vanilla ice cream
  Gumdrops

Combine honey, milk, and spices in blender container. Cover and blend at low speed for 30 seconds. Pour into 4 tall glasses and top with a scoop of ice cream. Top with sliced gumdrops. Makes 4 servings.

CHOCOLATE FLOAT

Combine 1½ or 2 tablespoons chocolate syrup with 1 cup milk. Beat with egg beater or electric mixer. Pour into glass and add 1 small scoop of vanilla, chocolate, or coffee ice cream. Makes 1 serving.

DUTCH DELIGHT FLOAT

1 cup milk
2 scoops vanilla ice cream
2 tablespoons creamy peanut butter
2 scoops chocolate ice cream

Combine milk, vanilla ice cream, and peanut butter in blender container. Whirl at high speed for 1 minute. Pour into tall glasses and top with chocolate ice cream. Makes 1 large drink.

BERRY FLOAT

1 package (10 ounces) frozen
  raspberries
3 cups milk, chilled
1 pint strawberry ice cream
½ teaspoon vanilla extract

Break up frozen raspberries; add with 1 cup milk to blender container. Cover and whirl at high speed until smooth. Add remaining milk, half of ice cream, and the vanilla. Blend until just mixed. Pour into tall glasses and top with remaining ice cream. Makes 4 servings.

Note: Must be prepared in a blender with at least a 5-cup capacity; or prepare half of recipe at one time.

FROSTED MINT CHOCOLATE FLOAT

Pour 1 cup chilled milk into tall glass. Add 1 to 2 tablespoons chocolate syrup and stir until blended. Add a drop or two of peppermint extract; top with a scoop of vanilla or chocolate ice cream and serve at once. Makes 1 serving.

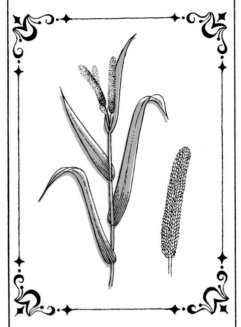

MILLET—Any of a large number of small-seeded cereal and forage grasses, or the grain or seed of these grasses. It is generally grown as a cereal in Asia and Africa, providing a diet staple for one third of the world's population. In Europe and North America it is used almost wholly as forage.

Millets, members of the *Gramineae,* or grass, family are thought to have been domesticated in eastern Asia over 4,000 years ago. Their importance as a grain and the extent of their spread and cultivation are indicated by the great variety of names applied to the major genera. *Panicum milaceum,* the common, or true, millet, is also known as Broom-corn, proso, Indian, and hog millet. Varieties of the millet genus *Echinochloa* are called Japanese barnyard millet; Deccan, Guinea, or barnyard grass, and Australian millet. *Setaria italica,* foxtail millet, is also known as Italian, Turkestan, German, Kursk, and Hungarian millet. *Pennisetum glaucum,* pearl millet, is called *bajri* in India, and is the cattail millet of the southeastern United States. This variety is a popular food in India, Egypt, and Africa, where it is grown during the rainy season. Flour made from the grain is used for bread and cake. *Eleusine coracana,* African millet, is also called *ragé* and finger millet. It is grown from Indonesia to North Africa and is especially important in India where flour made from it is used for puddings and cakes, and a fermented beverage is made from the grain.

Availability—In health and specialty food stores and in oriental food stores, as whole grain, grits, and ground millet.

Storage

☐ Kitchen shelf, dry: 6 months
☐ Refrigerator shelf, cooked and covered: 2 to 4 days

Nutritive Food Values—High in carbohydrates and proteins.

☐ Whole grain, 3½ ounces, uncooked = 327 calories

Basic Preparation—Boil like rice or barley, or brown first and then add liquid. Use like rice, barley, and other cereals for porridge or in pilafs.

MILLET PORRIDGE

½ cup shelled millet seed
1 cup water
½ teaspoon salt

Bring all ingredients to a boil and boil for 1 minute. Cover and simmer for 15 minutes, or until soft. Millet thickens in cooking; if necessary thin with a little hot milk or water. Serve as any hot cereal with cream, honey, syrup, raisins, or other fruit. Makes 3 or 4 servings.

MILLET PILAF

1 cup shelled millet seed
1 medium onion, chopped
1 teaspoon salt
¼ teaspoon pepper
¼ cup butter or margarine
3 cups boiling water or beef or
  chicken bouillon

Put millet into a dry heavy skillet or top-stove casserole. Over medium heat, cook millet, stirring constantly, for 2 minutes, or until golden-brown. Add remaining ingredients; millet will sizzle. Simmer, tightly covered, over low heat for 15 minutes or until liquid is absorbed. Stir occasionally, and if necessary, add a little more boiling water to prevent sticking. Serve instead of potatoes. Makes 4 servings.

MINCE—A method of cutting food into very small pieces. When a food is minced, the pieces still retain some shape in comparison to ground food, in which all shape is lost, and to chopped food, in which the pieces are larger. Food is minced so that it can be more easily incorporated with other foods or cooked more quickly.

MINCEMEAT—A cooked mixture of minced foods and spices. Mincemeats were originally developed as an alternative to smoking or drying as a method of preserving meat, but over the years many meatless versions have evolved. A typical mincemeat always contains raisins, a mixture of spices, and a fruit such as apples, pears, or tomatoes. It may contain meat, currants, candied fruits, and brandy, rum, or other liquor.

Commercially prepared mincemeats include ready-to-use varieties plain or with brandy or rum added, which are available in jars; and dried, condensed mincemeats which are packaged. The latter are reconstituted by the addition of water, or can be crumbled and used dry, as one would use any minced dried fruit. Also available, canned, is mincemeat pie filling.

PILGRIM MINCEMEAT

3½ pounds boneless brisket of beef
2 tablespoons salt
Water
1¼ pounds suet
7½ pounds firm apples
3 quarts cider
5 pounds sugar
½ teaspoon white pepper
2 tablespoons each of ground cloves, cinnamon, and grated nutmeg
1 tablespoon each of allspice and mace
Juice of 3 medium oranges
2 (15-ounce) packages seeded raisins
2 pounds currants
3 ounces each of candied orange peel, lemon peel, and citron
¼ pound each of candied pineapple and cherries

Simmer beef with 1 tablespoon salt in enough water to cover for 2½ hours. Allow to cool in same water. Remove tissue from suet. Peel and core apples. Force lean beef, suet, and apples through food chopper, using medium knife. Boil 2 quarts cider down to 1 quart. Add sugar. When mixture boils again, add suet, beef, and apples. Cook over low heat for 20 minutes, stirring often. Add spices, orange juice, chopped fruit, remaining salt, and cider. Mix thoroughly and bring to a boil, stirring constantly. Pack into hot sterilized pint jars and seal. One pint jar makes enough filling for an 8-inch pie. If desired, 1 pint brandy and 1 pint sherry may be used in place of the last quart of cider. Bring mincemeat to a boil after fruit has been added, cool and mix in brandy and sherry before packing mincemeat in jars. Makes about 16 pints.

ENGLISH MINCEMEAT

4¾ cups (1½ pounds) dried currants
4½ cups (2 pounds) seedless raisins
2 cups (¾ pound) mixed fruit peel
1 cup (⅓ pound) blanched almonds
6 large apples
¼ cup fresh lemon juice
1½ cups firmly packed brown sugar
1 teaspoon grated lemon peel
1 teaspoon salt
1 teaspoon each of ground allspice, cinnamon, and nutmeg
6 bananas
1 cup butter or margarine
½ cup (¼ pound) glacé cherries, chopped
½ cup brandy or rum

Clean currants and raisins; chop mixed peel and almonds. Grate apples without

removing the skins. Combine with lemon juice, brown sugar, lemon peel, salt, and spices. Peel bananas and fry in butter; add with remaining ingredients to fruit mixture. Turn into a large covered jar. Do not keep for more than 2 weeks. Makes 4 quarts.

MEATLESS MINCEMEAT

1 large orange
1 small lemon
1 box (15 ounces) seedless raisins
3 pounds (9 medium) tart apples, cored
1½ cups cider
3 cups firmly packed brown sugar
1½ teaspoons salt
1½ teaspoons each of powdered cinnamon, nutmeg, and cloves

Remove seeds from orange and lemon. Using coarse blade, force fruit through food chopper with raisins and unpeeled apples. Add cider. Put in kettle and bring to boil. Simmer, uncovered, for 15 minutes. Add remaining ingredients, and simmer for 20 minutes longer, or until thick. Makes enough filling for three 9-inch pies.

GREEN-TOMATO MINCEMEAT

4 quarts (after grinding) green tomatoes
4 quarts chopped peeled tart apples
2 pounds raisins, chopped or coarsely ground
1 cup ground beef suet
1 cup vinegar
2 tablespoons each of cinnamon and salt
1 teaspoon each of ground cloves and allspice
2 pounds brown sugar
½ cup molasses

Force tomatoes through food chopper. Drain. Put in large kettle, and cover with boiling water. Boil for 5 minutes. Drain, and repeat. Drain, and add remaining ingredients. Bring to boil; simmer until thick. Put in hot sterilized jars and seal. Makes about 8 pints.

■ For Pie—Sprinkle mincemeat with seedless raisins, and dot with 2 tablespoons butter. Adjust top crust, and bake in preheated hot oven (425°F.) for about 30 minutes.

SPICY PEAR MINCEMEAT

5 pounds firm winter pears
1 pound seedless raisins
4 cups sugar
¾ cup cider vinegar
1½ tablespoons each of ground cinnamon, nutmeg, and allspice
2 teaspoons ground cloves

Wash and peel pears. Force through food chopper, using coarse blade. There should be about 8 cups. Put in large saucepan with remaining ingredients. Cook, uncovered, for 2 hours, or until thick and pears are transparent, stirring frequently. Ladle into hot sterilized jars and seal at once. Makes about 2 quarts.

Spicy Apple Mincemeat

Follow recipe above, substituting 5 pounds baking apples for pears.

Mincemeat Glamour

by Marion Flexner

MAKE-YOUR-OWN MINCEMEAT
From an 18th-century recipe

1 pound lean beef (top round or chuck), ground
Water
5 cups firmly packed shredded peeled apples
¾ cup each of diced candied lemon peel, orange peel, and citron
1 pound raisins, seeded or seedless, or ½ pound of each
1 pound dried currants
1 large orange, juice and grated rind
1 lemon, juice and grated rind
½ pound finely ground beef suet, all skin removed
1½ pounds (3⅜ cups) dark brown sugar
1½ teaspoons salt
1½ teaspoons each of ground allspice, cinnamon, cloves, coriander, mace, and nutmeg
1 cup bourbon or brandy
1 cup rum or sherry

Simmer beef in 2 cups of water, covered, for about 10 minutes. Put beef and broth in a large kettle and add all other ingredients except liquors. Let come to a hard boil; then turn heat low and simmer for about 5 minutes, stirring to keep from sticking and to assure even distribution of spices and fat through the mixture. Let cool; then add spirits. Place in jars or a single gallon jar and store in a cool dark place for 3 weeks before using. Frozen, it will keep up to 6 months. Makes 4 quarts.

■ For Pie—Fill pastry-lined pie pan with mincemeat. Adjust top crust or lattice top, and bake in preheated hot oven (425°F.) for about 30 minutes.

DRESSED-UP BOUGHT MINCEMEAT

To 2 cups bought mincemeat add ½ cup shredded peeled apple; about 1 teaspoon mixed spices, especially ground cinnamon, nutmeg, and coriander; 2 tablespoons each of diced candied citron, orange peel, and lemon peel; 2 teaspoons fresh orange juice and 1 teaspoon fresh lemon juice; 2 tablespoons whisky or brandy; 1 to 2 tablespoons (to taste) rum or sherry. Mix well, cover, and let set for at least 24 hours before using.

Note: If using dry mincemeat, reconstitute before "dressing up."

OLD COLONY GINGERBREAD

1 cup plus 2 tablespoons sifted
all-purpose flour
1¼ teaspoons baking powder
¼ teaspoon baking soda
1 teaspoon ground ginger
¼ teaspoon each of ground cloves
and nutmeg
¾ teaspoon ground cinnamon
⅛ teaspoon salt
⅓ cup butter and lard mixed, or use
shortening in place of lard
½ cup boiling water or coffee
⅓ cup firmly packed dark brown sugar
½ cup unsulphured dark molasses
1 egg, well beaten
⅓ cup mincemeat

Sift dry ingredients together. Add shortenings to boiling water and stir until dissolved. Then add sugar and molasses. Combine with dry ingredients, adding egg and beating until batter is smooth. Fold in mincemeat. Pour batter into lightly buttered and floured 9-inch square cake pan. Bake in preheated moderate oven (350°F.) for 35 to 40 minutes. Cut into squares and serve warm or cool, plain or with a lemon sauce. Makes 8 to 9 servings.

MINCEMEAT DELIGHT

2 cups shelled pecans
⅔ cup firmly packed light brown sugar
½ teaspoon instant coffee powder
½ teaspoon ground cinnamon
¼ cup melted butter
Eggnog Chiffon Filling

Measure pecans, then put through finest blade of the food chopper along with the sugar which you add a little at a time. Add next 3 ingredients and mix well with your fingers. This forms a thick sticky paste. Butter a 9-inch springform pan very lightly. With fingers, press nut paste over bottom and sides of pan until they are completely covered. Patch any holes to prevent the filling leaking out. Press paste to make it firm. Bake in preheated moderate oven (350°F.) for 12 to 15 minutes, or until paste seems to just hold together. Do not overcook. The sides will brown before the bottom, but no matter. Remove from oven and cool. (You can use half the recipe in a 9-inch pie pan. Then 8 to 10 minutes should bake this crust.) Now spoon the whole Eggnog Chiffon Filling into baked pecan crust. Set in refrigerator. When filling is semifirm, decorate top with candied fruits and nuts. Chill until firm. To serve, place springform on round serving platter, remove sides, and bring to the table. Makes 12 to 16 servings.

Eggnog Chiffon Filling

2 envelopes unflavored gelatin
1½ cups milk
6 eggs, separated
½ cup sugar, or more to taste
1 cup mincemeat
2 tablespoons whisky or brandy
2 tablespoons rum or sherry
Few grains of salt

1 cup heavy cream
Candied fruits and nuts for garnishing
(optional)

Using a custard cup, soften gelatin in ½ cup of the milk. Stir quickly. Set cup in a small saucepan ¼ full of water and heat until gelatin melts. While the gelatin is melting, beat egg yolks with sugar. (Use an electric beater or rotary egg beater.) Add the rest of milk and the mincemeat, which have been allowed to boil for 1 minute in a saucepan. Place mixture in top part of a double boiler and cook, stirring constantly, until mixture is of the consistency of boiled custard and just coats the spoon. Add dissolved gelatin and set aside to cool to room temperature. Add the spirits to custard. Beat egg whites with salt. When very stiff, fold by hand into custard mixture. Beat cream until stiff but not buttery. Fold cream into custard mixture.

MINCEMEAT TEA LOAF

2 cups sifted all-purpose flour
½ teaspoon salt
½ teaspoon baking soda
1 teaspoon baking powder
¼ cup butter or margarine
⅔ cup firmly packed light brown sugar
2 eggs
3 tablespoons dairy sour cream
1 cup mincemeat
½ cup coarsely chopped pecans or
walnuts

Sift first 4 ingredients and set aside. Cream softened butter and sugar with an electric mixer, if handy. Add eggs, one at a time, beating well. Add sour cream. Fold into dry ingredients by hand, but do not overmix; this is a stiff batter. Fold in mincemeat and nuts. Place batter in lightly buttered loaf pan (9 x 5 x 3 inches). Press batter with back of spoon to pack solidly and to even it. Bake in preheated moderate oven (350°F.) until bread tests done, 50 to 60 minutes. Loosen edges with a dull knife if any batter has stuck to sides of pan. Let cool on a wire cake rack before slicing.
Note: This loaf slices beautifully the same day it is made, and when properly wrapped and stored in a tin box with a tight-fitting lid, it keeps for several weeks. Frozen, it keeps almost indefinitely.

MINCEMEAT LANE CAKES

Make any white cake—use your own recipe or a packaged mix. Spoon batter into lightly buttered and floured muffin pans and bake in preheated moderate oven (350°F.) until cakes test done, 20 to 25 minutes for average size. Cool. Remove centers. Then frost cupcakes with 7-minute frosting or any boiled white icing, being careful not to cover the holes in the centers. While frosting is still soft, sprinkle the top and sides generously with freshly grated coconut. Then fill the centers with this custard: Cream ½ cup

sugar with ½ cup butter. Gradually add 4 egg yolks. (Use an electric beater, if handy.) Add 1 rounded tablespoon flour, ½ cup mincemeat, few grains of salt, and ¼ cup sherry or bourbon. Pour into top part of a double boiler and cook, stirring constantly, until of the consistency of thick boiled custard. Remove from stove. Fold in ½ cup coarsely chopped toasted pecans. Cool. Makes 12 cupcakes.

MINCEMEAT ALASKA PIE

Bake an open 9-inch mincemeat pie, but use a deep pan. Cool. Just before serving, spread with 1 pint firm vanilla ice cream; slice it over top in 1-inch hunks. Spread immediately with Meringue, being sure to cover the rim to insulate the pie thoroughly. Place in preheated very hot oven (450°F.) until meringue turns golden.

Meringue

Beat 4 egg whites with a few grains of salt until stiff. Gradually add 1 cup sugar while beating; use an electric mixer if possible. Beat in 1 teaspoon each of vinegar and vanilla extract.

MINESTRONE—A thick Italian vegetable soup served with grated cheese. It may or may not contain meat and frequently contains pasta or rice. These last two are added for thickening and if omitted, dried beans or dried peas or both are added for the same purpose.

The word minestrone comes from *minestra,* which means soup and *one,* a suffix meaning "big." For many Italians minestrone is often the main dish at either supper or dinner. It is served with bread and followed by cheese and fruit.

There are definite regional differences in the contents of minestrone. The most famous minestrone comes from Milan, and it contains rice. The minestrone from Genoa contains basil. Generally, minestrones represent northern Italian cooking.

As with all basic dishes, there are many ways of making minestrone. Any vegetable ingredient and seasoning is all right if it suits the taste. Water may be used instead of beef bouillon, olive oil rather than butter, and so on. And also as with all dishes of this kind, feelings run high about what makes the best combination of ingredients. Some say that the vegetables should be cooked in the bouillon, and the oil or butter added later; others debate whether it is eaten hot or cold. Prudence and experience bring one to the conclusion that all minestrone is good if it is made with fresh ingredients and cooked slowly.

MINESTRONE MILANESE ALLA SAVINI

¼ cup butter
¼ cup olive oil
⅓ cup salt pork, diced

1 large onion, chopped
1 large carrot, diced
½ cup sliced zucchini
½ medium cabbage, shredded
3 quarts beef bouillon
½ pound red kidney beans, soaked and
ready to cook
2 medium potatoes, diced
1 cup uncooked rice
2 tablespoons minced parsley
1 garlic clove, mashed
¼ teaspoon ground thyme
½ cup grated Parmesan cheese

Heat butter and olive oil in deep kettle. Cook salt pork and onion in it until onion is soft and golden. Do not brown. Add carrot, zucchini, and cabbage. Cook, covered, for 5 minutes, stirring occasionally. Add bouillon and kidney beans. Simmer, covered, over low heat for 2 hours, or until beans are tender; add potatoes and rice. Cook over medium heat for 30 minutes, stirring frequently. Add parsley, garlic, and thyme. Lower heat and simmer, covered, for another 30 minutes, stirring occasionally. If soup is too thick, add a little hot water. Serve with grated Parmesan cheese. Makes 5 quarts.

MINESTRONE ALLA GENOVESE

1 cup white beans, washed and drained
2 tablespoons butter
2 tablespoons olive oil
1 large onion, thinly sliced
3 tablespoons chopped fresh basil
leaves, or basil to taste, or 1
tablespoon dried basil
3 tablespoons chopped parsley
2 medium fresh tomatoes, peeled and
chopped
½ cup diced celery
1 cup chopped raw escarole or Swiss
chard
1 large carrot, diced
1 large garlic clove, minced
2 quarts beef bouillon
Salt and pepper
¼ cup grated Parmesan cheese

Cook beans until tender according to package directions, reserving cooking water. In deep kettle heat butter and olive oil, add onion, herbs, other vegetables, and garlic, and cook for 15 minutes, stirring frequently. Add bouillon, beans and bean water, and salt and pepper to taste. Simmer, covered, over low heat for 1 hour. Serve with Parmesan cheese. Makes 2½ quarts.

MINESTRONE ALLA ROMANA

1 tablespoon olive oil
¼ cup minced salt pork
1 onion, minced
1 garlic clove, minced
1 celery stalk, minced
2 fresh tomatoes, peeled and cut into
pieces, or 2 large canned tomatoes
1 teaspoon salt
½ teaspoon pepper
¼ teaspoon ground sage
4 cups hot water or bouillon
2 cups cooked dried white beans
1 cup elbow macaroni
Grated Parmesan or Romano cheese

Heat oil in deep kettle. Add salt pork, onion, garlic, and celery. Cook over low heat until vegetables are soft, stirring

frequently. Add remaining ingredients except macaroni and cheese. Cook over low heat for 10 minutes. Bring to a boil, add macaroni, and cook until macaroni is soft. Serve with cheese. Makes 1½ quarts.

MINT *(Mentha)*—A fragrant herb of which there are over thirty species, a dozen of them cultivated in the United States. Among the most popular varieties of this upright plant with red-veined stems and sharply aromatic leaves are the well known peppermint and spearmint, as well as American apple mint, bergamot mint, curly mint, and red mint. The names indicate the difference either in flavor or in shape of the mint leaves.

The uses of mint leaves for cooking are indeed as many as the "sparks from Vulcan's furnace," the number which a 9th-century herbalist claimed represented the number of varieties of mint. The leaves, fresh or dried, add flavor to such appetizers as cranberry juice and fruit cup, and to soups, especially pea. Lamb, ham, and veal ragouts use mint, and fish is different and delicious when cooked with it. Cottage cheese perks up with mint added, as do cabbage, carrots, celery, potatoes, beans, or jellied salads. French dressing or vinegar may be flavored with mint and it is indispensable for the mint sauce (vinegar and chopped mint) traditionally served with lamb and for mint jelly, also served with lamb. Desserts such as custards, fruit compotes, and ice cream are flavored with mint; or it may be put in fruit punch, sugar syrup for beverages, and currant jelly. It forms the basis for the delicious and popular mint julep. The dried leaves make a refreshing tea, much drunk in Europe and among the Pennsylvania Dutch.

In addition to their leaves, mints have valuable essential oils which are made

into commercial flavoring for candy, chewing gum, and various medicinal remedies.

This popular herb was named by the Greeks and Romans. They believed that Pluto, the god of the underworld, had fallen in love with a beautiful nymph, Menthe. Persephone, Pluto's wife, in a fit of wifely pique changed the maiden into a plant that would grow where it could be stepped on. Since that day many people have had cause to be grateful to Persephone, for mint has been highly esteemed ever since.

Mint was so valuable that it is mentioned in the Bible as forming part of a tithe. It was used by the Assyrians as early as 3,000 B.C. for religious incantations. Later, the Greeks and Romans found many uses for the aromatic mint leaves. The 1st-century Roman cook book of Apicius records many recipes using mint, either fresh or dried: meat sauces, vegetables, and fish dishes were flavored with it.

Mint was probably introduced into Britain at the time of the Roman conquest. It was used by the people of the Middle Ages for many common ailments. One herbalist reports that "if it be oft eaten, it will slay worms." One does not know how often "oft" is, but it could hardly be more often than the sequence advised earlier by Pliny for the spleen. He had suggested mint would be of help "if tasted in the garden nine days consecutively, without plucking it, the person who bites it saying at the same time that he does so for the benefit of the spleen."

Mint, first as the popular spearmint, was brought very early to the American colonies by the English, who evidently could not do without the aromatic plant. It now grows wild here extensively, as it does in most countries where it is also cultivated.

Fresh mint can be grown in pots or in a shady, damp patch without great trouble. Mint is sold fresh or dried. The dried mint comes in leaves, and is never ground. Both fresh and dried mint should be crushed before using. Start with a little and add more to taste, or the dish may become too fragrant. For each serving ¼ to ½ teaspoon fresh mint, crushed before use, suffices. Less may be needed with dried mint.

Oil of peppermint and oil of spearmint and extracts of both of these are also available. These products should be used sparingly since they represent mint flavor in more concentrated form, the oils being even more concentrated than the extracts.

TRADITIONAL ENGLISH MINT
SAUCE FOR ROAST LAMB

1 cup fresh mint leaves

2 tablespoons fine granulated sugar
½ cup hot water
½ cup mild vinegar (not wine vinegar)

Crush mint leaves with 1 tablespoon of the sugar. Add hot water and remaining sugar. When dissolved, add vinegar. The sauce must be thick with mint. Let stand for about 2 hours before serving. Makes 1½ cups.

MINT JELLY
1½ cups firmly packed fresh mint leaves and stems
2¼ cups water
2 tablespoons strained fresh lemon juice
Green food coloring
3½ cups sugar
½ bottle liquid pectin

Wash mint leaves and stems, and put in a large saucepan; crush with a masher or drinking glass. Add the water and bring quickly to a boil. Remove from heat, cover, and let stand for 10 minutes. Strain and measure 1⅔ cups into large saucepan. Add lemon juice and a few drops of food coloring. Stir in sugar, put over high heat and bring to a boil, stirring constantly. At once stir in pectin. Then bring to a *full rolling boil and boil hard for 1 minute,* stirring constantly. Remove from heat, skim off foam with metal spoon, and pour quickly into hot sterilized jars. Seal. Makes about four ½-pint jars.

MINTED ONIONS
2 cups thinly sliced onions
Ice water
2 tablespoons chopped fresh mint
1 cup vinegar
⅔ cup sugar
½ teaspoon salt

Cover onion slices with ice water and let stand in refrigerator overnight. Drain, and add remaining ingredients. Serve as a relish, or on lettuce as a salad. Makes 2 cups, or 6 servings.

GREEN MINT VINEGAR
Bring 4 cups cider vinegar to a boil. Add 1 cup sugar and 2 cups spearmint leaves and young stem tips. Stir and crush. Boil for 4 or 5 minutes. Strain, and bottle in hot sterilized jars. Makes about 2 pints. Use in iced or fruit punches, or in salad dressings.

MINTED MELON WITH COINTREAU
Chill small ripe cantaloupes. When ready to serve, halve melons and remove seeds. Fill centers with orange sherbet. Pour 1 teaspoon Cointreau over each and sprinkle with chopped mint.

MINT PARFAIT
1 cup sugar
1 cup water
1 cup chopped fresh mint leaves
3 egg whites
Green food coloring
2 cups heavy cream, whipped

Make a syrup of sugar and water by boiling them together rapidly for 5 minutes. Remove from heat. Add mint leaves.

Cover and let steep for 1 hour. Strain through cheesecloth. Bring syrup to a boil and pour in a fine stream into stiffly beaten egg whites, beating constantly. Add 2 or 3 drops of green coloring. Fold in whipped cream. Pour into 2 freezer trays and freeze. Makes 8 to 10 servings.

PINEAPPLE-MINT SHERBET
1 teaspoon unflavored gelatin
¾ cup water
1 cup canned pineapple juice
½ cup sugar
About 1 cup (one 9-ounce can) crushed pineapple
1 tablespoon minced fresh mint
Juice of 1 lemon
Dash of salt
2 egg whites
Mint sprigs

Turn refrigerator control to coldest setting. Sprinkle gelatin on ¼ cup of the water and let stand for 5 minutes. Mix remaining ½ cup water, pineapple juice, and sugar; boil for 3 minutes. Add gelatin and stir until dissolved. Cool. Add remaining ingredients except last 2. Pour into refrigerator tray and freeze until mushy. Turn into chilled bowl; add unbeaten salted egg whites and whip until stiff. Pour into refrigerator tray and freeze until firm. Serve garnished with mint sprigs. Makes 4 to 6 servings.

MINT COOKIES
½ cup butter or margarine
½ cup sugar
1 egg
1 tablespoon crumbled dried mint
1 cup sifted all-purpose flour
1 teaspoon baking powder
¼ teaspoon salt

Cream butter and sugar; add egg and mint and mix well. Mix in sifted dry ingredients and drop by teaspoons onto ungreased cookie sheets. Bake in preheated moderate oven (375°F.) for 10 minutes. Makes 2 dozen.

THIN MINTS
3 cups sugar
1½ cups water
2½ tablespoons light corn syrup
Dash of salt
¼ teaspoon cream of tartar
½ teaspoon glycerin (buy in drugstore)
1 tablespoon shortening
Spearmint and peppermint extracts
Red and green food colorings

Mix sugar and water in saucepan. Bring to boil, stirring until sugar is dissolved. Cover tightly for 3 minutes to steam down crystals. Add corn syrup, salt, and cream of tartar. Cook without stirring until small amount of mixture forms a soft ball when dropped into very cold water (236°F. on a candy thermometer). Cool to lukewarm. Then beat with electric mixer or stir until stiff. Knead until free from lumps. Store in covered container for about 24 hours. Divide into halves. Put half in top part of double boiler and add ¼ teaspoon glycerin and 1½ teaspoons shortening. Add a few

drops of spearmint extract and red coloring to tint a delicate pink. Put over hot water and stir constantly until melted. Mixture should be just about as hot as the finger can stand. If too hot, mints will be hard and white spots will form on them. If not hot enough, they will be too soft. Drop from teaspoon onto wax paper to make thin round mints. Let harden. Repeat with other half of mixture, adding peppermint extract and tinting fondant a delicate green. Makes about 6 dozen.

MIREPOIX—The culinary term for an essence or concentrate of diced carrot, onion, and celery, cooked in butter with or without ham or bacon. It is added to sauces, soups, or stews to make them more flavorsome. It is always used in making a basic brown sauce which in its turn is used in making many other French sauces. Proportions are: ½ cup each of diced carrot, onion, and celery with ¼ cup diced ham cooked in ¼ cup butter until vegetables are very tender. Butter is drained off and used later with flour to thicken the sauce.

MIX—To blend several ingredients thoroughly into a homogeneous mixture. A spoon, fork, whisk, beater, or blender can be used for mixing.

The word mix is also used to describe a commercial blending of various ingredients. Mixes eliminate several steps in preparation and cooking: a time saver for the busy homemaker. The variety of mixes is endless, and more appear every day. They include gelatins, puddings, pie fillings, rennet desserts, dessert-topping mixes, and frostings; biscuit, muffin, popover, pancake, roll, pie, cookie, and cake mixes; as well as potato, rice, pasta, soup, salad dressing, gravy, and sauce mixes. Many meats, vegetables, and fruits come in mixes, and so do beverages, from coffee and cream to lemonade.

MOCHA—The word mocha originally referred to a certain kind of coffee grown in the Yemen district of Arabia and exported from the port of Mocha on the Red Sea. Mocha coffee beans are very fragrant and have been grown in Yemen since the 13th century. The town prospered by its shipping in the 16th and 17th centuries. Now, with coffee produced in huge commercial quantities in Brazil, Central America, and Africa, Mocha's trade has declined but its name still stands for top-quality coffee.

Alexander Pope, writing in the 18th century, declared: "As long as Mocha's happy tree shall grow,/While berries crackle, or while mills shall go . . ./ Or graceful bitters shall delight the taste/ So long her honors, name, and praise shall last."

The legendary discoverer of mocha was Hadjii Omar, who is said to have been exiled from the town, but who returned there when he was shown the fragrant coffee bush by Mohammed. The Moslems praise coffee in poem and prose. Abd-al-Kadir wrote: "Coffee! You dissolve all our cares. You are the drink of friends and of the chosen of Allah. You give health to all who seek learning."

When Solomon Aga, the ambassador of the Sultan to the court of Louis XIV, introduced mocha to France, Mme. de Sevigné, the famous letter writer, wrote in 1669: "Frenchmen will never swallow . . . coffee." She was wrong.

It may well be the French who are responsible for the use of the word mocha to describe the flavored beverage mocha which is a combination of coffee and chocolate. Chocolate had been brought to France by Maria Theresa, the wife of Louis XIV, when she came from Spain to marry the monarch. And it was the Marquis de Louvois, Louis' Minister of War, who lent his name to Café Louvois, a mixture of half coffee and half chocolate, served in large demitasses with whipped cream.

Today, mocha is the accepted term for a mixture of coffee and chocolate whether it is used as a beverage or as a flavoring.

MOCHA CHOCOLATE

- 2 squares (2 ounces) unsweetened chocolate
- ¾ cup water
- ⅓ cup sugar
- ⅛ teaspoon salt
- 2½ cups milk
- ¾ cup double-strength coffee
- 1 teaspoon vanilla extract

Put first 4 ingredients in saucepan and bring to boil, stirring until chocolate is melted. Increase heat and boil for 3 minutes, stirring constantly. Reduce heat and gradually stir in milk. Add coffee and heat to scalding (do not boil). Stir in vanilla. Makes 4 servings.

MOCHA-ALMOND CAKE

This is a very popular Italian cake that you can duplicate in your own kitchen. Buy two 8-inch dessert sponge layers. (You can, of course, make them, if you prefer.) Place one layer on platter on which it is to be served. Now make Mocha Cream and spread half on bottom layer of cake. Gently place top layer over filling and frost whole cake with remaining Mocha Cream. While frosting is still soft, sprinkle top and sides of cake with ½ cup toasted chopped almonds.

Mocha Cream

- 1 cup sugar
- ¼ cup all-purpose flour
- 1 tablespoon cocoa
- 1¼ cups milk
- 1 tablespoon instant coffee powder
- ½ cup butter or ¼ cup butter and ¼ cup margarine
- 1 teaspoon vanilla extract

Mix sugar, flour, and cocoa thoroughly; add milk gradually. Blend until smooth. Pour into top part of double boiler and cook over high heat at first; then when water boils, lower heat. Stir until mixture is very thick. Remove from heat, add coffee, and stir until dissolved. Cover; refrigerate to cool. Soften butter to room temperature and whip it, with an electric beater if possible. Add cold stiff Mocha Cream, a little at a time, beating until incorporated into butter. Stir in vanilla. Divide mixture in halves.

MOCHA CHIFFON PIE

- 1 cup milk
- 1 envelope unflavored gelatin
- 2 ounces (2 squares) unsweetened chocolate
- ¾ cup sugar
- ¼ teaspoon salt
- 4 eggs, separated
- 1 teaspoon vanilla extract
- 2 tablespoons instant coffee powder
  Baked 9-inch Crumb Crust

Put milk in top part of small double boiler. Sprinkle gelatin on milk and let stand for 5 minutes. Add chocolate. Stir until melted. Beat ¼ cup sugar and the salt with the egg yolks. Beat sauce into egg yolks. Put over simmering water and cook, stirring constantly, until mixture is thickened and coats a metal spoon. Remove from heat and add vanilla and coffee. Chill until thickened but not firm. Beat egg whites until foamy; gradually add remaining sugar, beating until stiff but not dry. Fold this meringue into gelatin mixture. Pile lightly in crumb crust; chill until firm. Serve plain, or spread with sweetened whipped cream. If desired, sprinkle with shaved chocolate, freshly ground nutmeg, chopped candied gingerroot, flaked coconut, chopped nuts, or crushed nut brittle.

Crumb Crust

On wax paper or in a plastic bag, roll enough graham crackers, gingersnaps, vanilla wafers, or zwieback to make 1¼ cups. (Or use crisp coconut macaroons and make 1½ cups crumbs.) With spoon or fingertips thoroughly mix crumbs with ⅓ cup soft (not melted) butter or margarine. Add ¼ cup sugar with grahams or 2 tablespoons with zwieback. Using back of spoon, press mixture firmly and evenly onto bottom and sides of buttered deep 9-inch pie pan. Press edge with fingertips, to extend a little above pan. Bake in preheated moderate oven (350°F.) for about 10 minutes; crust should not brown. Chill.

MOCHA MOUSSE

- 3 ounces (3 squares) unsweetened chocolate
- ⅓ cup water
- ¾ cup sugar
- ⅛ teaspoon salt
- 3 egg yolks
- 1 tablespoon instant coffee powder
- 1 teaspoon vanilla extract
- 2 cups heavy cream, whipped

Turn refrigerator control to coldest setting. Put chocolate and water in saucepan. Bring to boil over low heat, stirring vigorously until blended. Add sugar and salt; simmer for 3 minutes, stirring. Gradually stir into well-beaten egg yolks; add coffee, and cool. Fold in vanilla and cream. Pour into refrigerator trays and freeze until firm. Makes 8 servings.

LOW-CALORIE MOCHA MOLDS

- 3 tablespoons cocoa
- 2 teaspoons cornstarch
- 1 tablespoon instant coffee powder
- ⅛ teaspoon salt
  Water
- 2 eggs, separated
- 1 envelope unflavored gelatin
- 2 teaspoons liquid noncaloric sweetener
- 1 teaspoon vanilla extract
  Whipped Topping

In top part of double boiler mix cocoa, cornstarch, coffee, and salt. Add 1¾ cups water, mix well; bring to boil over direct heat. Cook, stirring, for 5 minutes. Remove from heat; cool. Beat egg yolks. Stir a little mixture very gradually into egg yolks. Put back in double boiler and put over boiling water. Cook for 2 or 3 minutes. Sprinkle gelatin on ¼ cup cold water; let stand for 5 minutes until softened. Stir into hot mixture. Add sweetener and vanilla. Chill until thickened. Beat egg whites stiff. Fold into chilled mixture. Pour into 4 molds and chill until firm. Serve with Whipped Topping. Makes 4 servings, about 100 calories each.

Whipped Topping

Mix ¼ cup each of instant nonfat dry-milk granules and cold water. Beat to form soft peaks. Add 1 tablespoon fresh lemon juice, and beat until stiff. Sweeten with noncaloric sweetener.

MOCHA SUNDAE SAUCE

Melt 4 ounces (4 squares) unsweetened chocolate in double boiler over boiling water; stir in 2 cups sugar. Add 1⅔ cups evaporated milk, undiluted, and dash of salt. Cover; cook over boiling water for 30 minutes. Beat until smooth. Add 2 tablespoons instant coffee and 1 teaspoon vanilla extract. Makes 3 cups.

MOCHA-BRANDY DELIGHT

- 4 cups hot chocolate
- 1½ cups strong hot coffee
- 1 cup brandy or rum
- 1 cup heavy cream, whipped with 2 tablespoons sugar

Beat together chocolate, coffee, and brandy. Fold in whipped cream. Serve at once. Makes about 8 cups.

100 Menus
to help you plan more varied meals for your family with the recipes in this volume

*Recipes for all starred dishes found in this volume.

BREAKFAST

Fruit Cup
Liver and Mushrooms*
Nebraska Spoon Bread*
Whipped Sweet Butter
Mocha Chocolate*

Sliced Oranges with
Whole Cranberry Sauce
Pancake Roll Ups*
(Made with Ham and Sour Cream)
Coffee

Orange-Milk Starter*
Rognoncini di Vitello
Trifolato*
Boiled Potatoes
Corn Bread   Butter
Beverage

Sliced Pears
Chicken-Liver Omelet*
Hot Tomato Slices*
Wigs*   Honey
Coffee

Mixed Vegetable Juice
Bacon and Scrambled Eggs
with Cheese
Cherry Muffins*   Butter
Beverage

Sauerkraut Juice
Broiled Ham Slice
Fried Yams
Cornish Fruited Saffron Bread*
Sweet Butter
Coffee or Tea

Millet Porridge*
with Raisins
Shirred Eggs
Crisp Sausage Links
Toasted Apple Bread*
Tea

Fresh Lime Froth*
Kippered Haddock
with Bacon*
Melba Rye Toast
Crullers*   Café au Lait

LUNCHES

Stewed Apricots
in Orange Juice
Crisp Fried Salt Pork
Fritti Rognoni*
Coffee Cake   Beverage

Orange-Milk Starter*
Domi Jun (Sea Bream Fried
in Egg Batter)*
Potatoes Lyonnaise*
Buttered Toasted
English Muffins
Blueberry Marmalade*
Coffee

Minted Grapefruit Juice
Lamb Hash de Luxe*
Corn Muffins   Mango Jam*
Beverage

Baked Apple with Dates
Canadian Style Bacon
Cheese Squares*
Coffee

Minestrone alla Genovese*
Garlic Italian Bread
Lemon and Orange Salad*

Lamb and Vegetable Soup*
Pineapple Blue-Cheese
Salad Ring*
Assorted Crisp Breads

Creole Vegetable Soup*
Ham and Swiss Cheese
Sandwiches on
Light Pumpernickel Bread*
Cocoa Kisses*

Cream-of-Lettuce Soup*
Danish Liver Pâté*
Toasted Saffron Bread*

Lima-Bean Soup
with Sausage Balls*
Corn Bread   Butter
Cherries in Currant Jelly*

Rock-Lobster Chowder*
Mace Cheese Puffs*
Blueberry Torte*

Thick Lentil and
Spinach Soup*
Jellied Lime
and Cheese Salad*
Hot Biscuits*   Butter
Loganberry Jam*

Fish and Macaroni Salad*
Wilted Lettuce*
Strawberry Fluff*

Tomato Juice
Bacon-Topped Macaroni
and Cheese*
Litchi Salad*
Whole-Wheat Wafers

Italian Rice Soup
with Chicken Livers*
Green-Lima-Bean Salad*
Olive Rolls
Lime-Grape Dessert*

Lamb Patties with
Cranberry Mint Sauce*
Cooked Vegetable Marrow*
Maple-Syrup Cake*

◆

Jellied Consommé Madrilene*
Macaroni and Cheese Soufflé*
Minted Fresh-Lime Mold
with Watermelon Balls*

Barley-Onion Soup
with Beef Balls*
Cottage Cheese and
Cucumber Salad*
Prune Kolache*

◆

Liverwurst Patties*
Omelette à la Lyonnaise*
Fresh Lemon Peach Cooler*

Grilled Frankfurters
Lentil and Potato Casserole*
Light Pumpernickel Bread*
Lemon Buttermilk Sherbet*

◆

Marrowbone Soup*
Lime Salmon-Salad Spread*
with Watercress
on Whole-wheat Toast
Frozen Maple-Graham Cream*

Kidney Turbigo*
Chili Limas*
Pear and Grape Salad
Mayonnaise*
Brown Sugar Fudge Cake*

◆

Smoked Boneless Pork Butt
Michigan Baked Beans*
Brown Bread
Pineapple-Strawberry Salad*
Black-Walnut
Chocolate Drops*

Lobster Bisque*
Piquant Liver
and Vegetables*
Hearts of Lettuce
Mixed Herb Mayonnaise*
Loganberry Ice*

◆

Lamb and Eggplant Stew*
Minted Onions*
Hard Rolls
Figs and Cling Peach
Halves on Chicory with
Fruit-Salad Dressing*

Kori Kuk (Oxtail Soup)*
Dak Chim (Steamed Chicken)*
Kim Kui (Toasted Seaweed)*
Kumquat, Orange
and Apple Compote*

◆

Kidney Casserole Jerez*
Cauliflower in Bread-
Crumb Sauce*
Macédoine of Vegetables*
Melon Simplicity*

Celery, Radishes, Olives
Deviled Lamb Riblets*
Millet Pilaf*
Sautéed Green Peppers*
Bird's-Nest Pudding*

◆

Herring in Sour Cream*
on Lettuce
Spareribs and Sauerkraut*
Farina Dumplings*
Rainbow Cake*

Roast Ham with Beer Glaze*
Super Lima-Bean Casserole*
Tomato, Green Pepper
and Cabbage Salad
Apple Dumplings*

◆

Party Pork Chops*   Rice
Green Onions, Peas
and Lettuce*
Molded Lime and
Blueberry Salad*
Chocolate-Filled
Eight-Layer Cake*

Anchovies on Pimientos
with Capers
Hearty Lasagna with
Meat Sauce*
Escarole
Lemon French Dressing*
Italian Whole-Wheat Bread
Pears Baked in Red Wine

◆

Barbecued Beef Patties*
Lima Beans with Cheese*
Hot Rolls
Fruit Salad
Lemon-Honey Dressing*
Chocolate Peppermint Cake*

Mushroom Liver Pâté
Melba Rounds
Red-Wine Beef
with Macaroni*
Patio Salad*
French Bread
Macaroon Angel Pudding*

◆

Greek Lemon Soup*
Hamburger, Macaroni and
Green-Bean Casserole*
Panama Radish Salad*
Corn Sticks
Peach Slices*

Creamed Lamb in
Puff Shells*
Minted Limas*
Cheese-Stuffed Lettuce Salad*
Cranberry Pudding with
Hot Butter Sauce*

◆

Skewered Shrimps
and Vegetables*
Macaroni Parmesan*
Pineapple-Strawberry Salad*
Fresh-Lime French Dressing*
Mocha Chiffon Pie*

Fresh Lime Melon Cup*
Crab-Stuffed Lobster*
Vegetable Platter*
Seeded Hard Rolls
Marron Soufflé*

◆

Glazed Roast Chicken*
Spiced Kohlrabi with Cheese*
Roasted Corn on the Cob*
Waldorf Salad on Shredded
Green Cabbage
Coffee Sponge*
Brazil-Nut Macaroons*

Beef Broth*
Rye Wafers
Steamed Lobster Tails*
Greek Potato Salad*
Mincemeat Alaska Pie*

◆

Sopa de Aguacate
(Avocado Soup)*
Chorizo (Mexican Sausage)*
Frijoles Refritos
(Crisp Fried Beans)*
Guadalajara Tostadas
(Guadalajara Toasts)*
Chocolate Mexicano*
Polvorónes (Tea Cakes)*

Thick Lentil Soup*
Butter-Stuffed Lake
Michigan Trout*
Green Peas and Lettuce*
Pickled Beets and Onion Rings
Lemon-Orange
Refrigerator Cake*

◆

Lamb Shanks Milanaise*
Sicilian Macaroni and
Eggplant Casserole*
Asparagus and Pimiento Salad
Garlic Dressing*
Italian Bread
Concord Grape Pie*

Sevice (Pickled Raw Fish)*
Mexican Lamb Stew*
Tortillas
Guayabas Rellenas
(Stuffed Guavas)*
Churros (Mexican Crullers)*

French-Fried
Butterfly Lobster*
Wild Rice Casserole*
Wilted Cucumbers, Radishes
Kumquat-Ginger Relish*
Jellied Litchi and
Peach Dessert*
Green Tea

Chicken Pie*
Creamy Gravy*
Biscuits*
Buttered Broccoli
Sliced Tomatoes
Cucumber Sauce*
Mint Parfait*
Cherry-Coconut Macaroons*

Kiek met Ballekens
(Flemish Fricasseed Chicken
with Meatballs)*
Rice
Green Peas with Mushrooms
Carrot and Cucumber Sticks
Banana Soufflé*

Barbecued Lamb Chops*
Braised Red and Green
Sweet Peppers
Lentil Salad*
Ladyfingers with Lemon Curd*

Stuffed Lamb Chops*
Tomato Sauce
Duchesse Potatoes*
Braised Radishes*
Mixed Greens
Sharp-Cheddar Dressing*
Creamy Strawberries
Maraschino*
Macaroons*

Baked Kingfish Steaks
au Gratin*
Potatoes Boulangère*
Braised Celery
Herb Buttered Baby Carrots
Melon India Relish*
Bavarois au Citron*

Hot Swiss-Cheese Appetizers*
Crab and Shell Chowder*
Pilot Crackers
Steamed Lemon Pudding*
Clear Lemon Sauce*

Cream Cheese-Stuffed Celery
Lamb Steaks in Marinade*
Herbed Pilaf
Tomatoes and Eggplant
Lemon Chiffon Pie*

Molded Egg-Lobster Salad*
Danish Macaroni Salad*
Radishes
Dilled Cucumbers
Stewed Mangoes*
Danish Macaroons*

Ham Loaf*
Lima Beans in Lemon Sauce*
Cheese-Tomato Grill*
Mocha Almond Cake*

Roast Fresh Ham with
Sour Cream Gravy*
Buttered Baby Peas
Whipped Potatoes
Stewed Apples*
Maple Cottage Pudding*

Leek Soup*
Polish Sausage
with Red Cabbage*
Hard Rolls
Lime Sherbet*
Poppy-Seed Mace Cookies*

Indonesian Skewered Pork*
Hashed Brown Potatoes
French-Fried Onion Rings
Hot Melon Chutney*
Garden Lettuce Salad
Blender Mayonnaise*
Angel Cake Lemon Delight*

Individual Ham Loaves*
Picnic Succotash*
Spinach Salad
Italian Bread
Parsleyed Onion Butter
Maple Freeze*

Ham Balls*
Macaroni, Bean
and Egg Salad*
Romaine Hearts
Cherry Tomatoes
Orange Cake*

Guacamole*
Corn Chips
Chicken in
Lemon-Caper Butter*
Whipped Sweet Potatoes
Stuffed Tomato Salad
Mocha Mousse*

Hot Consommé Madrilene*
Make-Ahead Chicken Lasagna*
Tomatoes and Okra
Belgian Endive
Baked Apricot Whip*

Veal Roast
Marron Purée*
Herbed Zucchini
Braised Radishes*
Savory Italian Bread Slices
Strawberry Schaumtorte*

Tartare Fish Loaf
with Caper Sauce*
Tossed Macaroni and Cheese*
Mixed Green Salad
French Dressing
Strawberry Frosted*

Planked Lake Superior
Whitefish*
Duchesse Potatoes*
Marinated Tomato Wedges
Asparagus Stalks
Glazed Baby Onions
Golden Lord Baltimore Cake*

Leek and Green-Pea Purée*
Baked Mackerel*
Tomato Sauce
Fried Noodles with
Grated Parmesan Cheese
Wilted Spinach Salad
with Curry Mayonnaise*
Lemon Meringue Pie*

Rib Roast (Rack) of Lamb
with Chutney Glaze*
Lima Beans with
Easy White Sauce*
Minted Baby Carrots
Seeded Dinner Rolls
Florida Lime Pie*

Layered Beef-and-Onion Loaf*
Country-Style Beans*
Orange, Artichoke Heart,
and Slivered-Almond Salad
French Dressing*
Low-Calorie Mocha Molds*

Sweet-and-Sour Beef and
Pork Meatballs*
Spiced Loquats*
Parsley New Potatoes
Braised Sweet Peppers
Spiced Squash Pudding*
Whipped Cream

◆

Vegetable Juice Cocktail
Rib Roast of Beef
on a Spit*
Browned Whole Potatoes
Corn on the Cob
Wilted Lettuce
Fresh-Lime Cream*
Madeleines*

Chopped Chicken Liver*
Lobster Casserole à la Costa*
Green-Bean and Carrot Salad*
Piquant Dressing*
Banana Frosted*
Coconut Kisses*

◆

Stuffed Mushrooms*
Curried Rock Lobster*
Rice
Spicy Mango Chutney*
Chopped Cashew Nuts
Pineapple Mint Sherbet*

Chicken Broth   Devil Balls*
Sweet-and-Sour Meatballs*
Rice
Fried Noodles
Vanilla Ice Cream
Candied Kumquats*

◆

Baked Stuffed
Breast of Lamb*
Buttered Carrot Slices
Curried Lima Salad*
Hot Biscuits with Sesame Seed
Minted Melon with Cointreau*

Cream-of-Lentil Soup*
Rice-Stuffed Lamb Shanks*
Simmered Tomatoes
and Cabbage*
Pear Salad
Blue Cheese Dressing*
Coffee Spice Cake*

◆

Sherry Crab Soup*
Bean and Bacon Casserole*
Boston Brown Bread
Red and Green Cabbage Salad
Cooked Salad Dressing*
Peach Marlow*

Herbed Lamb Shoulder*
Mint Jelly*
Corn Pudding*
Spinach and Beet Salad
Tomato Salad Dressing*
Key Lime Pie*

◆

Lobster Newburg*
Lentil Curry with Rice*
Tomato Wedges, Cucumber
and Radish Slices in
Marinade for Vegetables*
Red-Currant Cobbler*

Kansas Corn Chowder*
Lamb Haricot*
Buttered Broccoli
Assorted Raw Relishes
Rye Bread
Cherry Coconut Squares*

◆

Chicken Loaf*
Cranberry Marmalade*
Curried Onions and Cucumber*
Garden Lettuce
with Bacon Dressing*
Hickory-Nut Graham Bread
Butter
Lemon-Cheese Pie*

Red Noodles and Lamb*
Green Beans, Cape Cod
Style*
Mixed Green Salad
Vienna Bread
Blueberry Topped
Cheese Cake*

◆

Lobster and Orange Cocktail*
Rare Roast Leg of Lamb*
Traditional English
Mint Sauce*
Creamy Succotash*
Buttered Swiss Chard
Chocolate Shadow Cake*

Minestrone Milanese
alla Savini*
Veal Scaloppine Milanese*
Buttered Noodles
Finocchio   Olives
Fruit-Preserve Layer Cake*

◆

Fish Steaks, Lemon Butter*
Macaroni Double-Cheese
Casserole*
Asparagus Salad
Chili Mayonnaise*
Corn Bread   Butter
Low-Calorie Peach Sherbert*
Maple Lace Wafers*

Tomato and Sauerkraut Juice
Larded Herb Pot Roast*
Mashed Rutabaga
Mustard Greens
Western Melon Conserve*
Florida Meringue
Orange Pudding*

◆

Individual Salmon
Casseroles*
Toast Rounds
Masked Tomato Salad*
(with Cottage Cheese)
Celery and Carrot Sticks
Mrs. Van's Dutch
Apple Cake*

Swedish Meatballs*
Boiled New Potatoes
with Dill
Tomato, Cucumber and Lettuce
Caper Dressing*
Light Rye Bread   Butter
Strawberry Cream Cake*

◆

Lamb-Bone and
Lima-Bean Soup*
Macaroni, Lobster
and Artichoke Salad*
Dill Pickle Sticks
Toasted Rye Wafers   Butter
Mincemeat Lane Cakes*

Scotch Cock-a-Leekie*
Crusty Bread   Sweet Butter
Mixed Green Salad with
Sliced Raw Mushrooms
French Dressing
Frozen Eggnog Pie*

◆

Baked-Chicken-Macaroni Salad*
Tomato Aspic, Cucumber
and Green Pepper Salad
Melba Toast   Butter
Mango Rum Sundae*
Chocolate Macaroons*

Marjoram Veal Chops*
Baked Macaroni with
Tomatoes and Cheese*
Romaine and
Watercress Salad
Mango Pie*

◆

Menudo (Tripe Stew*) with
Whole Hominy
Ensalada de Naranjas
(Orange, Cucumber and
Pepper Salad)*
Empanadas de Dulce
(Sweet Turnovers)*

Mochomas (Minced Pork)*
Arroz Mexicano
(Mexican Rice)*
Colache (Vegetable Medley)*
Tortillas de Harina
(Flour Tortillas)*

◆

Chile con Carne
(Chili with Meat)*
Ensalada de Coliflor con
Aguacate (Cauliflower Salad
with Ham and Avocado)*
Tortillas de Maiz
(Corn Tortillas)*
Fresh Pineapple

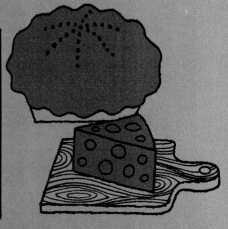

*Recipes for all starred dishes found in this volume.

GENERAL INFORMATION

The Ingredients and Measurements Used in Recipes

All recipes in this book have been tested in the Woman's Day Kitchens with standard American measuring cups (8 ounces = 16 tablespoons), measuring spoons (1 tablespoon = 3 teaspoons), and other standard kitchen equipment. All measurements are level. Liquids are measured in standard 8-ounce glass measuring cups, at eye level.

All sugar is granulated white sugar unless otherwise specified.

All flours, cake and all-purpose, are sifted before measuring unless otherwise specified. No self-rising flour is used.

All baking powder is double-acting baking powder.

All brown sugar is firmly packed when measured.

All confectioners' sugar is sifted before measuring.

All pepper is ground black pepper unless otherwise specified.

Fats and shortening are measured at room temperature, packed firmly into measuring cup and leveled with a straight knife. They are scraped out with a rubber spatula.

Salted butter or margarine, packed in ¼-pound sticks, is used unless otherwise specified. 1 stick = ½ cup = 8 tablespoons = ¼ pound.

1 tall can evaporated milk (14½ ounces) contains 1⅔ cups undiluted evaporated milk. Sweetened condensed milk is an entirely different product, and cannot be used interchangeably with evaporated milk.

⅓ to ½ teaspoon dried herbs can be substituted for each tablespoon fresh herbs. Crumble herbs before using to release flavor.

Before starting to cook or to bake, read the recipes carefully. Assemble all ingredients and equipment. Follow recipe exactly. Do not increase or decrease recipe unless you are a skilled enough cook to recognize what adjustments must be made as to ingredients, pan sizes, and/or cooking time.

Cooking Temperatures and Times

Cooking temperatures and times are approximate for meat. They depend not only on the weight and kind of meat, but also on its shape, temperature, and its bone and fat contents. A meat thermometer was used in testing.

Cooking times for meats are as recommended by the National Live Stock and Meat Board, 36 Wabash Avenue, Chicago, Illinois 60603.

Oven Temperatures

TEMPERATURES (Degree F.)	TERM
250 to 275	VERY SLOW
300 to 325	SLOW
350 to 375	MODERATE
400 to 425	HOT
450 to 475	VERY HOT
500 to 525	EXTREMELY HOT

Important—Preheat oven for 10 to 15 minutes before placing food in it. Many a cake has been spoiled by being placed in a barely heated oven. Baking times are based on the assumption that the oven is already at the stated temperature.

Check the oven temperature control frequently, especially if baking times vary from those given in recipes. (This can be done with a portable oven thermometer.) If a control is consistently off, call your public utility. They should be able to reset the oven temperature control.

Caloric Values

The caloric values, where mentioned, for each food are based on 100 grams, about 3½ ounces edible portion, as mentioned in Composition of Foods, Agriculture Handbook No. 8, Agricultural Service of the United States Department of Agriculture, Washington, D. C., revised December 1963.